DON'T STAND WHERE THE COMET IS ASSUMED TO STRIKE OIL

Other DILBERT books from Andrews McMeel Publishing

Words You Don't Want to Hear During Your Annual Performance Review
ISBN: 0-7407-3805-4

When Body Language Goes Bad
ISBN: 0-7407-3298-6

What Do You Call a Sociopath in a Cubicle? Answer: A Coworker
ISBN: 0-7407-2663-3

Another Day in Cubicle Paradise
ISBN: 0-7407-2194-1

When Did Ignorance Become a Point of View?
ISBN: 0-7407-1839-8

Excuse Me While I Wag
ISBN: 0-7407-1390-6

Dilbert—A Treasury of Sunday Strips: Version 00
ISBN: 0-7407-0531-8

Random Acts of Management
ISBN: 0-7407-0453-2

Dilbert Gives You the Business
ISBN: 0-7407-0338-2 hardcover
ISBN: 0-7407-0003-0 paperback

Don't Step in the Leadership
ISBN: 0-8362-7844-5

Journey to Cubeville
ISBN: 0-8362-7175-0 hardcover
ISBN: 0-8362-6745-1 paperback

I'm Not Anti-Business, I'm Anti-Idiot
ISBN: 0-8362-5182-2

Seven Years of Highly Defective People
ISBN: 0-8362-5129-6 hardcover
ISBN: 0-8362-3668-8 paperback

Casual Day Has Gone Too Far
ISBN: 0-8362-2899-5

Fugitive from the Cubicle Police
ISBN: 0-8362-2119-2

Still Pumped from Using the Mouse
ISBN: 0-8362-1026-3

It's Obvious You Won't Survive by Your Wits Alone
ISBN: 0-8362-0415-8

Bring Me the Head of Willy the Mailboy!
ISBN: 0-8362-1779-9

Shave the Whales
ISBN: 0-8362-1740-3

Dogbert's Clues for the Clueless
ISBN: 0-8362-1737-3

Build a Better Life by Stealing Office Supplies
ISBN: 0-8362-1757-8

Always Postpone Meetings with Time-Wasting Morons
ISBN: 0-8362-1758-6

For ordering information, call 1-800-223-2336.

DON'T STAND WHERE THE COMET IS ASSUMED TO STRIKE OIL

A DILBERT™ BOOK
BY SCOTT ADAMS

**Andrews McMeel
Publishing**

Kansas City

04 05 06 07 08 BBG 10 9 8 7 6 5 4 3 2 1

ISBN: 0-7407-4539-5

Library of Congress Control Number: 2003116547

www.dilbert.com

For a woman who thinks *crafts* and *crap* are completely different concepts

Introduction

You've probably noticed that the population of earth can be divided into smart people and dumb people. That would be a handy distinction if there were any way you could tell which group you were in. I mean, how can you know whether you are really a smart person or actually so dumb that you think you are smart? I have to assume it all feels the same.

It's easier to tell if other people are dumb. A good test is to announce at your next gathering that you have discovered an herbal treatment for ugliness, fatness, baldness, impotence, hair loss, and unhappiness. Say that it involves eating grass while repeating a special mantra in your head: "moo."

Dumb people will assume that you are highly qualified to dispense medical advice, especially if you say you tried something and it worked, or you saw it on *Oprah*. Then they'll drop on all fours and scurry out to the backyard to begin the cure. Smart people will ask you what scientific evidence you have to back up your ridiculous claim. That's where the fun begins. I like to take that conversation in this direction:

Smart Person: What evidence do you have of your claim?

Me: What evidence do you have of anything you think you know?

Smart Person: I rely on scientific evidence.

Me: How many double-blind studies have you performed?

Smart Person: Well, none, but I read about them.

Me: So you rely on writers you don't know to describe research you don't fully understand, performed by people who often have financial incentives to mislead you?

Smart Person: You have exposed me for the hypocrite and fraud that I am. I'll be out on the lawn.

Me: Very good. Stay away from the grass near the trees. We have dogs.

Actually, it doesn't usually have that happy ending. There's typically some blather about repeatable results, peer reviews, and how science isn't perfect but it's better than guessing, blah, blah, blah. Then I point out how it all boils down to "someone that you don't know told you it was true." Pretty soon there are fisticuffs, corrective lenses go flying, children cry. My point is that I don't get invited to parties and I don't know why.

But you're invited to the only party that counts. If you sign up for the free *Dilbert* newsletter, written by me whenever I feel like it—usually five times a year—then you will automatically be a member of Dogbert's New Ruling Class. When Dogbert conquers the world, you will be in the ruling elite just like you always wanted to be.

To subscribe, go to www.Dilbert.com and follow the links. If you have any trouble subscribing, send an e-mail to newsletter@unitedmedia.com.

S. Adams

Scott Adams

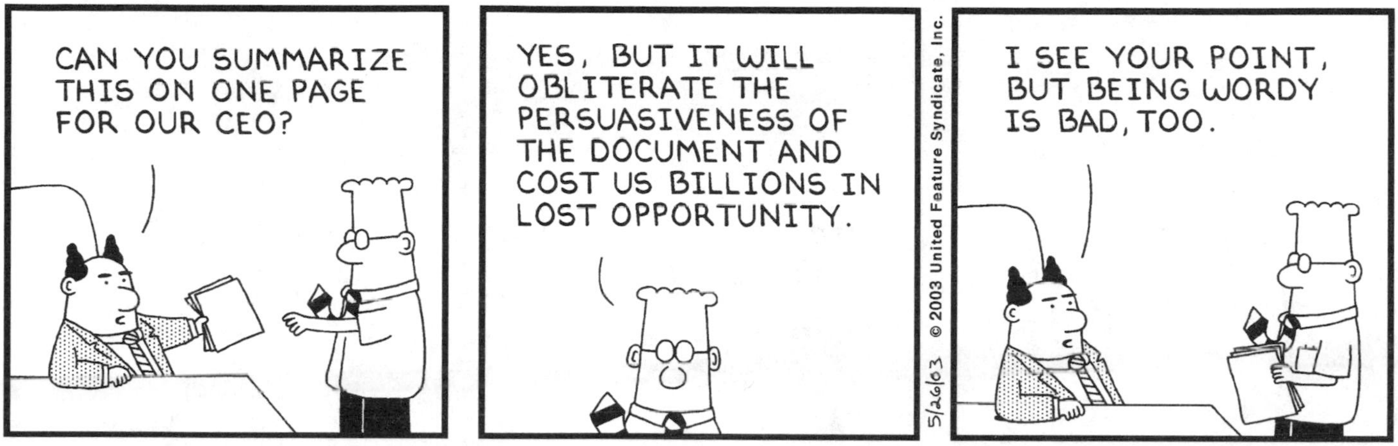
CAN YOU SUMMARIZE THIS ON ONE PAGE FOR OUR CEO?
YES, BUT IT WILL OBLITERATE THE PERSUASIVENESS OF THE DOCUMENT AND COST US BILLIONS IN LOST OPPORTUNITY.
5/26/03 © 2003 United Feature Syndicate, Inc.
I SEE YOUR POINT, BUT BEING WORDY IS BAD, TOO.

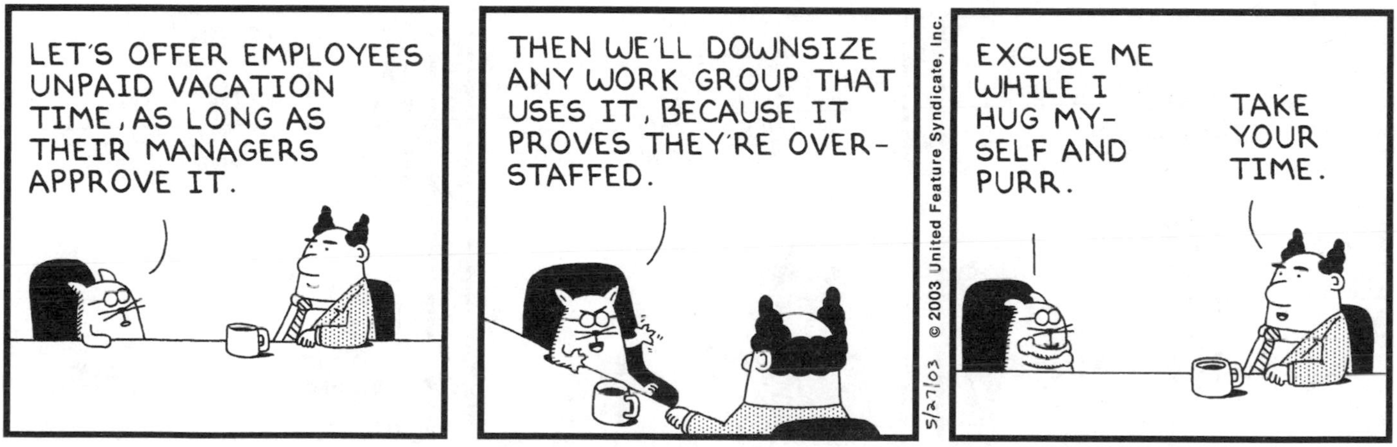
LET'S OFFER EMPLOYEES UNPAID VACATION TIME, AS LONG AS THEIR MANAGERS APPROVE IT.
THEN WE'LL DOWNSIZE ANY WORK GROUP THAT USES IT, BECAUSE IT PROVES THEY'RE OVER-STAFFED.
5/27/03 © 2003 United Feature Syndicate, Inc.
EXCUSE ME WHILE I HUG MY-SELF AND PURR.
TAKE YOUR TIME.

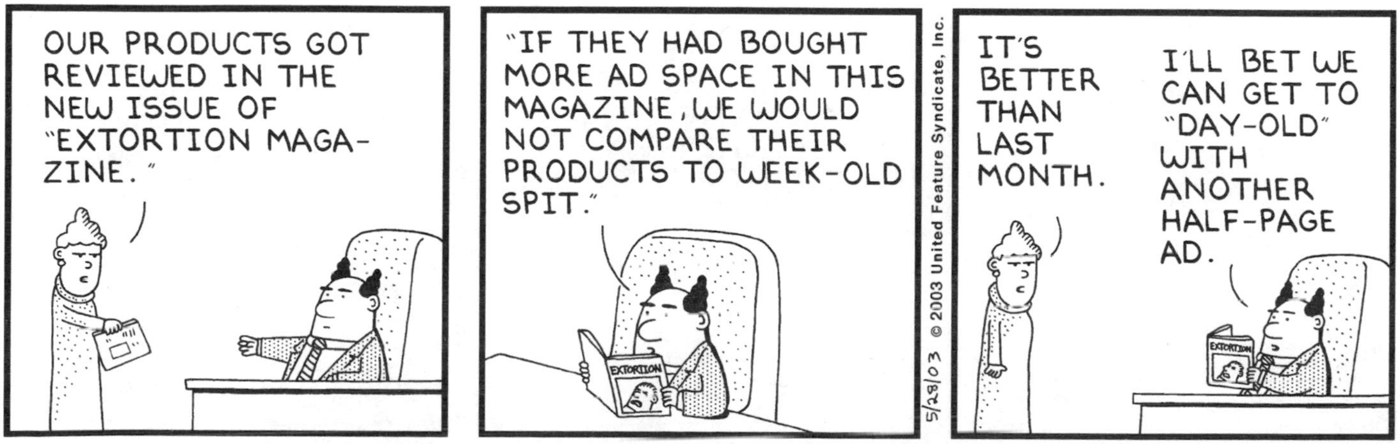
OUR PRODUCTS GOT REVIEWED IN THE NEW ISSUE OF "EXTORTION MAGA-ZINE."
"IF THEY HAD BOUGHT MORE AD SPACE IN THIS MAGAZINE, WE WOULD NOT COMPARE THEIR PRODUCTS TO WEEK-OLD SPIT."
EXTORTION
5/28/03 © 2003 United Feature Syndicate, Inc.
IT'S BETTER THAN LAST MONTH.
I'LL BET WE CAN GET TO "DAY-OLD" WITH ANOTHER HALF-PAGE AD.
EXTORTION

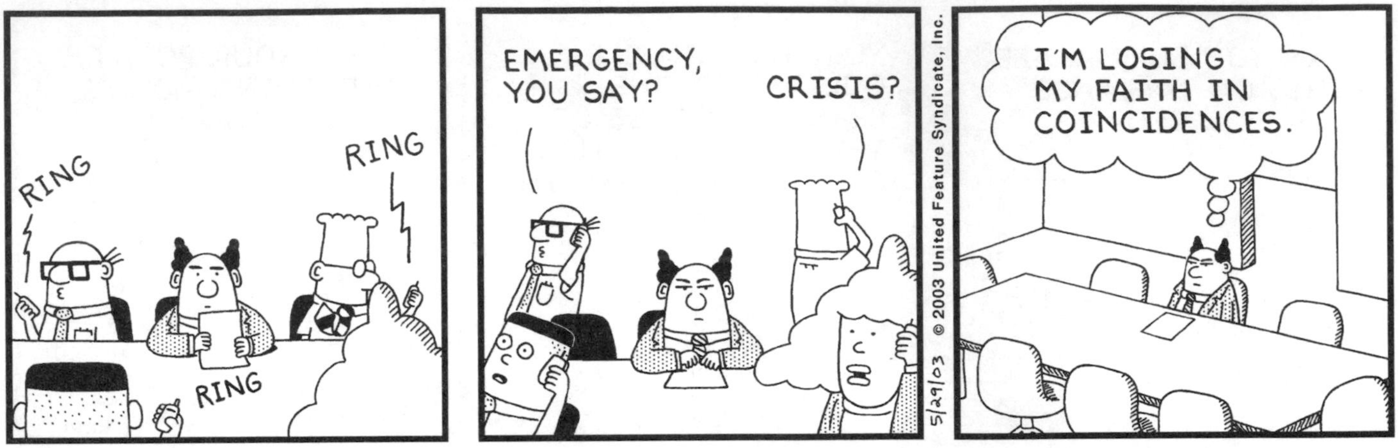
RING
RING
RING
EMERGENCY, YOU SAY?
CRISIS?
5/29/03 © 2003 United Feature Syndicate, Inc.
I'M LOSING MY FAITH IN COINCIDENCES.

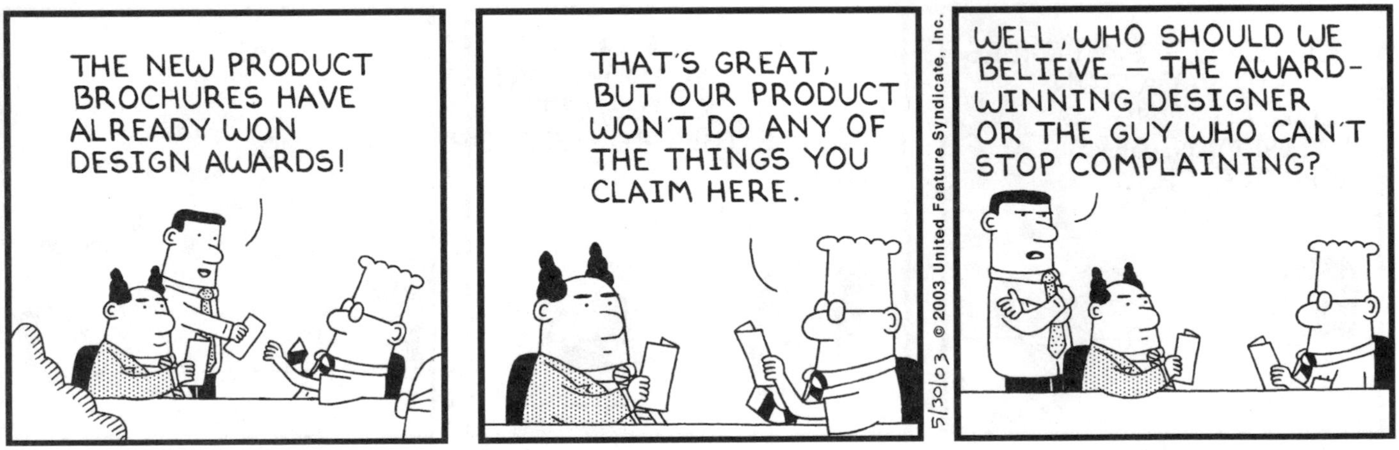
THE NEW PRODUCT BROCHURES HAVE ALREADY WON DESIGN AWARDS!
THAT'S GREAT, BUT OUR PRODUCT WON'T DO ANY OF THE THINGS YOU CLAIM HERE.
5/30/03 © 2003 United Feature Syndicate, Inc.
WELL, WHO SHOULD WE BELIEVE — THE AWARD-WINNING DESIGNER OR THE GUY WHO CAN'T STOP COMPLAINING?

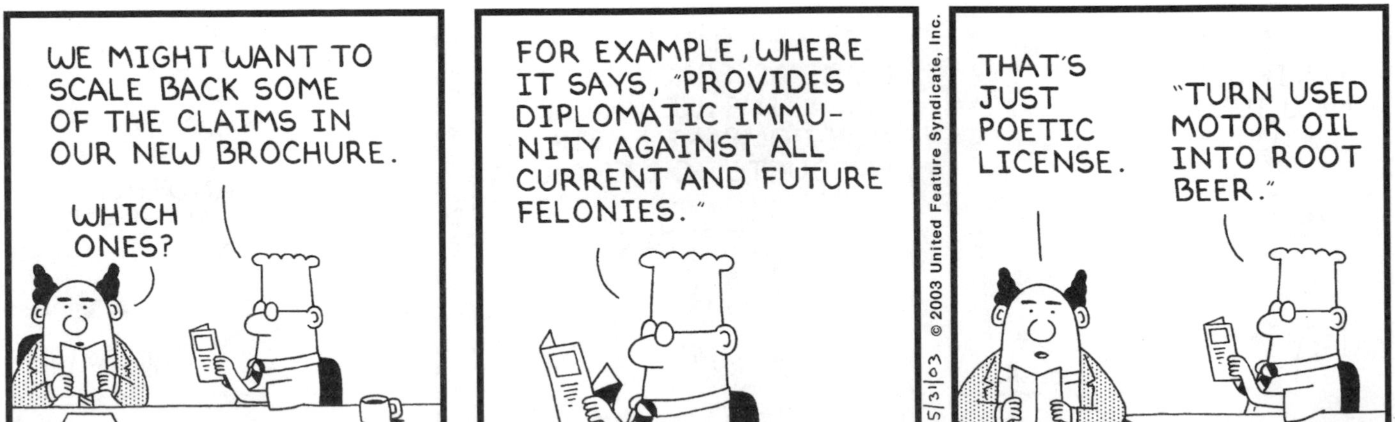
WE MIGHT WANT TO SCALE BACK SOME OF THE CLAIMS IN OUR NEW BROCHURE.
WHICH ONES?
FOR EXAMPLE, WHERE IT SAYS, "PROVIDES DIPLOMATIC IMMUNITY AGAINST ALL CURRENT AND FUTURE FELONIES."
5/31/03 © 2003 United Feature Syndicate, Inc.
THAT'S JUST POETIC LICENSE.
"TURN USED MOTOR OIL INTO ROOT BEER."

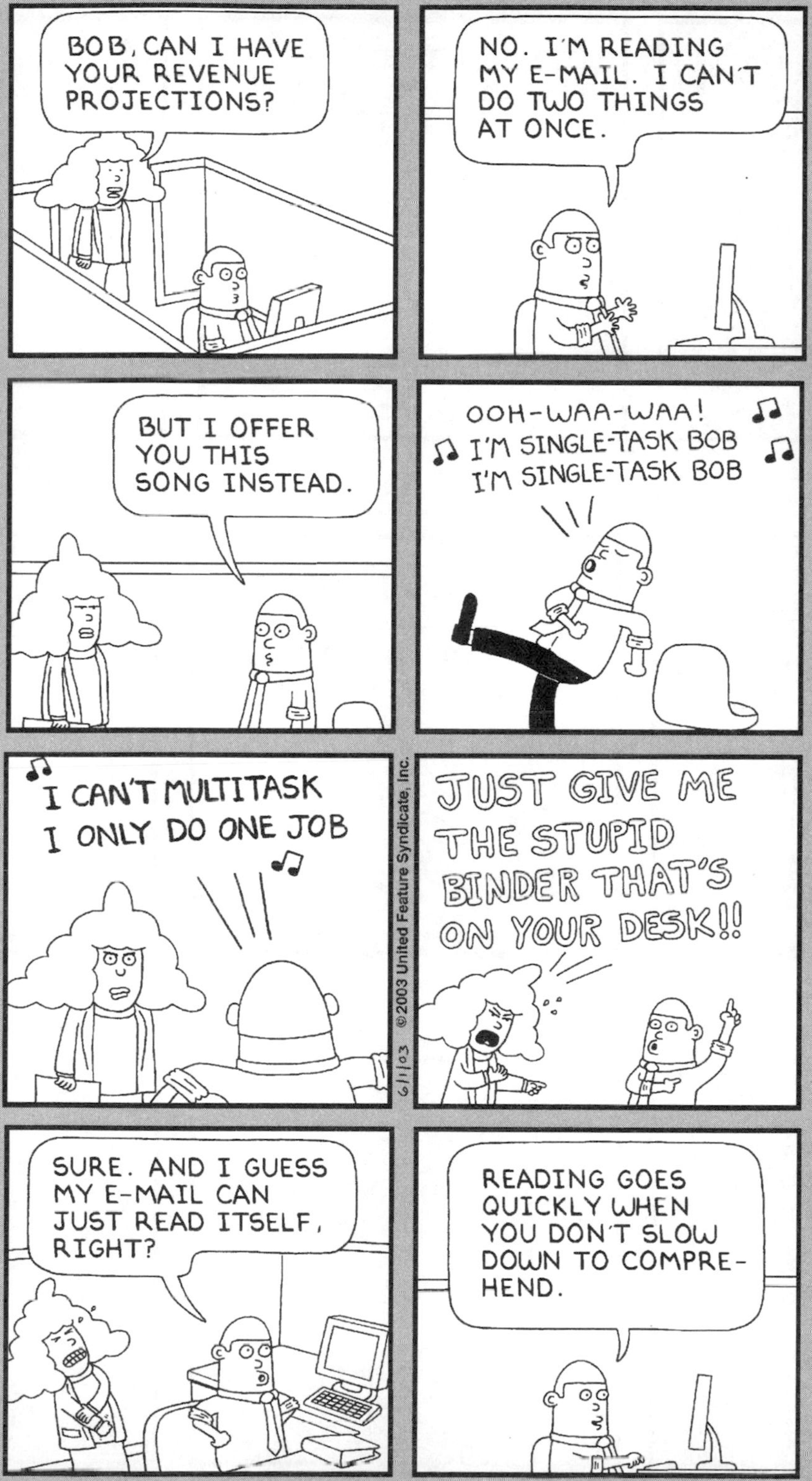
BOB, CAN I HAVE YOUR REVENUE PROJECTIONS?
NO. I'M READING MY E-MAIL. I CAN'T DO TWO THINGS AT ONCE.
BUT I OFFER YOU THIS SONG INSTEAD.
OOH-WAA-WAA!
I'M SINGLE-TASK BOB
I'M SINGLE-TASK BOB
I CAN'T MULTITASK
I ONLY DO ONE JOB
JUST GIVE ME THE STUPID BINDER THAT'S ON YOUR DESK!!
SURE. AND I GUESS MY E-MAIL CAN JUST READ ITSELF, RIGHT?
READING GOES QUICKLY WHEN YOU DON'T SLOW DOWN TO COMPRE-HEND.
©2003 United Feature Syndicate, Inc.
6/1/03

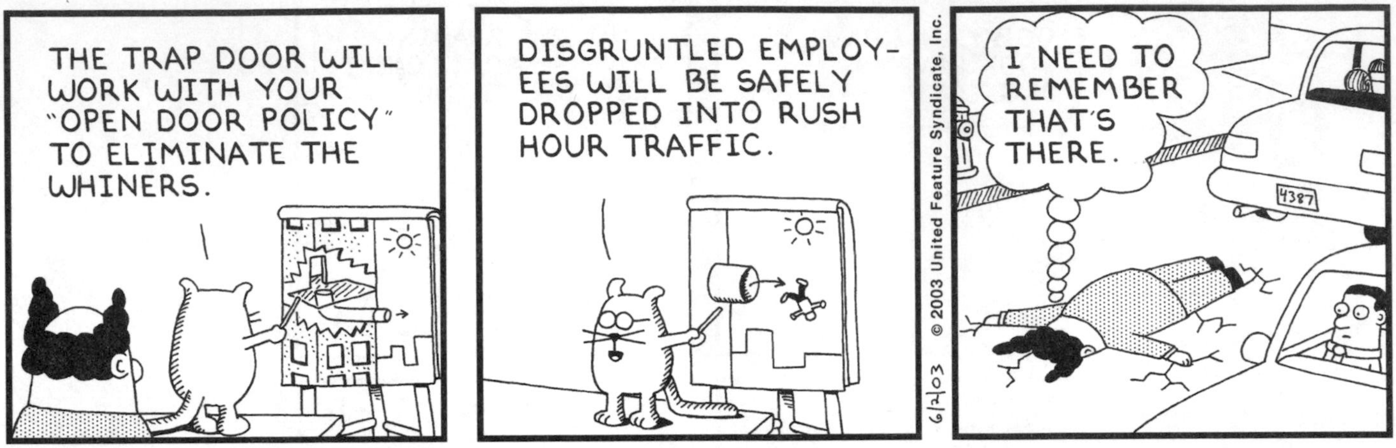
THE TRAP DOOR WILL WORK WITH YOUR "OPEN DOOR POLICY" TO ELIMINATE THE WHINERS.
DISGRUNTLED EMPLOY-EES WILL BE SAFELY DROPPED INTO RUSH HOUR TRAFFIC.
6/2/03 © 2003 United Feature Syndicate, Inc.
I NEED TO REMEMBER THAT'S THERE.
4387

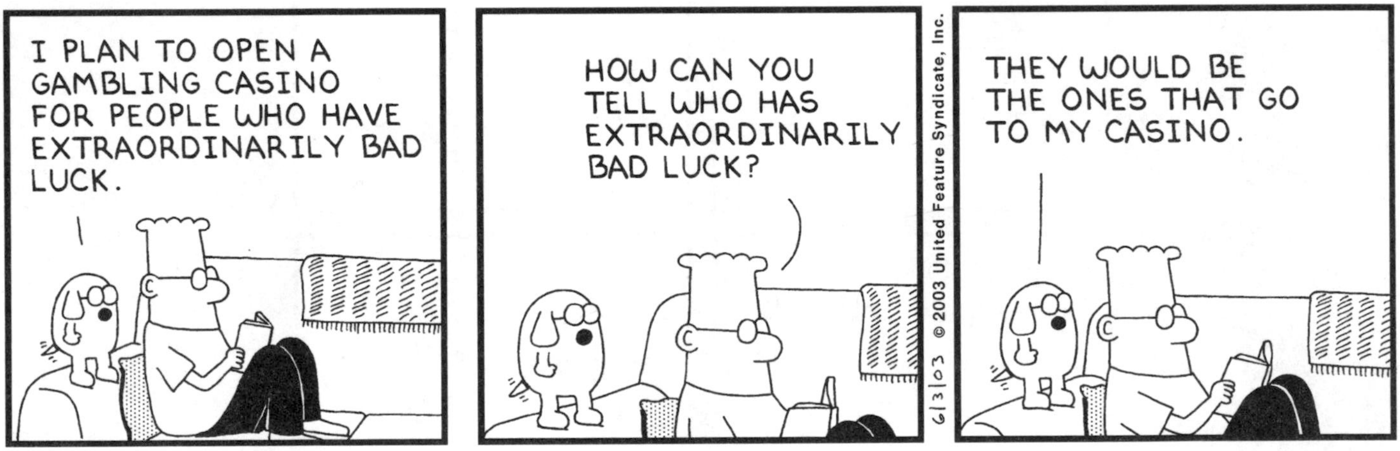
I PLAN TO OPEN A GAMBLING CASINO FOR PEOPLE WHO HAVE EXTRAORDINARILY BAD LUCK.
HOW CAN YOU TELL WHO HAS EXTRAORDINARILY BAD LUCK?
6/3/03 © 2003 United Feature Syndicate, Inc.
THEY WOULD BE THE ONES THAT GO TO MY CASINO.

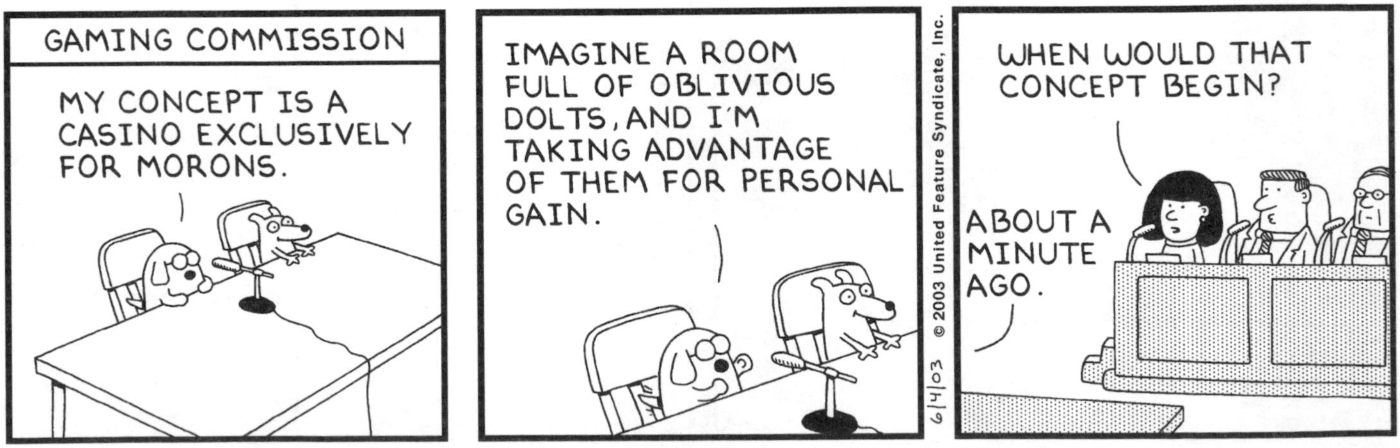
GAMING COMMISSION
MY CONCEPT IS A CASINO EXCLUSIVELY FOR MORONS.
IMAGINE A ROOM FULL OF OBLIVIOUS DOLTS, AND I'M TAKING ADVANTAGE OF THEM FOR PERSONAL GAIN.
6/4/03 © 2003 United Feature Syndicate, Inc.
WHEN WOULD THAT CONCEPT BEGIN?
ABOUT A MINUTE AGO.

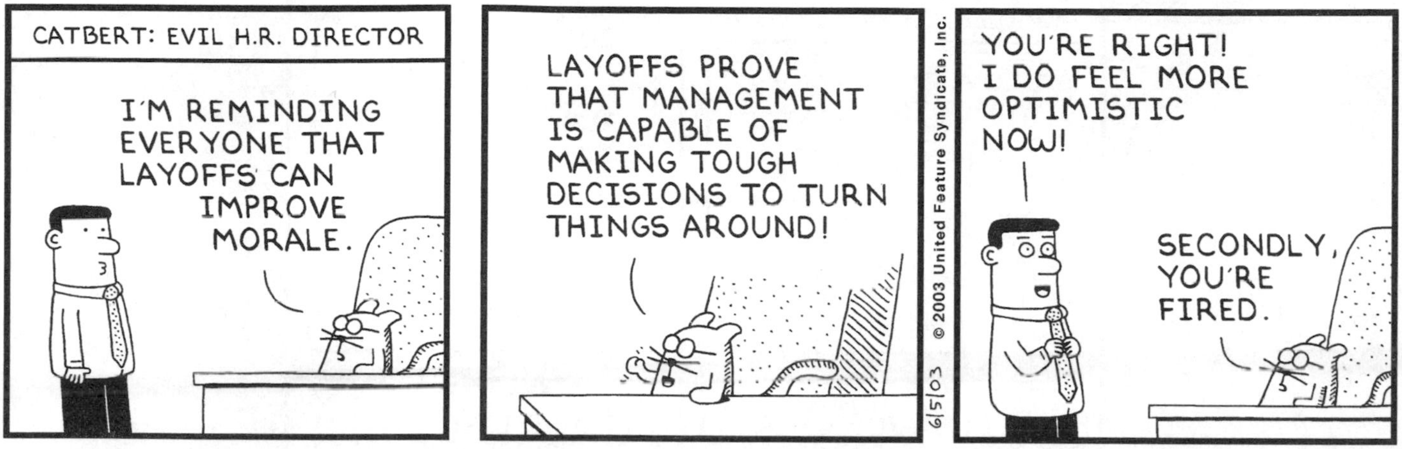
CATBERT: EVIL H.R. DIRECTOR
I'M REMINDING EVERYONE THAT LAYOFFS CAN IMPROVE MORALE.
LAYOFFS PROVE THAT MANAGEMENT IS CAPABLE OF MAKING TOUGH DECISIONS TO TURN THINGS AROUND!
6/5/03 © 2003 United Feature Syndicate, Inc.
YOU'RE RIGHT! I DO FEEL MORE OPTIMISTIC NOW!
SECONDLY, YOU'RE FIRED.

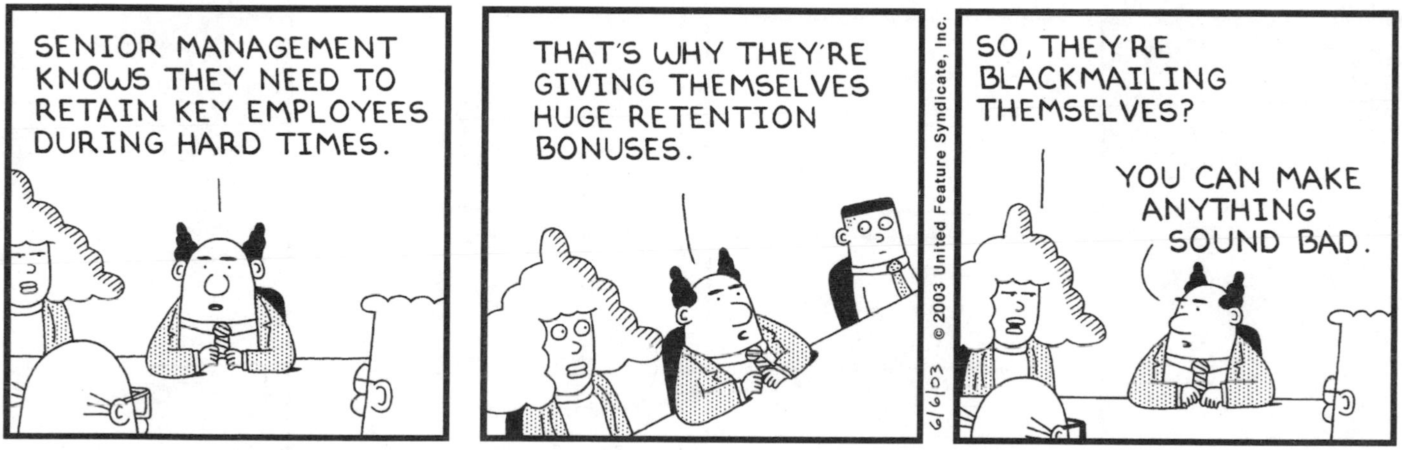
SENIOR MANAGEMENT KNOWS THEY NEED TO RETAIN KEY EMPLOYEES DURING HARD TIMES.
THAT'S WHY THEY'RE GIVING THEMSELVES HUGE RETENTION BONUSES.
6/6/03 © 2003 United Feature Syndicate, Inc.
SO, THEY'RE BLACKMAILING THEMSELVES?
YOU CAN MAKE ANYTHING SOUND BAD.

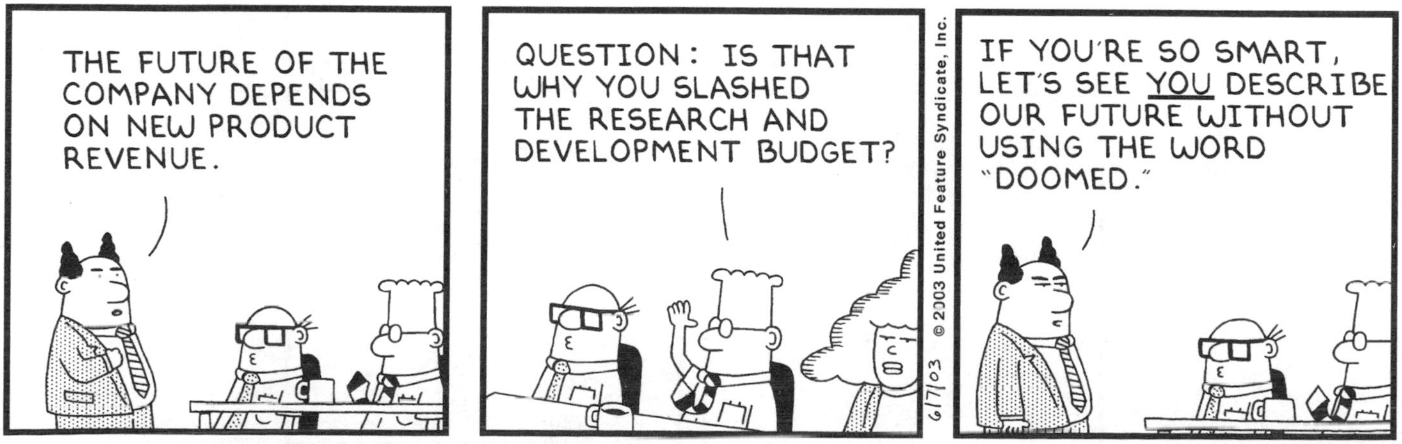
THE FUTURE OF THE COMPANY DEPENDS ON NEW PRODUCT REVENUE.
QUESTION: IS THAT WHY YOU SLASHED THE RESEARCH AND DEVELOPMENT BUDGET?
6/7/03 © 2003 United Feature Syndicate, Inc.
IF YOU'RE SO SMART, LET'S SEE YOU DESCRIBE OUR FUTURE WITHOUT USING THE WORD "DOOMED."

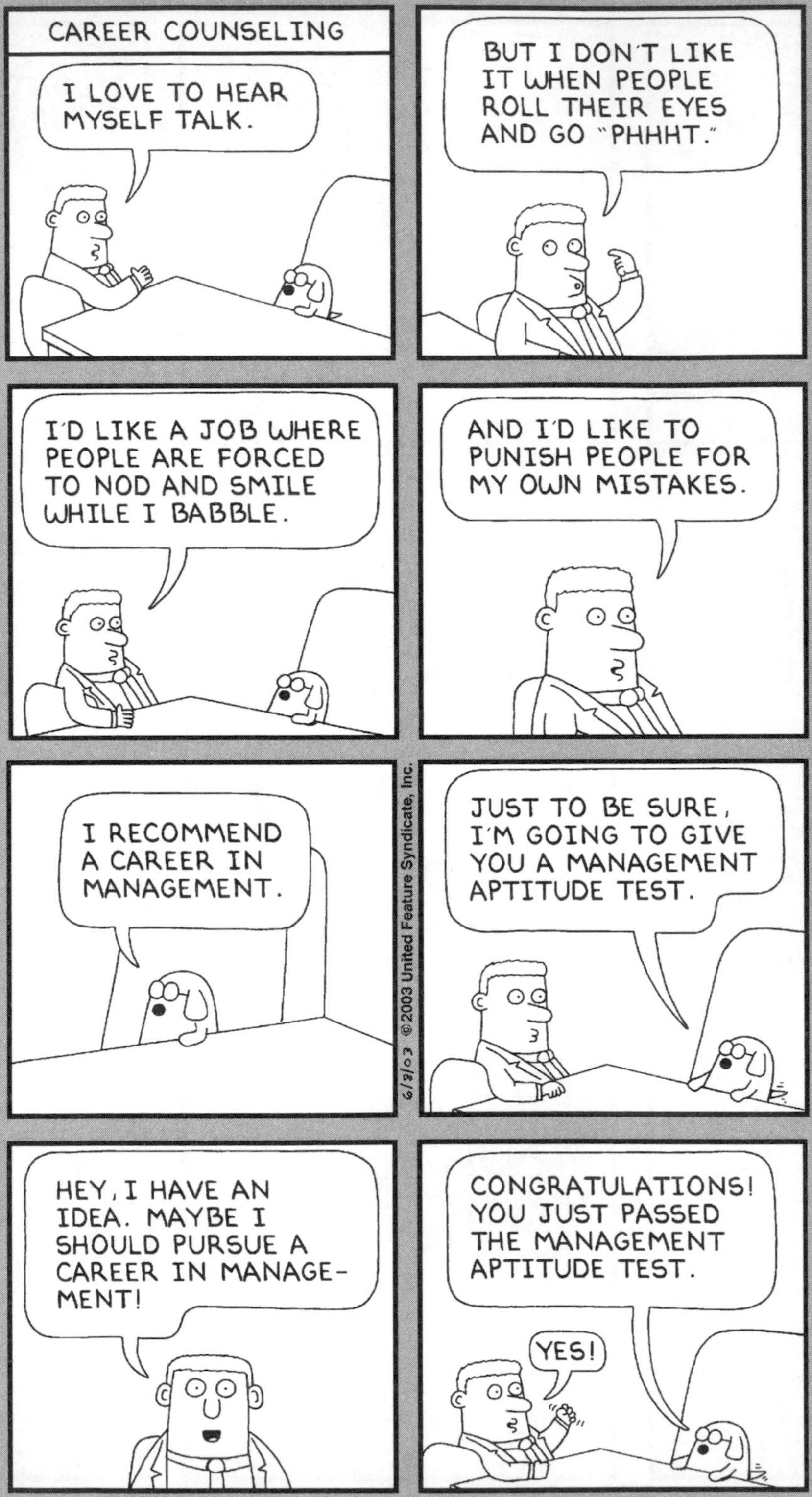
CAREER COUNSELING
I LOVE TO HEAR MYSELF TALK.
BUT I DON'T LIKE IT WHEN PEOPLE ROLL THEIR EYES AND GO "PHHHT."
I'D LIKE A JOB WHERE PEOPLE ARE FORCED TO NOD AND SMILE WHILE I BABBLE.
AND I'D LIKE TO PUNISH PEOPLE FOR MY OWN MISTAKES.
I RECOMMEND A CAREER IN MANAGEMENT.
6/8/03 ©2003 United Feature Syndicate, Inc.
JUST TO BE SURE, I'M GOING TO GIVE YOU A MANAGEMENT APTITUDE TEST.
HEY, I HAVE AN IDEA. MAYBE I SHOULD PURSUE A CAREER IN MANAGE-MENT!
CONGRATULATIONS! YOU JUST PASSED THE MANAGEMENT APTITUDE TEST.
YES!

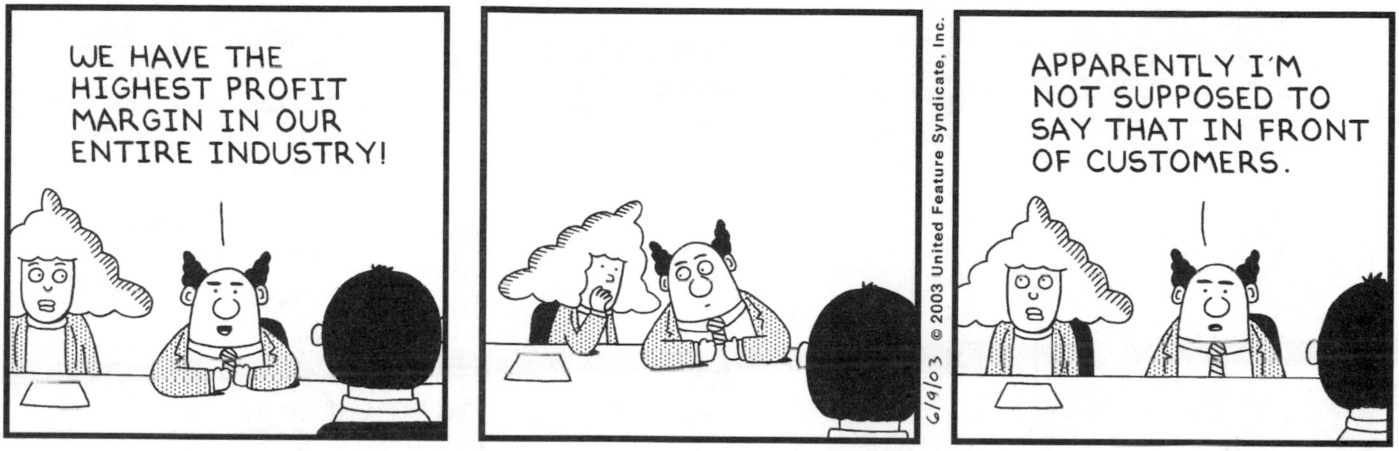
WE HAVE THE HIGHEST PROFIT MARGIN IN OUR ENTIRE INDUSTRY!
6/9/03 © 2003 United Feature Syndicate, Inc.
APPARENTLY I'M NOT SUPPOSED TO SAY THAT IN FRONT OF CUSTOMERS.

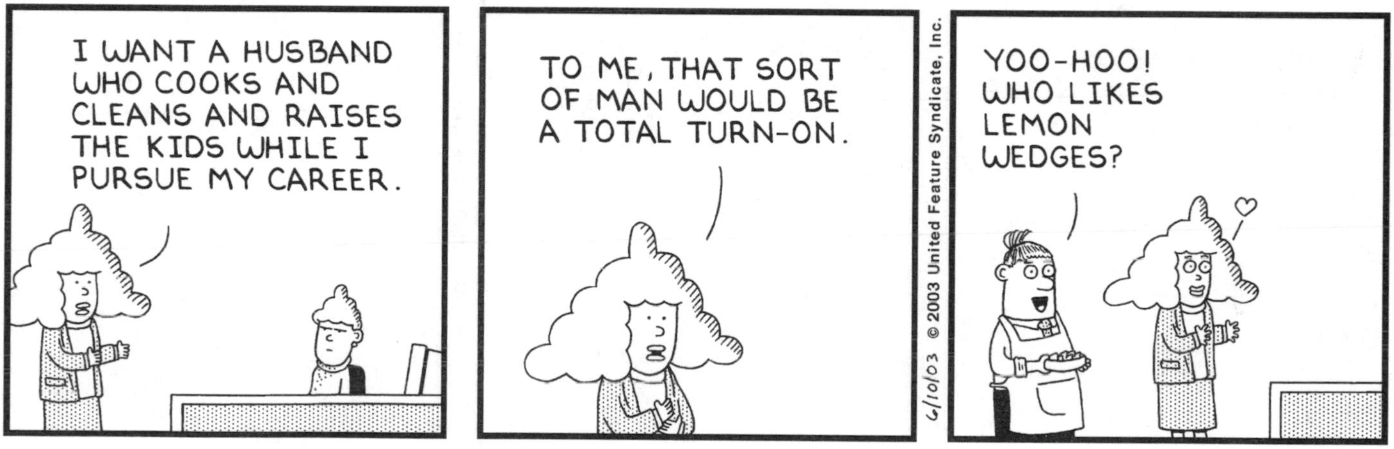
I WANT A HUSBAND WHO COOKS AND CLEANS AND RAISES THE KIDS WHILE I PURSUE MY CAREER.
TO ME, THAT SORT OF MAN WOULD BE A TOTAL TURN-ON.
6/10/03 © 2003 United Feature Syndicate, Inc.
YOO-HOO! WHO LIKES LEMON WEDGES?

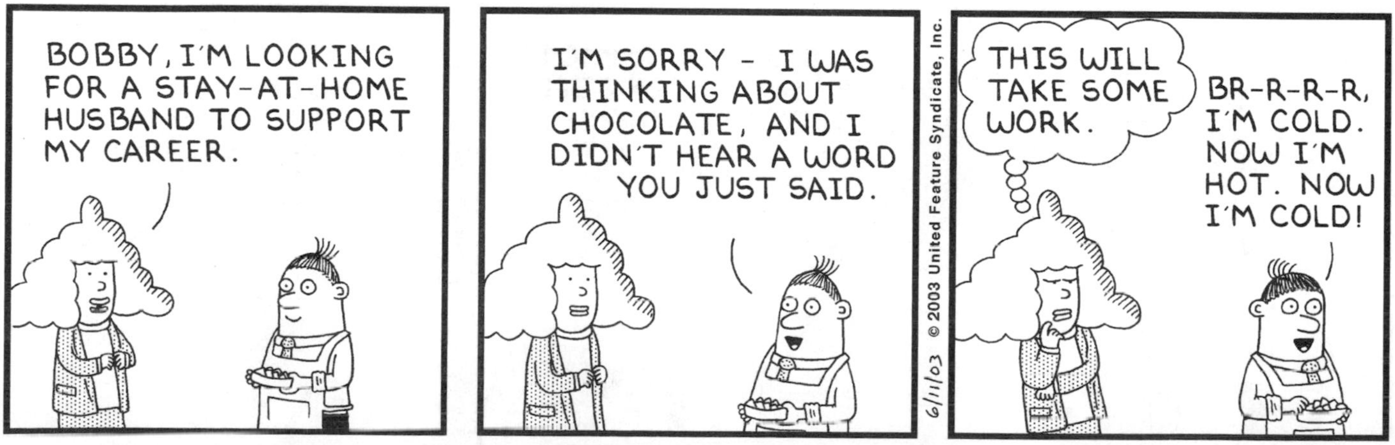
BOBBY, I'M LOOKING FOR A STAY-AT-HOME HUSBAND TO SUPPORT MY CAREER.
I'M SORRY - I WAS THINKING ABOUT CHOCOLATE, AND I DIDN'T HEAR A WORD YOU JUST SAID.
6/11/03 © 2003 United Feature Syndicate, Inc.
THIS WILL TAKE SOME WORK.
BR-R-R-R, I'M COLD. NOW I'M HOT. NOW I'M COLD!

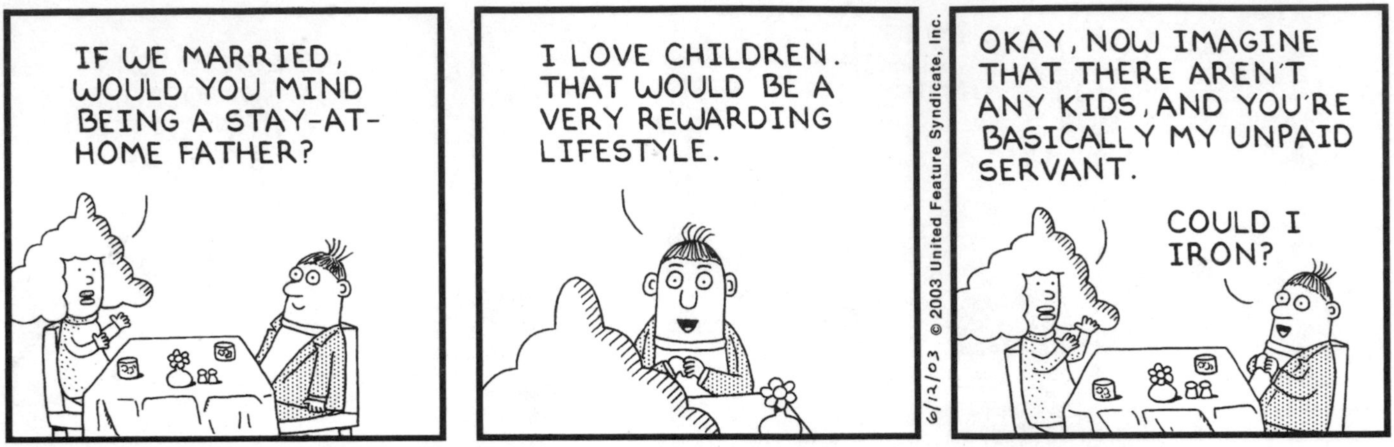
IF WE MARRIED, WOULD YOU MIND BEING A STAY-AT-HOME FATHER?
I LOVE CHILDREN. THAT WOULD BE A VERY REWARDING LIFESTYLE.
6/12/03 © 2003 United Feature Syndicate, Inc.
OKAY, NOW IMAGINE THAT THERE AREN'T ANY KIDS, AND YOU'RE BASICALLY MY UNPAID SERVANT.
COULD I IRON?

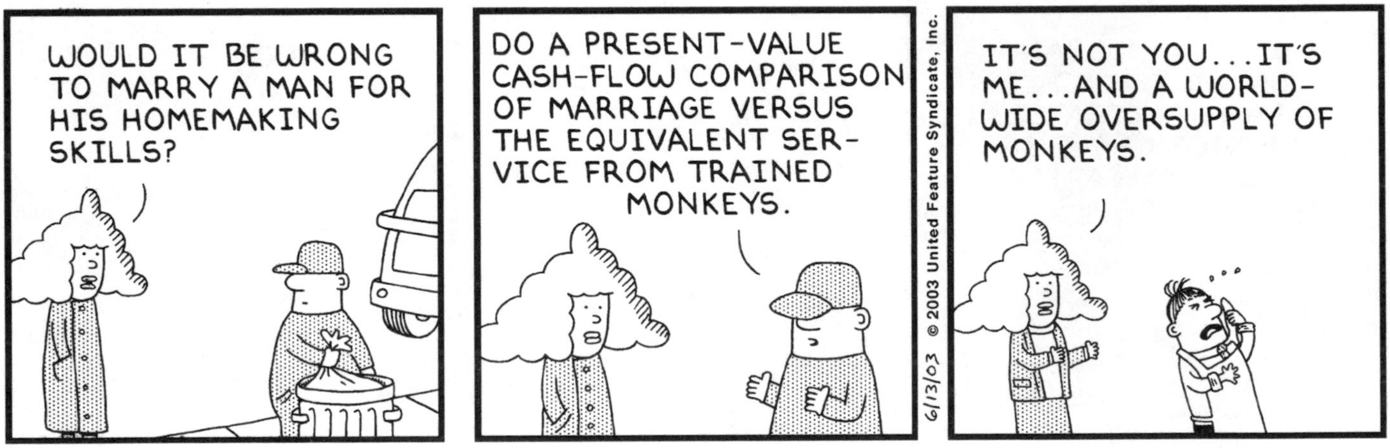
WOULD IT BE WRONG TO MARRY A MAN FOR HIS HOMEMAKING SKILLS?
DO A PRESENT-VALUE CASH-FLOW COMPARISON OF MARRIAGE VERSUS THE EQUIVALENT SERVICE FROM TRAINED MONKEYS.
6/13/03 © 2003 United Feature Syndicate, Inc.
IT'S NOT YOU...IT'S ME...AND A WORLD-WIDE OVERSUPPLY OF MONKEYS.

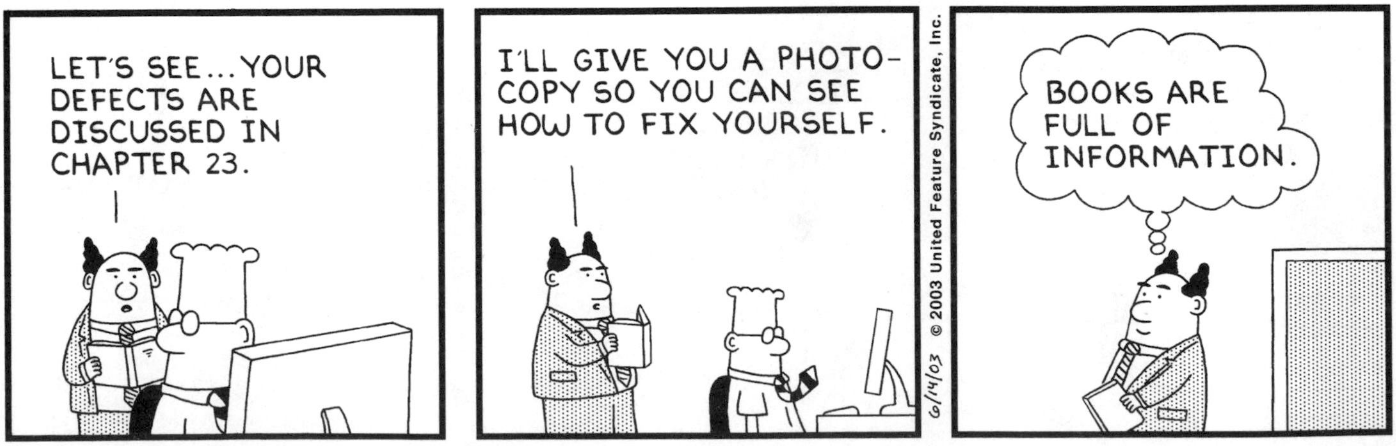
LET'S SEE...YOUR DEFECTS ARE DISCUSSED IN CHAPTER 23.
I'LL GIVE YOU A PHOTOCOPY SO YOU CAN SEE HOW TO FIX YOURSELF.
6/14/03 © 2003 United Feature Syndicate, Inc.
BOOKS ARE FULL OF INFORMATION.

IT'S NOT JUST MY DESK; IT'S THE CHAIR, TOO!
DILBERT, COME HERE!
EVERYTHING IN MY OFFICE FEELS CLAMMY.
I FIRST NOTICED WHEN I TOUCHED MY PHONE...THEN MY MOUSE.
ALL CLAMMY.
WHAT COULD IT MEAN?
6/15/03 ©2003 United Feature Syndicate, Inc.
IT COULD MEAN YOUR HANDS ARE CLAMMY.
YOU MUST NEVER SPEAK OF THIS.
HAVE YOU EVER NOTICED THAT EVERY-THING YOU SIT ON FEELS LIKE UNDERPANTS?

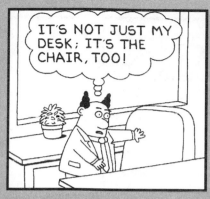

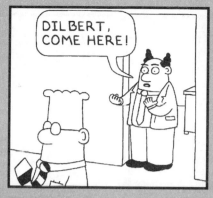

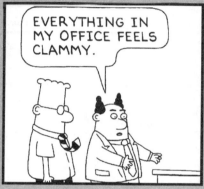

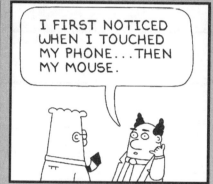

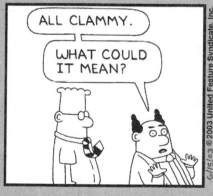

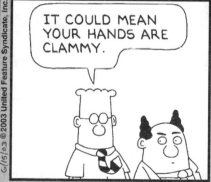

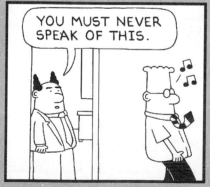

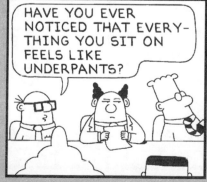

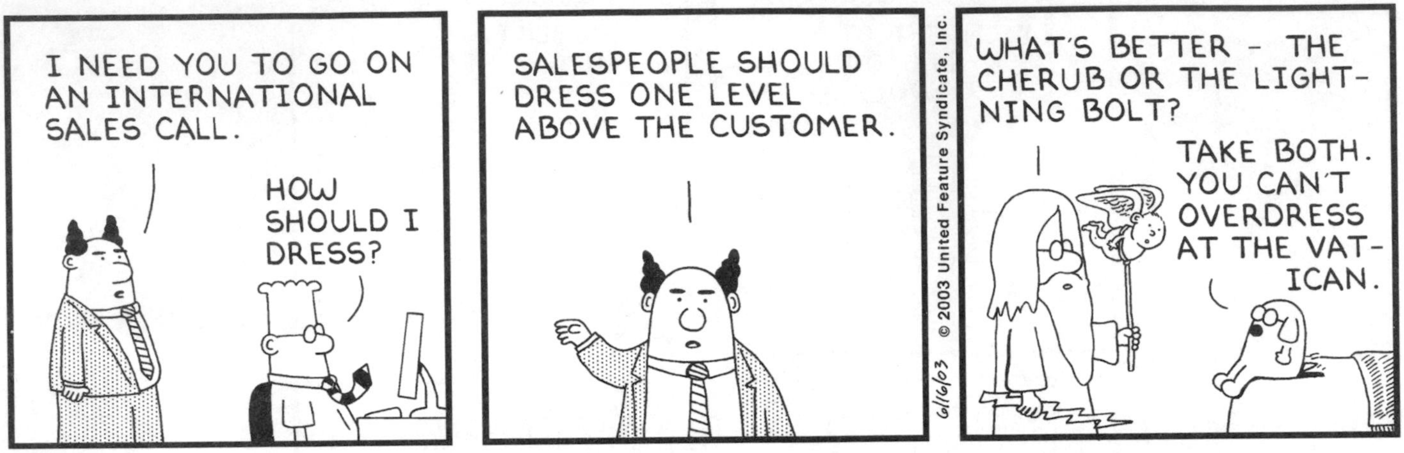
I NEED YOU TO GO ON AN INTERNATIONAL SALES CALL.
HOW SHOULD I DRESS?
SALESPEOPLE SHOULD DRESS ONE LEVEL ABOVE THE CUSTOMER.
WHAT'S BETTER - THE CHERUB OR THE LIGHT-NING BOLT?
TAKE BOTH. YOU CAN'T OVERDRESS AT THE VAT-ICAN.
6/16/03 © 2003 United Feature Syndicate, Inc.

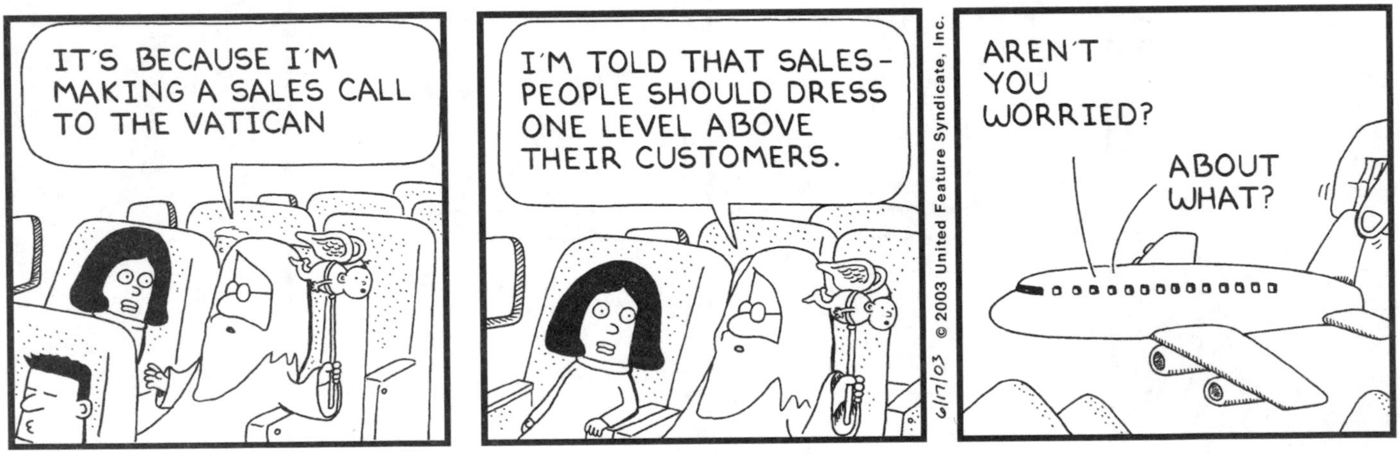
IT'S BECAUSE I'M MAKING A SALES CALL TO THE VATICAN
I'M TOLD THAT SALES-PEOPLE SHOULD DRESS ONE LEVEL ABOVE THEIR CUSTOMERS.
AREN'T YOU WORRIED?
ABOUT WHAT?
6/17/03 © 2003 United Feature Syndicate, Inc.

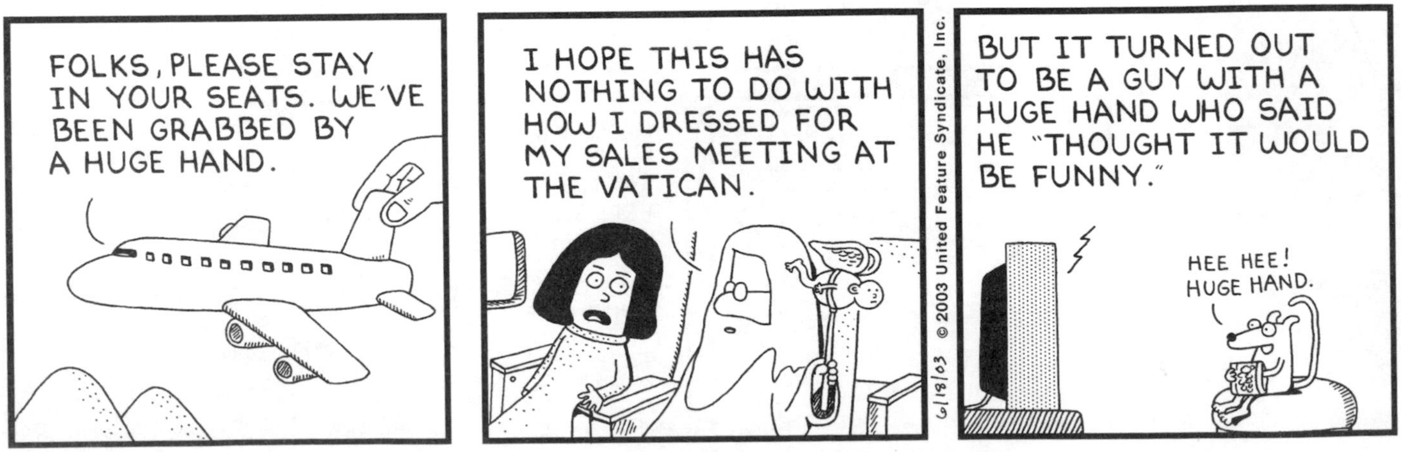
FOLKS, PLEASE STAY IN YOUR SEATS. WE'VE BEEN GRABBED BY A HUGE HAND.
I HOPE THIS HAS NOTHING TO DO WITH HOW I DRESSED FOR MY SALES MEETING AT THE VATICAN.
BUT IT TURNED OUT TO BE A GUY WITH A HUGE HAND WHO SAID HE "THOUGHT IT WOULD BE FUNNY."
HEE HEE! HUGE HAND.
6/18/03 © 2003 United Feature Syndicate, Inc.

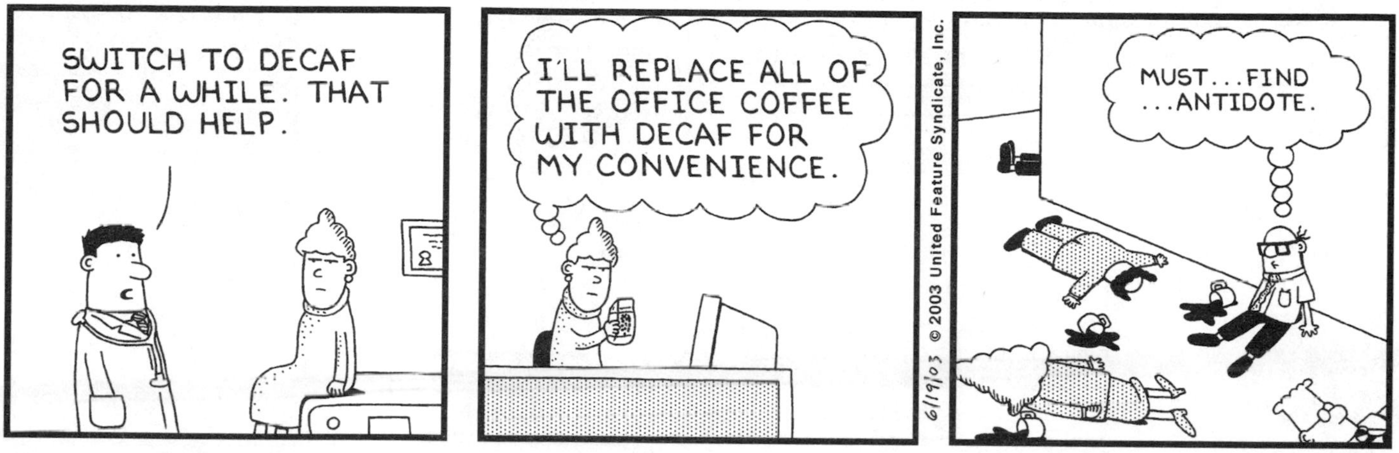
SWITCH TO DECAF FOR A WHILE. THAT SHOULD HELP.
I'LL REPLACE ALL OF THE OFFICE COFFEE WITH DECAF FOR MY CONVENIENCE.
6/19/03 © 2003 United Feature Syndicate, Inc.
MUST...FIND ...ANTIDOTE.

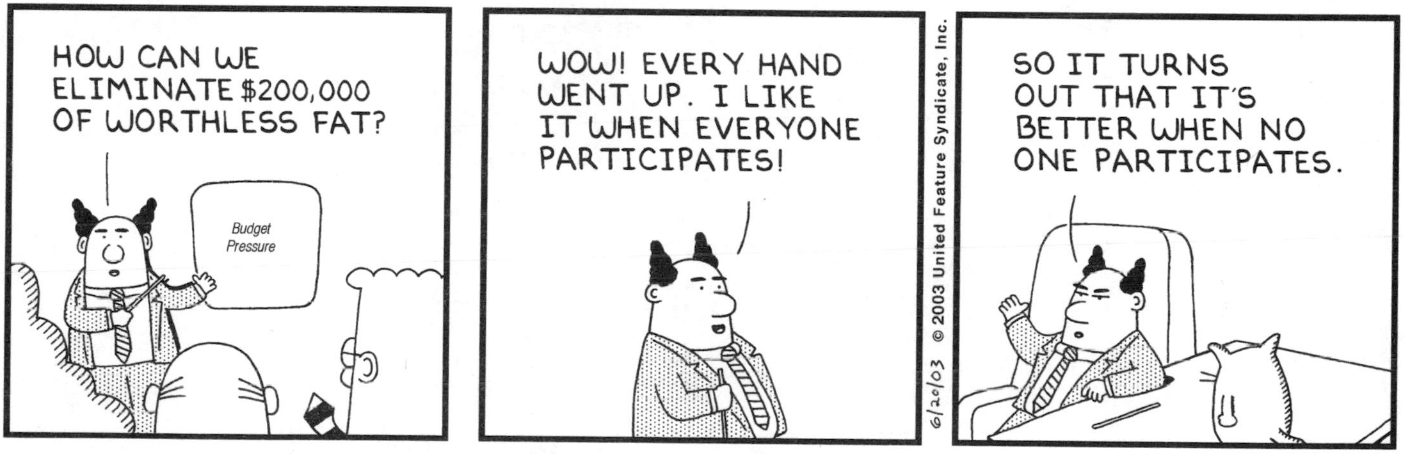
HOW CAN WE ELIMINATE $200,000 OF WORTHLESS FAT?
Budget Pressure
WOW! EVERY HAND WENT UP. I LIKE IT WHEN EVERYONE PARTICIPATES!
6/20/03 © 2003 United Feature Syndicate, Inc.
SO IT TURNS OUT THAT IT'S BETTER WHEN NO ONE PARTICIPATES.

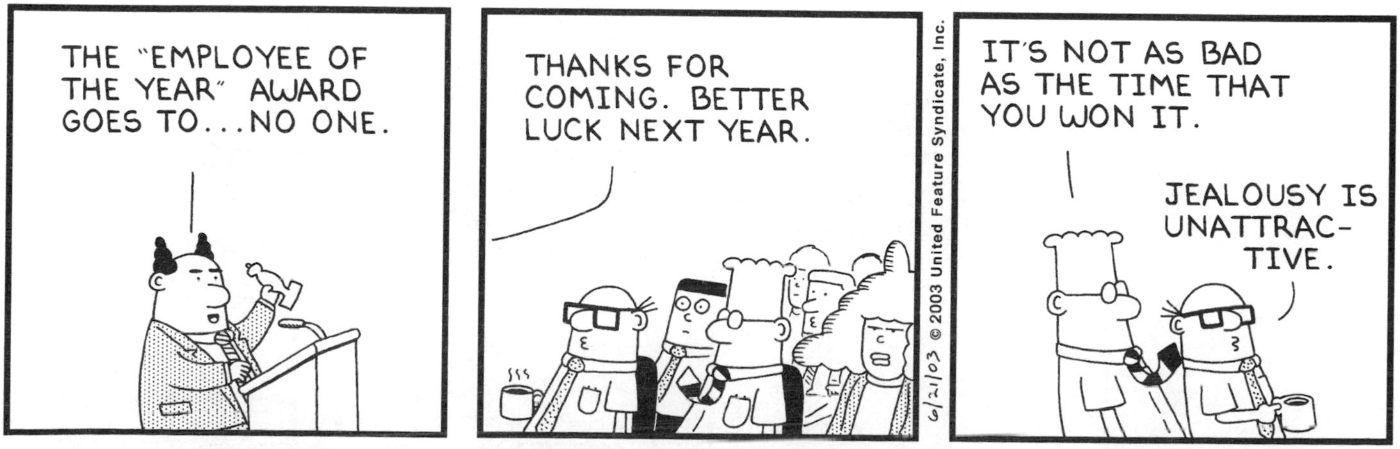
THE "EMPLOYEE OF THE YEAR" AWARD GOES TO...NO ONE.
THANKS FOR COMING. BETTER LUCK NEXT YEAR.
6/21/03 © 2003 United Feature Syndicate, Inc.
IT'S NOT AS BAD AS THE TIME THAT YOU WON IT.
JEALOUSY IS UNATTRAC- TIVE.

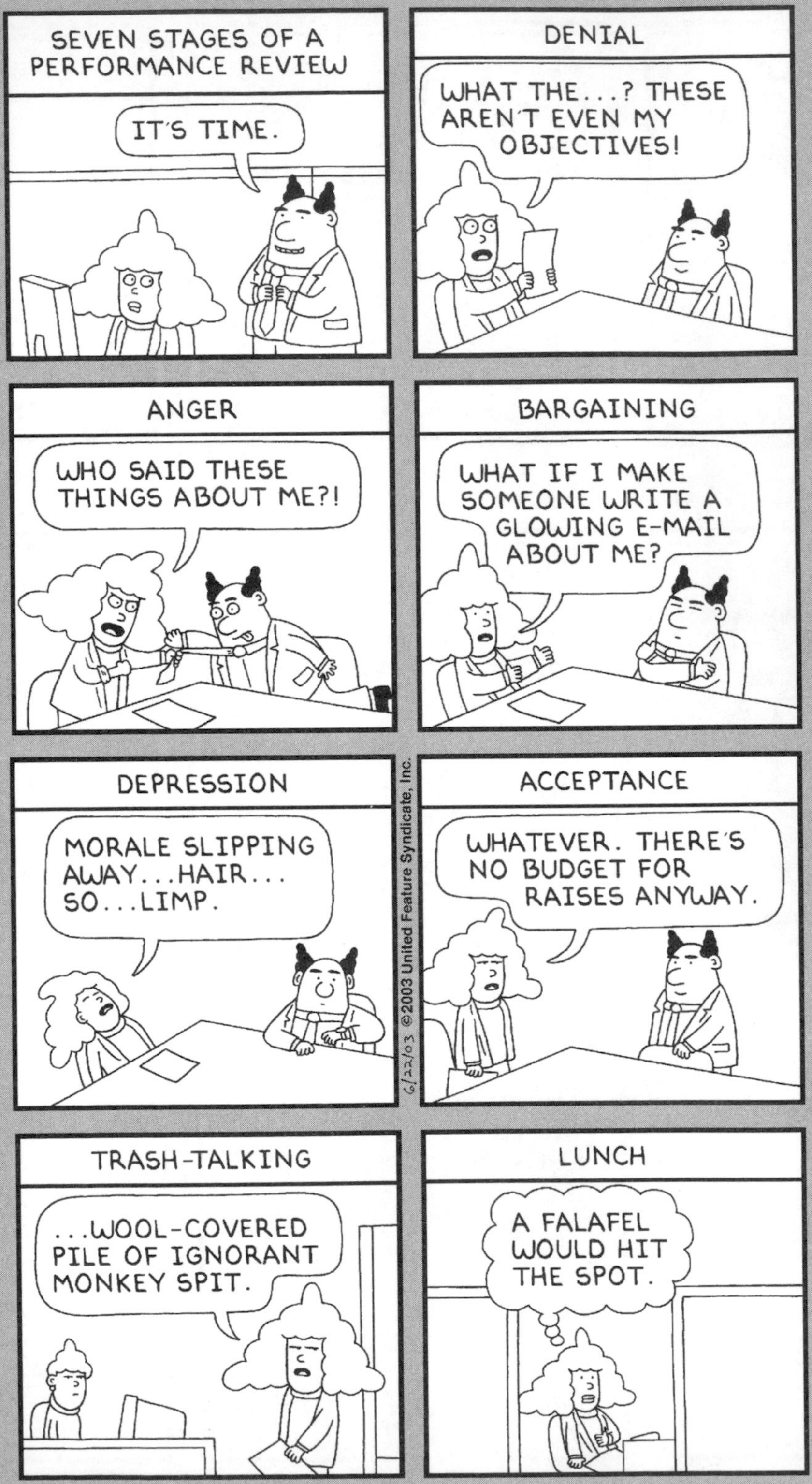
SEVEN STAGES OF A PERFORMANCE REVIEW
IT'S TIME.
DENIAL
WHAT THE...? THESE AREN'T EVEN MY OBJECTIVES!
ANGER
WHO SAID THESE THINGS ABOUT ME?!
BARGAINING
WHAT IF I MAKE SOMEONE WRITE A GLOWING E-MAIL ABOUT ME?
DEPRESSION
MORALE SLIPPING AWAY...HAIR... SO...LIMP.
ACCEPTANCE
WHATEVER. THERE'S NO BUDGET FOR RAISES ANYWAY.
TRASH-TALKING
...WOOL-COVERED PILE OF IGNORANT MONKEY SPIT.
LUNCH
A FALAFEL WOULD HIT THE SPOT.
6/22/03 ©2003 United Feature Syndicate, Inc.

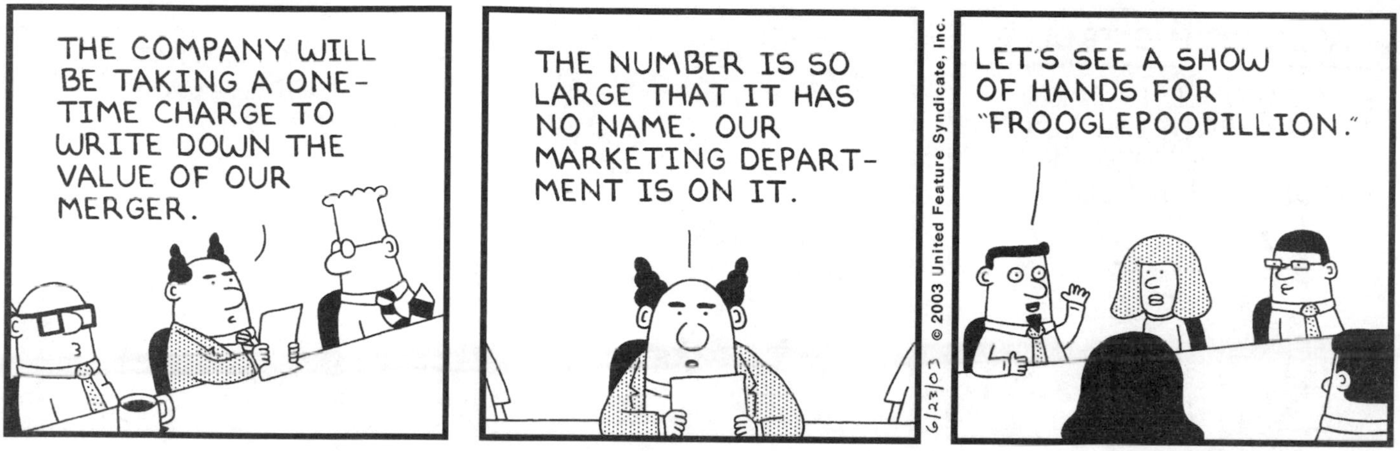
THE COMPANY WILL BE TAKING A ONE-TIME CHARGE TO WRITE DOWN THE VALUE OF OUR MERGER.
THE NUMBER IS SO LARGE THAT IT HAS NO NAME. OUR MARKETING DEPARTMENT IS ON IT.
6/23/03 © 2003 United Feature Syndicate, Inc.
LET'S SEE A SHOW OF HANDS FOR "FROOGLEPOOPILLION."

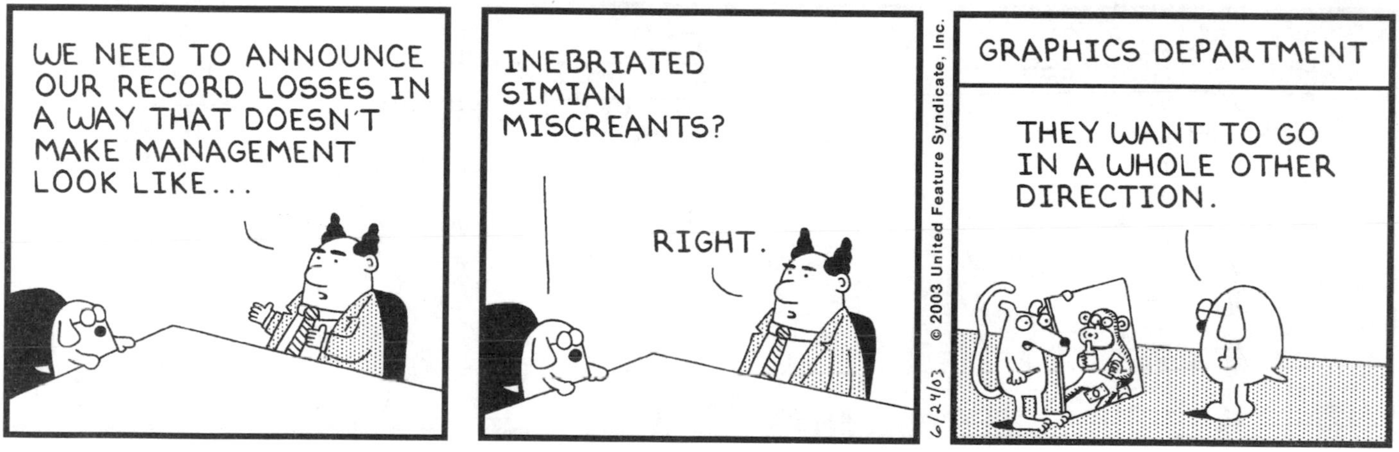
WE NEED TO ANNOUNCE OUR RECORD LOSSES IN A WAY THAT DOESN'T MAKE MANAGEMENT LOOK LIKE...
INEBRIATED SIMIAN MISCREANTS?
RIGHT.
6/24/03 © 2003 United Feature Syndicate, Inc.
GRAPHICS DEPARTMENT
THEY WANT TO GO IN A WHOLE OTHER DIRECTION.

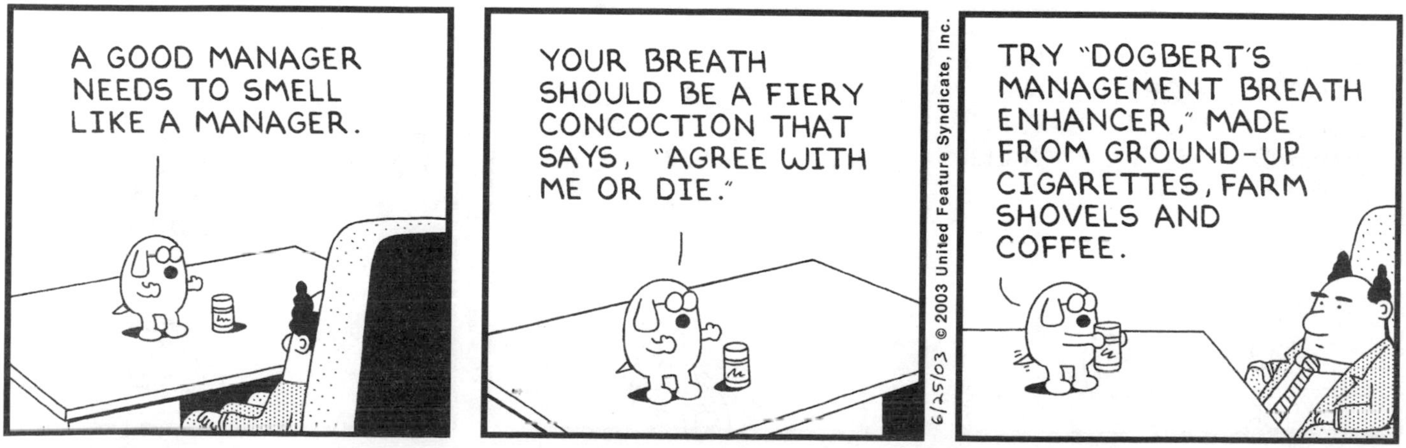
A GOOD MANAGER NEEDS TO SMELL LIKE A MANAGER.
YOUR BREATH SHOULD BE A FIERY CONCOCTION THAT SAYS, "AGREE WITH ME OR DIE."
6/25/03 © 2003 United Feature Syndicate, Inc.
TRY "DOGBERT'S MANAGEMENT BREATH ENHANCER," MADE FROM GROUND-UP CIGARETTES, FARM SHOVELS AND COFFEE.

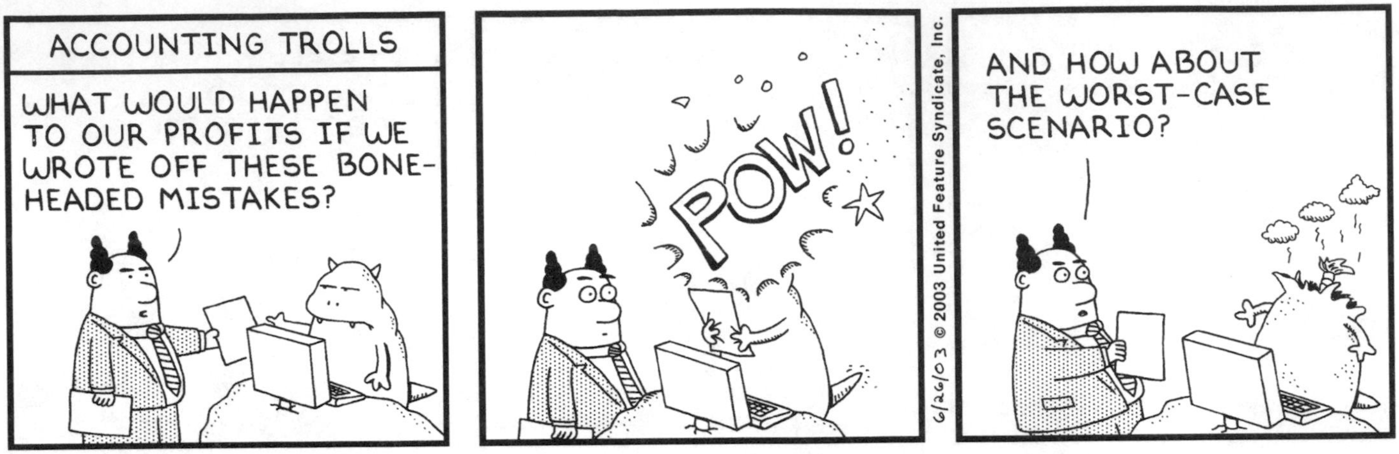
ACCOUNTING TROLLS
WHAT WOULD HAPPEN TO OUR PROFITS IF WE WROTE OFF THESE BONE-HEADED MISTAKES?
POW!
AND HOW ABOUT THE WORST-CASE SCENARIO?
6/26/03 © 2003 United Feature Syndicate, Inc.

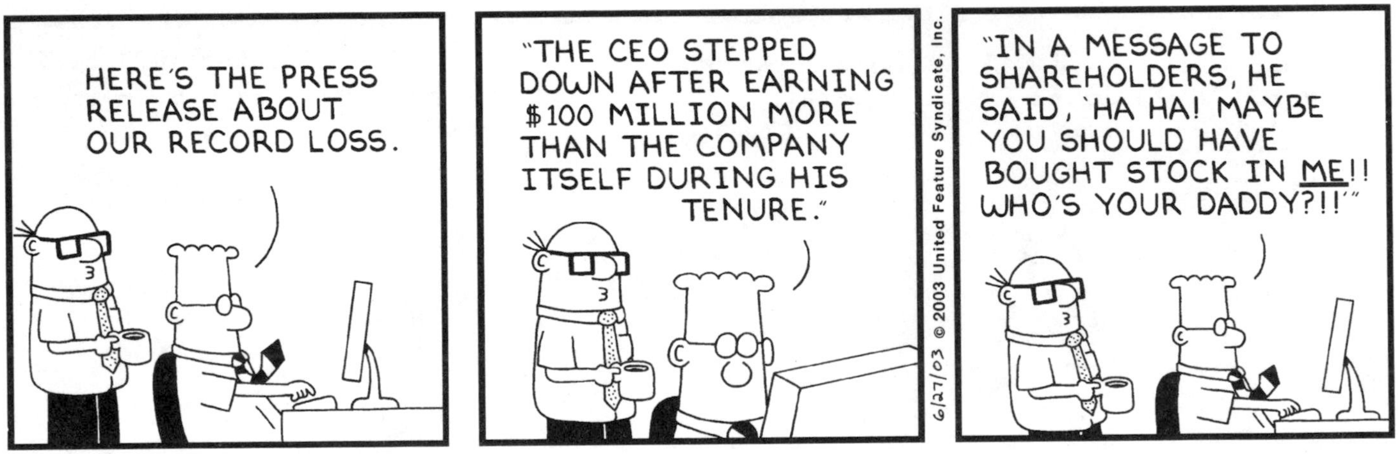
HERE'S THE PRESS RELEASE ABOUT OUR RECORD LOSS.
"THE CEO STEPPED DOWN AFTER EARNING $100 MILLION MORE THAN THE COMPANY ITSELF DURING HIS TENURE."
"IN A MESSAGE TO SHAREHOLDERS, HE SAID, 'HA HA! MAYBE YOU SHOULD HAVE BOUGHT STOCK IN ME!! WHO'S YOUR DADDY?!!'"
6/27/03 © 2003 United Feature Syndicate, Inc.

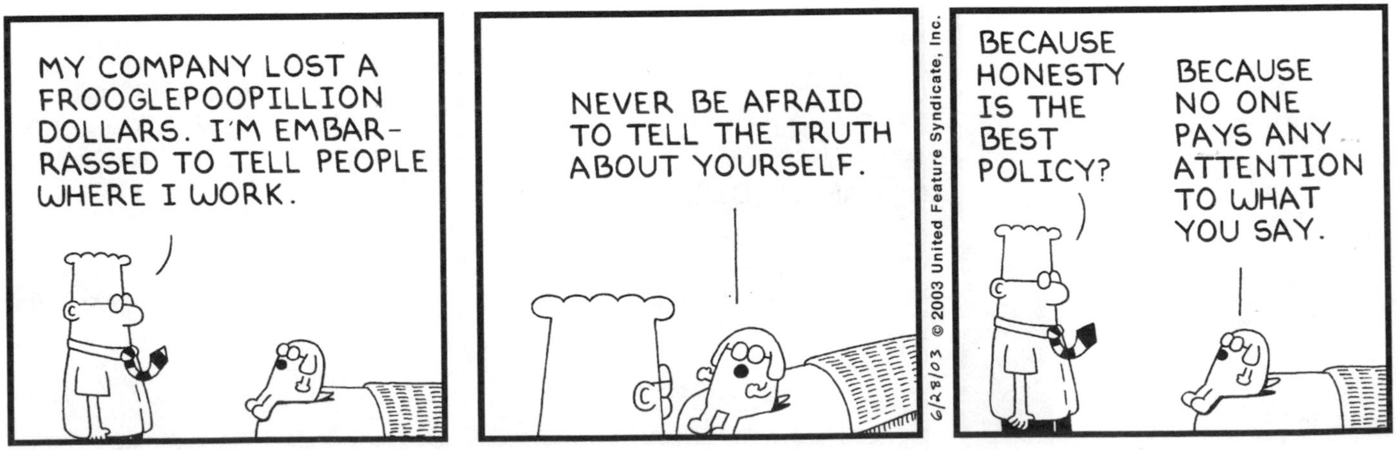
MY COMPANY LOST A FROOGLEPOOPILLION DOLLARS. I'M EMBARRASSED TO TELL PEOPLE WHERE I WORK.
NEVER BE AFRAID TO TELL THE TRUTH ABOUT YOURSELF.
BECAUSE HONESTY IS THE BEST POLICY?
BECAUSE NO ONE PAYS ANY ATTENTION TO WHAT YOU SAY.
6/28/03 © 2003 United Feature Syndicate, Inc.

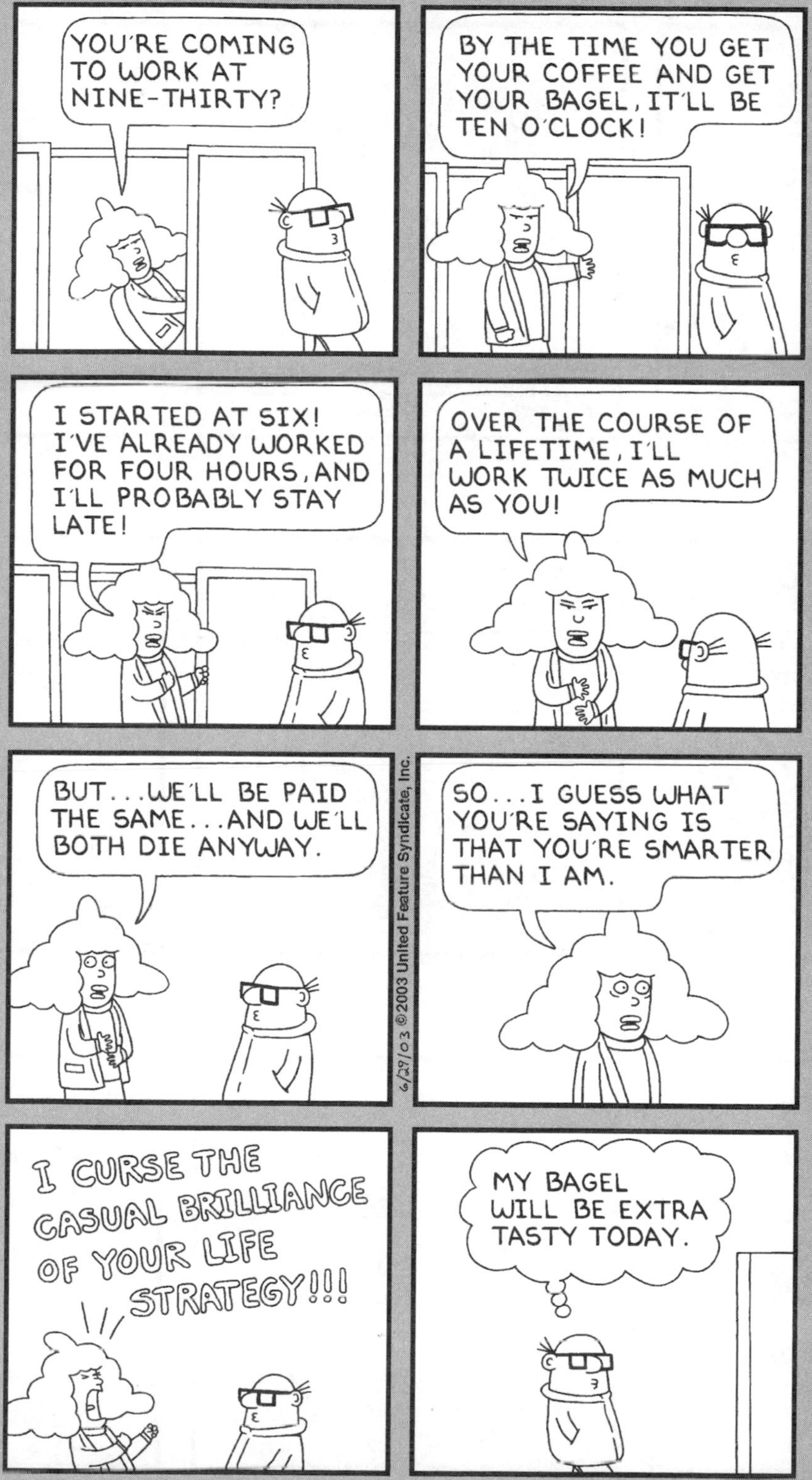
YOU'RE COMING TO WORK AT NINE-THIRTY?
BY THE TIME YOU GET YOUR COFFEE AND GET YOUR BAGEL, IT'LL BE TEN O'CLOCK!
I STARTED AT SIX! I'VE ALREADY WORKED FOR FOUR HOURS, AND I'LL PROBABLY STAY LATE!
OVER THE COURSE OF A LIFETIME, I'LL WORK TWICE AS MUCH AS YOU!
BUT...WE'LL BE PAID THE SAME...AND WE'LL BOTH DIE ANYWAY.
SO...I GUESS WHAT YOU'RE SAYING IS THAT YOU'RE SMARTER THAN I AM.
I CURSE THE CASUAL BRILLIANCE OF YOUR LIFE STRATEGY!!!
MY BAGEL WILL BE EXTRA TASTY TODAY.
6/27/03 ©2003 United Feature Syndicate, Inc.

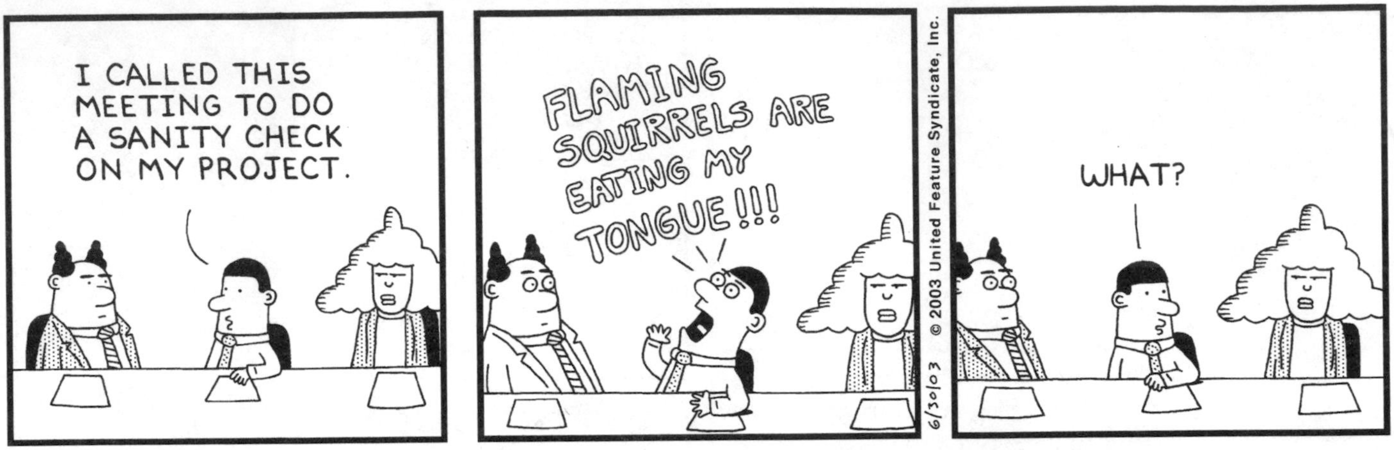
I CALLED THIS MEETING TO DO A SANITY CHECK ON MY PROJECT.
FLAMING SQUIRRELS ARE EATING MY TONGUE!!!
WHAT?
6/30/03 © 2003 United Feature Syndicate, Inc.

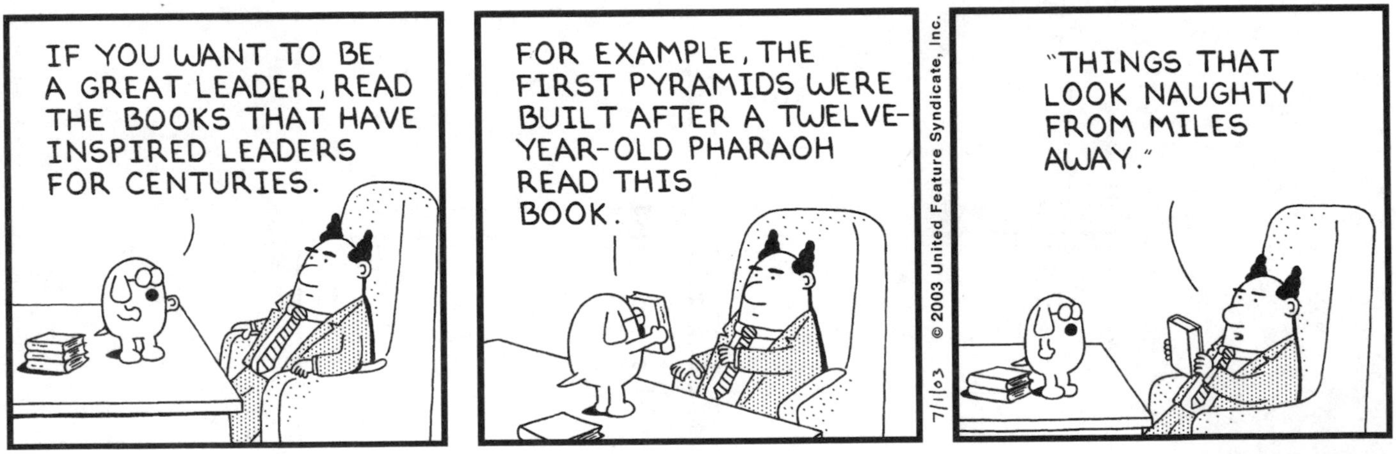
IF YOU WANT TO BE A GREAT LEADER, READ THE BOOKS THAT HAVE INSPIRED LEADERS FOR CENTURIES.
FOR EXAMPLE, THE FIRST PYRAMIDS WERE BUILT AFTER A TWELVE-YEAR-OLD PHARAOH READ THIS BOOK.
"THINGS THAT LOOK NAUGHTY FROM MILES AWAY."
7/1/03 © 2003 United Feature Syndicate, Inc.

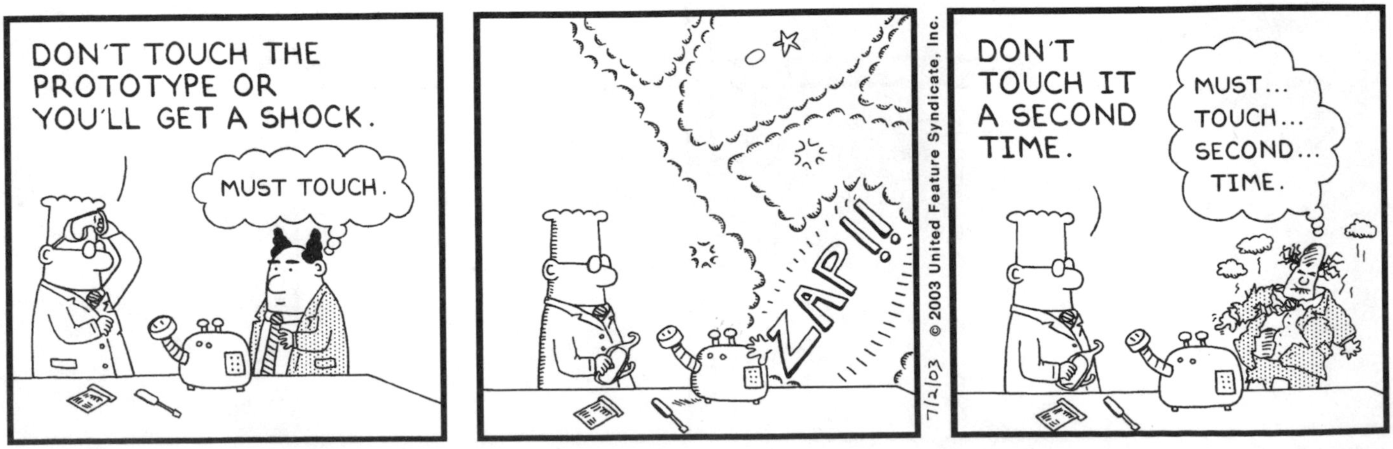
DON'T TOUCH THE PROTOTYPE OR YOU'LL GET A SHOCK.
MUST TOUCH.
ZAP!!
DON'T TOUCH IT A SECOND TIME.
MUST... TOUCH... SECOND... TIME.
7/2/03 © 2003 United Feature Syndicate, Inc.

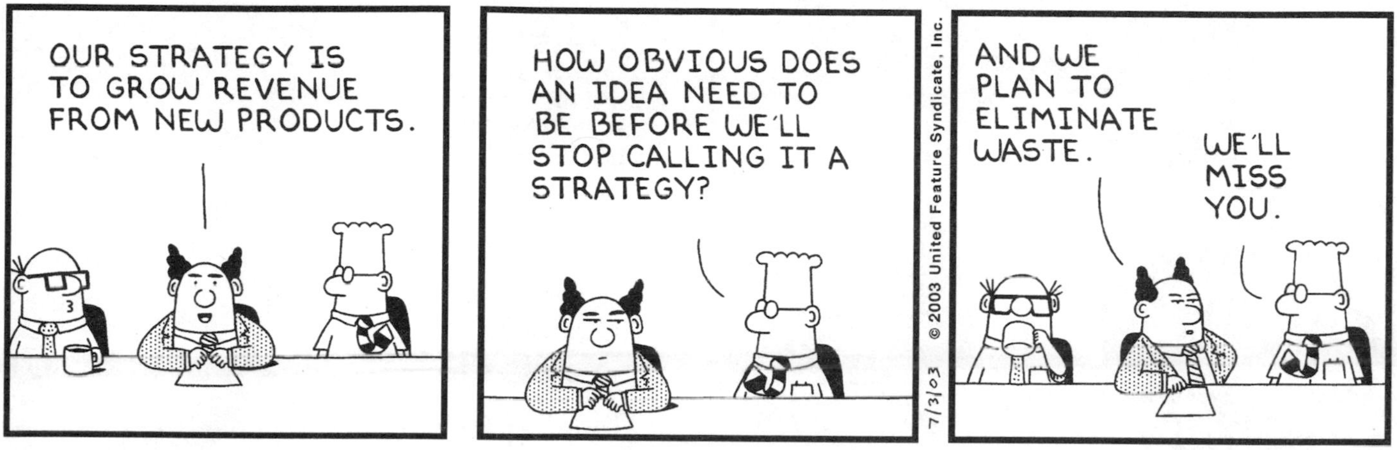
OUR STRATEGY IS TO GROW REVENUE FROM NEW PRODUCTS.
HOW OBVIOUS DOES AN IDEA NEED TO BE BEFORE WE'LL STOP CALLING IT A STRATEGY?
© 2003 United Feature Syndicate, Inc.
7/3/03
AND WE PLAN TO ELIMINATE WASTE.
WE'LL MISS YOU.

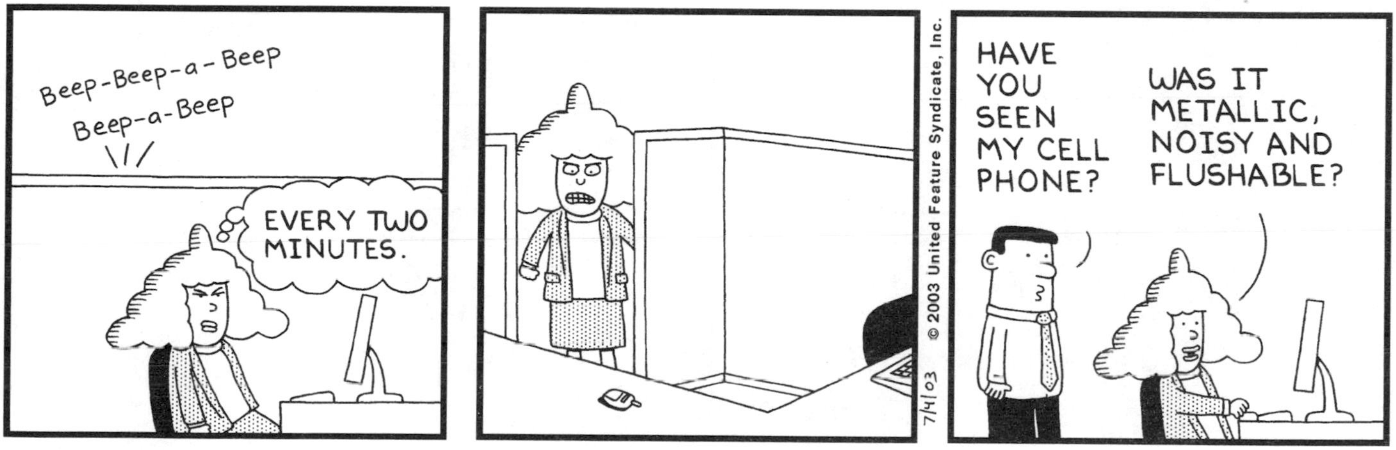
Beep-Beep-a-Beep
Beep-a-Beep
EVERY TWO MINUTES.
© 2003 United Feature Syndicate, Inc.
7/4/03
HAVE YOU SEEN MY CELL PHONE?
WAS IT METALLIC, NOISY AND FLUSHABLE?

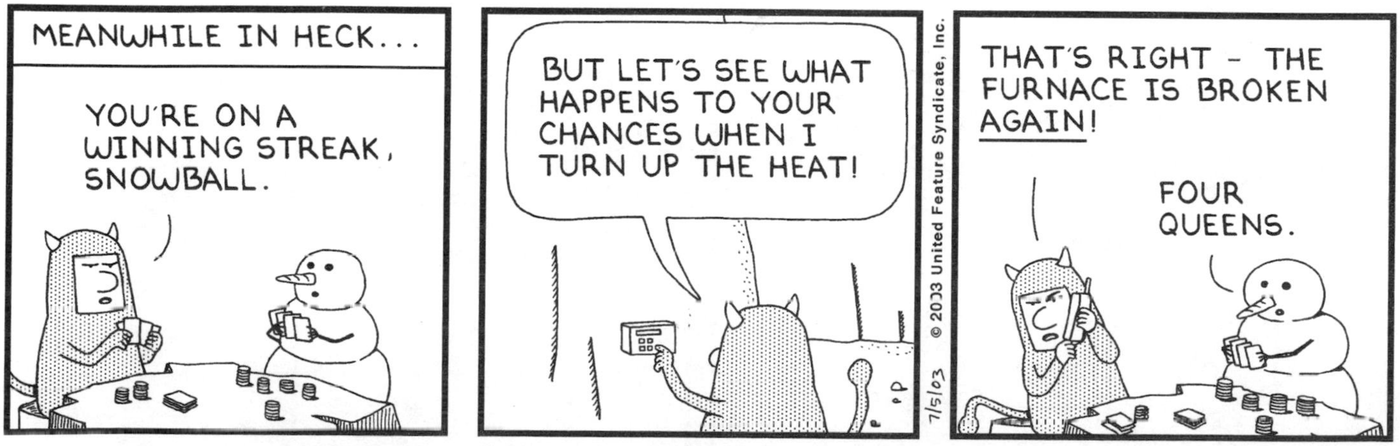
MEANWHILE IN HECK...
YOU'RE ON A WINNING STREAK, SNOWBALL.
BUT LET'S SEE WHAT HAPPENS TO YOUR CHANCES WHEN I TURN UP THE HEAT!
© 2003 United Feature Syndicate, Inc.
7/5/03
THAT'S RIGHT - THE FURNACE IS BROKEN AGAIN!
FOUR QUEENS.

THANKS FOR TESTING MY NEW INVENTION.
IF THIS THING WORKS, IT WILL CHANGE FOREVER THE WAY THAT MOTHERS USE THE TELEPHONE.
WE'VE BEEN ON THE PHONE FOR HALF A MINUTE. THE NOISE SHOULD START AT ANY MOMENT.
HERE IT COMES.
HEY! WHAT ARE YOU DOING ON THE PHONE?!
CAN I EAT TEN COOKIES? I THINK MY ARM IS BROKEN! WHERE'S MY TOY?!!
© 2003 United Feature Syndicate, Inc.
7/6/03
WAAAAAAAAAAAA!!
NOW PRESS THE TODDLER NOISE CANCELLATION BUTTON.
IT STOPPED THE NOISE, BUT YOU NEED TO DO SOMETHING ABOUT THE VISUAL.

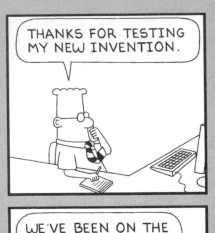

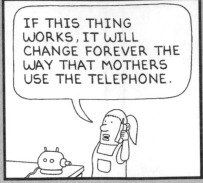

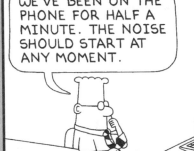

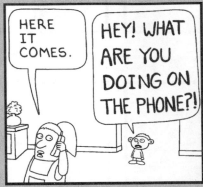

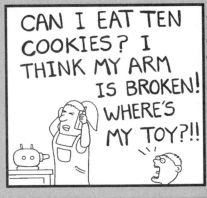

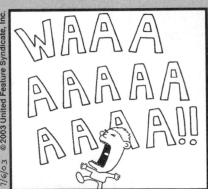

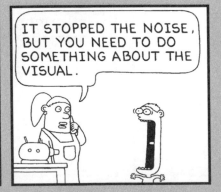

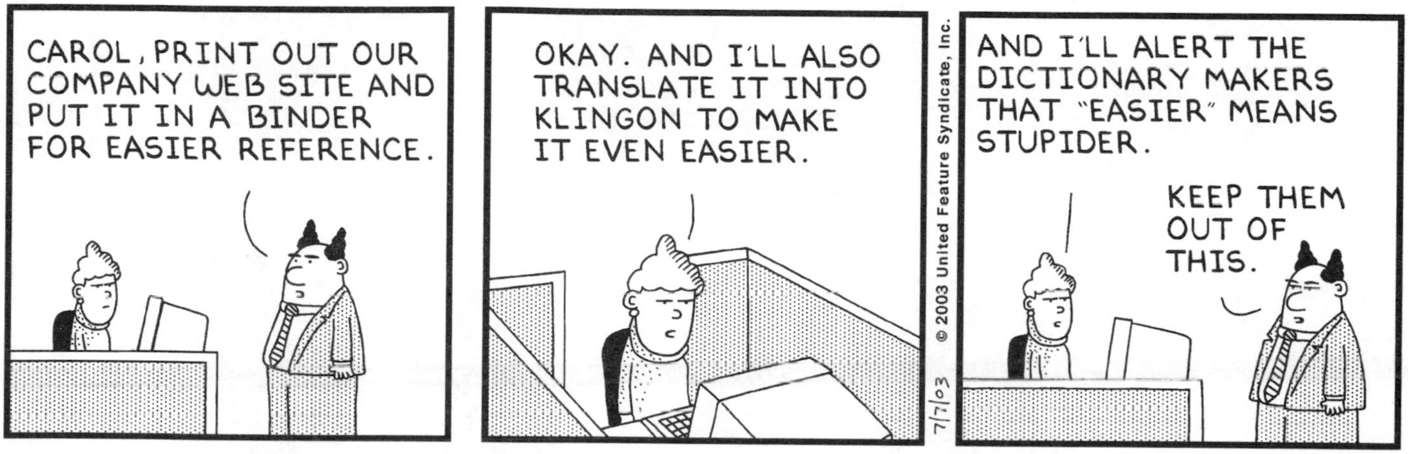
CAROL, PRINT OUT OUR COMPANY WEB SITE AND PUT IT IN A BINDER FOR EASIER REFERENCE.
OKAY. AND I'LL ALSO TRANSLATE IT INTO KLINGON TO MAKE IT EVEN EASIER.
7/7/03 © 2003 United Feature Syndicate, Inc.
AND I'LL ALERT THE DICTIONARY MAKERS THAT "EASIER" MEANS STUPIDER.
KEEP THEM OUT OF THIS.

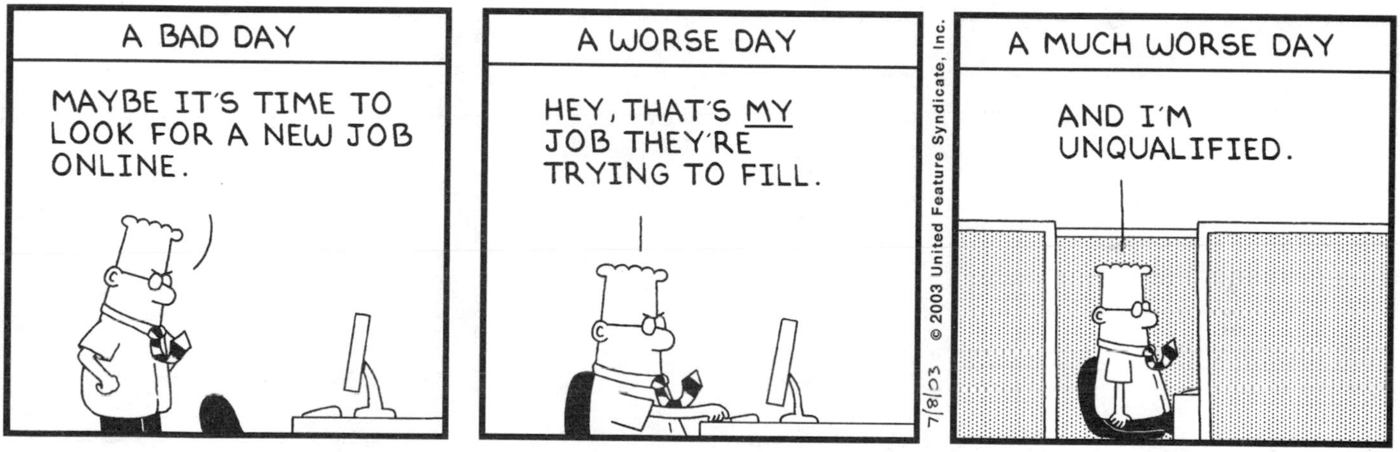
A BAD DAY
MAYBE IT'S TIME TO LOOK FOR A NEW JOB ONLINE.
A WORSE DAY
HEY, THAT'S MY JOB THEY'RE TRYING TO FILL.
7/8/03 © 2003 United Feature Syndicate, Inc.
A MUCH WORSE DAY
AND I'M UNQUALIFIED.

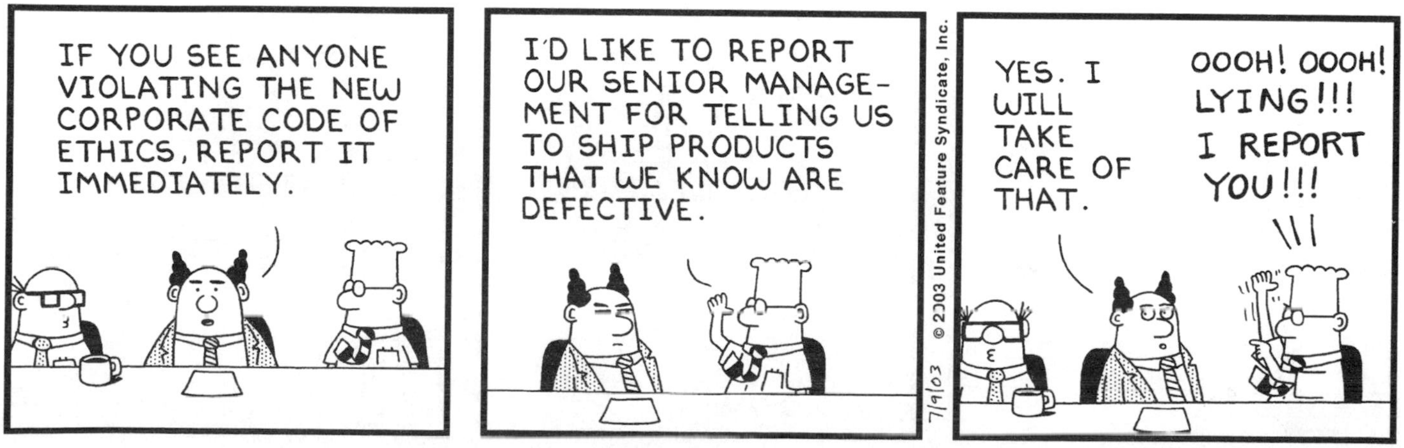
IF YOU SEE ANYONE VIOLATING THE NEW CORPORATE CODE OF ETHICS, REPORT IT IMMEDIATELY.
I'D LIKE TO REPORT OUR SENIOR MANAGEMENT FOR TELLING US TO SHIP PRODUCTS THAT WE KNOW ARE DEFECTIVE.
7/9/03 © 2303 United Feature Syndicate, Inc.
YES. I WILL TAKE CARE OF THAT.
OOOH! OOOH! LYING!!! I REPORT YOU!!!

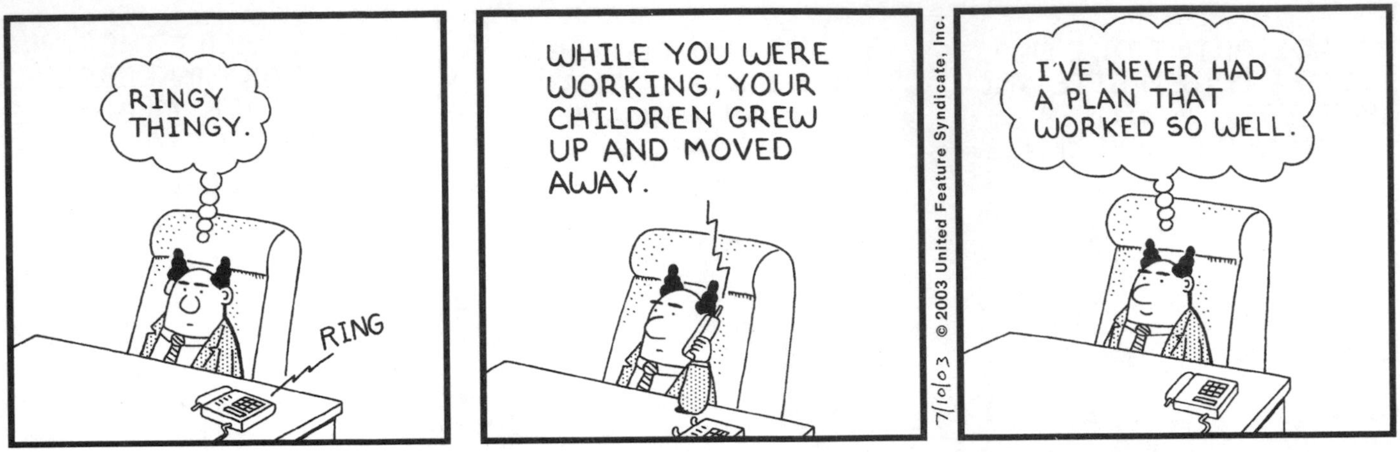
RINGY THINGY.
RING
WHILE YOU WERE WORKING, YOUR CHILDREN GREW UP AND MOVED AWAY.
7/10/03 © 2003 United Feature Syndicate, Inc.
I'VE NEVER HAD A PLAN THAT WORKED SO WELL.

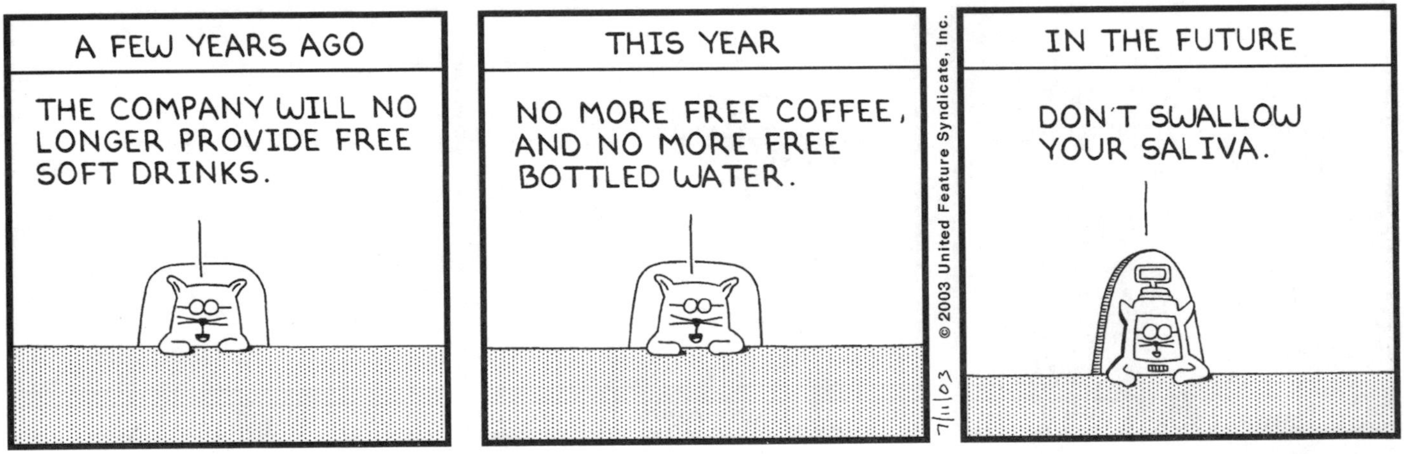
A FEW YEARS AGO
THE COMPANY WILL NO LONGER PROVIDE FREE SOFT DRINKS.
THIS YEAR
NO MORE FREE COFFEE, AND NO MORE FREE BOTTLED WATER.
7/11/03 © 2003 United Feature Syndicate, Inc.
IN THE FUTURE
DON'T SWALLOW YOUR SALIVA.

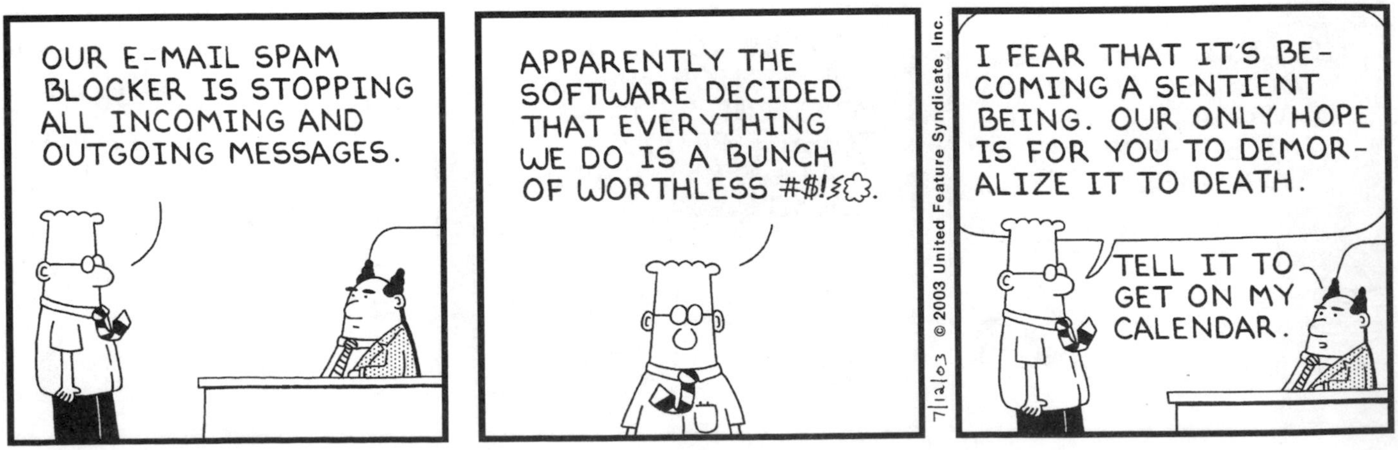
OUR E-MAIL SPAM BLOCKER IS STOPPING ALL INCOMING AND OUTGOING MESSAGES.
APPARENTLY THE SOFTWARE DECIDED THAT EVERYTHING WE DO IS A BUNCH OF WORTHLESS #$!
7/12/03 © 2003 United Feature Syndicate, Inc.
I FEAR THAT IT'S BECOMING A SENTIENT BEING. OUR ONLY HOPE IS FOR YOU TO DEMORALIZE IT TO DEATH.
TELL IT TO GET ON MY CALENDAR.

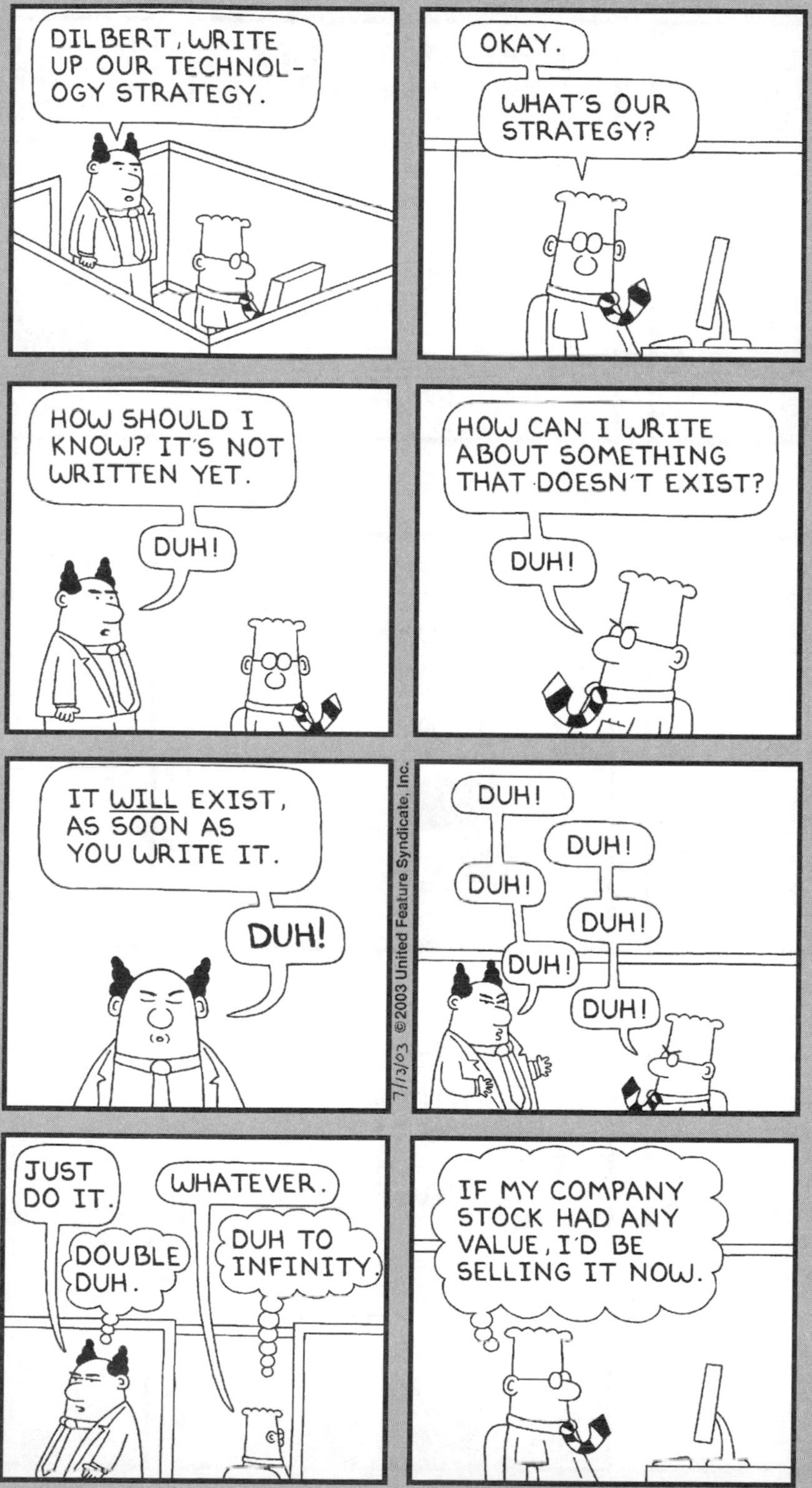
DILBERT, WRITE UP OUR TECHNOLOGY STRATEGY.
OKAY.
WHAT'S OUR STRATEGY?
HOW SHOULD I KNOW? IT'S NOT WRITTEN YET.
DUH!
HOW CAN I WRITE ABOUT SOMETHING THAT DOESN'T EXIST?
DUH!
IT WILL EXIST, AS SOON AS YOU WRITE IT.
DUH!
7/13/03 ©2003 United Feature Syndicate, Inc.
DUH!
DUH!
DUH!
DUH!
DUH!
DUH!
JUST DO IT.
DOUBLE DUH.
WHATEVER.
DUH TO INFINITY.
IF MY COMPANY STOCK HAD ANY VALUE, I'D BE SELLING IT NOW.

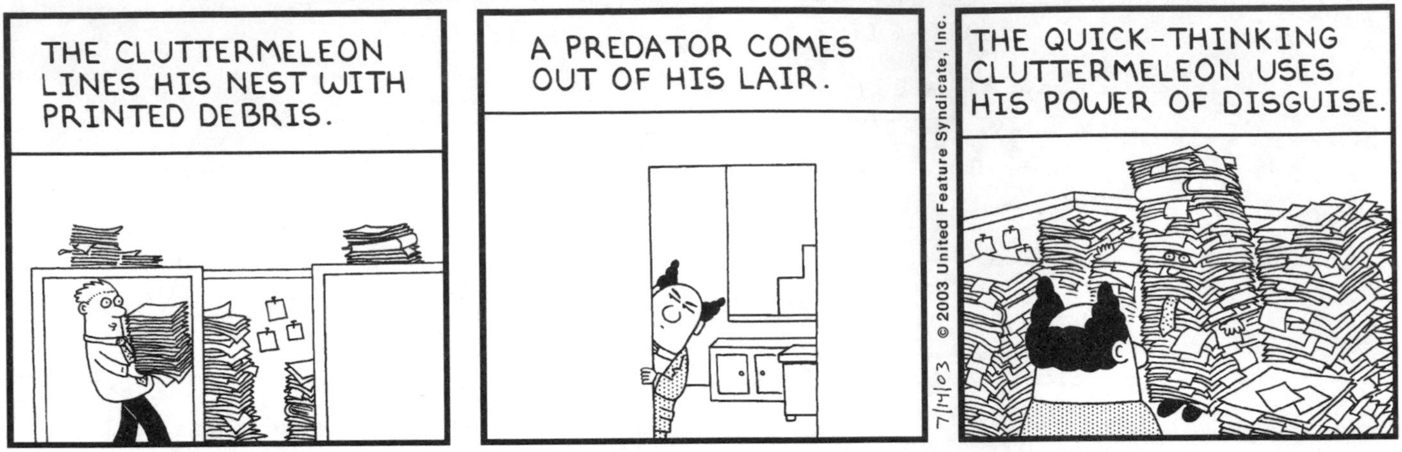
THE CLUTTERMELEON LINES HIS NEST WITH PRINTED DEBRIS.
A PREDATOR COMES OUT OF HIS LAIR.
7/14/03 © 2003 United Feature Syndicate, Inc.
THE QUICK-THINKING CLUTTERMELEON USES HIS POWER OF DISGUISE.

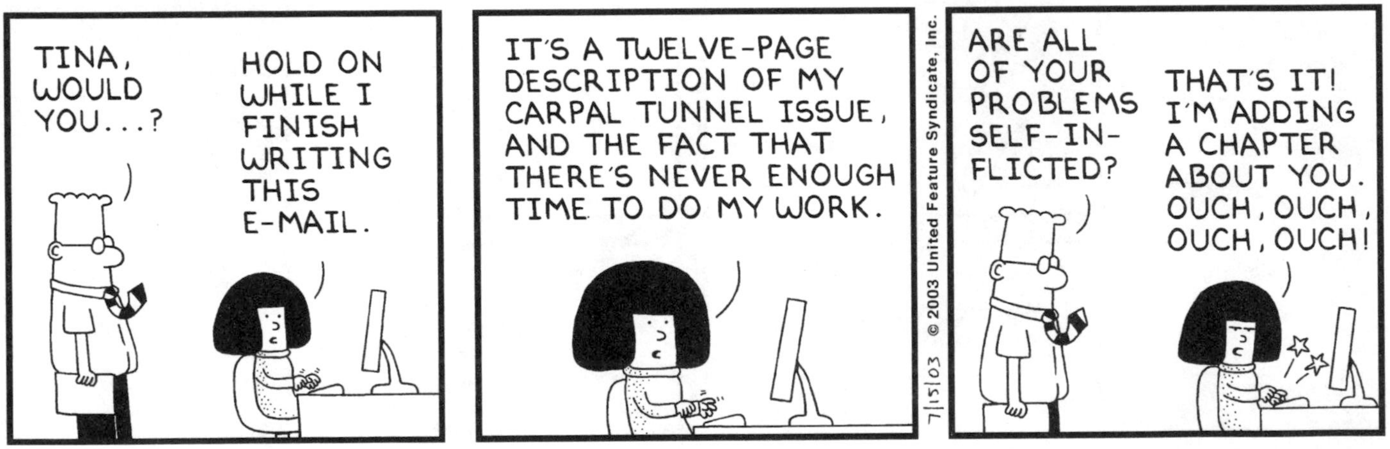
TINA, WOULD YOU...?
HOLD ON WHILE I FINISH WRITING THIS E-MAIL.
IT'S A TWELVE-PAGE DESCRIPTION OF MY CARPAL TUNNEL ISSUE, AND THE FACT THAT THERE'S NEVER ENOUGH TIME TO DO MY WORK.
7/15/03 © 2003 United Feature Syndicate, Inc.
ARE ALL OF YOUR PROBLEMS SELF-INFLICTED?
THAT'S IT! I'M ADDING A CHAPTER ABOUT YOU. OUCH, OUCH, OUCH, OUCH!

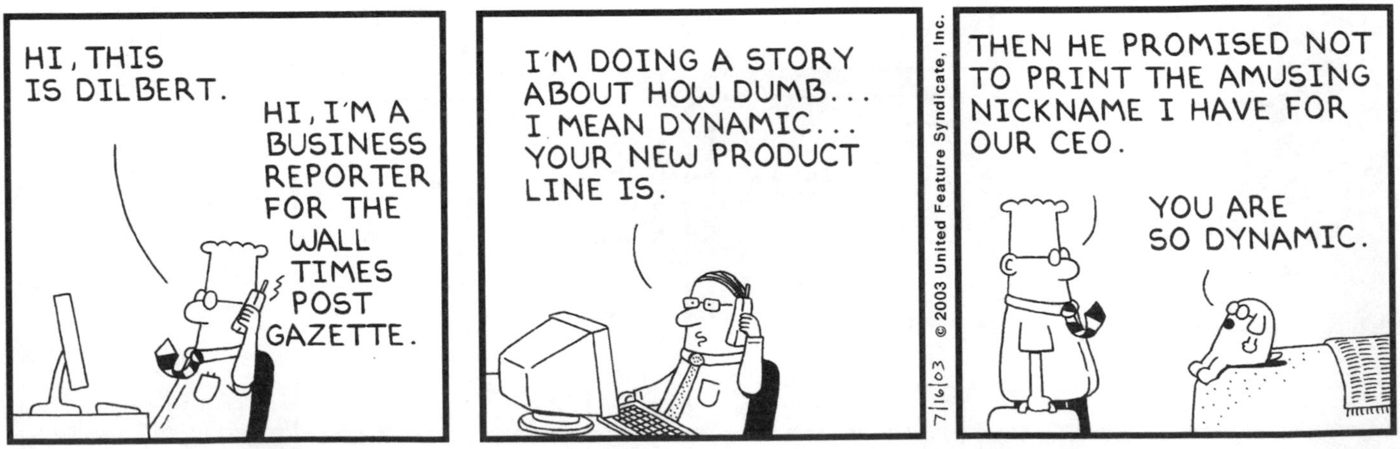
HI, THIS IS DILBERT.
HI, I'M A BUSINESS REPORTER FOR THE WALL TIMES POST GAZETTE.
I'M DOING A STORY ABOUT HOW DUMB... I MEAN DYNAMIC... YOUR NEW PRODUCT LINE IS.
7/16/03 © 2003 United Feature Syndicate, Inc.
THEN HE PROMISED NOT TO PRINT THE AMUSING NICKNAME I HAVE FOR OUR CEO.
YOU ARE SO DYNAMIC.

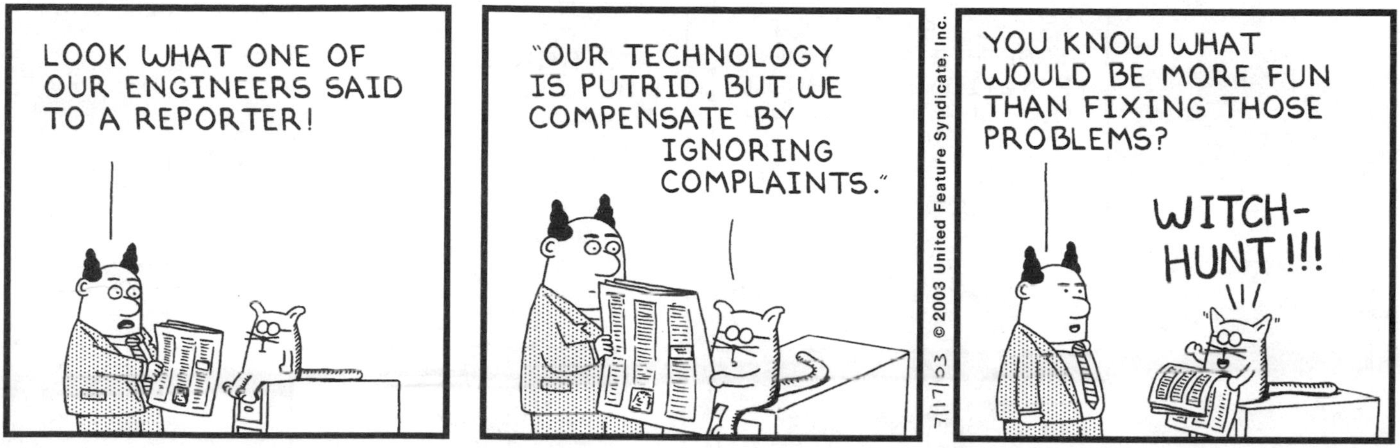
LOOK WHAT ONE OF OUR ENGINEERS SAID TO A REPORTER!
"OUR TECHNOLOGY IS PUTRID, BUT WE COMPENSATE BY IGNORING COMPLAINTS."
7/17/03 © 2003 United Feature Syndicate, Inc.
YOU KNOW WHAT WOULD BE MORE FUN THAN FIXING THOSE PROBLEMS?
WITCH-HUNT!!!

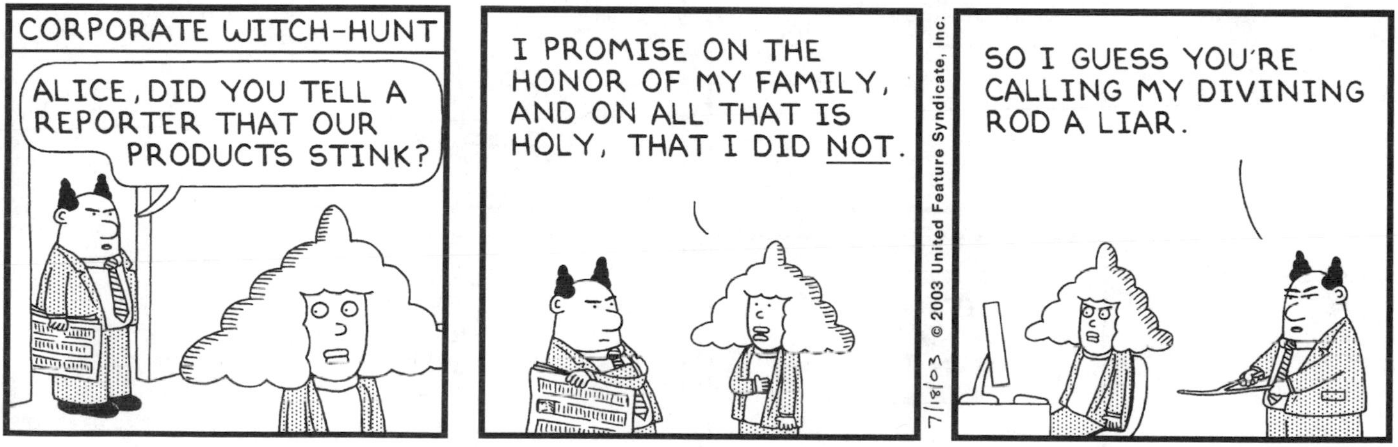
CORPORATE WITCH-HUNT
ALICE, DID YOU TELL A REPORTER THAT OUR PRODUCTS STINK?
I PROMISE ON THE HONOR OF MY FAMILY, AND ON ALL THAT IS HOLY, THAT I DID NOT.
7/18/03 © 2003 United Feature Syndicate, Inc.
SO I GUESS YOU'RE CALLING MY DIVINING ROD A LIAR.

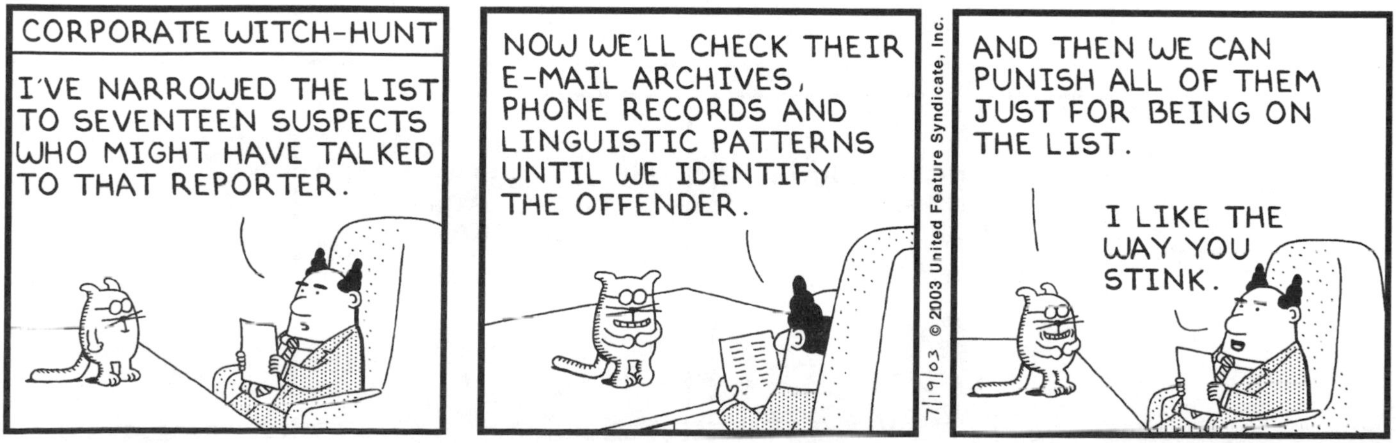
CORPORATE WITCH-HUNT
I'VE NARROWED THE LIST TO SEVENTEEN SUSPECTS WHO MIGHT HAVE TALKED TO THAT REPORTER.
NOW WE'LL CHECK THEIR E-MAIL ARCHIVES, PHONE RECORDS AND LINGUISTIC PATTERNS UNTIL WE IDENTIFY THE OFFENDER.
7/19/03 © 2003 United Feature Syndicate, Inc.
AND THEN WE CAN PUNISH ALL OF THEM JUST FOR BEING ON THE LIST.
I LIKE THE WAY YOU STINK.

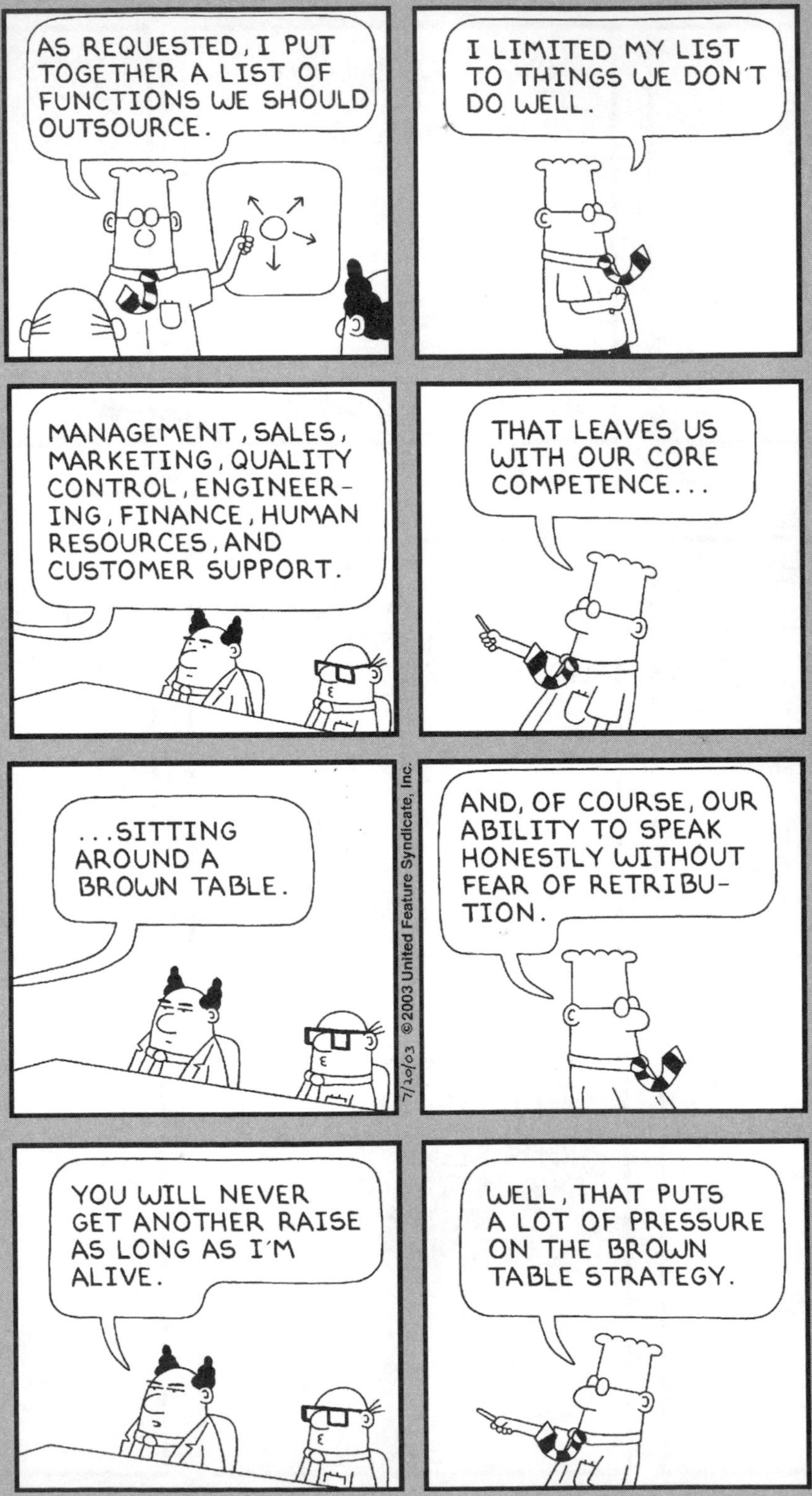
AS REQUESTED, I PUT TOGETHER A LIST OF FUNCTIONS WE SHOULD OUTSOURCE.
I LIMITED MY LIST TO THINGS WE DON'T DO WELL.
MANAGEMENT, SALES, MARKETING, QUALITY CONTROL, ENGINEERING, FINANCE, HUMAN RESOURCES, AND CUSTOMER SUPPORT.
THAT LEAVES US WITH OUR CORE COMPETENCE...
...SITTING AROUND A BROWN TABLE.
AND, OF COURSE, OUR ABILITY TO SPEAK HONESTLY WITHOUT FEAR OF RETRIBUTION.
YOU WILL NEVER GET ANOTHER RAISE AS LONG AS I'M ALIVE.
WELL, THAT PUTS A LOT OF PRESSURE ON THE BROWN TABLE STRATEGY.
7/20/03 ©2003 United Feature Syndicate, Inc.

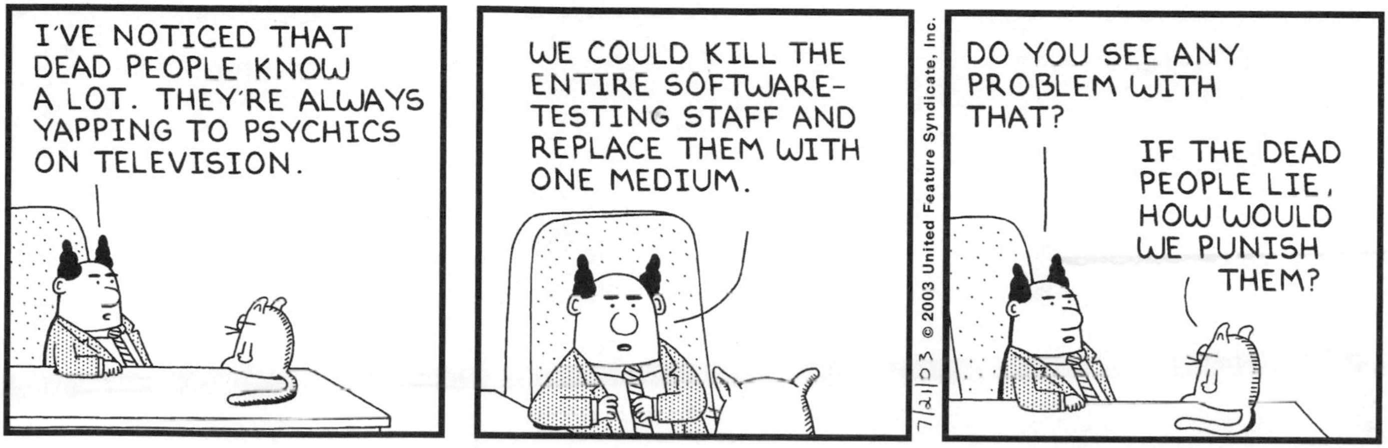
I'VE NOTICED THAT DEAD PEOPLE KNOW A LOT. THEY'RE ALWAYS YAPPING TO PSYCHICS ON TELEVISION.
WE COULD KILL THE ENTIRE SOFTWARE-TESTING STAFF AND REPLACE THEM WITH ONE MEDIUM.
7/21/03 © 2003 United Feature Syndicate, Inc.
DO YOU SEE ANY PROBLEM WITH THAT?
IF THE DEAD PEOPLE LIE, HOW WOULD WE PUNISH THEM?

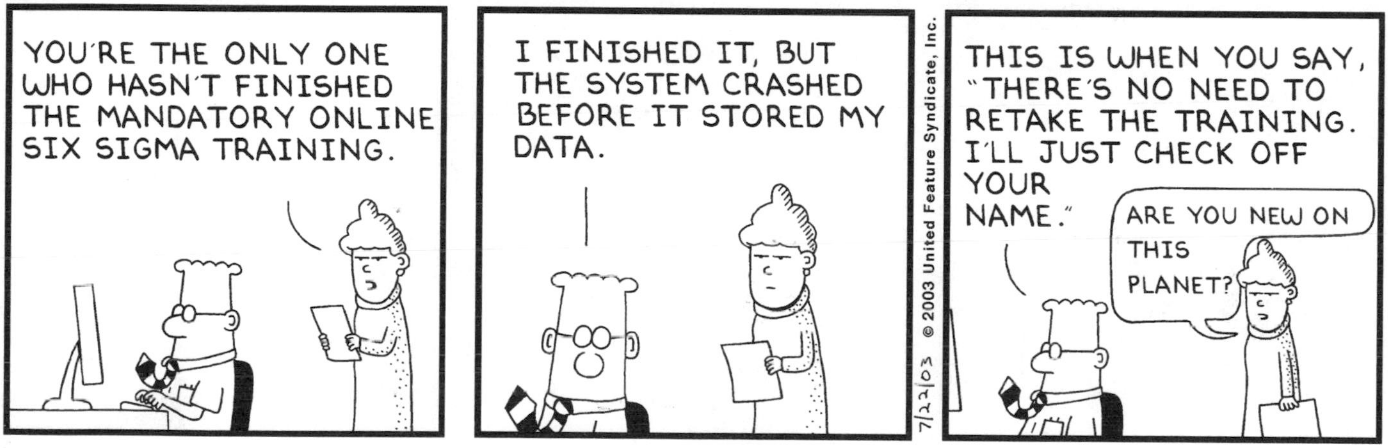
YOU'RE THE ONLY ONE WHO HASN'T FINISHED THE MANDATORY ONLINE SIX SIGMA TRAINING.
I FINISHED IT, BUT THE SYSTEM CRASHED BEFORE IT STORED MY DATA.
7/22/03 © 2003 United Feature Syndicate, Inc.
THIS IS WHEN YOU SAY, "THERE'S NO NEED TO RETAKE THE TRAINING. I'LL JUST CHECK OFF YOUR NAME."
ARE YOU NEW ON THIS PLANET?

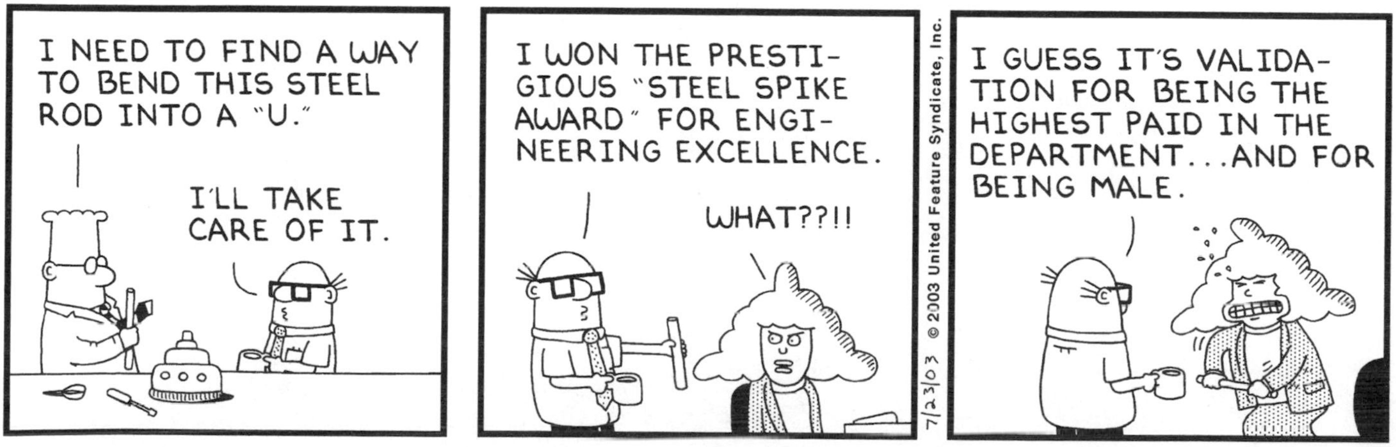
I NEED TO FIND A WAY TO BEND THIS STEEL ROD INTO A "U."
I'LL TAKE CARE OF IT.
I WON THE PRESTIGIOUS "STEEL SPIKE AWARD" FOR ENGINEERING EXCELLENCE.
WHAT??!!
7/23/03 © 2003 United Feature Syndicate, Inc.
I GUESS IT'S VALIDATION FOR BEING THE HIGHEST PAID IN THE DEPARTMENT...AND FOR BEING MALE.

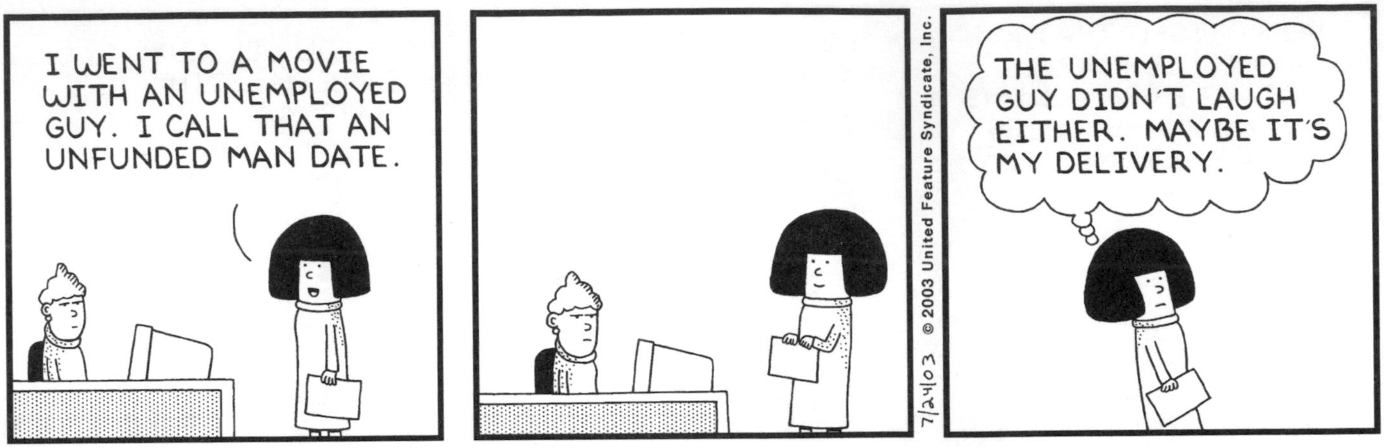
I WENT TO A MOVIE WITH AN UNEMPLOYED GUY. I CALL THAT AN UNFUNDED MAN DATE.
7/24/03 © 2003 United Feature Syndicate, Inc.
THE UNEMPLOYED GUY DIDN'T LAUGH EITHER. MAYBE IT'S MY DELIVERY.

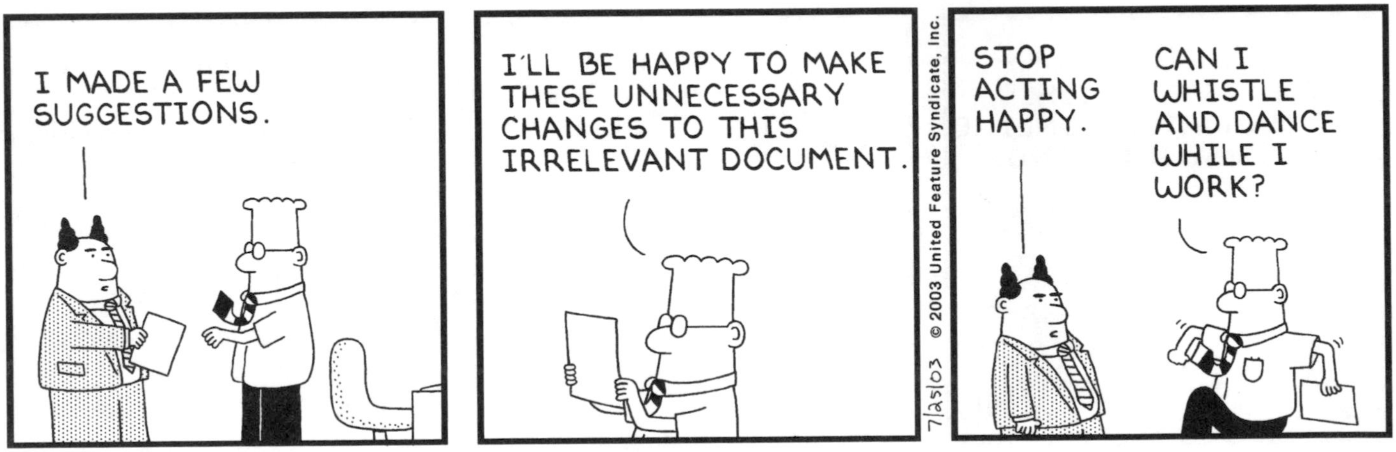
I MADE A FEW SUGGESTIONS.
I'LL BE HAPPY TO MAKE THESE UNNECESSARY CHANGES TO THIS IRRELEVANT DOCUMENT.
7/25/03 © 2003 United Feature Syndicate, Inc.
STOP ACTING HAPPY.
CAN I WHISTLE AND DANCE WHILE I WORK?

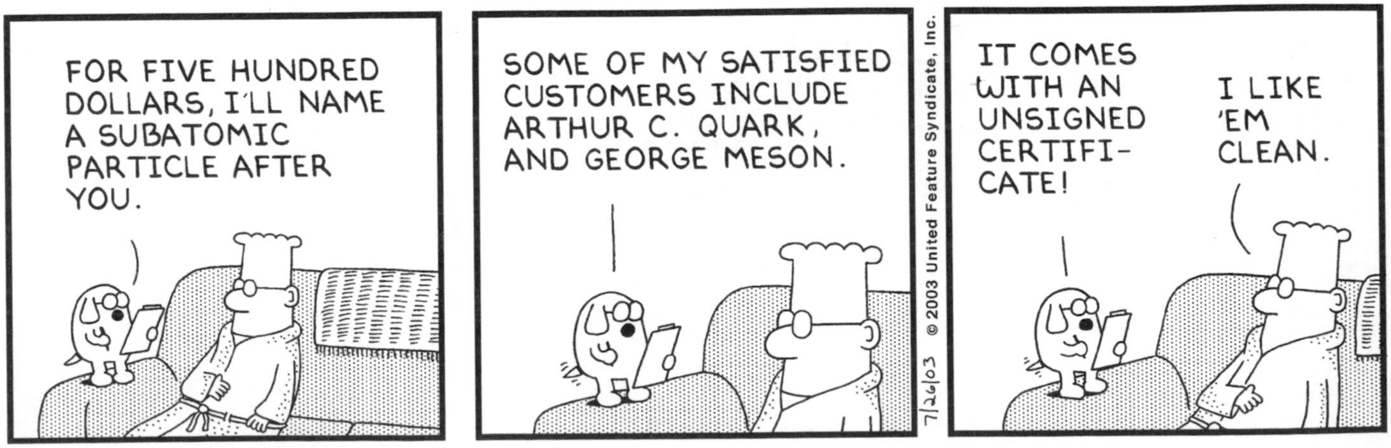
FOR FIVE HUNDRED DOLLARS, I'LL NAME A SUBATOMIC PARTICLE AFTER YOU.
SOME OF MY SATISFIED CUSTOMERS INCLUDE ARTHUR C. QUARK, AND GEORGE MESON.
7/26/03 © 2003 United Feature Syndicate, Inc.
IT COMES WITH AN UNSIGNED CERTIFI-CATE!
I LIKE 'EM CLEAN.

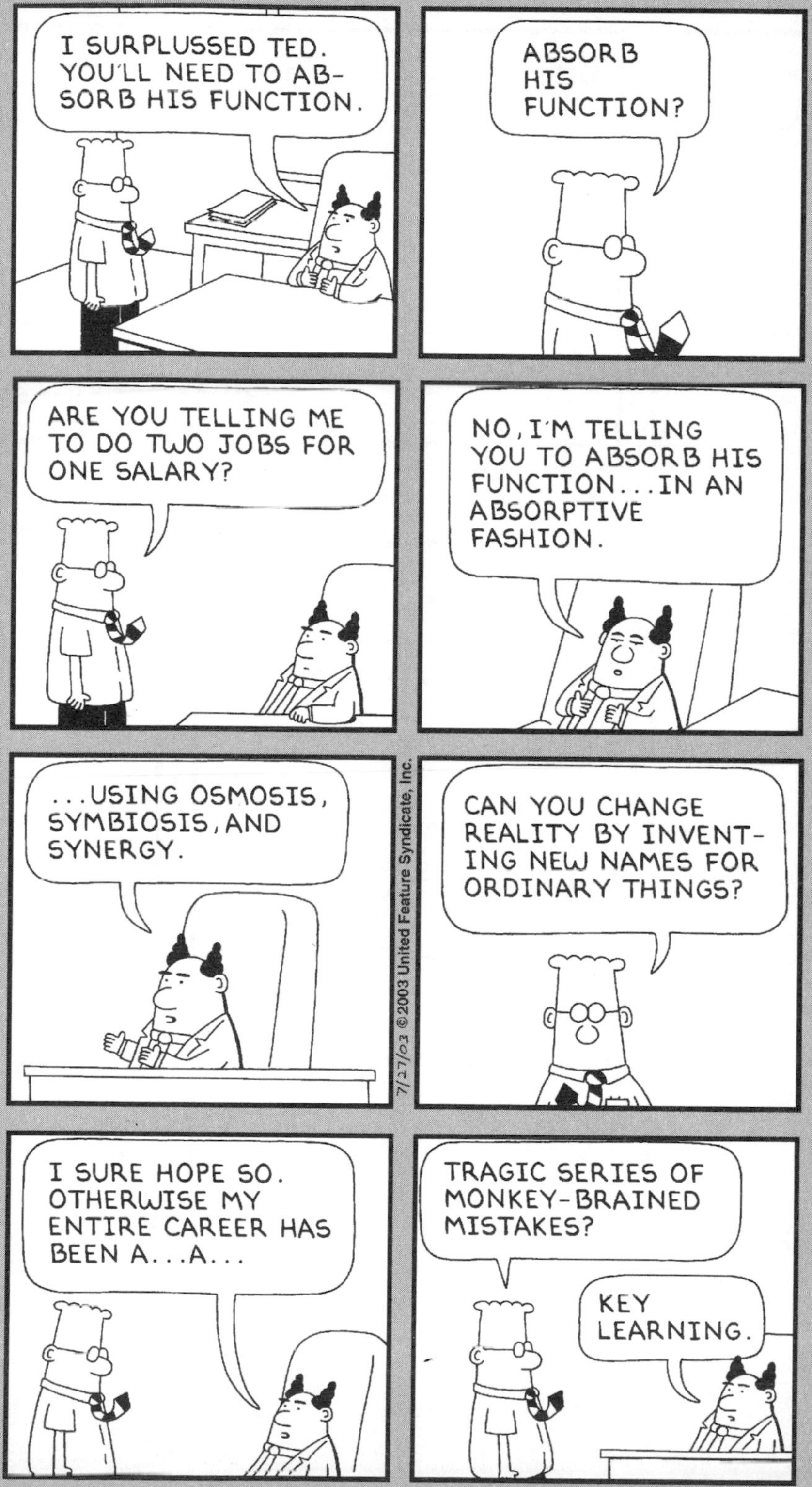

I SURPLUSSED TED. YOU'LL NEED TO ABSORB HIS FUNCTION.
ABSORB HIS FUNCTION?
ARE YOU TELLING ME TO DO TWO JOBS FOR ONE SALARY?
NO, I'M TELLING YOU TO ABSORB HIS FUNCTION...IN AN ABSORPTIVE FASHION.
...USING OSMOSIS, SYMBIOSIS, AND SYNERGY.
7/27/03 ©2003 United Feature Syndicate, Inc.
CAN YOU CHANGE REALITY BY INVENTING NEW NAMES FOR ORDINARY THINGS?
I SURE HOPE SO. OTHERWISE MY ENTIRE CAREER HAS BEEN A...A...
TRAGIC SERIES OF MONKEY-BRAINED MISTAKES?
KEY LEARNING.

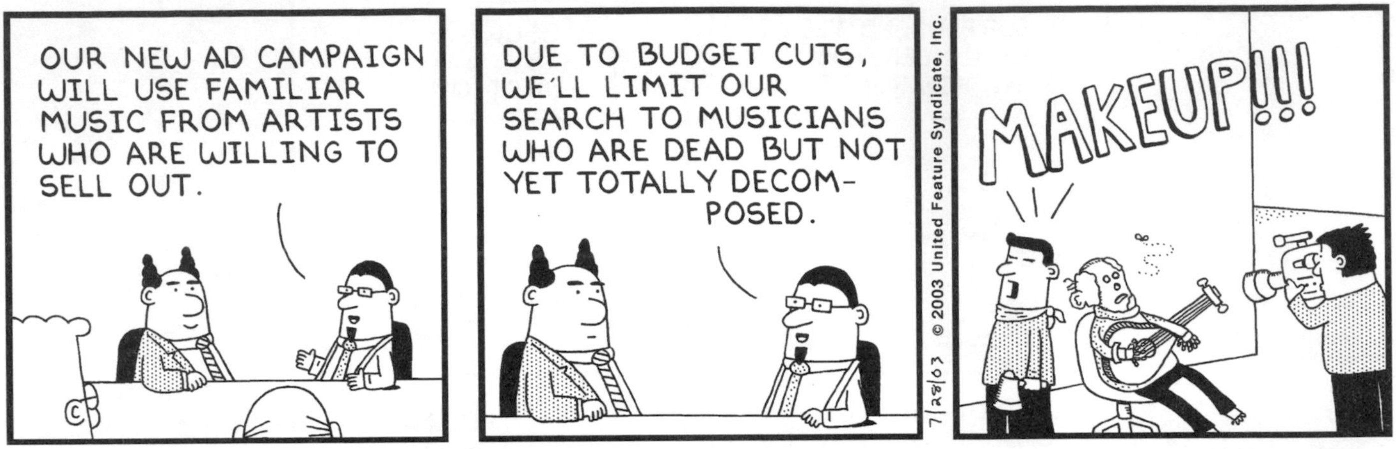
OUR NEW AD CAMPAIGN WILL USE FAMILIAR MUSIC FROM ARTISTS WHO ARE WILLING TO SELL OUT.
DUE TO BUDGET CUTS, WE'LL LIMIT OUR SEARCH TO MUSICIANS WHO ARE DEAD BUT NOT YET TOTALLY DECOM-POSED.
7/28/03 © 2003 United Feature Syndicate, Inc.
MAKEUP!!!

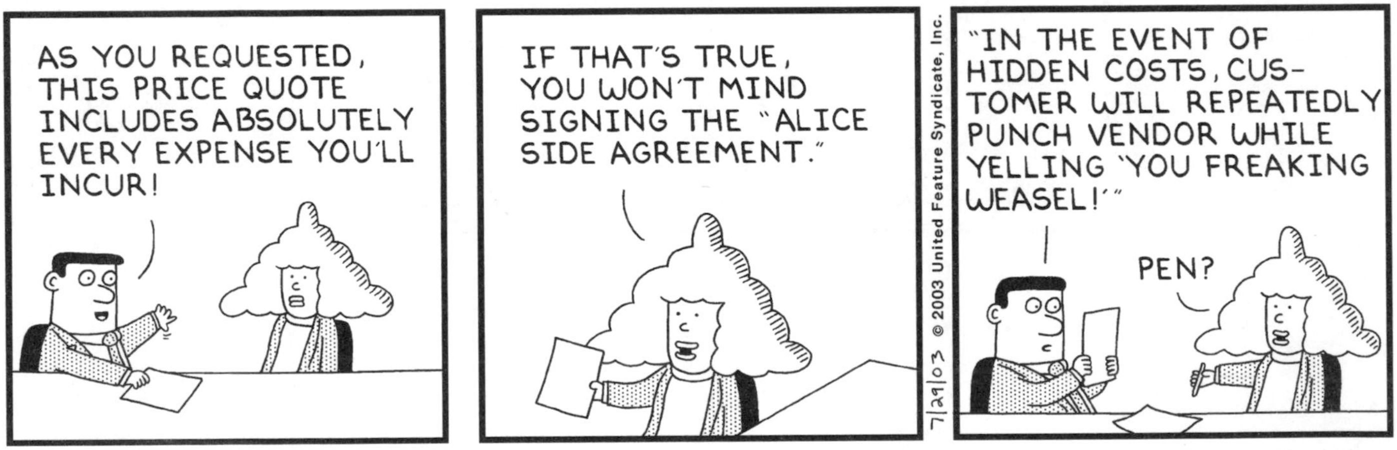
AS YOU REQUESTED, THIS PRICE QUOTE INCLUDES ABSOLUTELY EVERY EXPENSE YOU'LL INCUR!
IF THAT'S TRUE, YOU WON'T MIND SIGNING THE "ALICE SIDE AGREEMENT."
7/29/03 © 2003 United Feature Syndicate, Inc.
"IN THE EVENT OF HIDDEN COSTS, CUS-TOMER WILL REPEATEDLY PUNCH VENDOR WHILE YELLING 'YOU FREAKING WEASEL!'"
PEN?

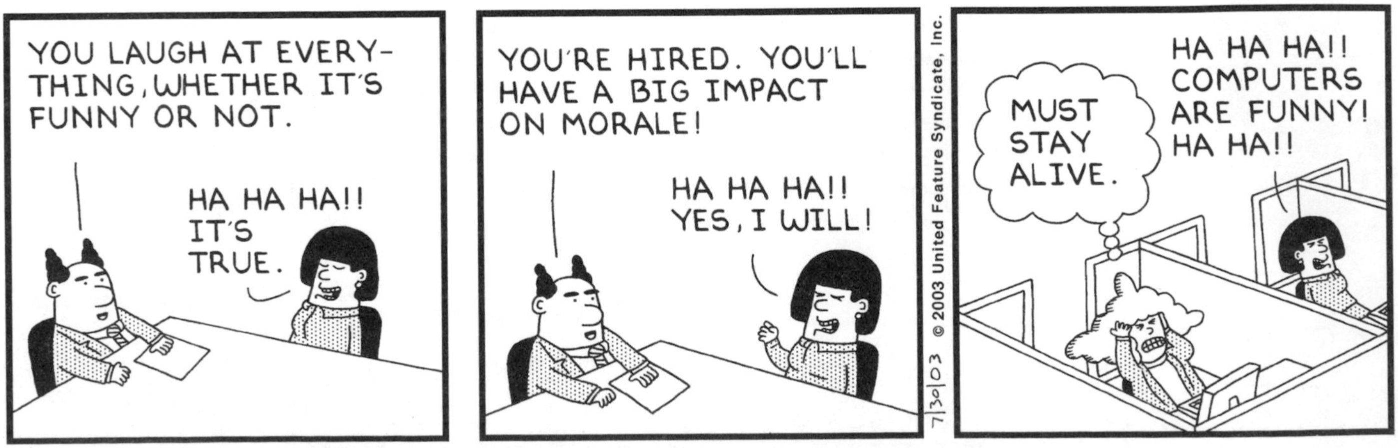
YOU LAUGH AT EVERY-THING, WHETHER IT'S FUNNY OR NOT.
HA HA HA!! IT'S TRUE.
YOU'RE HIRED. YOU'LL HAVE A BIG IMPACT ON MORALE!
HA HA HA!! YES, I WILL!
7/30/03 © 2003 United Feature Syndicate, Inc.
MUST STAY ALIVE.
HA HA HA!! COMPUTERS ARE FUNNY! HA HA!!

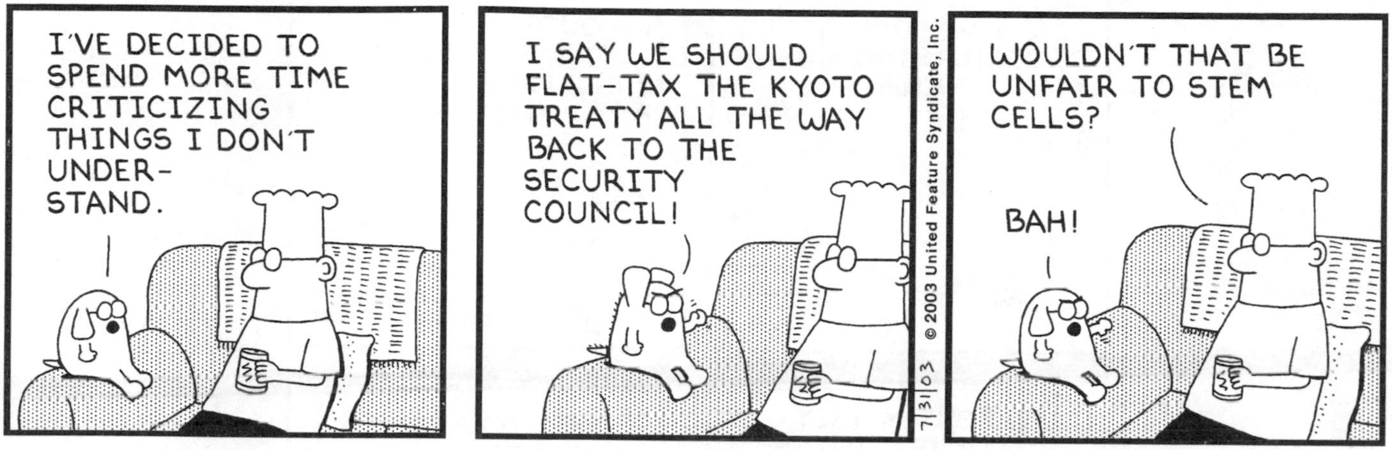
I'VE DECIDED TO SPEND MORE TIME CRITICIZING THINGS I DON'T UNDER-STAND.
I SAY WE SHOULD FLAT-TAX THE KYOTO TREATY ALL THE WAY BACK TO THE SECURITY COUNCIL!
7/31/03 © 2003 United Feature Syndicate, Inc.
WOULDN'T THAT BE UNFAIR TO STEM CELLS?
BAH!

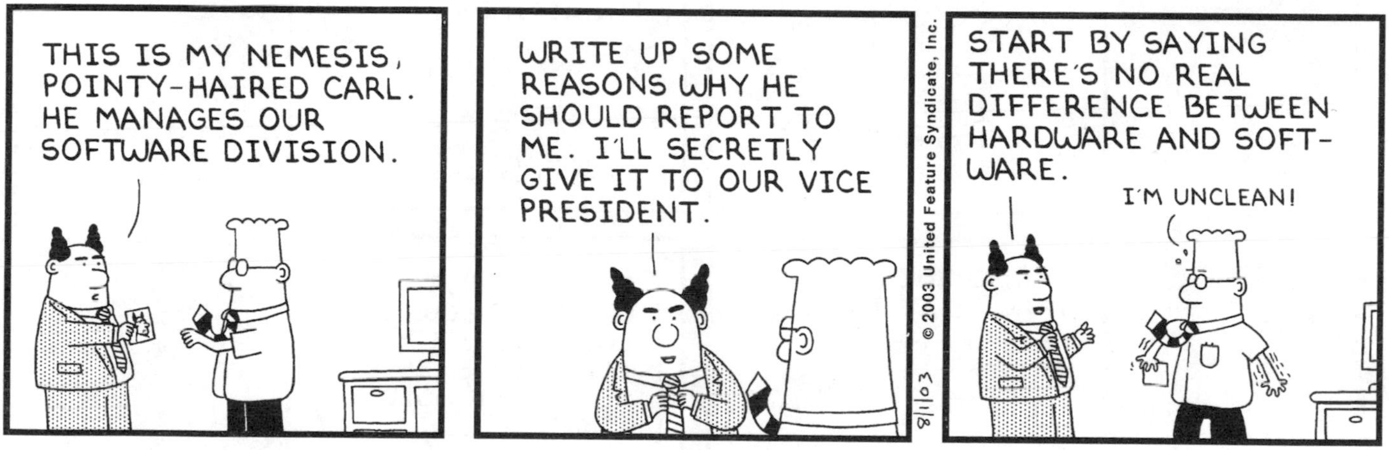
THIS IS MY NEMESIS, POINTY-HAIRED CARL. HE MANAGES OUR SOFTWARE DIVISION.
WRITE UP SOME REASONS WHY HE SHOULD REPORT TO ME. I'LL SECRETLY GIVE IT TO OUR VICE PRESIDENT.
8/1/03 © 2003 United Feature Syndicate, Inc.
START BY SAYING THERE'S NO REAL DIFFERENCE BETWEEN HARDWARE AND SOFT-WARE.
I'M UNCLEAN!

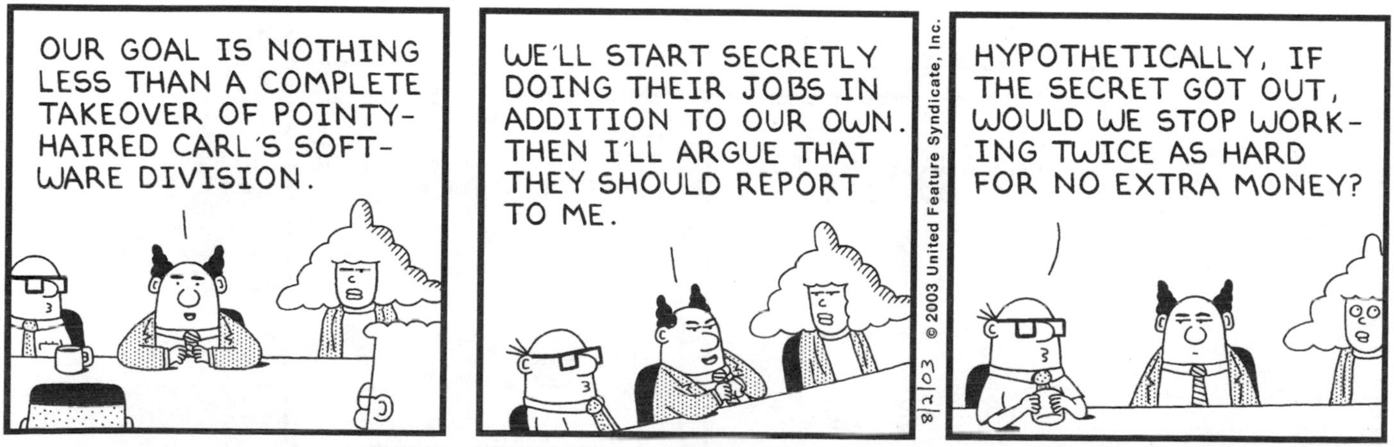
OUR GOAL IS NOTHING LESS THAN A COMPLETE TAKEOVER OF POINTY-HAIRED CARL'S SOFT-WARE DIVISION.
WE'LL START SECRETLY DOING THEIR JOBS IN ADDITION TO OUR OWN. THEN I'LL ARGUE THAT THEY SHOULD REPORT TO ME.
8/2/03 © 2003 United Feature Syndicate, Inc.
HYPOTHETICALLY, IF THE SECRET GOT OUT, WOULD WE STOP WORK-ING TWICE AS HARD FOR NO EXTRA MONEY?

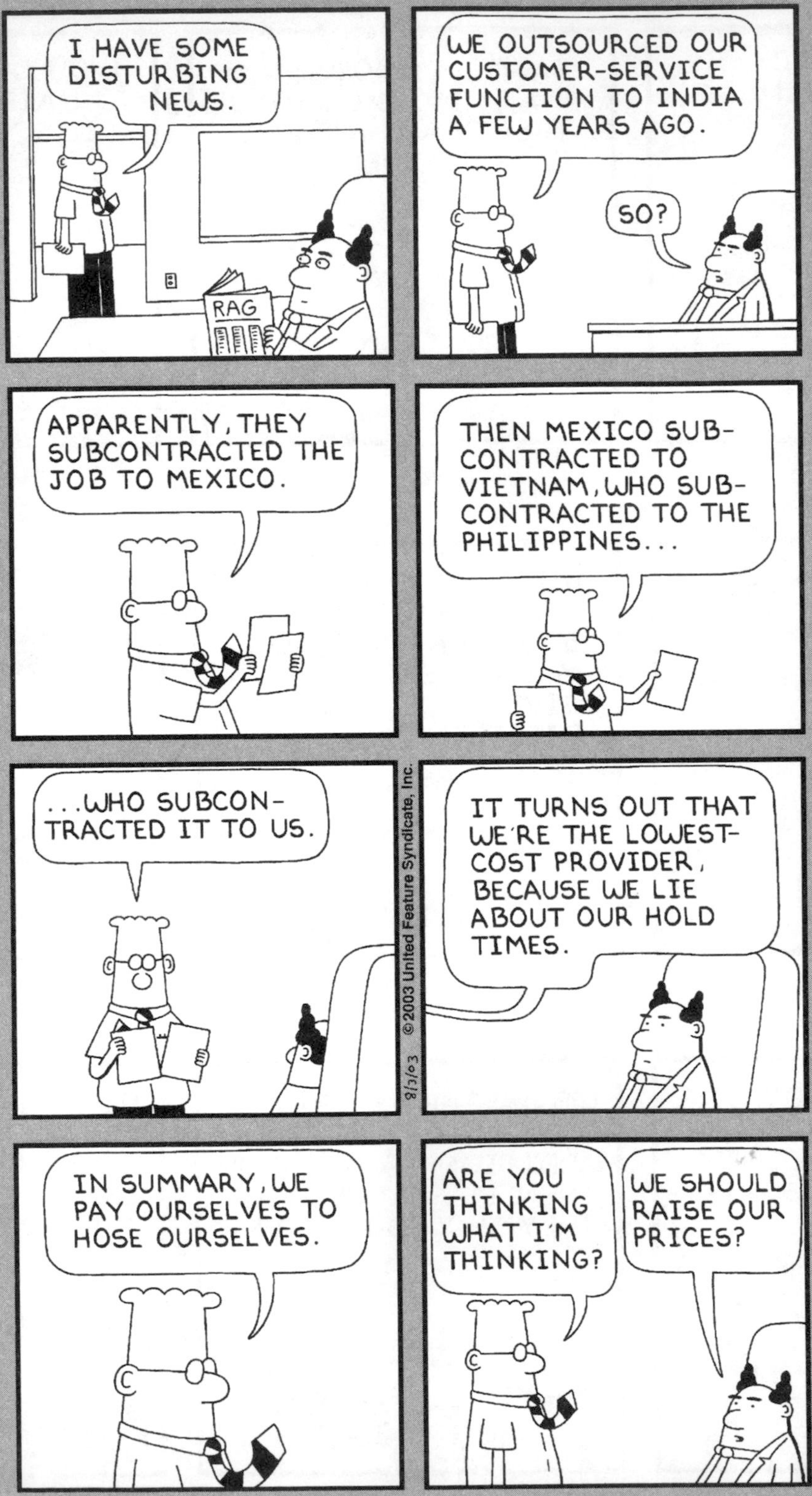
I HAVE SOME DISTURBING NEWS.
RAG
WE OUTSOURCED OUR CUSTOMER-SERVICE FUNCTION TO INDIA A FEW YEARS AGO.
SO?
APPARENTLY, THEY SUBCONTRACTED THE JOB TO MEXICO.
THEN MEXICO SUB-CONTRACTED TO VIETNAM, WHO SUB-CONTRACTED TO THE PHILIPPINES...
...WHO SUBCON-TRACTED IT TO US.
©2003 United Feature Syndicate, Inc.
8/3/03
IT TURNS OUT THAT WE'RE THE LOWEST-COST PROVIDER, BECAUSE WE LIE ABOUT OUR HOLD TIMES.
IN SUMMARY, WE PAY OURSELVES TO HOSE OURSELVES.
ARE YOU THINKING WHAT I'M THINKING?
WE SHOULD RAISE OUR PRICES?

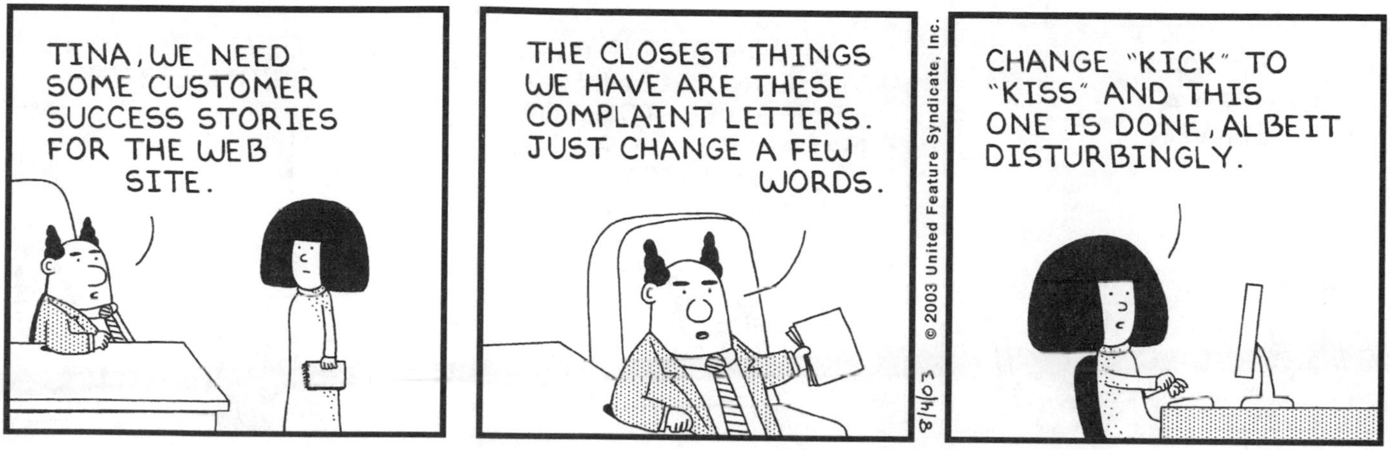
TINA, WE NEED SOME CUSTOMER SUCCESS STORIES FOR THE WEB SITE.
THE CLOSEST THINGS WE HAVE ARE THESE COMPLAINT LETTERS. JUST CHANGE A FEW WORDS.
© 2003 United Feature Syndicate, Inc.
8/4/03
CHANGE "KICK" TO "KISS" AND THIS ONE IS DONE, ALBEIT DISTURBINGLY.

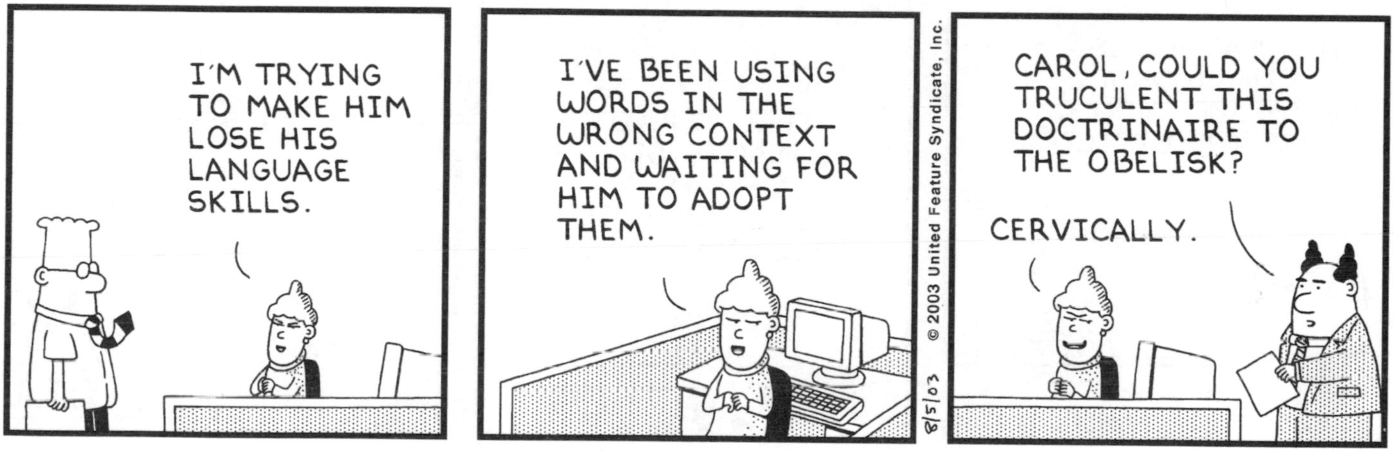
I'M TRYING TO MAKE HIM LOSE HIS LANGUAGE SKILLS.
I'VE BEEN USING WORDS IN THE WRONG CONTEXT AND WAITING FOR HIM TO ADOPT THEM.
© 2003 United Feature Syndicate, Inc.
8/5/03
CAROL, COULD YOU TRUCULENT THIS DOCTRINAIRE TO THE OBELISK?
CERVICALLY.

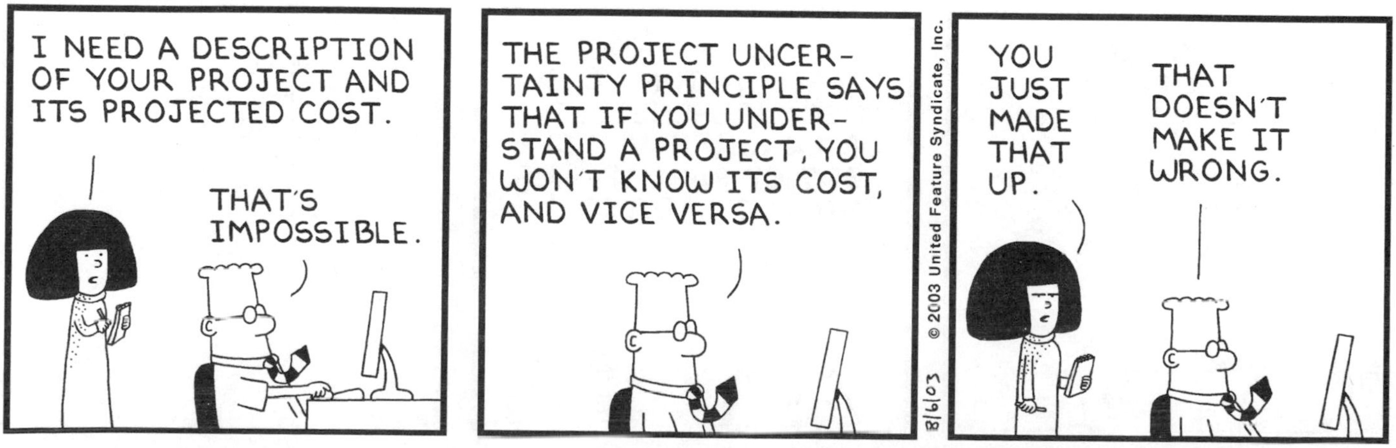
I NEED A DESCRIPTION OF YOUR PROJECT AND ITS PROJECTED COST.
THAT'S IMPOSSIBLE.
THE PROJECT UNCERTAINTY PRINCIPLE SAYS THAT IF YOU UNDERSTAND A PROJECT, YOU WON'T KNOW ITS COST, AND VICE VERSA.
© 2003 United Feature Syndicate, Inc.
8/6/03
YOU JUST MADE THAT UP.
THAT DOESN'T MAKE IT WRONG.

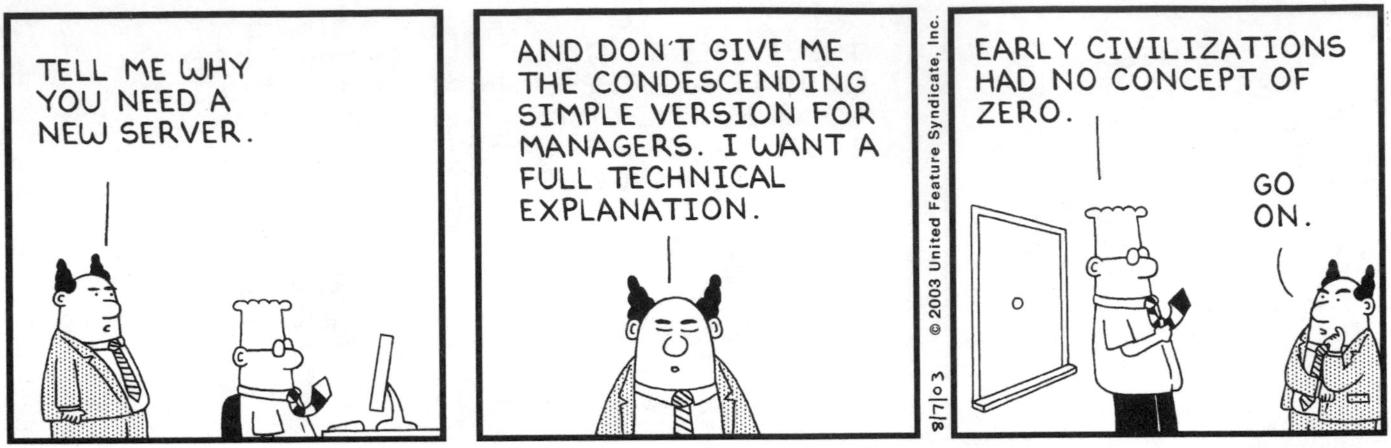
TELL ME WHY YOU NEED A NEW SERVER.
AND DON'T GIVE ME THE CONDESCENDING SIMPLE VERSION FOR MANAGERS. I WANT A FULL TECHNICAL EXPLANATION.
EARLY CIVILIZATIONS HAD NO CONCEPT OF ZERO.
GO ON.
8/7/03 © 2003 United Feature Syndicate, Inc.

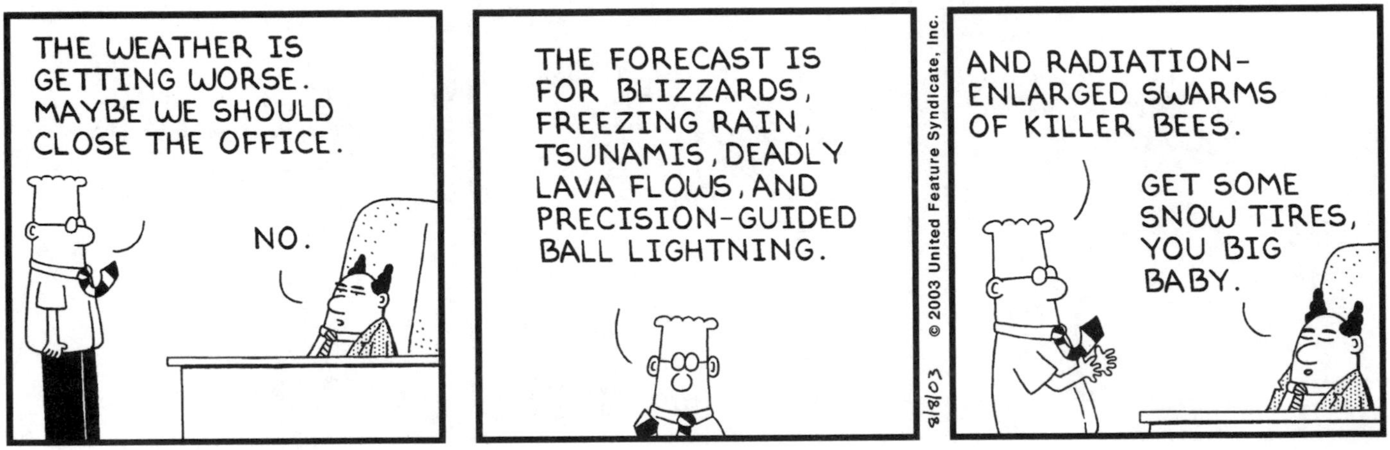
THE WEATHER IS GETTING WORSE. MAYBE WE SHOULD CLOSE THE OFFICE.
NO.
THE FORECAST IS FOR BLIZZARDS, FREEZING RAIN, TSUNAMIS, DEADLY LAVA FLOWS, AND PRECISION-GUIDED BALL LIGHTNING.
AND RADIATION-ENLARGED SWARMS OF KILLER BEES.
GET SOME SNOW TIRES, YOU BIG BABY.
8/8/03 © 2003 United Feature Syndicate, Inc.

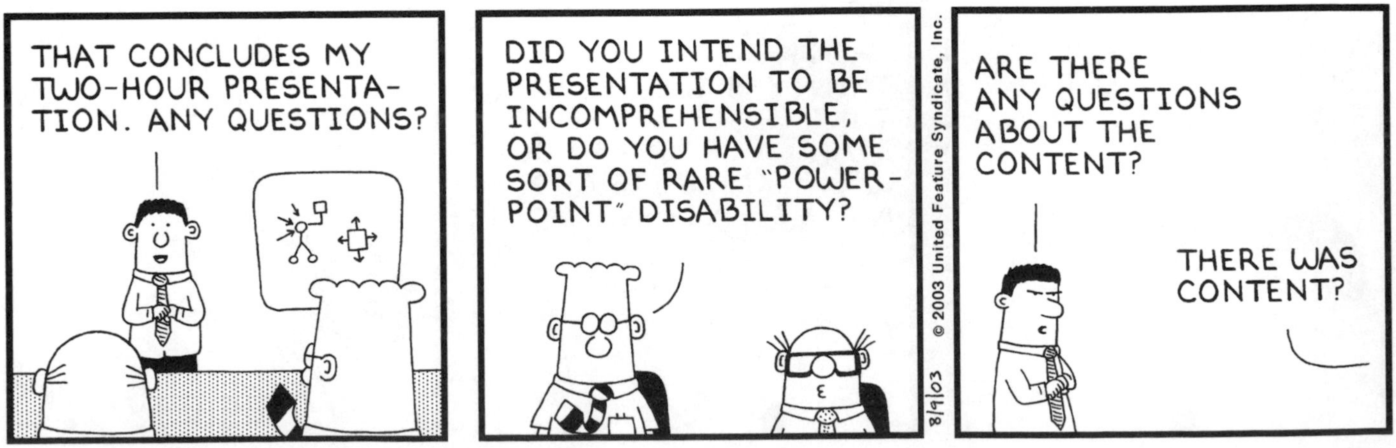
THAT CONCLUDES MY TWO-HOUR PRESENTATION. ANY QUESTIONS?
DID YOU INTEND THE PRESENTATION TO BE INCOMPREHENSIBLE, OR DO YOU HAVE SOME SORT OF RARE "POWERPOINT" DISABILITY?
ARE THERE ANY QUESTIONS ABOUT THE CONTENT?
THERE WAS CONTENT?
8/9/03 © 2003 United Feature Syndicate, Inc.

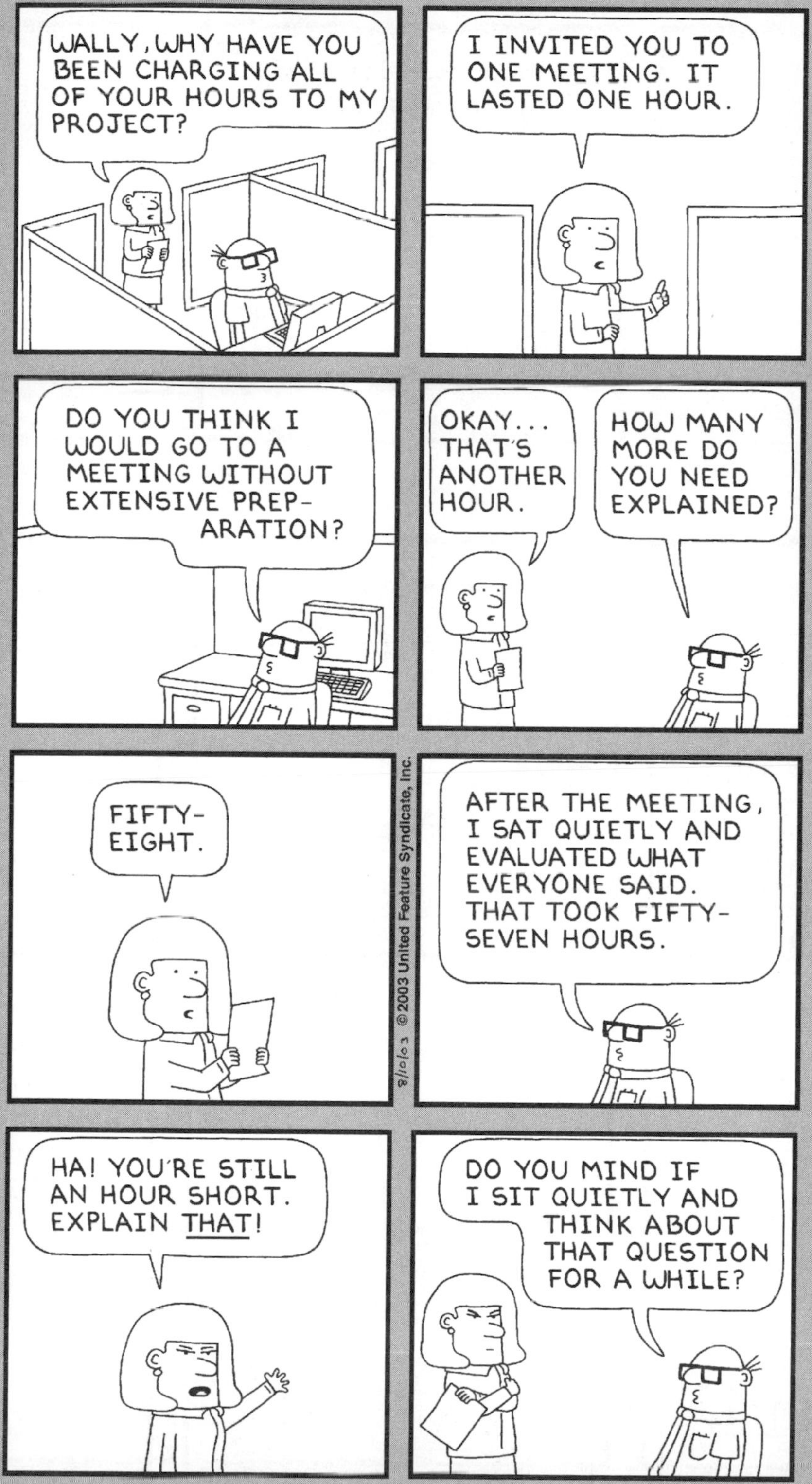
WALLY, WHY HAVE YOU BEEN CHARGING ALL OF YOUR HOURS TO MY PROJECT?
I INVITED YOU TO ONE MEETING. IT LASTED ONE HOUR.
DO YOU THINK I WOULD GO TO A MEETING WITHOUT EXTENSIVE PREP-ARATION?
OKAY... THAT'S ANOTHER HOUR.
HOW MANY MORE DO YOU NEED EXPLAINED?
FIFTY-EIGHT.
AFTER THE MEETING, I SAT QUIETLY AND EVALUATED WHAT EVERYONE SAID. THAT TOOK FIFTY-SEVEN HOURS.
HA! YOU'RE STILL AN HOUR SHORT. EXPLAIN THAT!
DO YOU MIND IF I SIT QUIETLY AND THINK ABOUT THAT QUESTION FOR A WHILE?
8/10/03 © 2003 United Feature Syndicate, Inc.

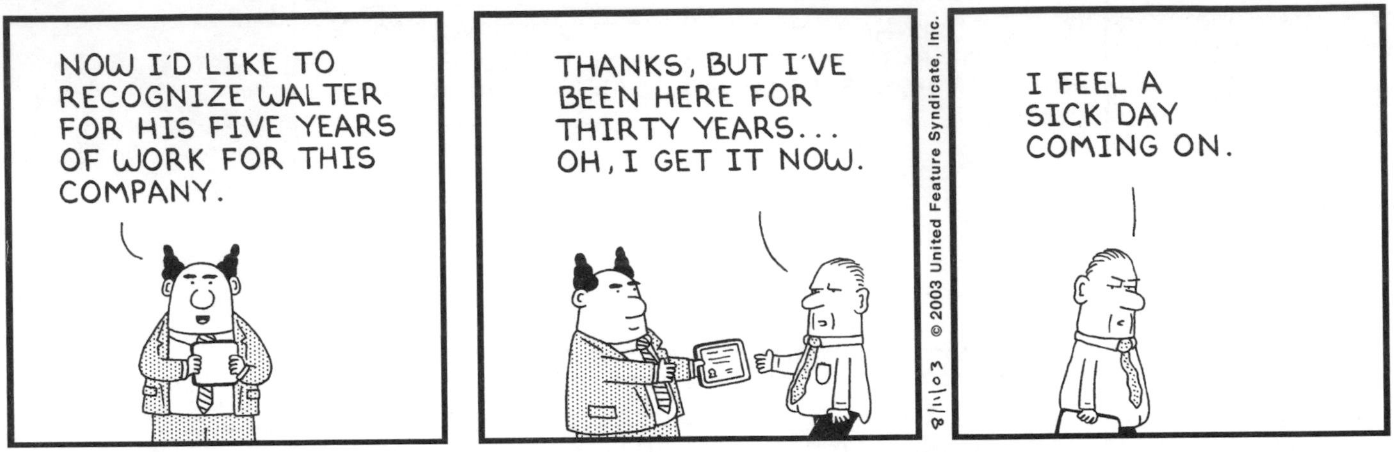
NOW I'D LIKE TO RECOGNIZE WALTER FOR HIS FIVE YEARS OF WORK FOR THIS COMPANY.
THANKS, BUT I'VE BEEN HERE FOR THIRTY YEARS... OH, I GET IT NOW.
8/11/03 © 2003 United Feature Syndicate, Inc.
I FEEL A SICK DAY COMING ON.

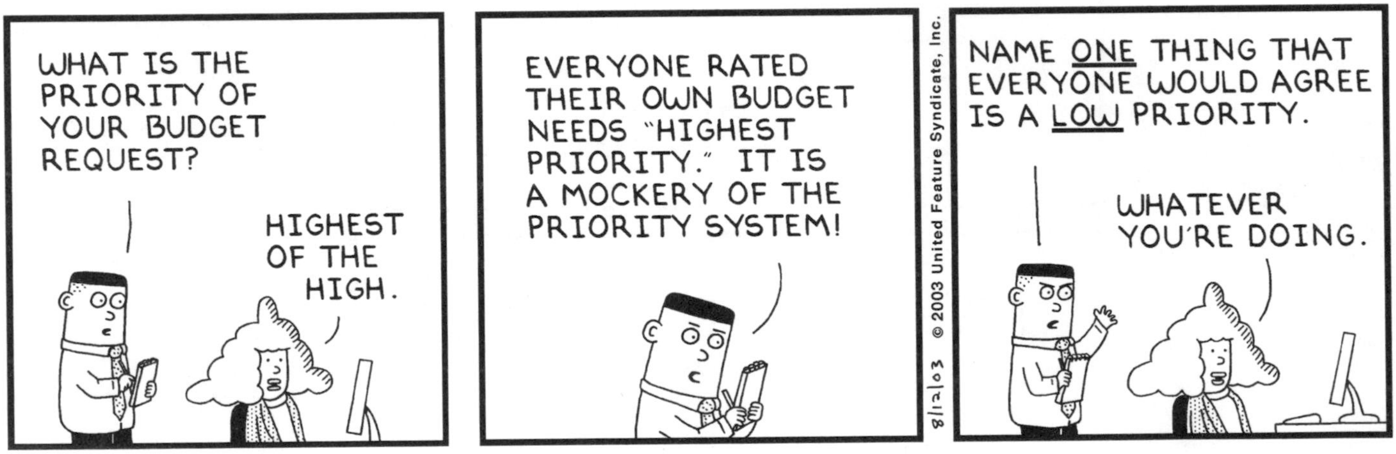
WHAT IS THE PRIORITY OF YOUR BUDGET REQUEST?
HIGHEST OF THE HIGH.
EVERYONE RATED THEIR OWN BUDGET NEEDS "HIGHEST PRIORITY." IT IS A MOCKERY OF THE PRIORITY SYSTEM!
8/12/03 © 2003 United Feature Syndicate, Inc.
NAME ONE THING THAT EVERYONE WOULD AGREE IS A LOW PRIORITY.
WHATEVER YOU'RE DOING.

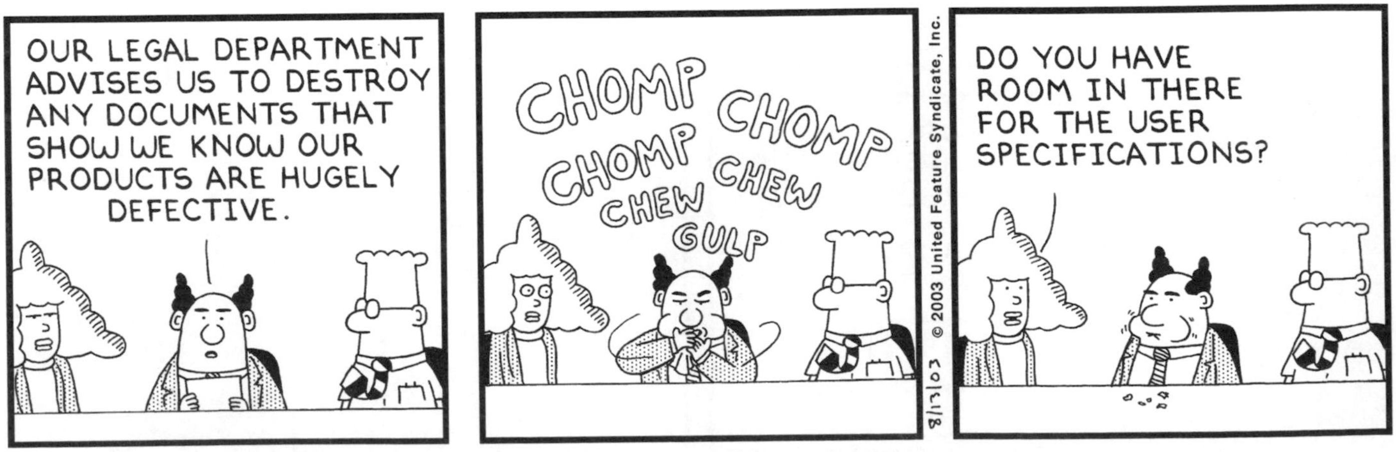
OUR LEGAL DEPARTMENT ADVISES US TO DESTROY ANY DOCUMENTS THAT SHOW WE KNOW OUR PRODUCTS ARE HUGELY DEFECTIVE.
CHOMP CHOMP
CHOMP
CHEW CHEW
GULP
8/13/03 © 2003 United Feature Syndicate, Inc.
DO YOU HAVE ROOM IN THERE FOR THE USER SPECIFICATIONS?

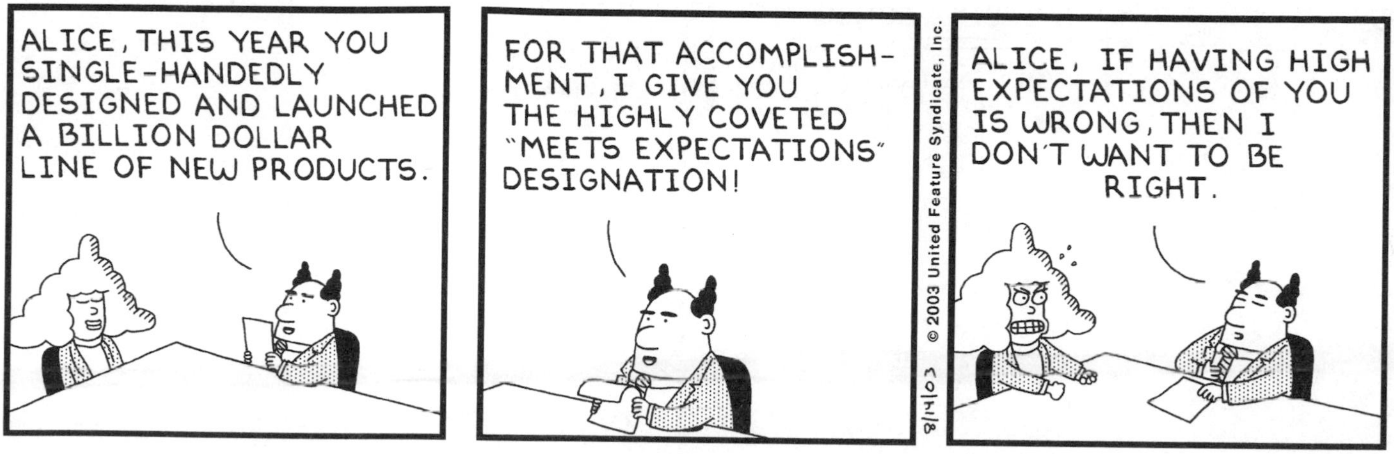
ALICE, THIS YEAR YOU SINGLE-HANDEDLY DESIGNED AND LAUNCHED A BILLION DOLLAR LINE OF NEW PRODUCTS.
FOR THAT ACCOMPLISHMENT, I GIVE YOU THE HIGHLY COVETED "MEETS EXPECTATIONS" DESIGNATION!
8/14/03 © 2003 United Feature Syndicate, Inc.
ALICE, IF HAVING HIGH EXPECTATIONS OF YOU IS WRONG, THEN I DON'T WANT TO BE RIGHT.

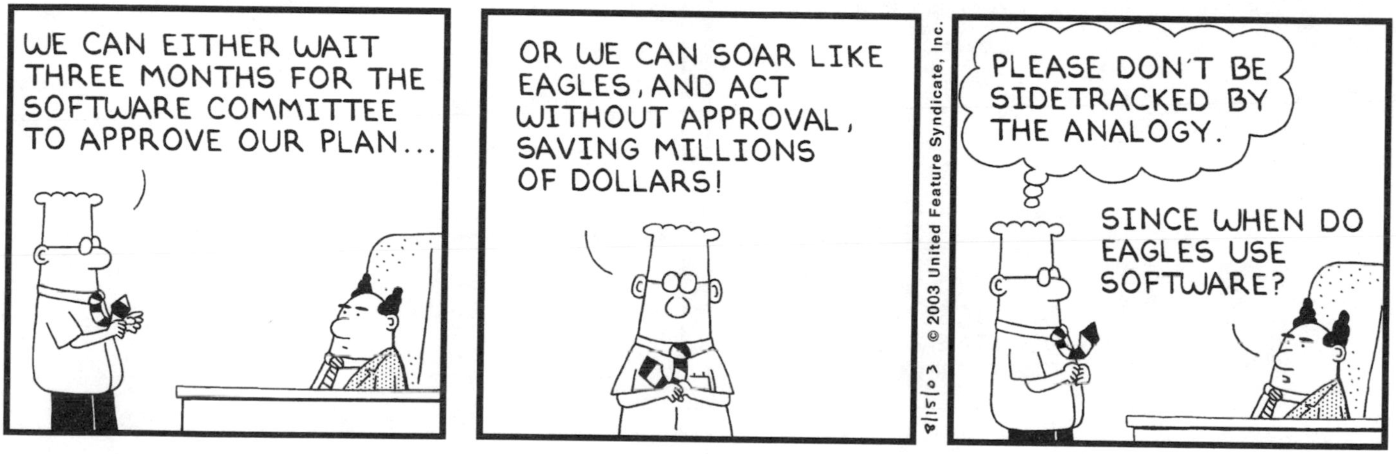
WE CAN EITHER WAIT THREE MONTHS FOR THE SOFTWARE COMMITTEE TO APPROVE OUR PLAN...
OR WE CAN SOAR LIKE EAGLES, AND ACT WITHOUT APPROVAL, SAVING MILLIONS OF DOLLARS!
8/15/03 © 2003 United Feature Syndicate, Inc.
PLEASE DON'T BE SIDETRACKED BY THE ANALOGY.
SINCE WHEN DO EAGLES USE SOFTWARE?

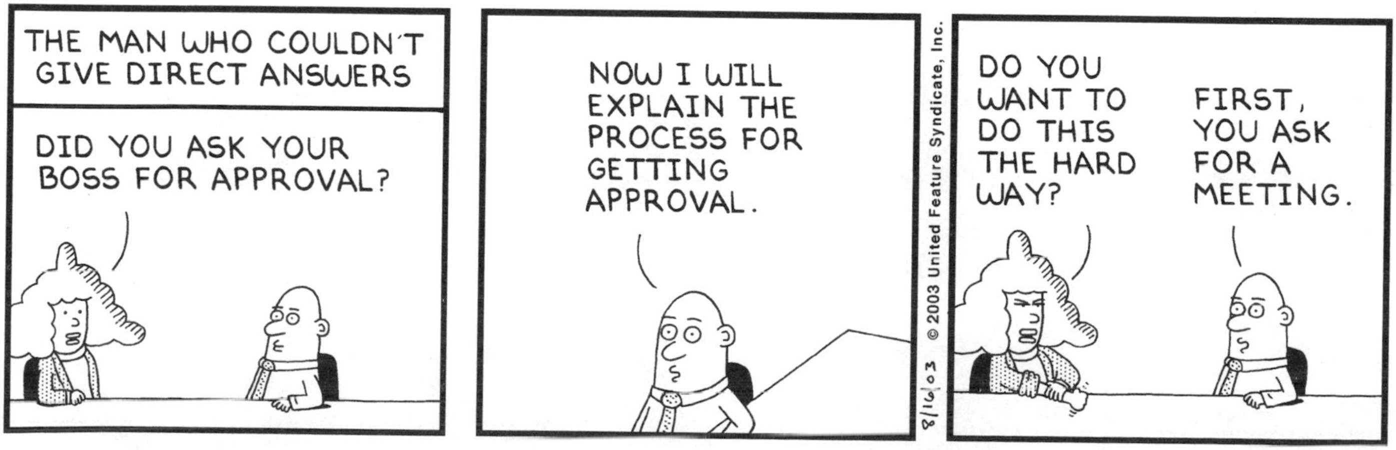
THE MAN WHO COULDN'T GIVE DIRECT ANSWERS
DID YOU ASK YOUR BOSS FOR APPROVAL?
NOW I WILL EXPLAIN THE PROCESS FOR GETTING APPROVAL.
8/16/03 © 2003 United Feature Syndicate, Inc.
DO YOU WANT TO DO THIS THE HARD WAY?
FIRST, YOU ASK FOR A MEETING.

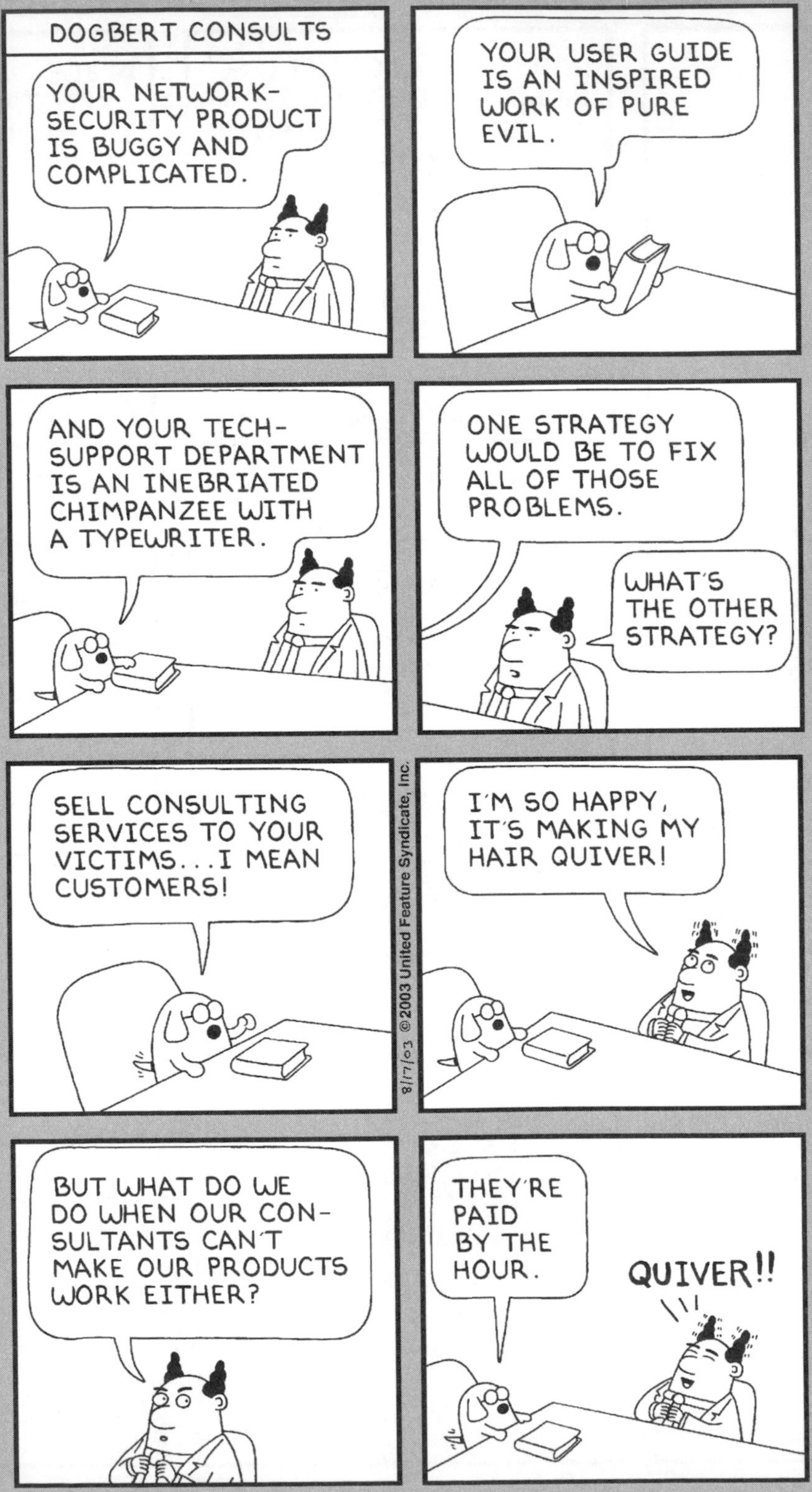
DOGBERT CONSULTS
YOUR NETWORK-SECURITY PRODUCT IS BUGGY AND COMPLICATED.
YOUR USER GUIDE IS AN INSPIRED WORK OF PURE EVIL.
AND YOUR TECH-SUPPORT DEPARTMENT IS AN INEBRIATED CHIMPANZEE WITH A TYPEWRITER.
ONE STRATEGY WOULD BE TO FIX ALL OF THOSE PROBLEMS.
WHAT'S THE OTHER STRATEGY?
SELL CONSULTING SERVICES TO YOUR VICTIMS...I MEAN CUSTOMERS!
I'M SO HAPPY, IT'S MAKING MY HAIR QUIVER!
BUT WHAT DO WE DO WHEN OUR CON-SULTANTS CAN'T MAKE OUR PRODUCTS WORK EITHER?
THEY'RE PAID BY THE HOUR.
QUIVER!!
©2003 United Feature Syndicate, Inc.

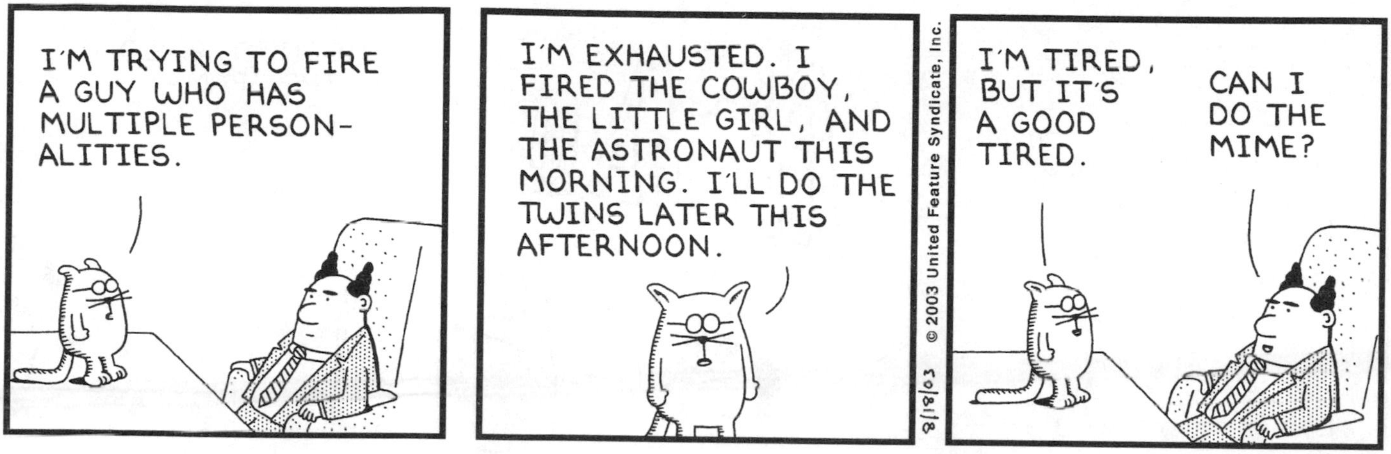
I'M TRYING TO FIRE A GUY WHO HAS MULTIPLE PERSON-ALITIES.
I'M EXHAUSTED. I FIRED THE COWBOY, THE LITTLE GIRL, AND THE ASTRONAUT THIS MORNING. I'LL DO THE TWINS LATER THIS AFTERNOON.
8/18/03 © 2003 United Feature Syndicate, Inc.
I'M TIRED, BUT IT'S A GOOD TIRED.
CAN I DO THE MIME?

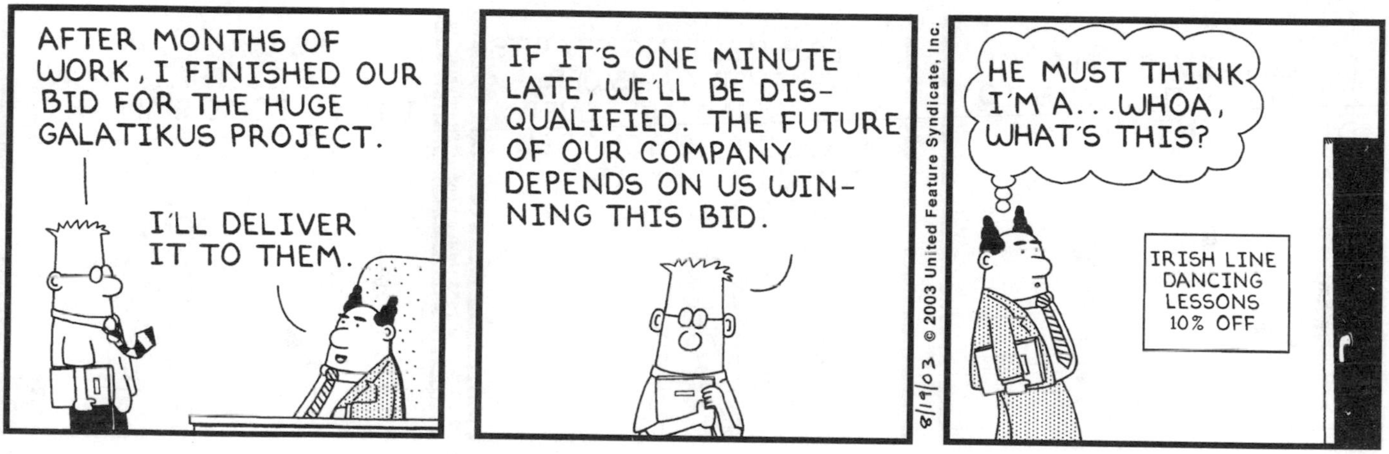
AFTER MONTHS OF WORK, I FINISHED OUR BID FOR THE HUGE GALATIKUS PROJECT.
I'LL DELIVER IT TO THEM.
IF IT'S ONE MINUTE LATE, WE'LL BE DIS-QUALIFIED. THE FUTURE OF OUR COMPANY DEPENDS ON US WIN-NING THIS BID.
8/19/03 © 2003 United Feature Syndicate, Inc.
HE MUST THINK I'M A...WHOA, WHAT'S THIS?
IRISH LINE DANCING LESSONS 10% OFF

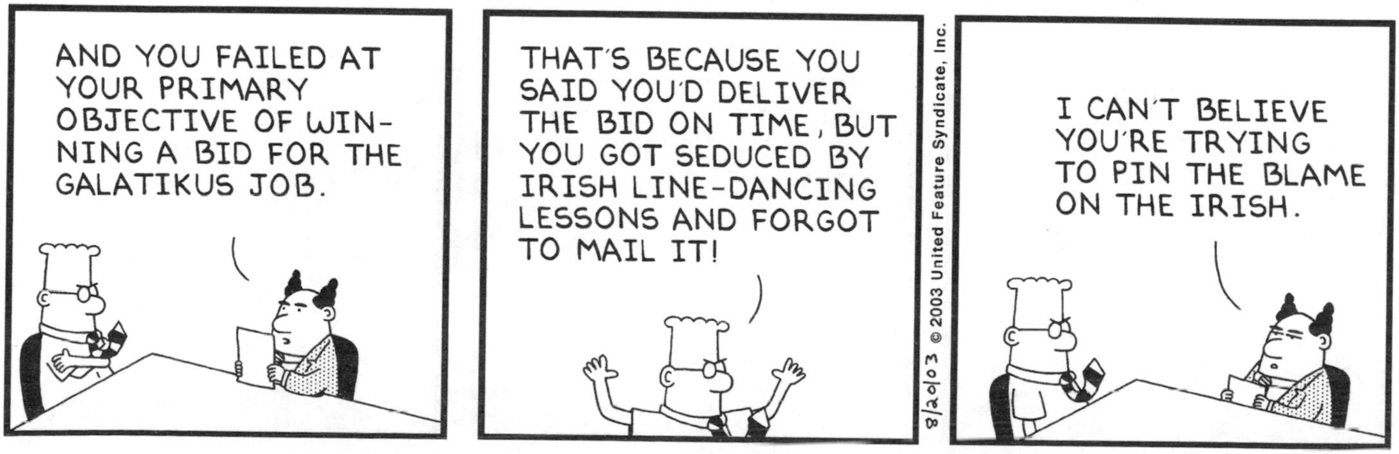
AND YOU FAILED AT YOUR PRIMARY OBJECTIVE OF WIN-NING A BID FOR THE GALATIKUS JOB.
THAT'S BECAUSE YOU SAID YOU'D DELIVER THE BID ON TIME, BUT YOU GOT SEDUCED BY IRISH LINE-DANCING LESSONS AND FORGOT TO MAIL IT!
8/20/03 © 2003 United Feature Syndicate, Inc.
I CAN'T BELIEVE YOU'RE TRYING TO PIN THE BLAME ON THE IRISH.

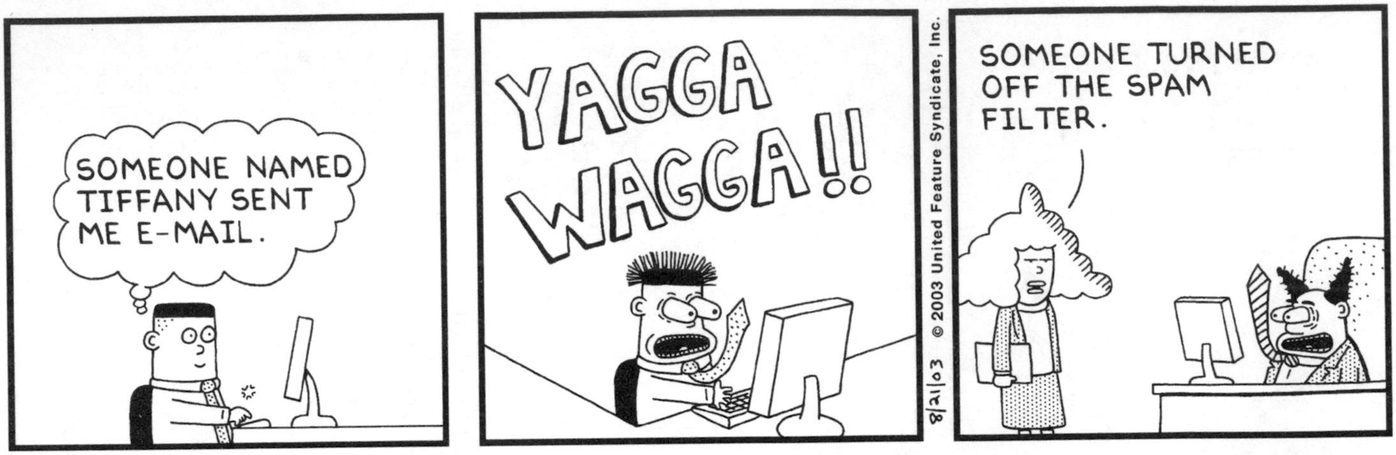
SOMEONE NAMED TIFFANY SENT ME E-MAIL.
YAGGA WAGGA!!
8/21/03 © 2003 United Feature Syndicate, Inc.
SOMEONE TURNED OFF THE SPAM FILTER.

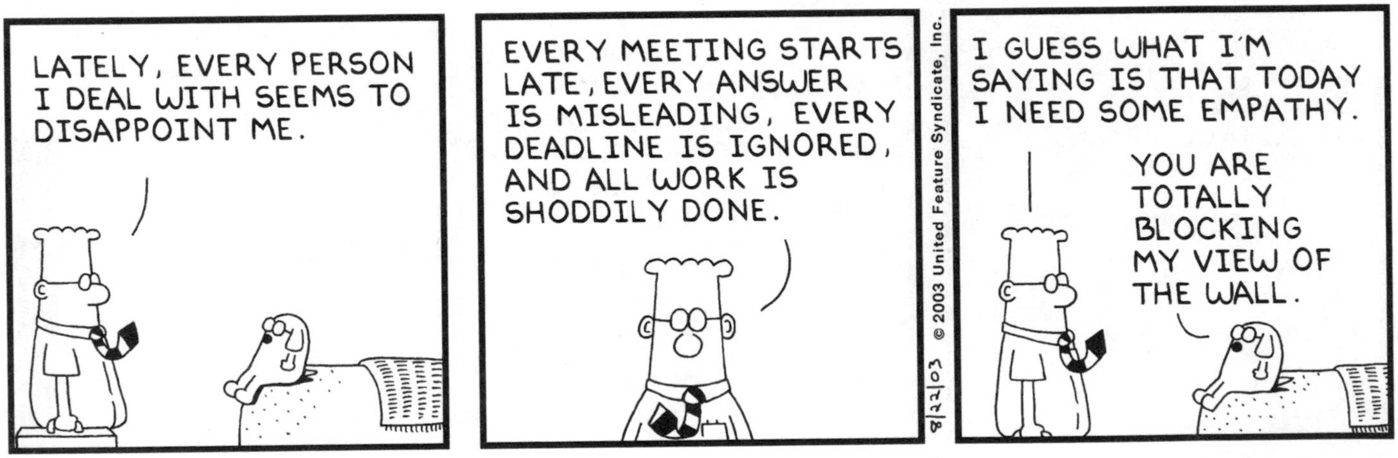
LATELY, EVERY PERSON I DEAL WITH SEEMS TO DISAPPOINT ME.
EVERY MEETING STARTS LATE, EVERY ANSWER IS MISLEADING, EVERY DEADLINE IS IGNORED, AND ALL WORK IS SHODDILY DONE.
8/22/03 © 2003 United Feature Syndicate, Inc.
I GUESS WHAT I'M SAYING IS THAT TODAY I NEED SOME EMPATHY.
YOU ARE TOTALLY BLOCKING MY VIEW OF THE WALL.

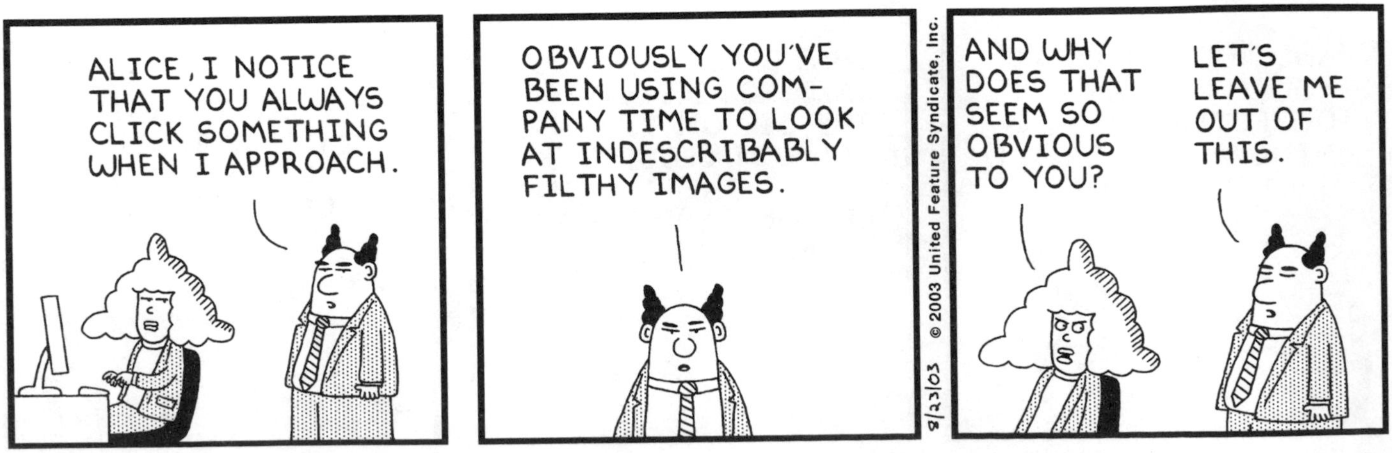
ALICE, I NOTICE THAT YOU ALWAYS CLICK SOMETHING WHEN I APPROACH.
OBVIOUSLY YOU'VE BEEN USING COM-PANY TIME TO LOOK AT INDESCRIBABLY FILTHY IMAGES.
8/23/03 © 2003 United Feature Syndicate, Inc.
AND WHY DOES THAT SEEM SO OBVIOUS TO YOU?
LET'S LEAVE ME OUT OF THIS.

WHEN I'M NOT HELPING TEAM MEMBERS, I LIKE TO FEED THE POOR OR READ TO BLIND PEOPLE.
I DON'T CARE ABOUT MONEY. ALL I WANT IS A CHANCE TO HELP HUMANITY REACH ITS FULLEST POTENTIAL.
YOU'RE SO WONDERFUL, IT'S MAKING ME CRY! YOU'RE HIRED.
EXCELLENT.
COME MEET THE TEAM.
I HAVE A SPECIAL SKILL FOR IDENTIFYING GOOD PEOPLE.
8/24/03 © 2003 United Feature Syndicate, Inc.
IT'S PART INSTINCT, PART EXPERIENCE.
AND YES, MAYBE JUST A LITTLE ESP.
WATCH THIS.
ALICE, YOUR FAVORITE COLOR IS... MITTEN?

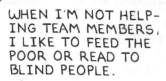

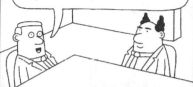

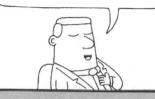

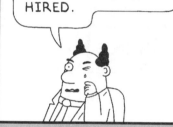

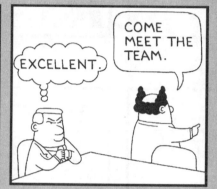

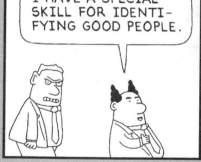

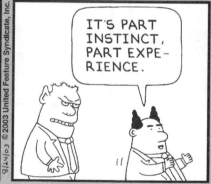

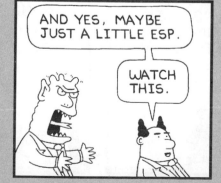

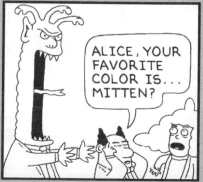

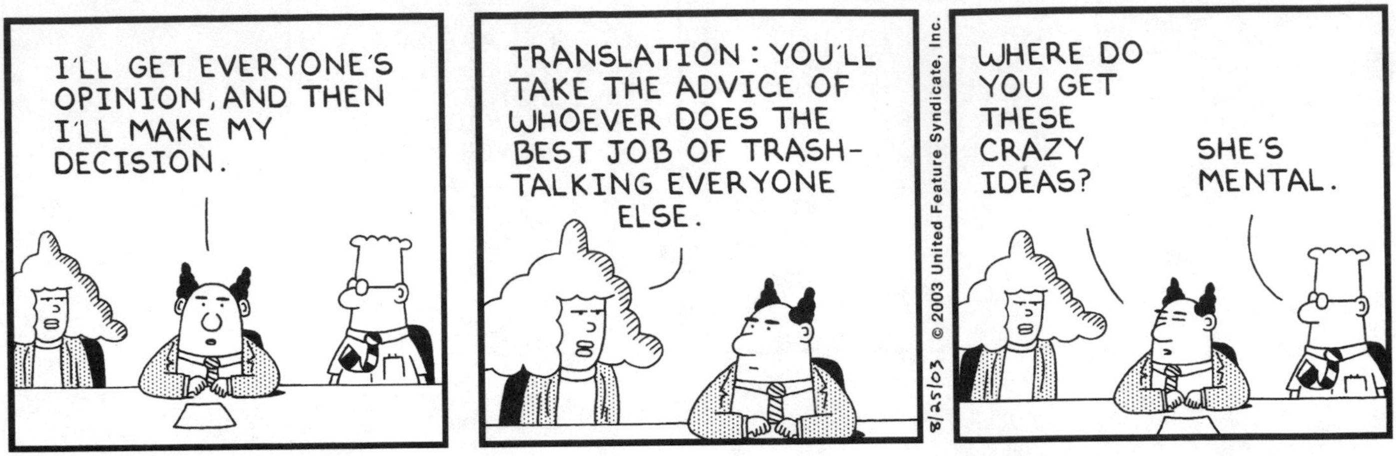
I'LL GET EVERYONE'S OPINION, AND THEN I'LL MAKE MY DECISION.
TRANSLATION: YOU'LL TAKE THE ADVICE OF WHOEVER DOES THE BEST JOB OF TRASH-TALKING EVERYONE ELSE.
8/25/03 © 2003 United Feature Syndicate, Inc.
WHERE DO YOU GET THESE CRAZY IDEAS?
SHE'S MENTAL.

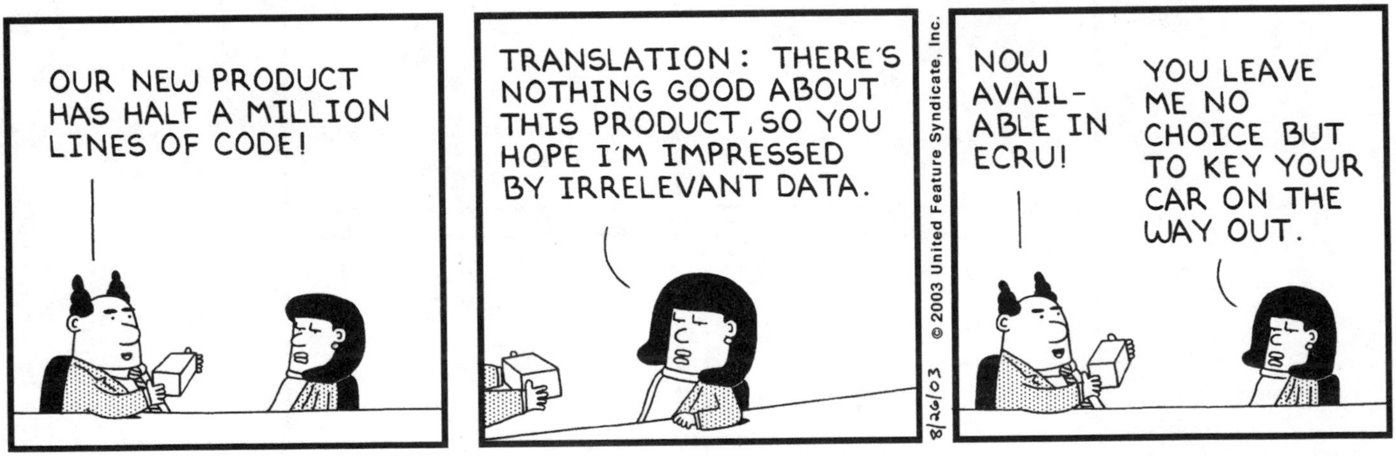
OUR NEW PRODUCT HAS HALF A MILLION LINES OF CODE!
TRANSLATION: THERE'S NOTHING GOOD ABOUT THIS PRODUCT, SO YOU HOPE I'M IMPRESSED BY IRRELEVANT DATA.
8/26/03 © 2003 United Feature Syndicate, Inc.
NOW AVAIL-ABLE IN ECRU!
YOU LEAVE ME NO CHOICE BUT TO KEY YOUR CAR ON THE WAY OUT.

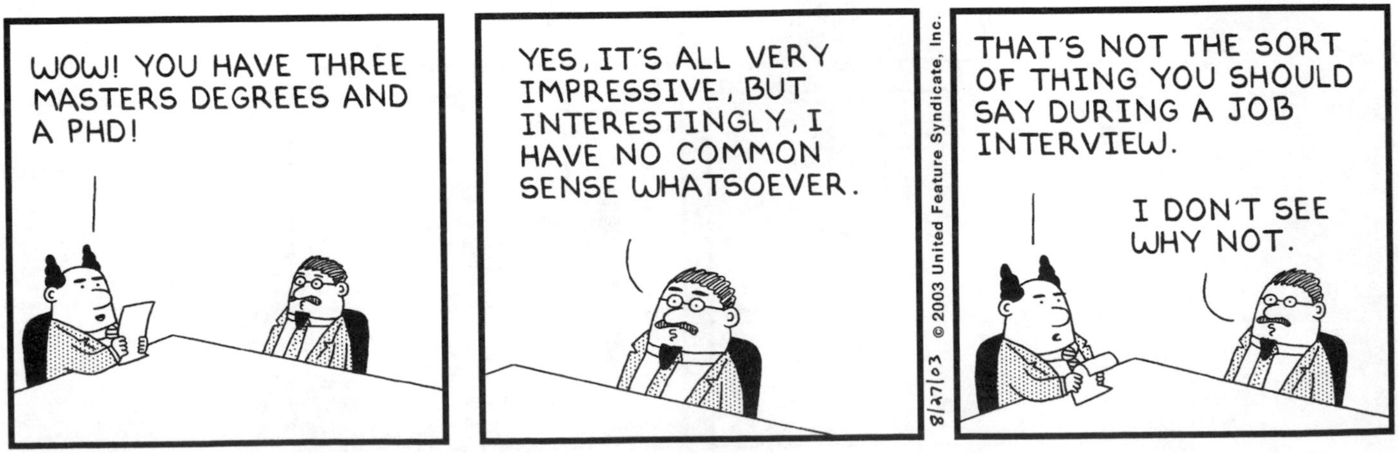
WOW! YOU HAVE THREE MASTERS DEGREES AND A PHD!
YES, IT'S ALL VERY IMPRESSIVE, BUT INTERESTINGLY, I HAVE NO COMMON SENSE WHATSOEVER.
8/27/03 © 2003 United Feature Syndicate, Inc.
THAT'S NOT THE SORT OF THING YOU SHOULD SAY DURING A JOB INTERVIEW.
I DON'T SEE WHY NOT.

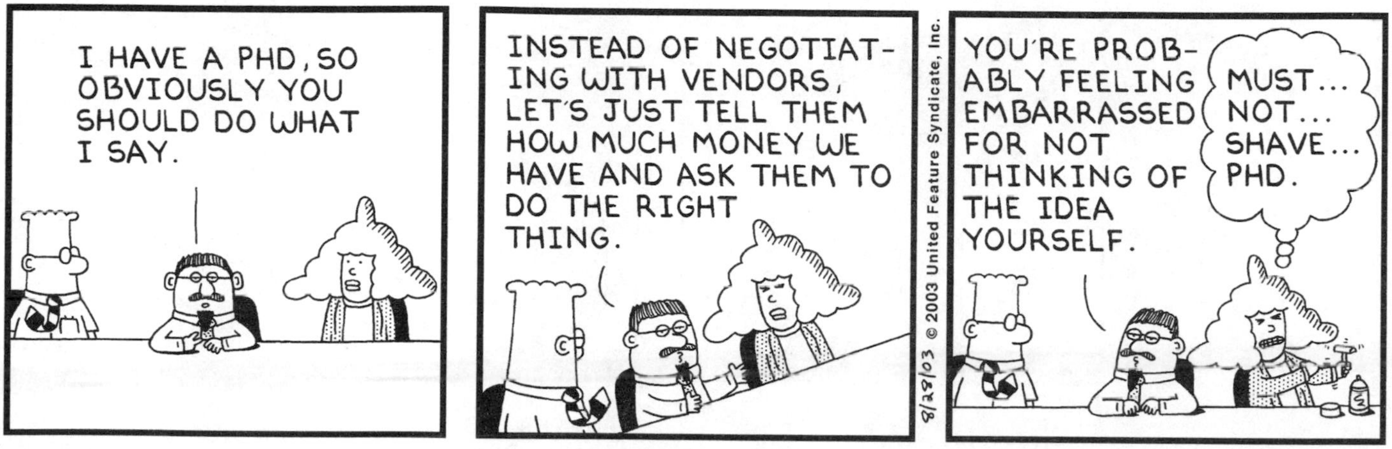
I HAVE A PHD, SO OBVIOUSLY YOU SHOULD DO WHAT I SAY.
INSTEAD OF NEGOTIATING WITH VENDORS, LET'S JUST TELL THEM HOW MUCH MONEY WE HAVE AND ASK THEM TO DO THE RIGHT THING.
8/28/03 © 2003 United Feature Syndicate, Inc.
YOU'RE PROBABLY FEELING EMBARRASSED FOR NOT THINKING OF THE IDEA YOURSELF.
MUST... NOT... SHAVE... PHD.

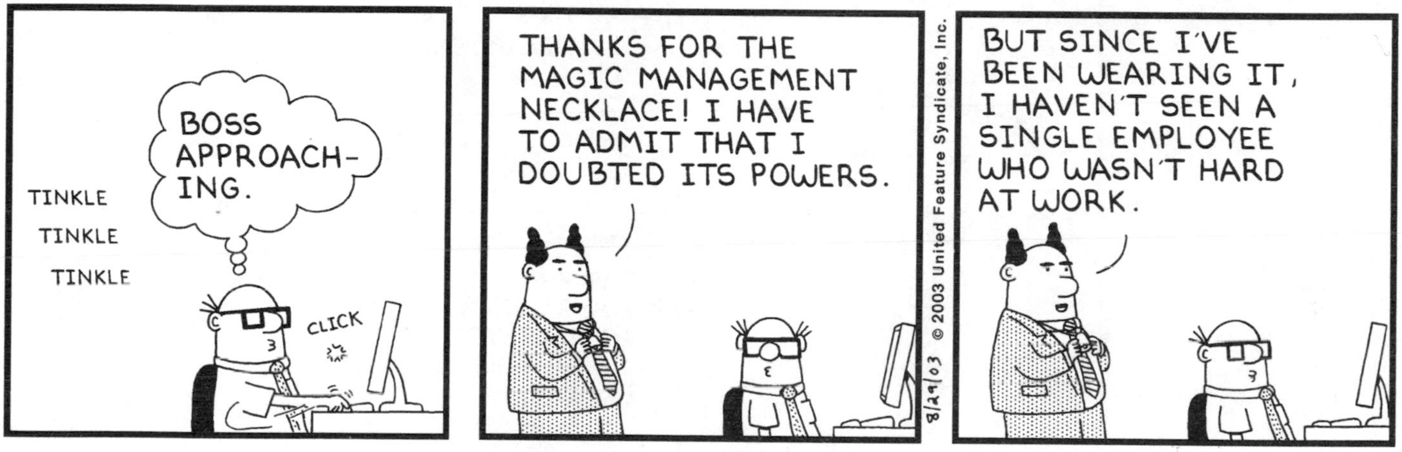
TINKLE
TINKLE
TINKLE
BOSS APPROACHING.
CLICK
THANKS FOR THE MAGIC MANAGEMENT NECKLACE! I HAVE TO ADMIT THAT I DOUBTED ITS POWERS.
8/29/03 © 2003 United Feature Syndicate, Inc.
BUT SINCE I'VE BEEN WEARING IT, I HAVEN'T SEEN A SINGLE EMPLOYEE WHO WASN'T HARD AT WORK.

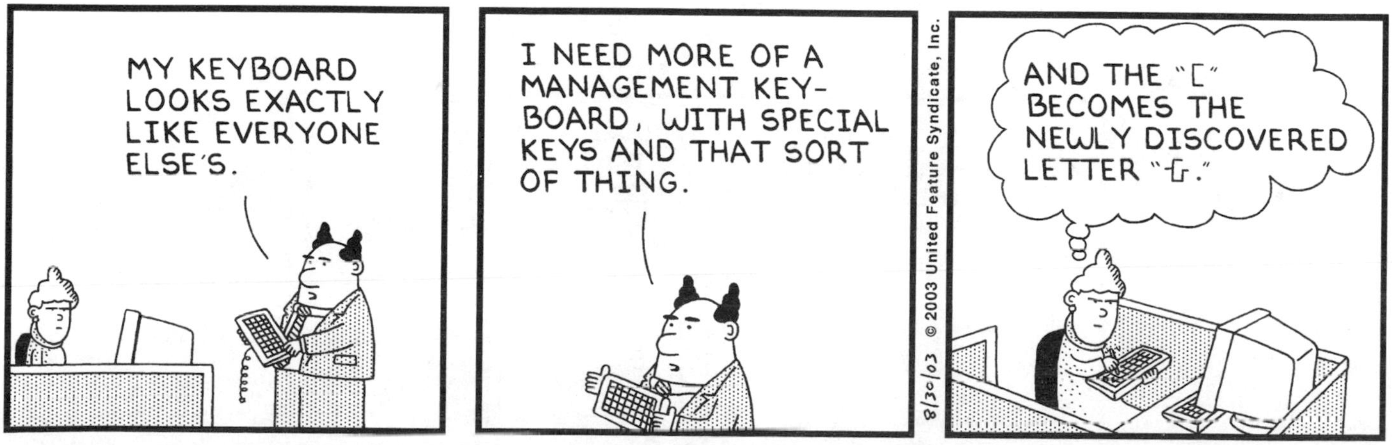
MY KEYBOARD LOOKS EXACTLY LIKE EVERYONE ELSE'S.
I NEED MORE OF A MANAGEMENT KEYBOARD, WITH SPECIAL KEYS AND THAT SORT OF THING.
8/30/03 © 2003 United Feature Syndicate, Inc.
AND THE "[" BECOMES THE NEWLY DISCOVERED LETTER

HI, I'M MATT. IT'S MY FIRST DAY HERE.
I'M DILBERT.
AND THIS IS...
I'D RATHER NOT SAY.
I PREFER TO REMAIN ANONYMOUS, SO YOU WON'T FEEL COMFORTABLE ASKING ME FOR ANYTHING LATER.
HERE'S MY CARD. IT'S BLANK.
THE PHRASE THAT YOU'RE LEAST LIKELY TO HEAR TODAY IS, "WE'RE JUST LIKE FAMILY."
©2003 United Feature Syndicate, Inc.
8/31/03
ARE YOU WORRIED THAT HE'LL TURN OVER THE CARD AND SEE YOUR NAME?
NO.
WAS THAT MY CARD?
I'VE BEEN HANDING THEM OUT FORYEARS.

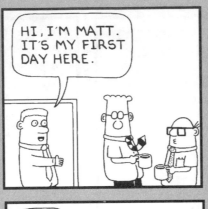

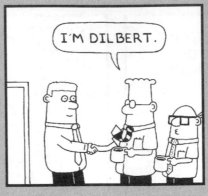

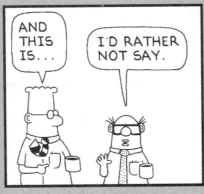

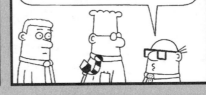

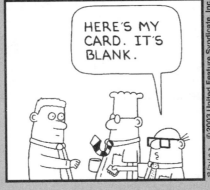

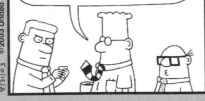

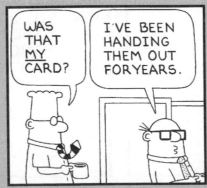

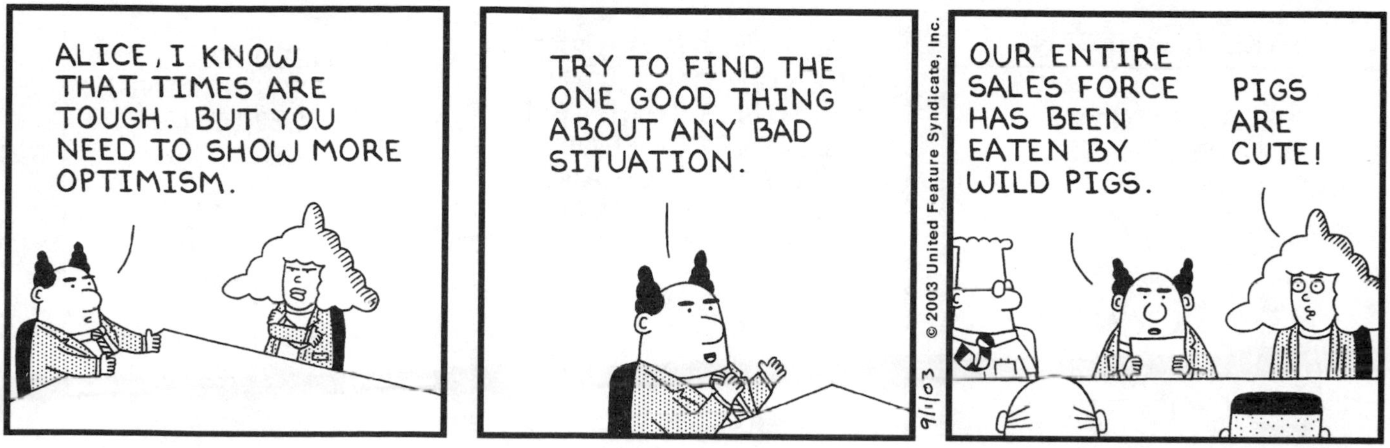
ALICE, I KNOW THAT TIMES ARE TOUGH. BUT YOU NEED TO SHOW MORE OPTIMISM.
TRY TO FIND THE ONE GOOD THING ABOUT ANY BAD SITUATION.
9/1/03
OUR ENTIRE SALES FORCE HAS BEEN EATEN BY WILD PIGS.
PIGS ARE CUTE!

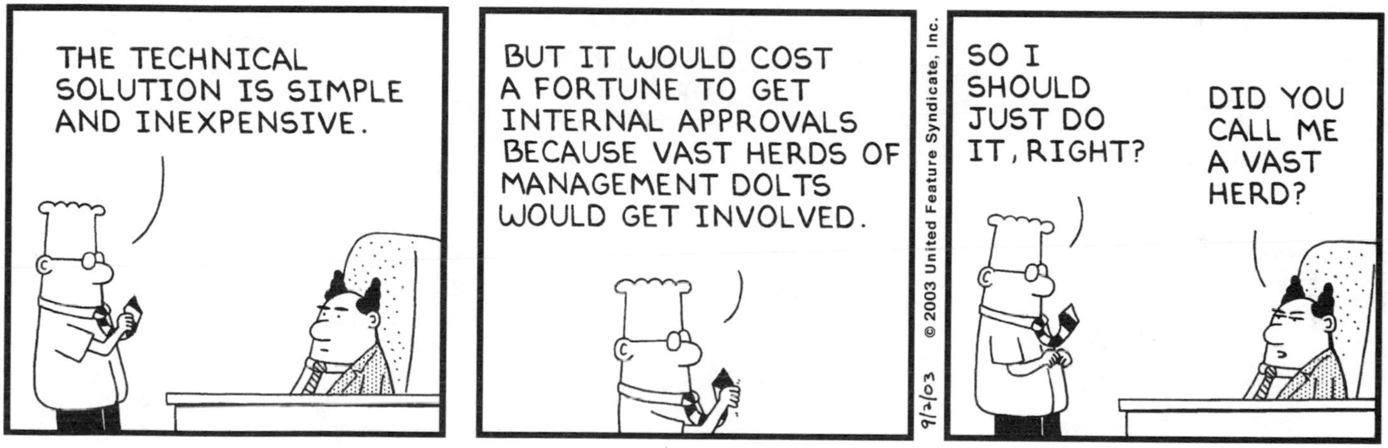
THE TECHNICAL SOLUTION IS SIMPLE AND INEXPENSIVE.
BUT IT WOULD COST A FORTUNE TO GET INTERNAL APPROVALS BECAUSE VAST HERDS OF MANAGEMENT DOLTS WOULD GET INVOLVED.
9/2/03
SO I SHOULD JUST DO IT, RIGHT?
DID YOU CALL ME A VAST HERD?

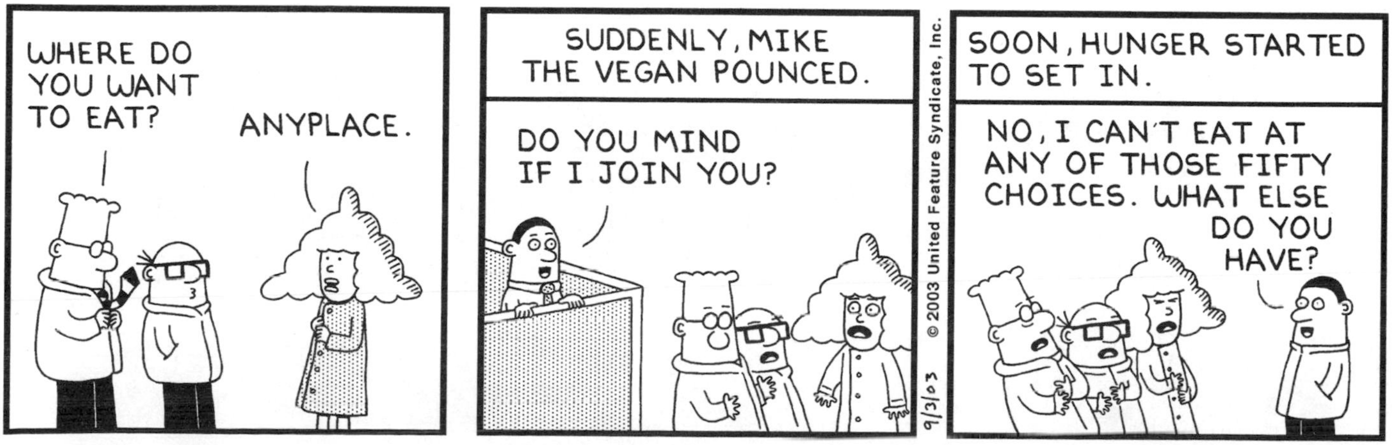
WHERE DO YOU WANT TO EAT?
ANYPLACE.
SUDDENLY, MIKE THE VEGAN POUNCED.
DO YOU MIND IF I JOIN YOU?
9/3/03
SOON, HUNGER STARTED TO SET IN.
NO, I CAN'T EAT AT ANY OF THOSE FIFTY CHOICES. WHAT ELSE DO YOU HAVE?

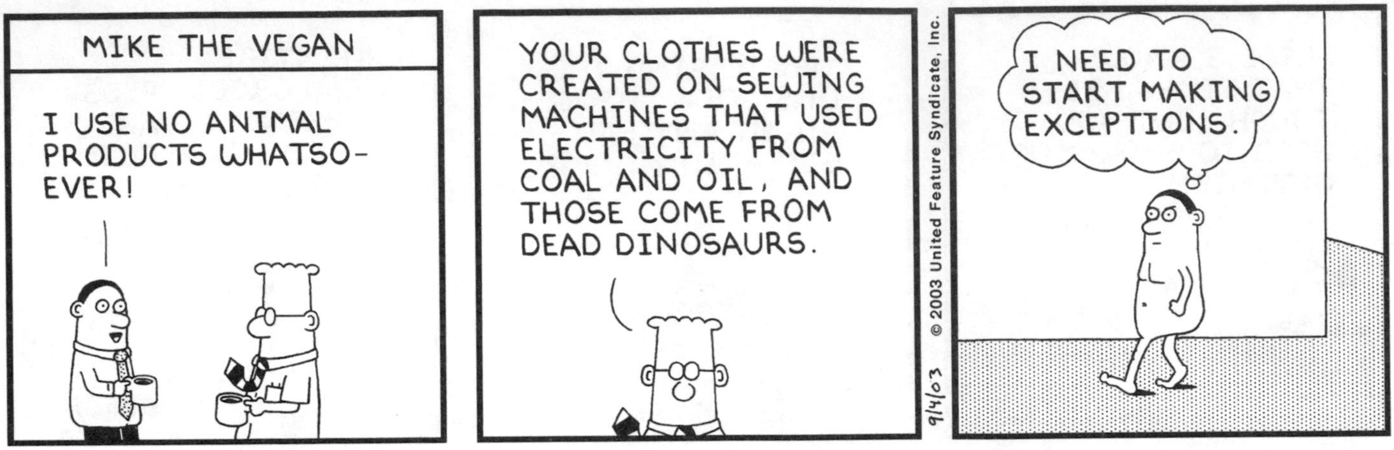
MIKE THE VEGAN
I USE NO ANIMAL PRODUCTS WHATSO-EVER!
YOUR CLOTHES WERE CREATED ON SEWING MACHINES THAT USED ELECTRICITY FROM COAL AND OIL, AND THOSE COME FROM DEAD DINOSAURS.
© 2003 United Feature Syndicate, Inc.
9/4/03
I NEED TO START MAKING EXCEPTIONS.

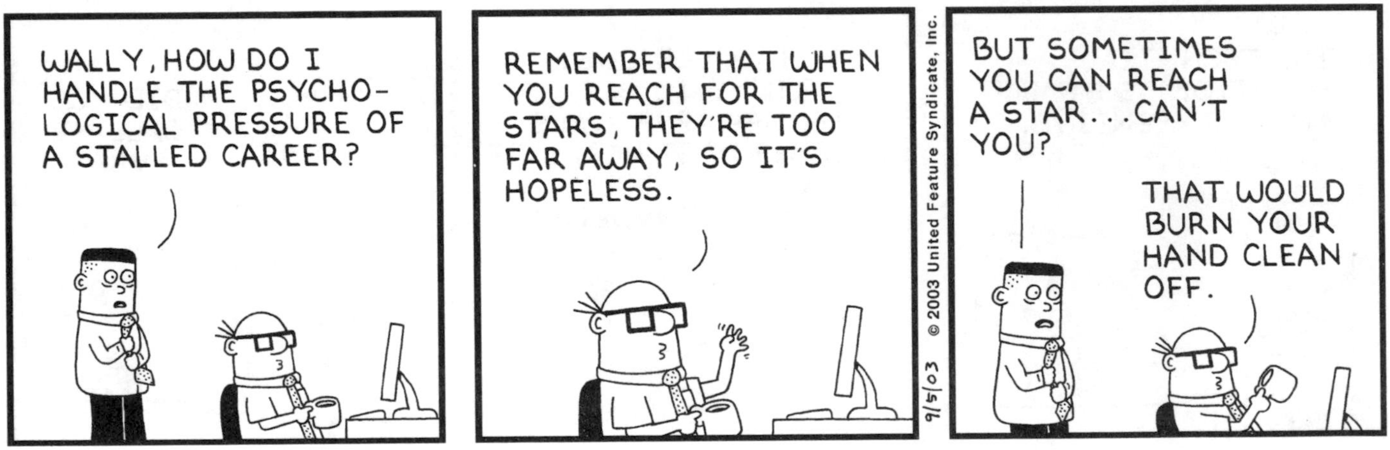
WALLY, HOW DO I HANDLE THE PSYCHO-LOGICAL PRESSURE OF A STALLED CAREER?
REMEMBER THAT WHEN YOU REACH FOR THE STARS, THEY'RE TOO FAR AWAY, SO IT'S HOPELESS.
© 2003 United Feature Syndicate, Inc.
9/5/03
BUT SOMETIMES YOU CAN REACH A STAR...CAN'T YOU?
THAT WOULD BURN YOUR HAND CLEAN OFF.

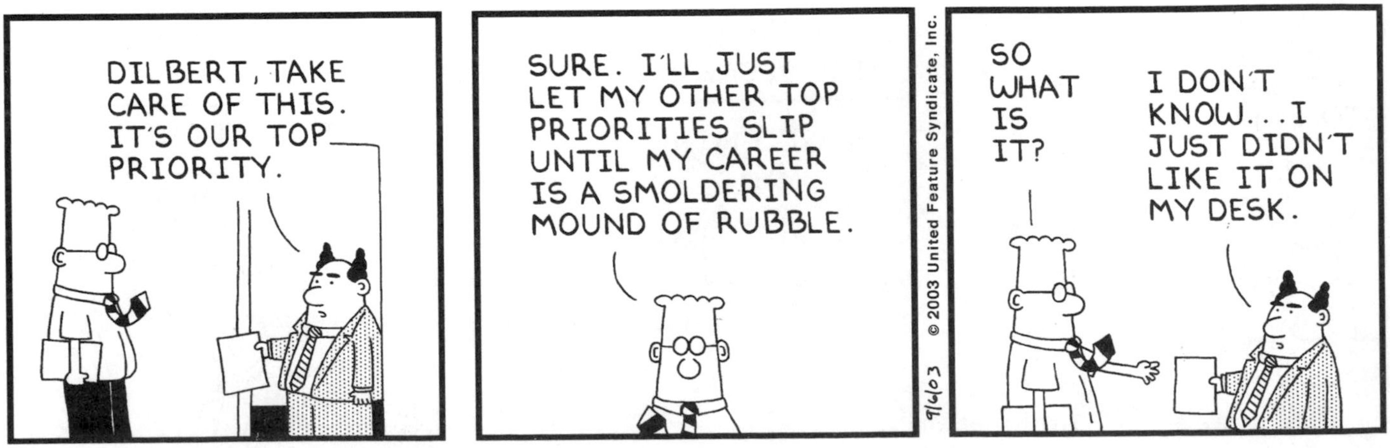
DILBERT, TAKE CARE OF THIS. IT'S OUR TOP PRIORITY.
SURE. I'LL JUST LET MY OTHER TOP PRIORITIES SLIP UNTIL MY CAREER IS A SMOLDERING MOUND OF RUBBLE.
© 2003 United Feature Syndicate, Inc.
9/6/03
SO WHAT IS IT?
I DON'T KNOW...I JUST DIDN'T LIKE IT ON MY DESK.

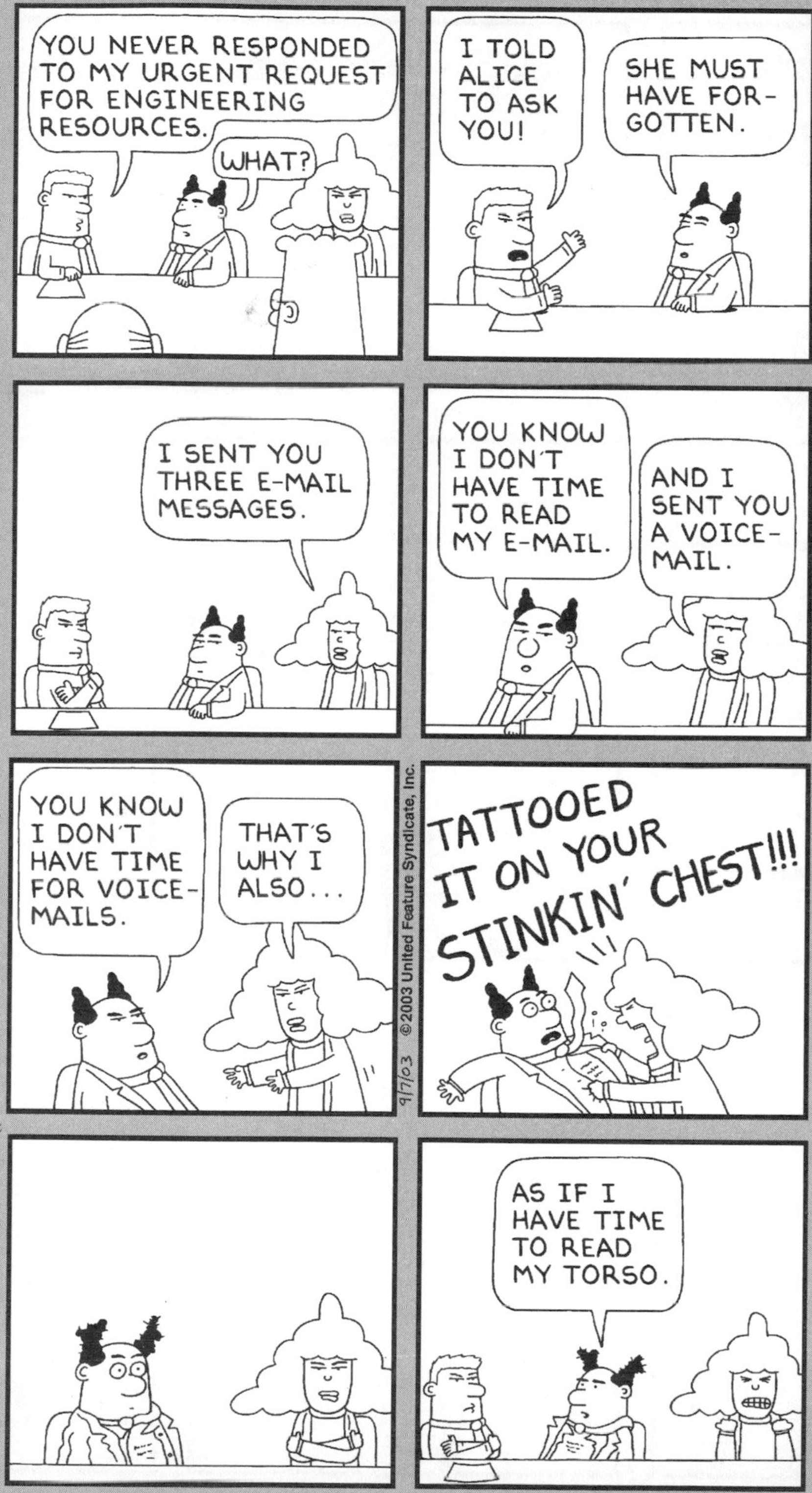
YOU NEVER RESPONDED TO MY URGENT REQUEST FOR ENGINEERING RESOURCES.
WHAT?
I TOLD ALICE TO ASK YOU!
SHE MUST HAVE FORGOTTEN.
I SENT YOU THREE E-MAIL MESSAGES.
YOU KNOW I DON'T HAVE TIME TO READ MY E-MAIL.
AND I SENT YOU A VOICE-MAIL.
YOU KNOW I DON'T HAVE TIME FOR VOICE-MAILS.
THAT'S WHY I ALSO...
©2003 United Feature Syndicate, Inc.
9/7/03
TATTOOED IT ON YOUR STINKIN' CHEST!!!
AS IF I HAVE TIME TO READ MY TORSO.

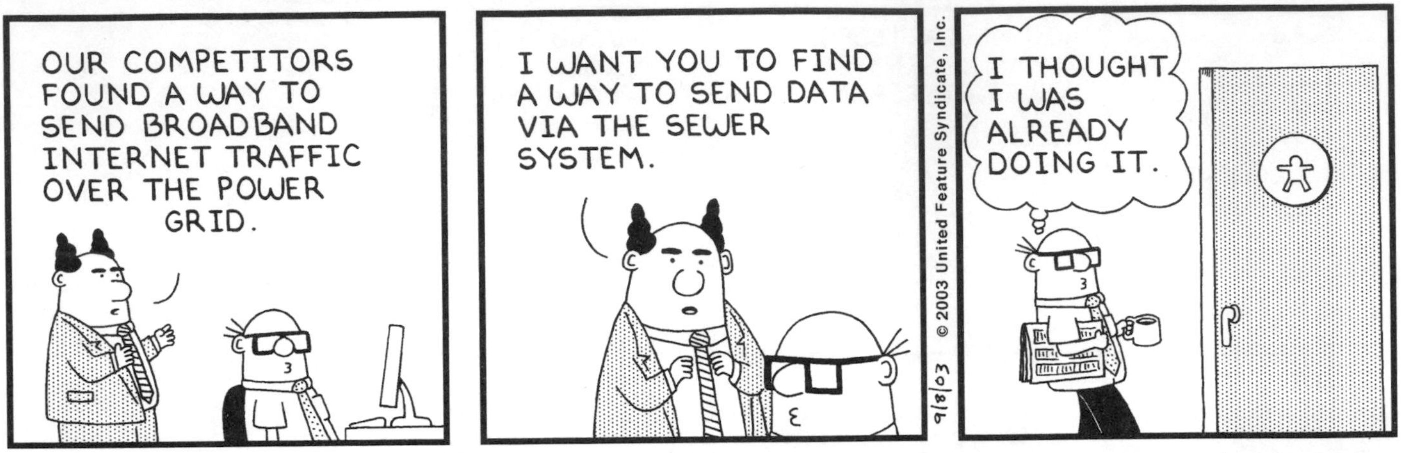
OUR COMPETITORS FOUND A WAY TO SEND BROADBAND INTERNET TRAFFIC OVER THE POWER GRID.
I WANT YOU TO FIND A WAY TO SEND DATA VIA THE SEWER SYSTEM.
I THOUGHT I WAS ALREADY DOING IT.
9/8/03

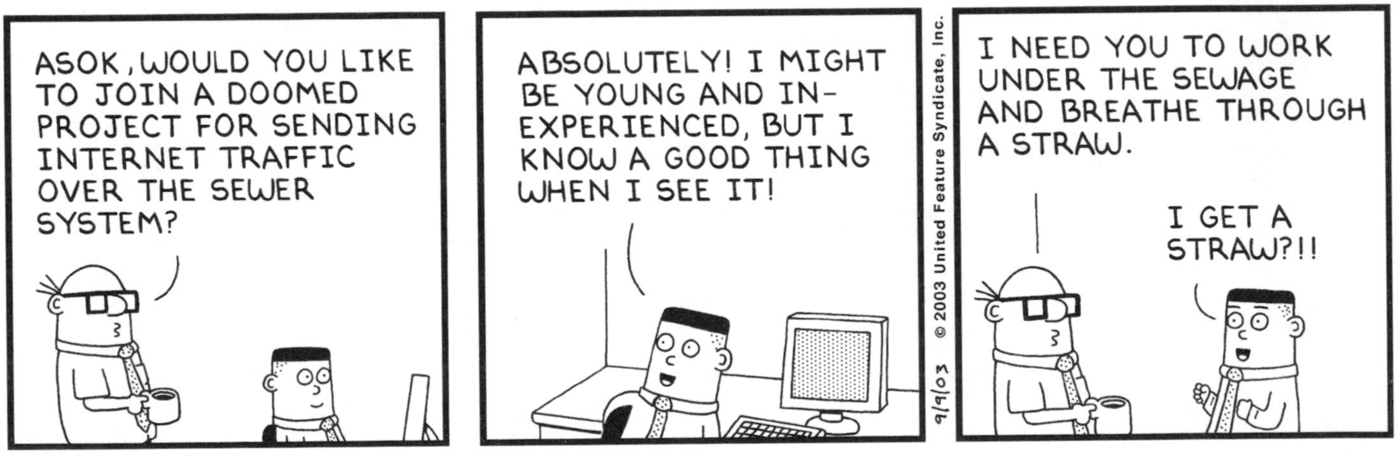
ASOK, WOULD YOU LIKE TO JOIN A DOOMED PROJECT FOR SENDING INTERNET TRAFFIC OVER THE SEWER SYSTEM?
ABSOLUTELY! I MIGHT BE YOUNG AND IN-EXPERIENCED, BUT I KNOW A GOOD THING WHEN I SEE IT!
I NEED YOU TO WORK UNDER THE SEWAGE AND BREATHE THROUGH A STRAW.
I GET A STRAW?!!
9/9/03

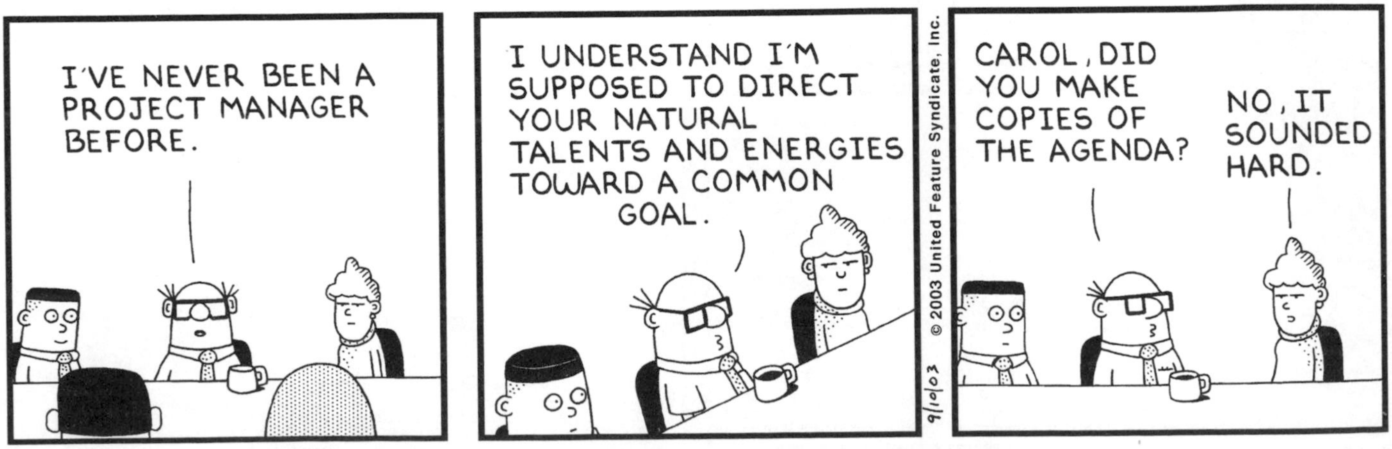
I'VE NEVER BEEN A PROJECT MANAGER BEFORE.
I UNDERSTAND I'M SUPPOSED TO DIRECT YOUR NATURAL TALENTS AND ENERGIES TOWARD A COMMON GOAL.
CAROL, DID YOU MAKE COPIES OF THE AGENDA?
NO, IT SOUNDED HARD.
9/10/03

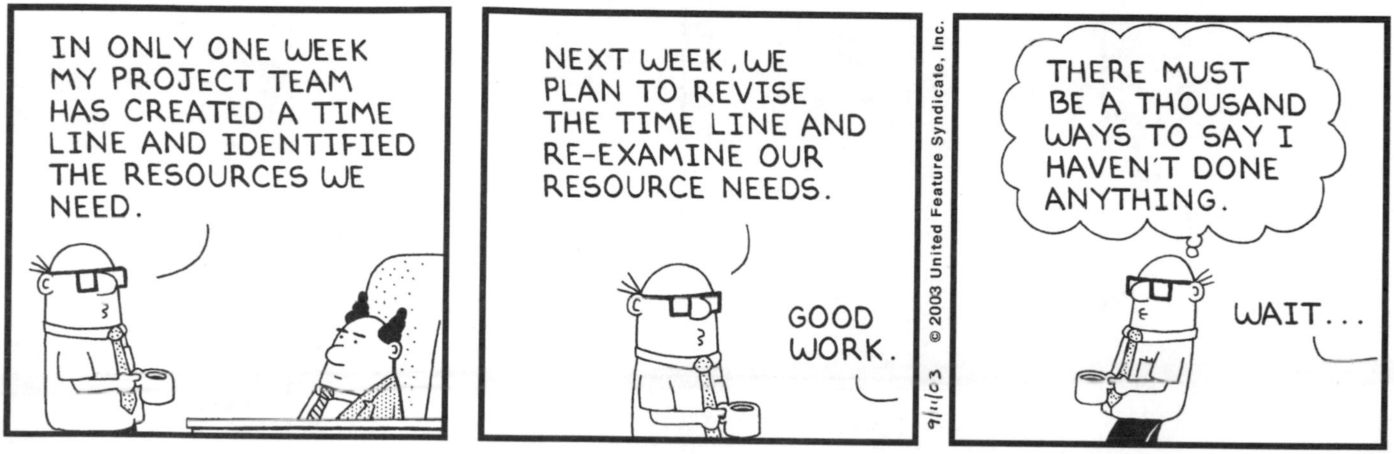
IN ONLY ONE WEEK MY PROJECT TEAM HAS CREATED A TIME LINE AND IDENTIFIED THE RESOURCES WE NEED.
NEXT WEEK, WE PLAN TO REVISE THE TIME LINE AND RE-EXAMINE OUR RESOURCE NEEDS.
GOOD WORK.
9/11/03
© 2003 United Feature Syndicate, Inc.
THERE MUST BE A THOUSAND WAYS TO SAY I HAVEN'T DONE ANYTHING.
WAIT...

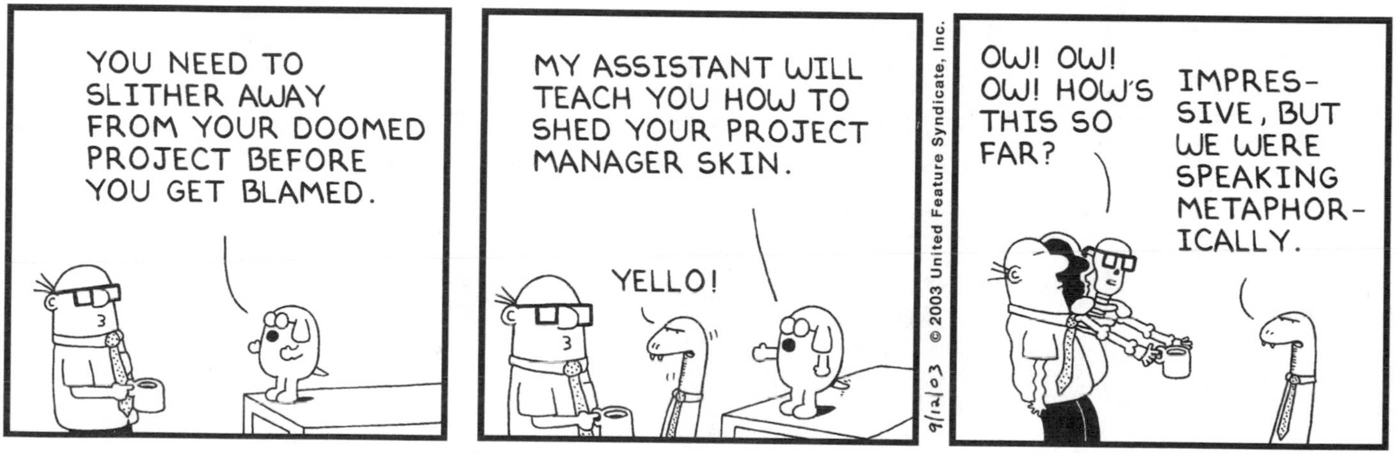
YOU NEED TO SLITHER AWAY FROM YOUR DOOMED PROJECT BEFORE YOU GET BLAMED.
MY ASSISTANT WILL TEACH YOU HOW TO SHED YOUR PROJECT MANAGER SKIN.
YELLO!
9/12/03
© 2003 United Feature Syndicate, Inc.
OW! OW! OW! HOW'S THIS SO FAR?
IMPRES-SIVE, BUT WE WERE SPEAKING METAPHOR-ICALLY.

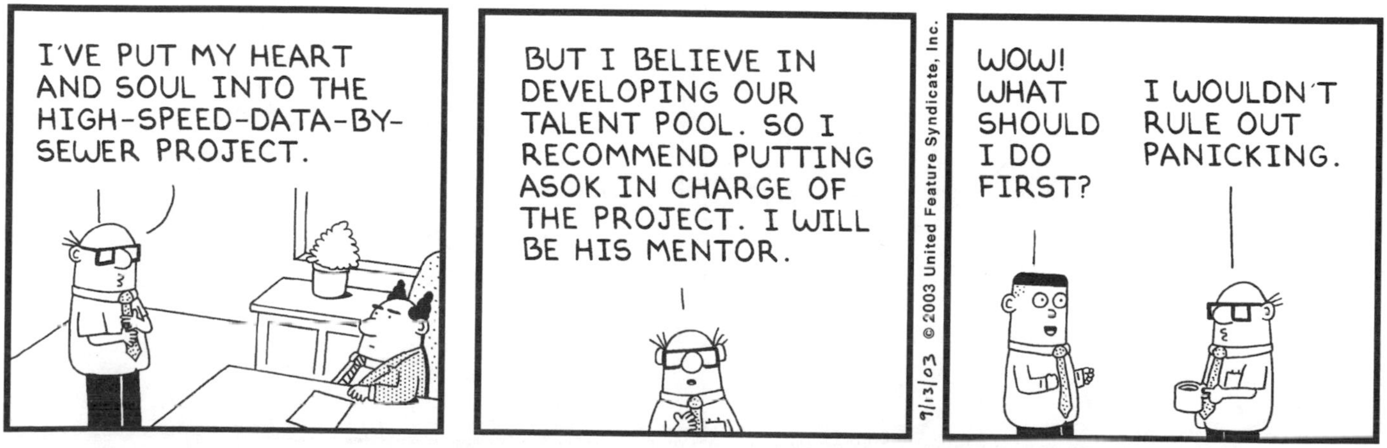
I'VE PUT MY HEART AND SOUL INTO THE HIGH-SPEED-DATA-BY-SEWER PROJECT.
BUT I BELIEVE IN DEVELOPING OUR TALENT POOL. SO I RECOMMEND PUTTING ASOK IN CHARGE OF THE PROJECT. I WILL BE HIS MENTOR.
9/13/03
© 2003 United Feature Syndicate, Inc.
WOW! WHAT SHOULD I DO FIRST?
I WOULDN'T RULE OUT PANICKING.

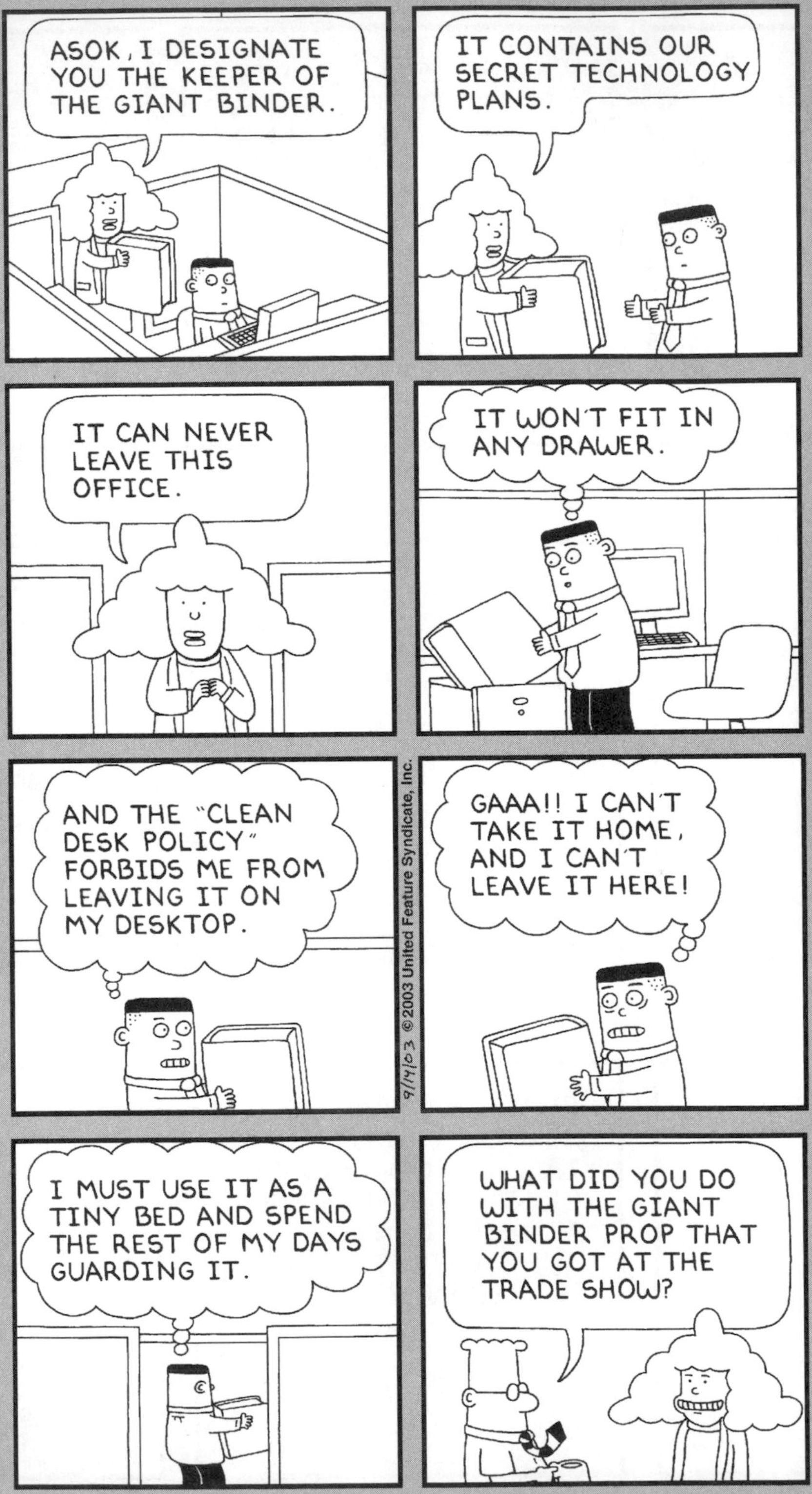
ASOK, I DESIGNATE YOU THE KEEPER OF THE GIANT BINDER.
IT CONTAINS OUR SECRET TECHNOLOGY PLANS.
IT CAN NEVER LEAVE THIS OFFICE.
IT WON'T FIT IN ANY DRAWER.
AND THE "CLEAN DESK POLICY" FORBIDS ME FROM LEAVING IT ON MY DESKTOP.
GAAA!! I CAN'T TAKE IT HOME, AND I CAN'T LEAVE IT HERE!
I MUST USE IT AS A TINY BED AND SPEND THE REST OF MY DAYS GUARDING IT.
WHAT DID YOU DO WITH THE GIANT BINDER PROP THAT YOU GOT AT THE TRADE SHOW?
9/14/03 © 2003 United Feature Syndicate, Inc.

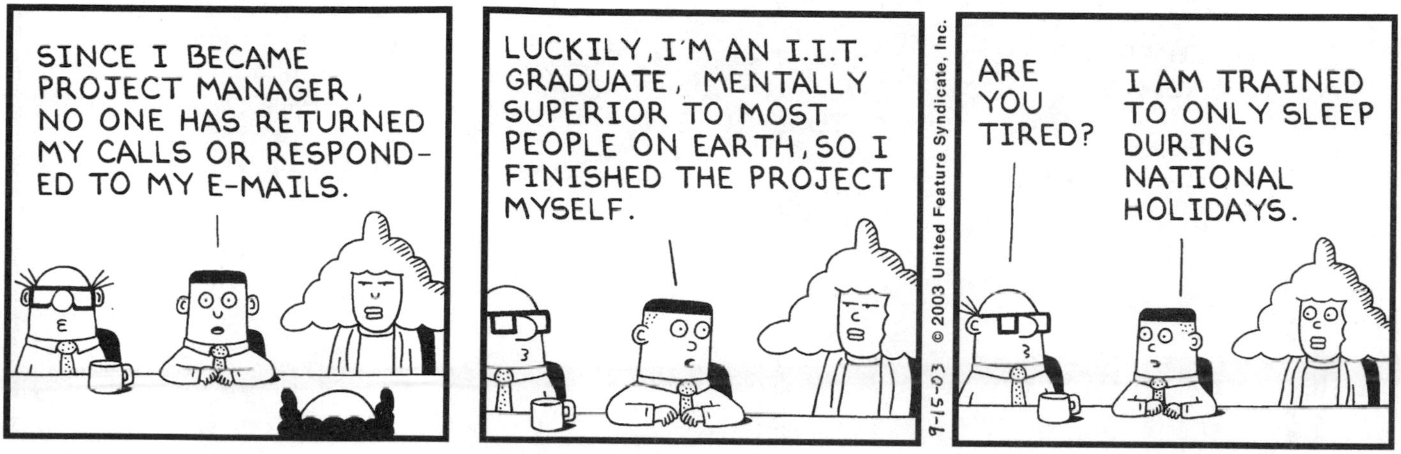
SINCE I BECAME PROJECT MANAGER, NO ONE HAS RETURNED MY CALLS OR RESPOND-ED TO MY E-MAILS.
LUCKILY, I'M AN I.I.T. GRADUATE, MENTALLY SUPERIOR TO MOST PEOPLE ON EARTH, SO I FINISHED THE PROJECT MYSELF.
ARE YOU TIRED?
I AM TRAINED TO ONLY SLEEP DURING NATIONAL HOLIDAYS.
9-15-03 © 2003 United Feature Syndicate, Inc.

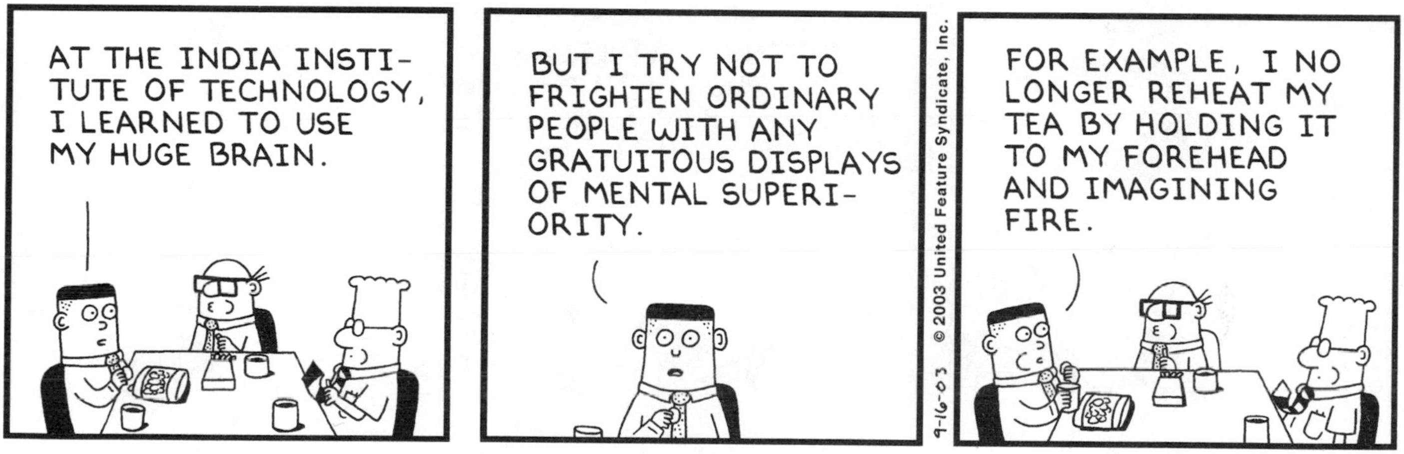
AT THE INDIA INSTI-TUTE OF TECHNOLOGY, I LEARNED TO USE MY HUGE BRAIN.
BUT I TRY NOT TO FRIGHTEN ORDINARY PEOPLE WITH ANY GRATUITOUS DISPLAYS OF MENTAL SUPERI-ORITY.
FOR EXAMPLE, I NO LONGER REHEAT MY TEA BY HOLDING IT TO MY FOREHEAD AND IMAGINING FIRE.
9-16-03 © 2003 United Feature Syndicate, Inc.

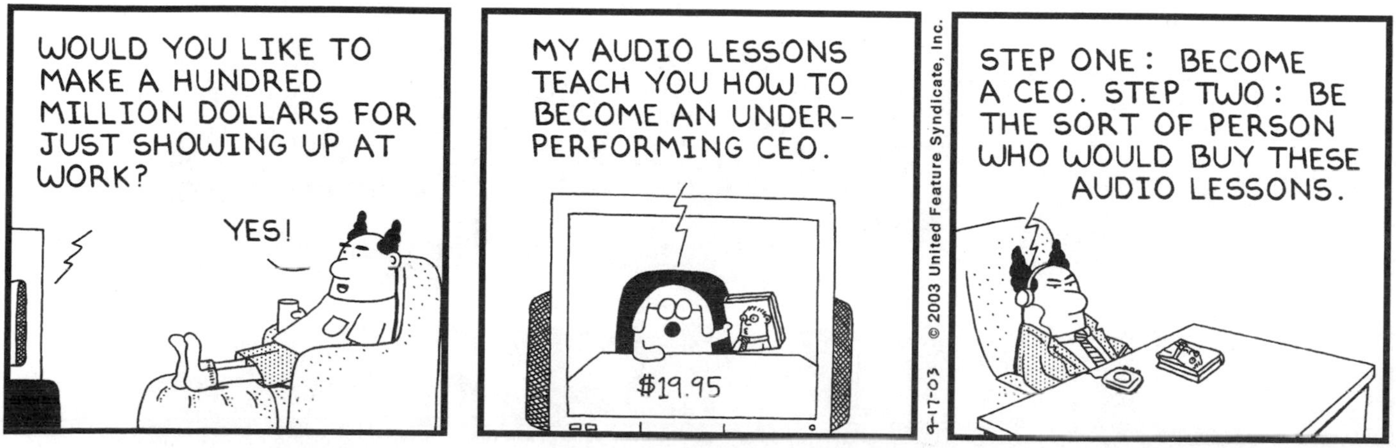
WOULD YOU LIKE TO MAKE A HUNDRED MILLION DOLLARS FOR JUST SHOWING UP AT WORK?
YES!
MY AUDIO LESSONS TEACH YOU HOW TO BECOME AN UNDER-PERFORMING CEO.
$19.95
STEP ONE: BECOME A CEO. STEP TWO: BE THE SORT OF PERSON WHO WOULD BUY THESE AUDIO LESSONS.
9-17-03 © 2003 United Feature Syndicate, Inc.

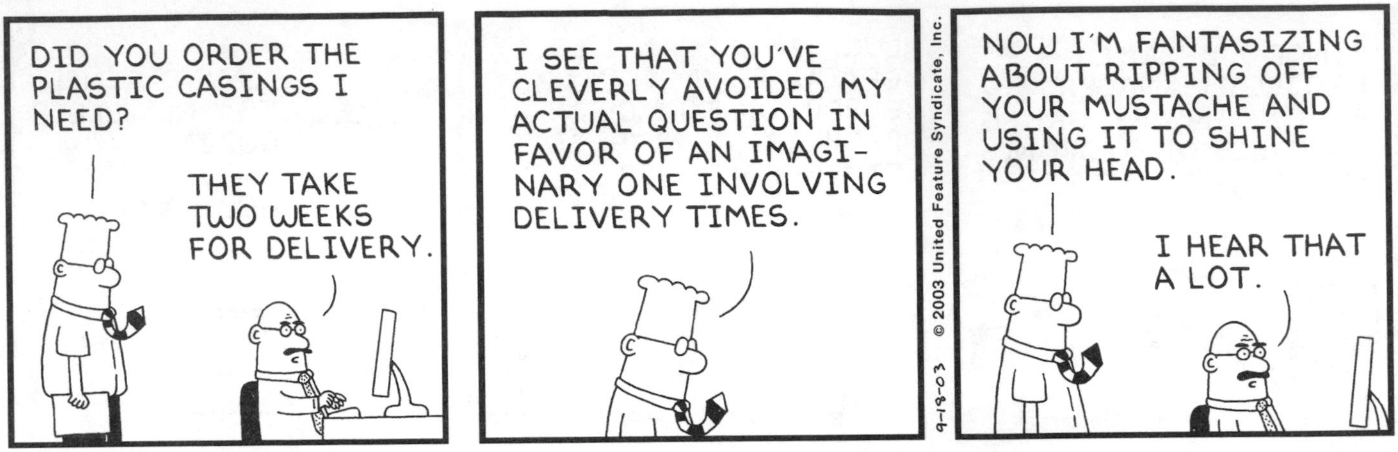
DID YOU ORDER THE PLASTIC CASINGS I NEED?
THEY TAKE TWO WEEKS FOR DELIVERY.
I SEE THAT YOU'VE CLEVERLY AVOIDED MY ACTUAL QUESTION IN FAVOR OF AN IMAGI- NARY ONE INVOLVING DELIVERY TIMES.
9-19-03 © 2003 United Feature Syndicate, Inc.
NOW I'M FANTASIZING ABOUT RIPPING OFF YOUR MUSTACHE AND USING IT TO SHINE YOUR HEAD.
I HEAR THAT A LOT.

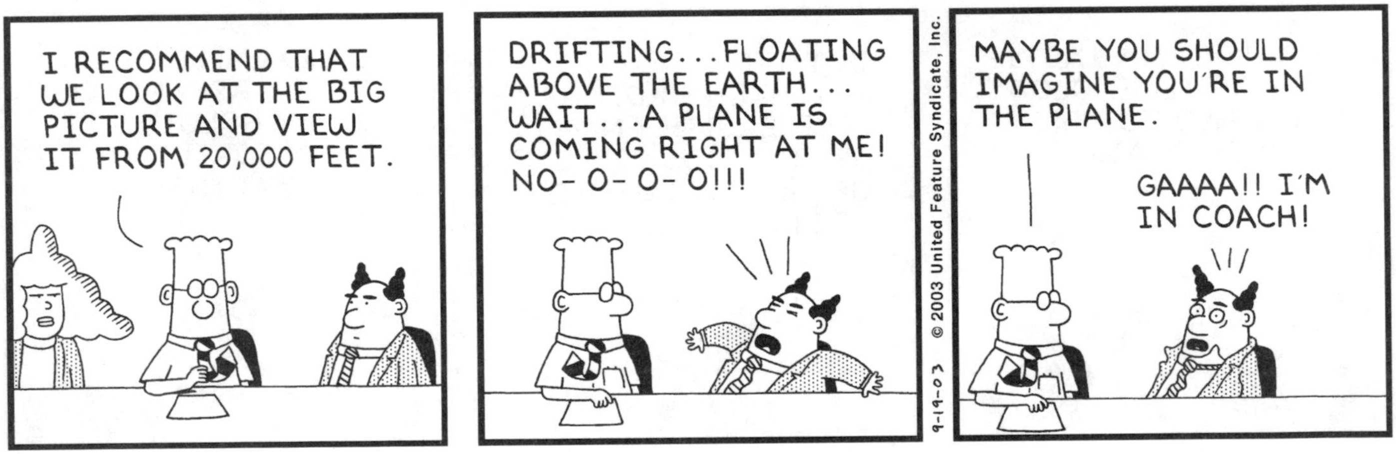
I RECOMMEND THAT WE LOOK AT THE BIG PICTURE AND VIEW IT FROM 20,000 FEET.
DRIFTING...FLOATING ABOVE THE EARTH... WAIT...A PLANE IS COMING RIGHT AT ME! NO- O- O- O!!!
9-19-03 © 2003 United Feature Syndicate, Inc.
MAYBE YOU SHOULD IMAGINE YOU'RE IN THE PLANE.
GAAAA!! I'M IN COACH!

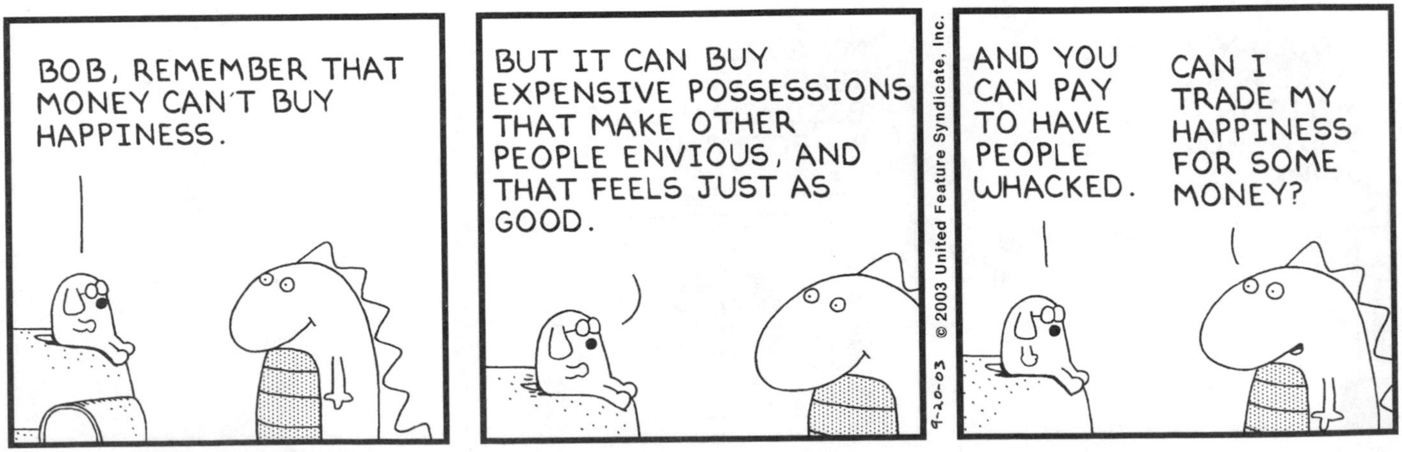
BOB, REMEMBER THAT MONEY CAN'T BUY HAPPINESS.
BUT IT CAN BUY EXPENSIVE POSSESSIONS THAT MAKE OTHER PEOPLE ENVIOUS, AND THAT FEELS JUST AS GOOD.
9-20-03 © 2003 United Feature Syndicate, Inc.
AND YOU CAN PAY TO HAVE PEOPLE WHACKED.
CAN I TRADE MY HAPPINESS FOR SOME MONEY?

I DON'T HAVE TIME TO WORK ON THE NANOBIT PROJECT.
NO PROBLEM. TELL DILBERT I SAID HE SHOULD TAKE OVER.
TWO MINUTES LATER
I'M WAY, WAY TOO BUSY.
FINE. TELL WALLY TO DO IT.
TWO MINUTES LATER
I'M UP TO YOUR FACE IN ALLIGATORS!
OKAY, OKAY... HAND IT OFF TO ASOK.
TWO MINUTES LATER
BUT ALREADY I ONLY HAVE TIME TO EAT ONE CRACKER A DAY.
TELL TED I SAID...
© 2003 United Feature Syndicate, Inc.
9/21/03
SURE, I'LL DO IT. NO PROBLEM.
MMM... CRACKER TIME.
I'M QUITTING TOMORROW.
I SOLVED FOUR PROBLEMS TODAY!

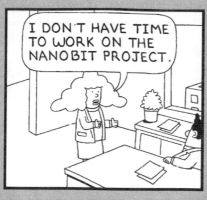

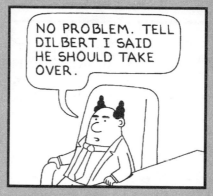

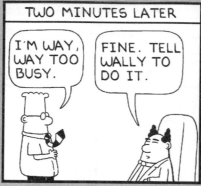

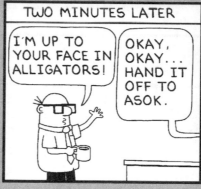

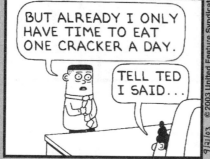

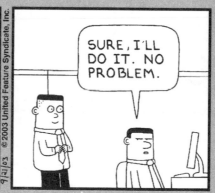

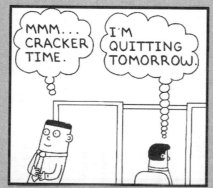

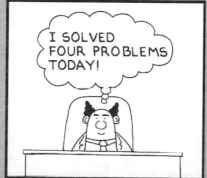

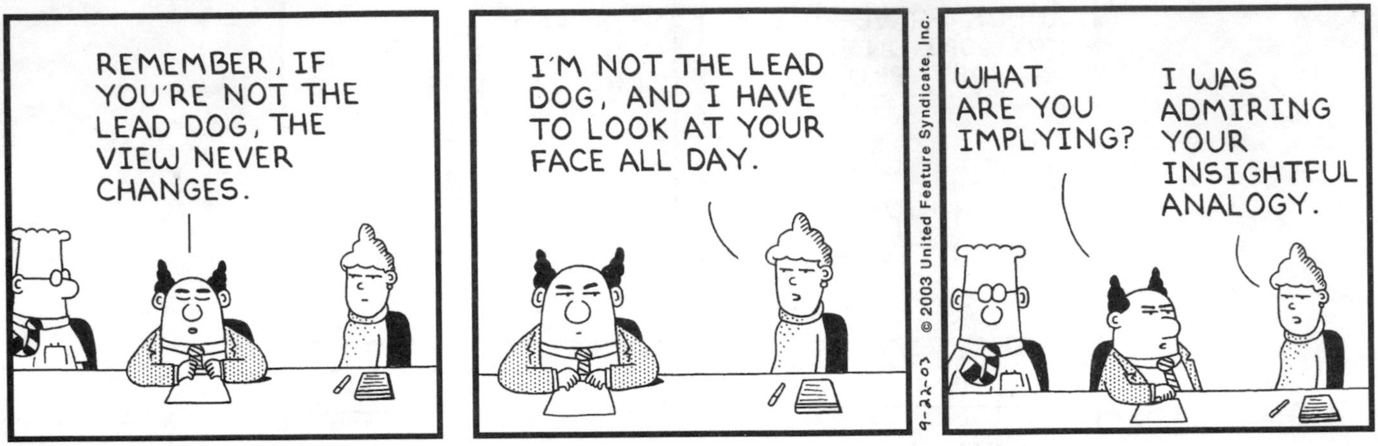
REMEMBER, IF YOU'RE NOT THE LEAD DOG, THE VIEW NEVER CHANGES.
I'M NOT THE LEAD DOG, AND I HAVE TO LOOK AT YOUR FACE ALL DAY.
9-22-03 © 2003 United Feature Syndicate, Inc.
WHAT ARE YOU IMPLYING?
I WAS ADMIRING YOUR INSIGHTFUL ANALOGY.

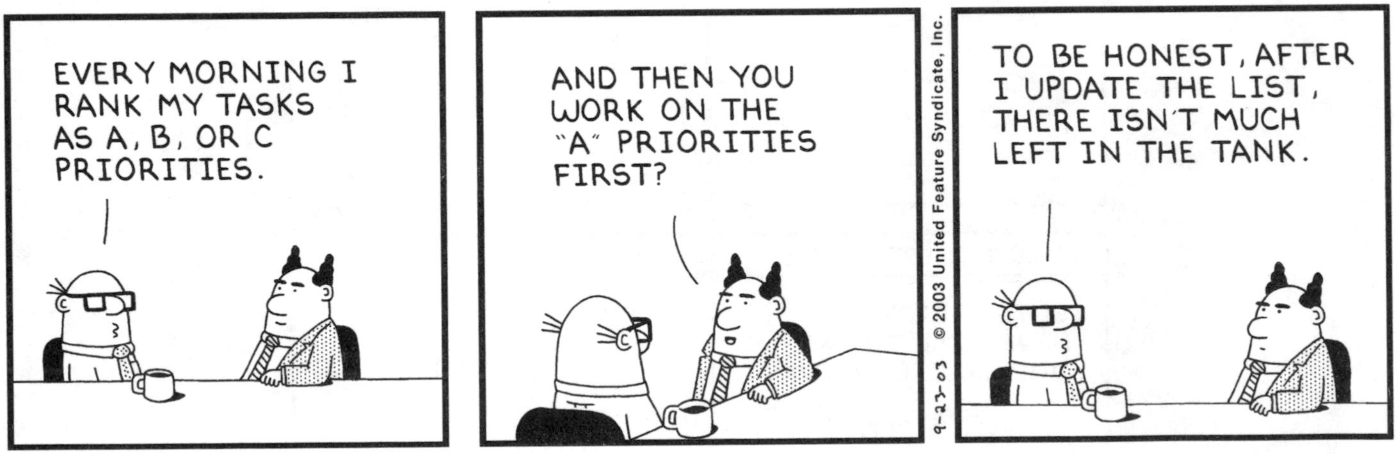
EVERY MORNING I RANK MY TASKS AS A, B, OR C PRIORITIES.
AND THEN YOU WORK ON THE "A" PRIORITIES FIRST?
9-23-03 © 2003 United Feature Syndicate, Inc.
TO BE HONEST, AFTER I UPDATE THE LIST, THERE ISN'T MUCH LEFT IN THE TANK.

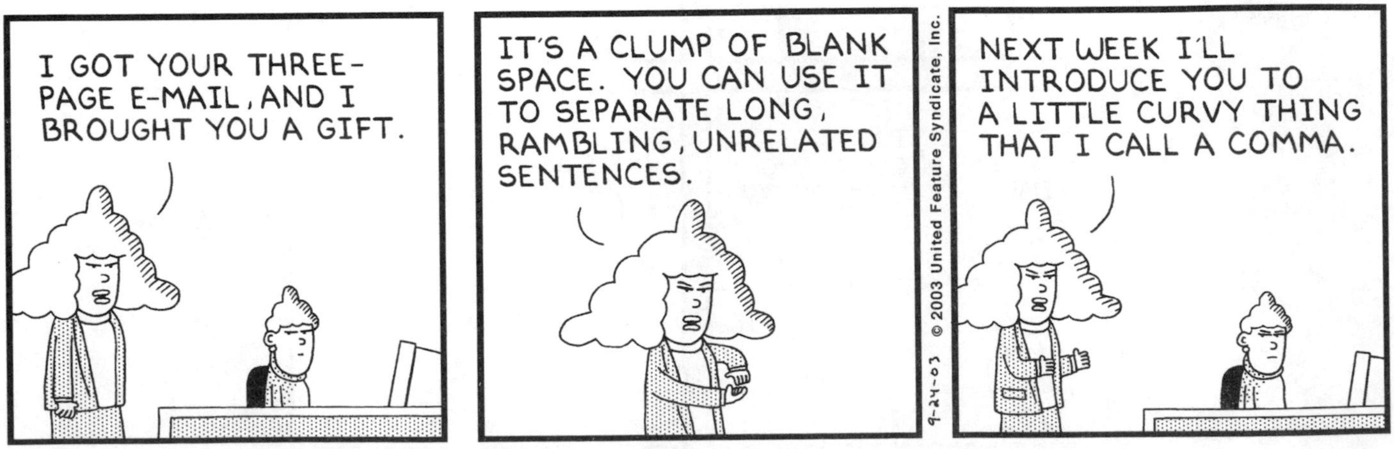
I GOT YOUR THREE-PAGE E-MAIL, AND I BROUGHT YOU A GIFT.
IT'S A CLUMP OF BLANK SPACE. YOU CAN USE IT TO SEPARATE LONG, RAMBLING, UNRELATED SENTENCES.
9-24-03 © 2003 United Feature Syndicate, Inc.
NEXT WEEK I'LL INTRODUCE YOU TO A LITTLE CURVY THING THAT I CALL A COMMA.

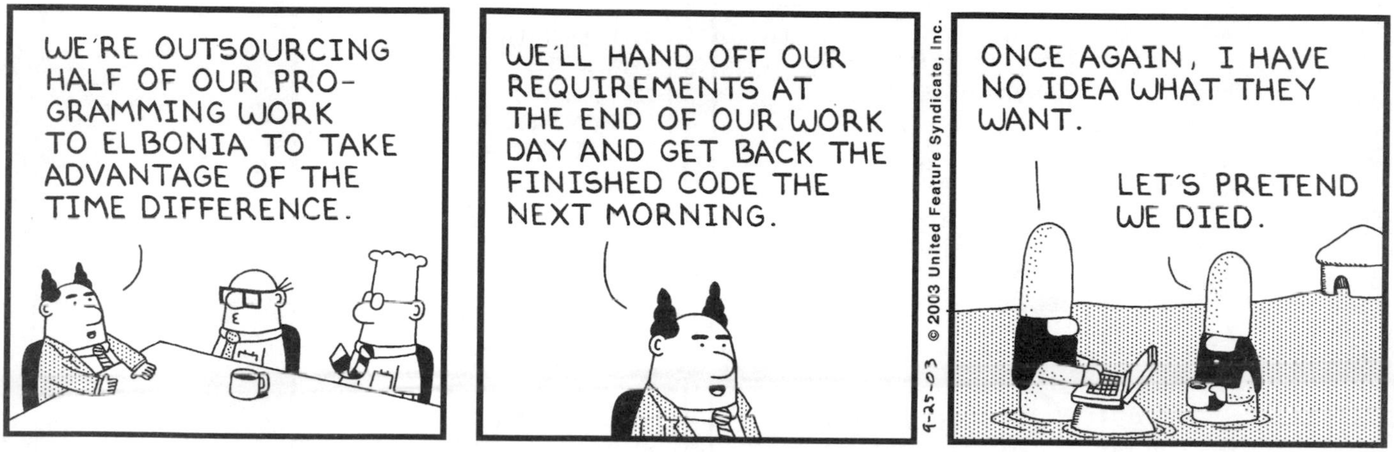
WE'RE OUTSOURCING HALF OF OUR PRO-GRAMMING WORK TO ELBONIA TO TAKE ADVANTAGE OF THE TIME DIFFERENCE.
WE'LL HAND OFF OUR REQUIREMENTS AT THE END OF OUR WORK DAY AND GET BACK THE FINISHED CODE THE NEXT MORNING.
9-25-03 © 2003 United Feature Syndicate, Inc.
ONCE AGAIN, I HAVE NO IDEA WHAT THEY WANT.
LET'S PRETEND WE DIED.

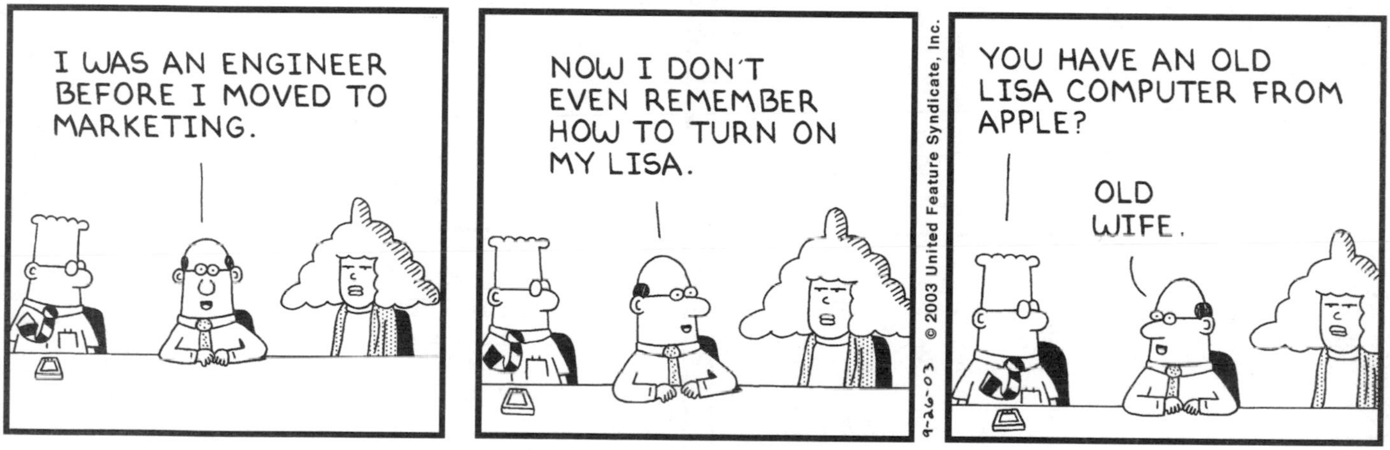
I WAS AN ENGINEER BEFORE I MOVED TO MARKETING.
NOW I DON'T EVEN REMEMBER HOW TO TURN ON MY LISA.
9-26-03 © 2003 United Feature Syndicate, Inc.
YOU HAVE AN OLD LISA COMPUTER FROM APPLE?
OLD WIFE.

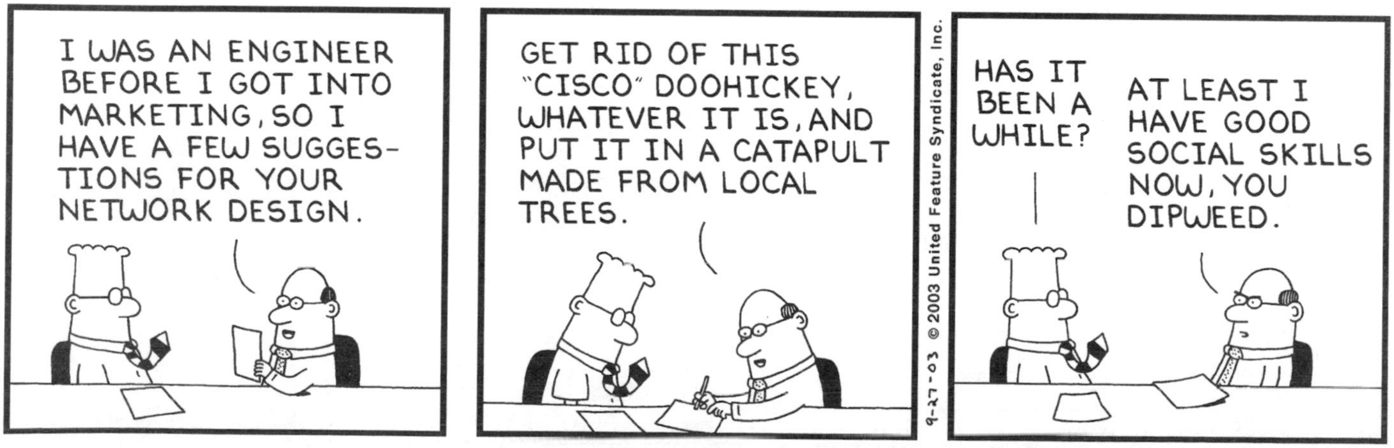
I WAS AN ENGINEER BEFORE I GOT INTO MARKETING, SO I HAVE A FEW SUGGES-TIONS FOR YOUR NETWORK DESIGN.
GET RID OF THIS "CISCO" DOOHICKEY, WHATEVER IT IS, AND PUT IT IN A CATAPULT MADE FROM LOCAL TREES.
9-27-03 © 2003 United Feature Syndicate, Inc.
HAS IT BEEN A WHILE?
AT LEAST I HAVE GOOD SOCIAL SKILLS NOW, YOU DIPWEED.

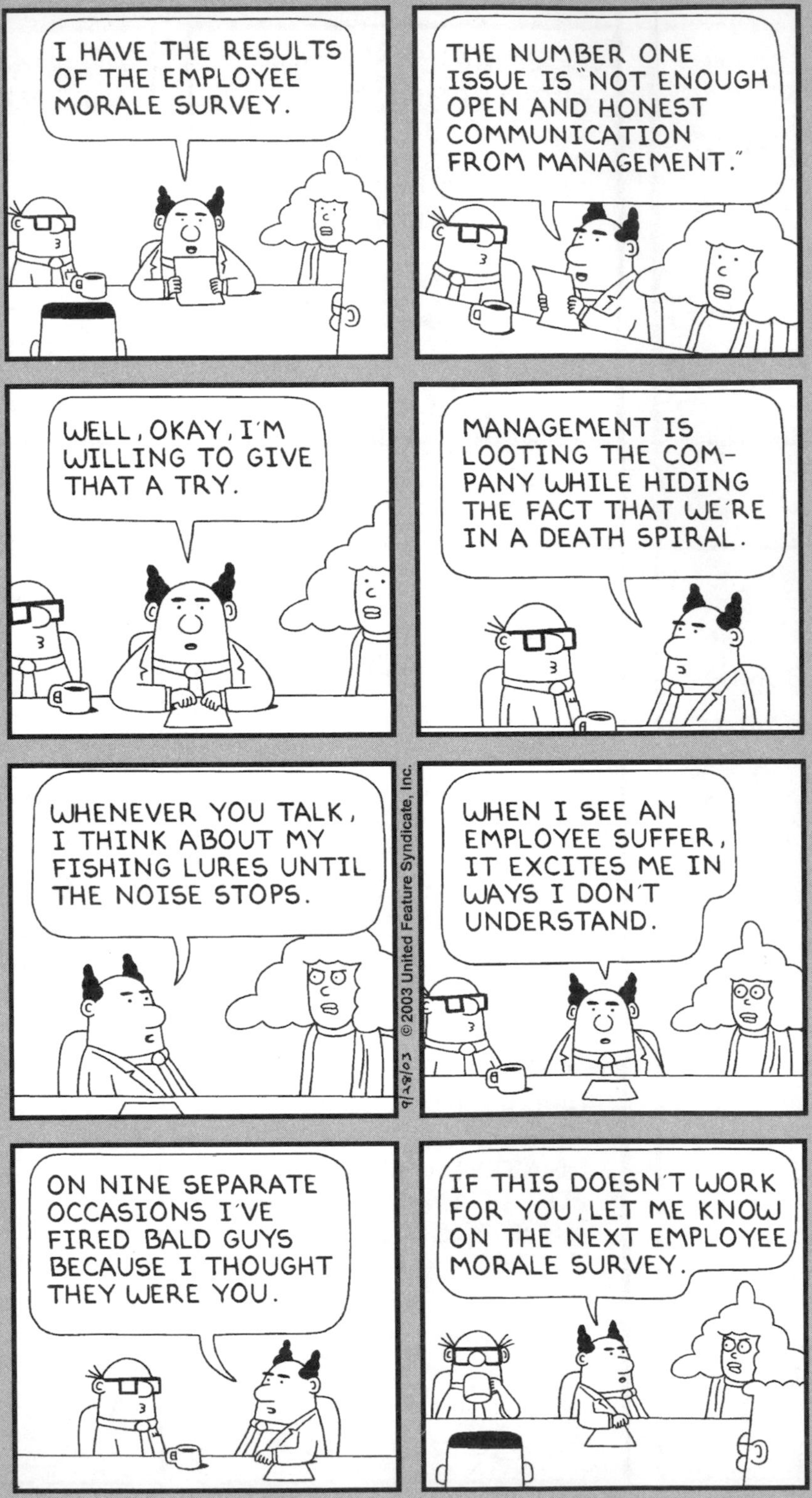
I HAVE THE RESULTS OF THE EMPLOYEE MORALE SURVEY.
THE NUMBER ONE ISSUE IS "NOT ENOUGH OPEN AND HONEST COMMUNICATION FROM MANAGEMENT."
WELL, OKAY, I'M WILLING TO GIVE THAT A TRY.
MANAGEMENT IS LOOTING THE COMPANY WHILE HIDING THE FACT THAT WE'RE IN A DEATH SPIRAL.
WHENEVER YOU TALK, I THINK ABOUT MY FISHING LURES UNTIL THE NOISE STOPS.
WHEN I SEE AN EMPLOYEE SUFFER, IT EXCITES ME IN WAYS I DON'T UNDERSTAND.
ON NINE SEPARATE OCCASIONS I'VE FIRED BALD GUYS BECAUSE I THOUGHT THEY WERE YOU.
IF THIS DOESN'T WORK FOR YOU, LET ME KNOW ON THE NEXT EMPLOYEE MORALE SURVEY.
9/28/03 © 2003 United Feature Syndicate, Inc.

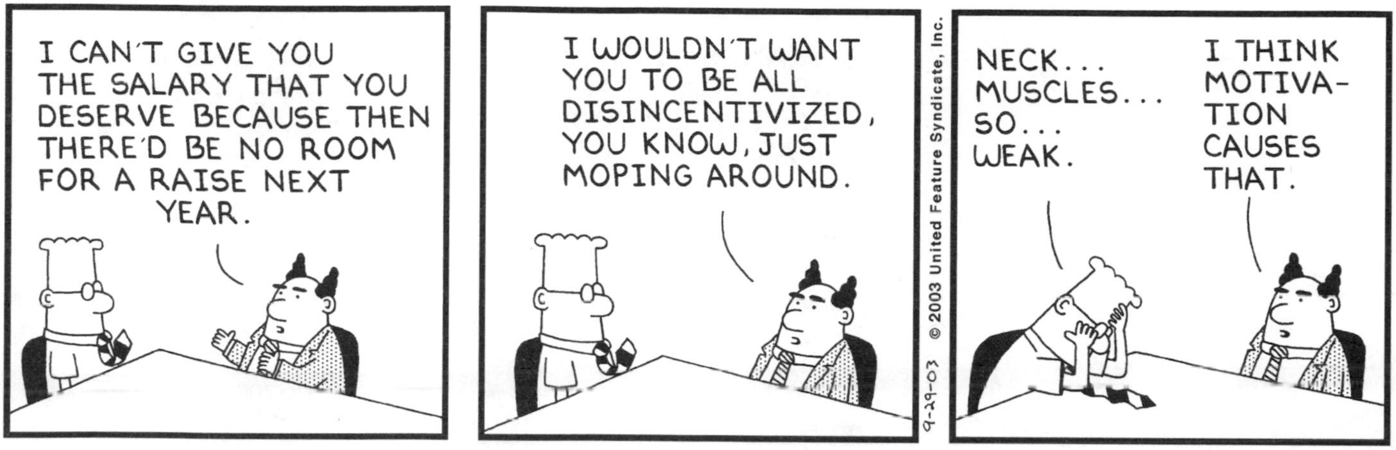
I CAN'T GIVE YOU THE SALARY THAT YOU DESERVE BECAUSE THEN THERE'D BE NO ROOM FOR A RAISE NEXT YEAR.
I WOULDN'T WANT YOU TO BE ALL DISINCENTIVIZED, YOU KNOW, JUST MOPING AROUND.
9-29-03 © 2003 United Feature Syndicate, Inc.
NECK... MUSCLES... SO... WEAK.
I THINK MOTIVATION CAUSES THAT.

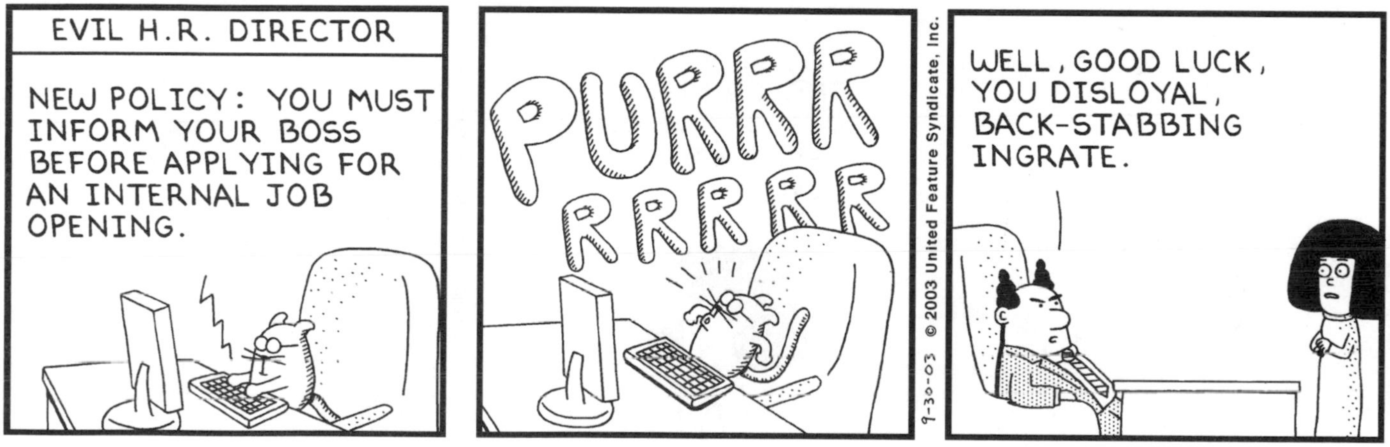
EVIL H.R. DIRECTOR
NEW POLICY: YOU MUST INFORM YOUR BOSS BEFORE APPLYING FOR AN INTERNAL JOB OPENING.
PURRR RRRRR
9-30-03 © 2003 United Feature Syndicate, Inc.
WELL, GOOD LUCK, YOU DISLOYAL, BACK-STABBING INGRATE.

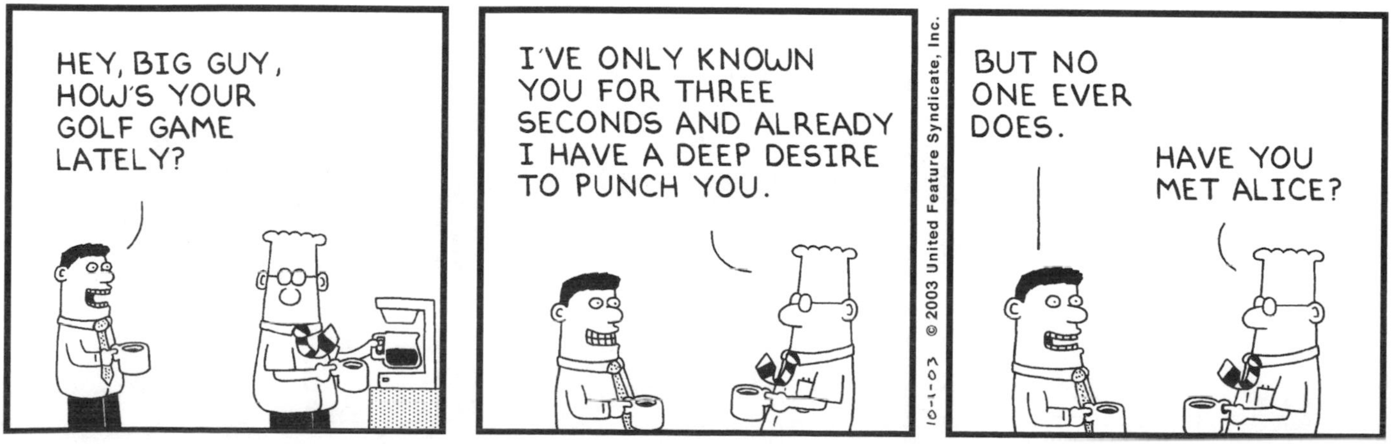
HEY, BIG GUY, HOW'S YOUR GOLF GAME LATELY?
I'VE ONLY KNOWN YOU FOR THREE SECONDS AND ALREADY I HAVE A DEEP DESIRE TO PUNCH YOU.
10-1-03 © 2003 United Feature Syndicate, Inc.
BUT NO ONE EVER DOES.
HAVE YOU MET ALICE?

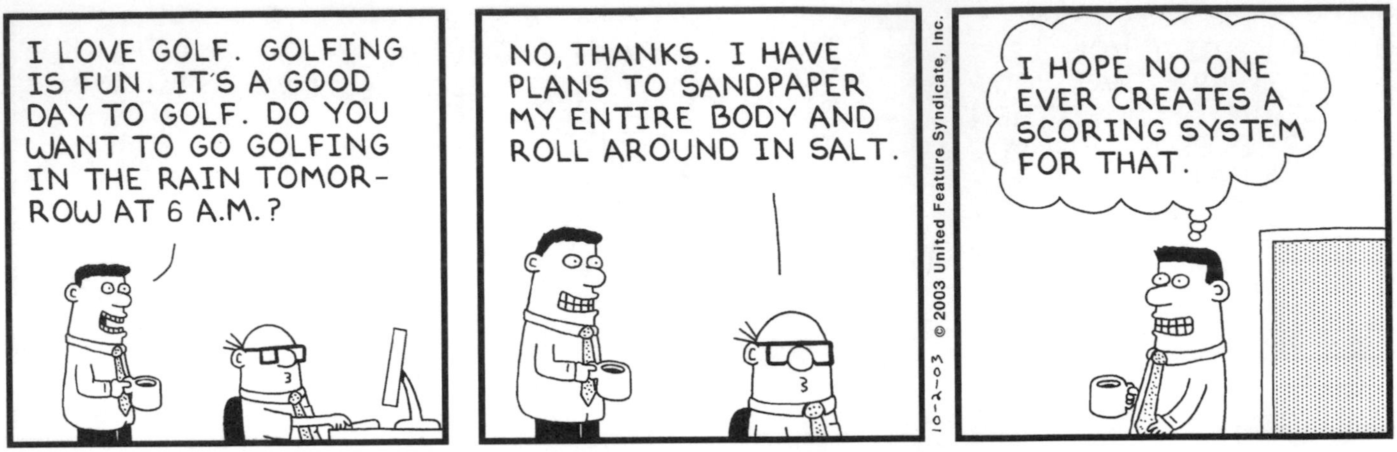
I LOVE GOLF. GOLFING IS FUN. IT'S A GOOD DAY TO GOLF. DO YOU WANT TO GO GOLFING IN THE RAIN TOMORROW AT 6 A.M.?
NO, THANKS. I HAVE PLANS TO SANDPAPER MY ENTIRE BODY AND ROLL AROUND IN SALT.
10-2-03 © 2003 United Feature Syndicate, Inc.
I HOPE NO ONE EVER CREATES A SCORING SYSTEM FOR THAT.

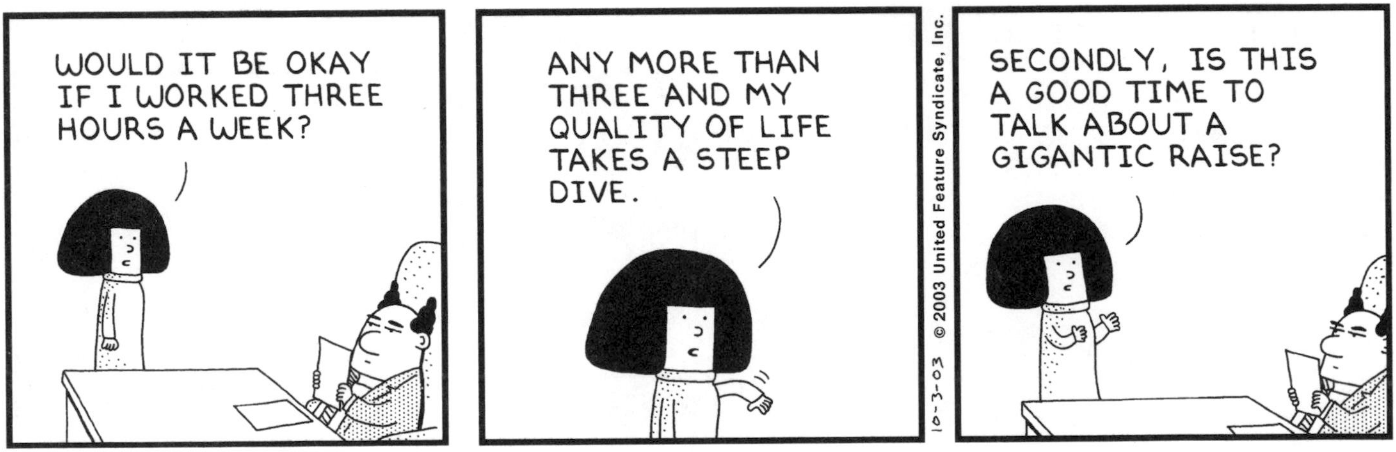
WOULD IT BE OKAY IF I WORKED THREE HOURS A WEEK?
ANY MORE THAN THREE AND MY QUALITY OF LIFE TAKES A STEEP DIVE.
10-3-03 © 2003 United Feature Syndicate, Inc.
SECONDLY, IS THIS A GOOD TIME TO TALK ABOUT A GIGANTIC RAISE?

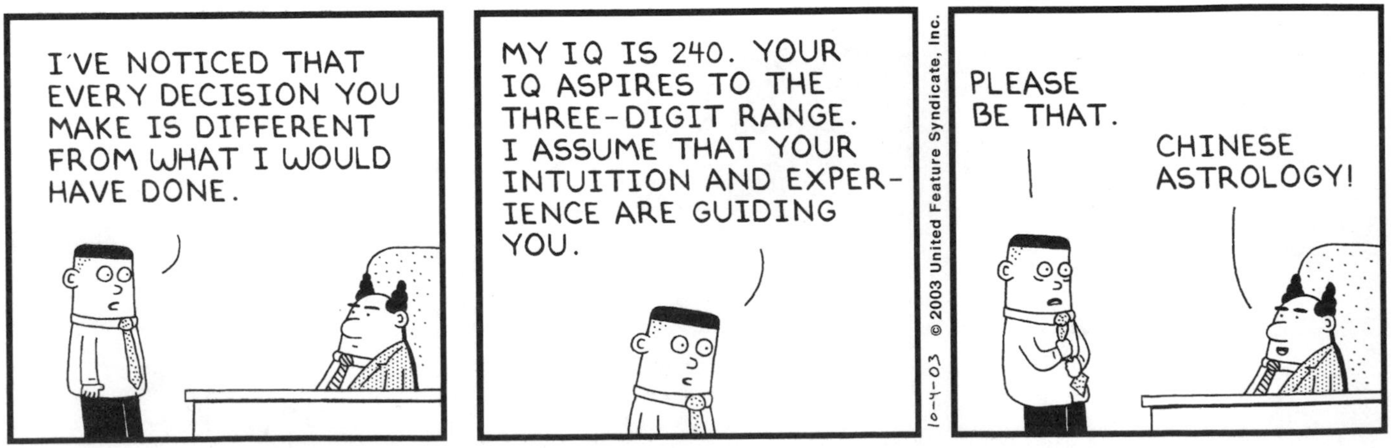
I'VE NOTICED THAT EVERY DECISION YOU MAKE IS DIFFERENT FROM WHAT I WOULD HAVE DONE.
MY IQ IS 240. YOUR IQ ASPIRES TO THE THREE-DIGIT RANGE. I ASSUME THAT YOUR INTUITION AND EXPERIENCE ARE GUIDING YOU.
10-4-03 © 2003 United Feature Syndicate, Inc.
PLEASE BE THAT.
CHINESE ASTROLOGY!

CATBERT, THE EVIL DIRECTOR OF HUMAN RESOURCES

YOUR 401K RETIREMENT PLAN WILL BE REPLACED WITH A 401A PLAN.

THE "A" STANDS FOR AFTERLIFE.

YOU'LL GET NO MONEY IN THIS LIFE, BUT THE COMPANY WILL REWARD YOU IN THE AFTERLIFE.

THE ODDS OF THAT HAPPENING SEEM LOW.

YES, BUT ON AN EXPECTED-VALUE BASIS, A HIGH POTENTIAL REWARD COMPENSATES FOR LOW ODDS.

FOR EXAMPLE, HOW MANY FREE SOFTWARE UPGRADES WOULD I NEED TO PROMISE YOU IN THE AFTERLIFE TO MAKE YOU WORK YOURSELF TO DEATH THIS YEAR?

SEVENTY VERSIONS.

I RESISTED HIS CHARISMA, BUT HE GOT ME WITH HIS MATH.

10/5/03 © 2003 United Feature Syndicate, Inc.

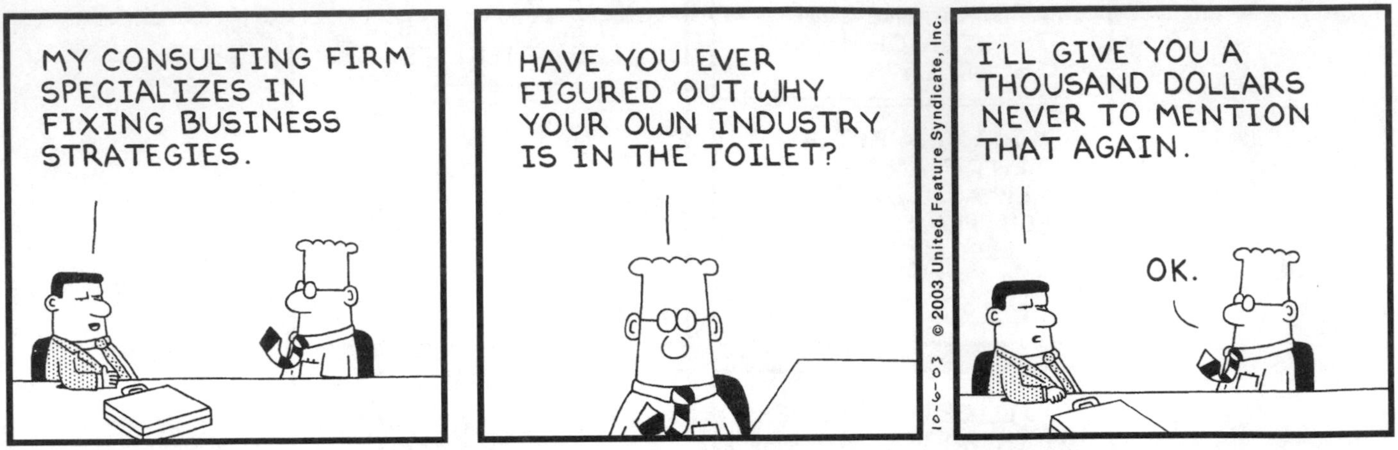
MY CONSULTING FIRM SPECIALIZES IN FIXING BUSINESS STRATEGIES.
HAVE YOU EVER FIGURED OUT WHY YOUR OWN INDUSTRY IS IN THE TOILET?
10-6-03 © 2003 United Feature Syndicate, Inc.
I'LL GIVE YOU A THOUSAND DOLLARS NEVER TO MENTION THAT AGAIN.
OK.

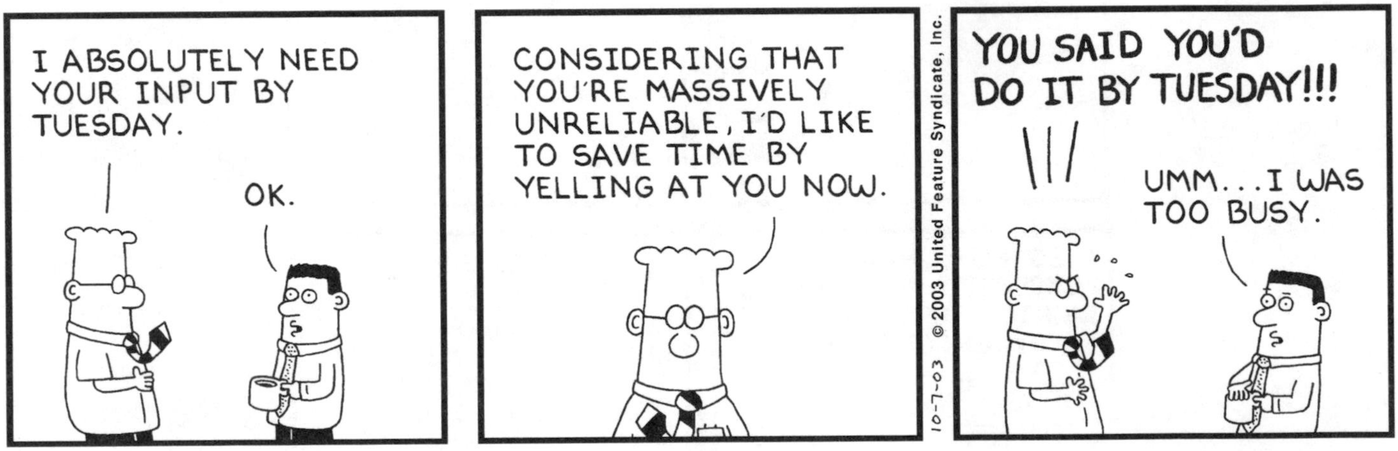
I ABSOLUTELY NEED YOUR INPUT BY TUESDAY.
OK.
CONSIDERING THAT YOU'RE MASSIVELY UNRELIABLE, I'D LIKE TO SAVE TIME BY YELLING AT YOU NOW.
10-7-03 © 2003 United Feature Syndicate, Inc.
YOU SAID YOU'D DO IT BY TUESDAY!!!
UMM...I WAS TOO BUSY.

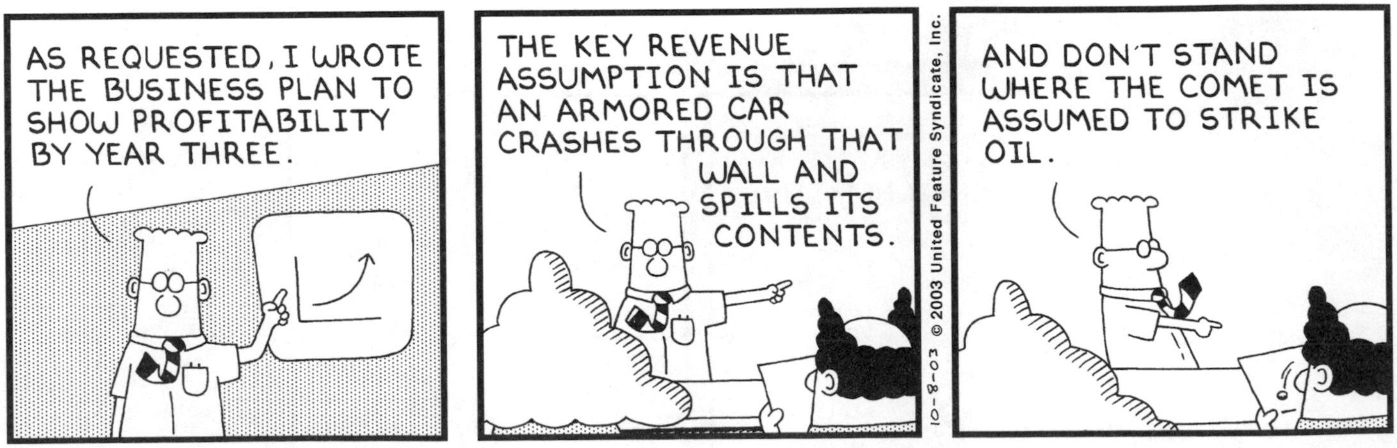
AS REQUESTED, I WROTE THE BUSINESS PLAN TO SHOW PROFITABILITY BY YEAR THREE.
THE KEY REVENUE ASSUMPTION IS THAT AN ARMORED CAR CRASHES THROUGH THAT WALL AND SPILLS ITS CONTENTS.
10-8-03 © 2003 United Feature Syndicate, Inc.
AND DON'T STAND WHERE THE COMET IS ASSUMED TO STRIKE OIL.

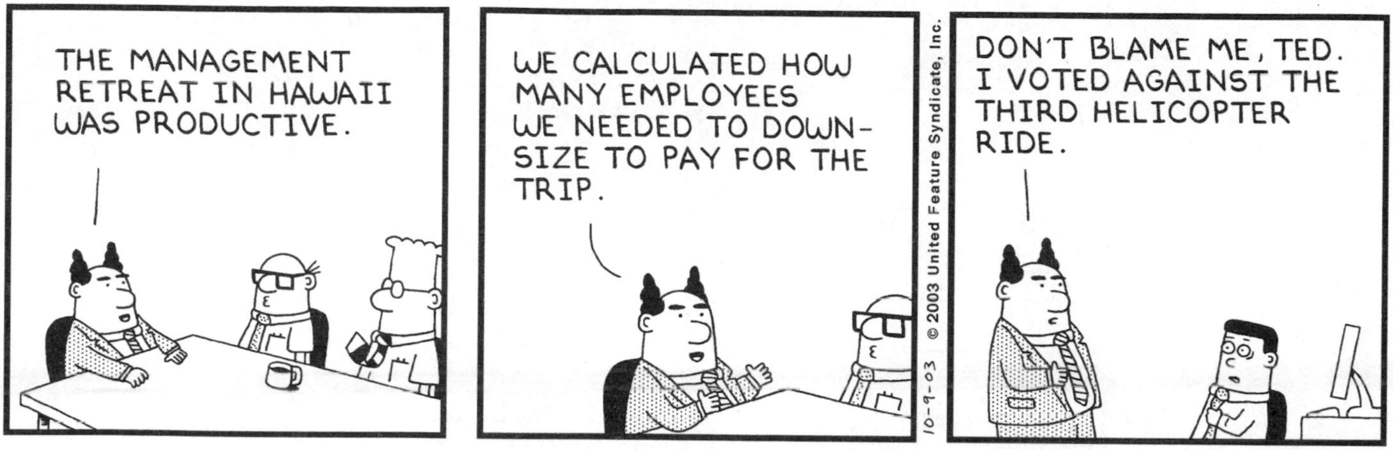
THE MANAGEMENT RETREAT IN HAWAII WAS PRODUCTIVE.
WE CALCULATED HOW MANY EMPLOYEES WE NEEDED TO DOWN-SIZE TO PAY FOR THE TRIP.
10-9-03 © 2003 United Feature Syndicate, Inc.
DON'T BLAME ME, TED. I VOTED AGAINST THE THIRD HELICOPTER RIDE.

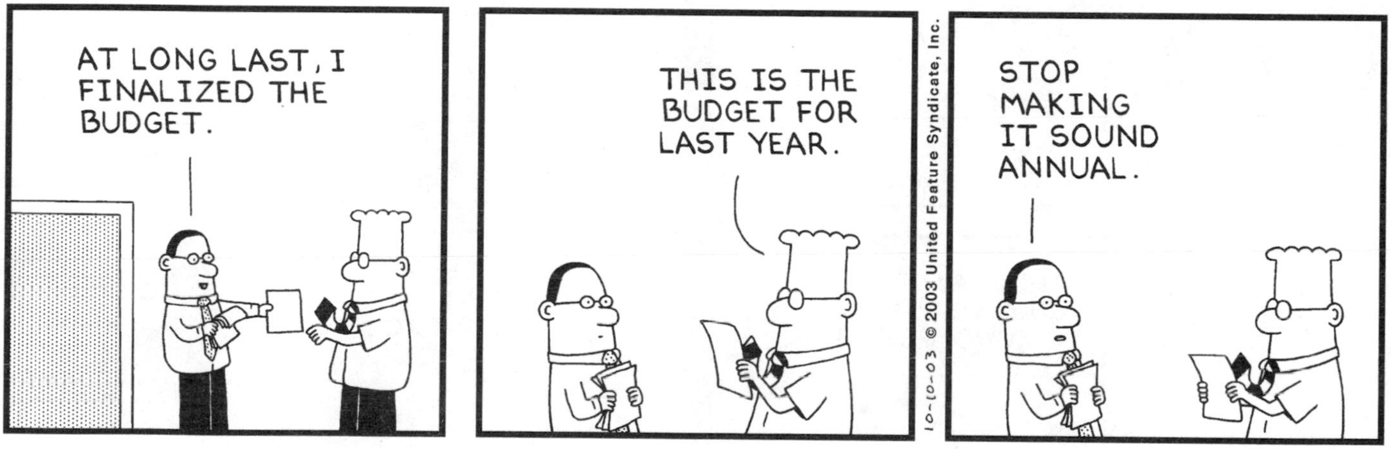
AT LONG LAST, I FINALIZED THE BUDGET.
THIS IS THE BUDGET FOR LAST YEAR.
10-10-03 © 2003 United Feature Syndicate, Inc.
STOP MAKING IT SOUND ANNUAL.

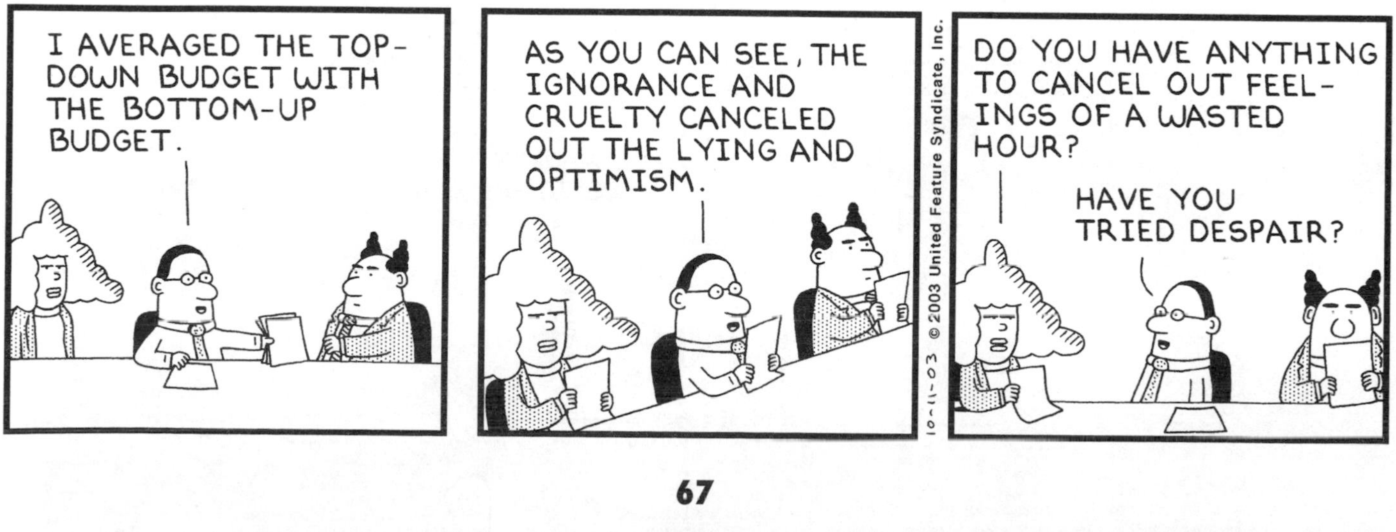
I AVERAGED THE TOP-DOWN BUDGET WITH THE BOTTOM-UP BUDGET.
AS YOU CAN SEE, THE IGNORANCE AND CRUELTY CANCELED OUT THE LYING AND OPTIMISM.
10-11-03 © 2003 United Feature Syndicate, Inc.
DO YOU HAVE ANYTHING TO CANCEL OUT FEEL-INGS OF A WASTED HOUR?
HAVE YOU TRIED DESPAIR?

HEY, IT'S A CUSTOMER!
YOU'RE IN LUCK; OUR NEXT VERSION HAS EVERY FEATURE YOU'LL EVER WANT!
IT DOES?
I WAS READY TO BUY YOUR CURRENT VERSION... BUT I GUESS I'LL WAIT.
WHEN WILL OUR NEW VERSION BE READY?
IN A YEAR.
THE NEW VERSION WILL LEAPFROG OUR COMPETITION.
LEAPFROG? THAT IMPLIES THAT THEY HAVE BETTER PROD-UCTS RIGHT NOW.
BUY OUR PRODUCT, YOU STINKIN' PILE OF CRUD!!
SLAP!
I HAVE TO RUN. TRY NOT TO BLOW THE SALE.

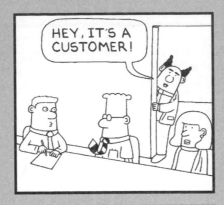

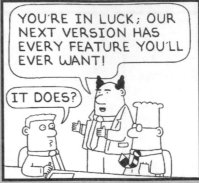

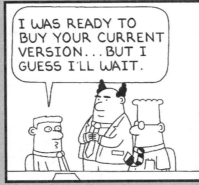

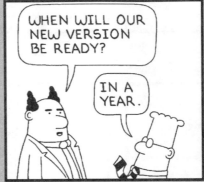

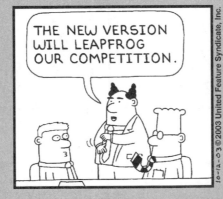

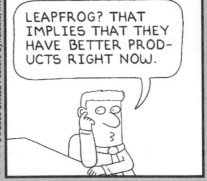

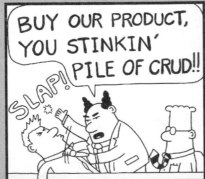

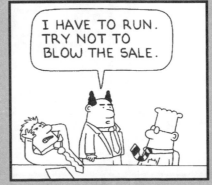

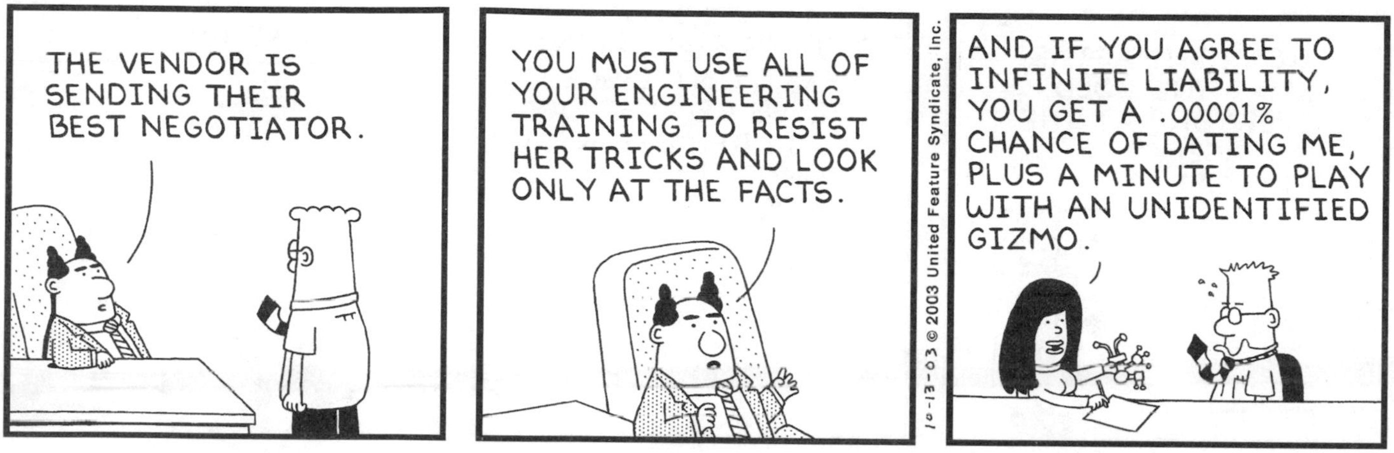
THE VENDOR IS SENDING THEIR BEST NEGOTIATOR.
YOU MUST USE ALL OF YOUR ENGINEERING TRAINING TO RESIST HER TRICKS AND LOOK ONLY AT THE FACTS.
10-13-03 © 2003 United Feature Syndicate, Inc.
AND IF YOU AGREE TO INFINITE LIABILITY, YOU GET A .00001% CHANCE OF DATING ME, PLUS A MINUTE TO PLAY WITH AN UNIDENTIFIED GIZMO.

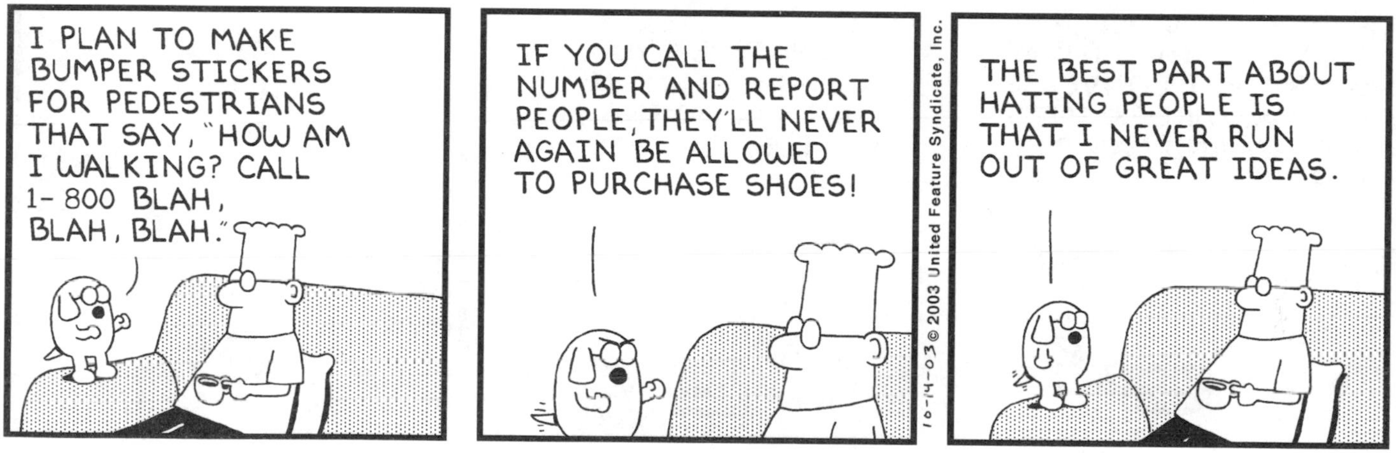
I PLAN TO MAKE BUMPER STICKERS FOR PEDESTRIANS THAT SAY, "HOW AM I WALKING? CALL 1-800 BLAH, BLAH, BLAH."
IF YOU CALL THE NUMBER AND REPORT PEOPLE, THEY'LL NEVER AGAIN BE ALLOWED TO PURCHASE SHOES!
10-14-03 © 2003 United Feature Syndicate, Inc.
THE BEST PART ABOUT HATING PEOPLE IS THAT I NEVER RUN OUT OF GREAT IDEAS.

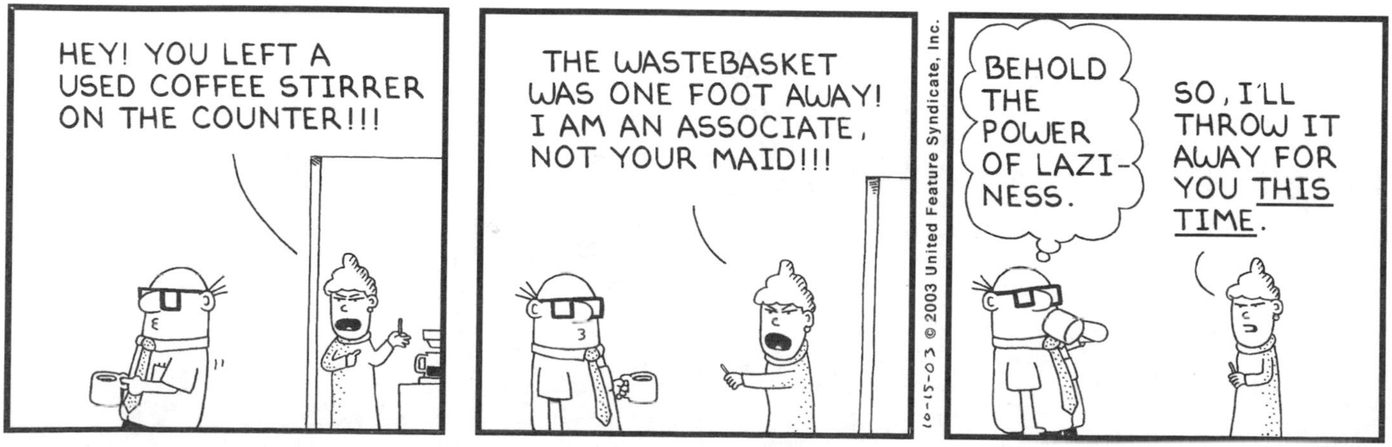
HEY! YOU LEFT A USED COFFEE STIRRER ON THE COUNTER!!!
THE WASTEBASKET WAS ONE FOOT AWAY! I AM AN ASSOCIATE, NOT YOUR MAID!!!
10-15-03 © 2003 United Feature Syndicate, Inc.
BEHOLD THE POWER OF LAZI-NESS.
SO, I'LL THROW IT AWAY FOR YOU THIS TIME.

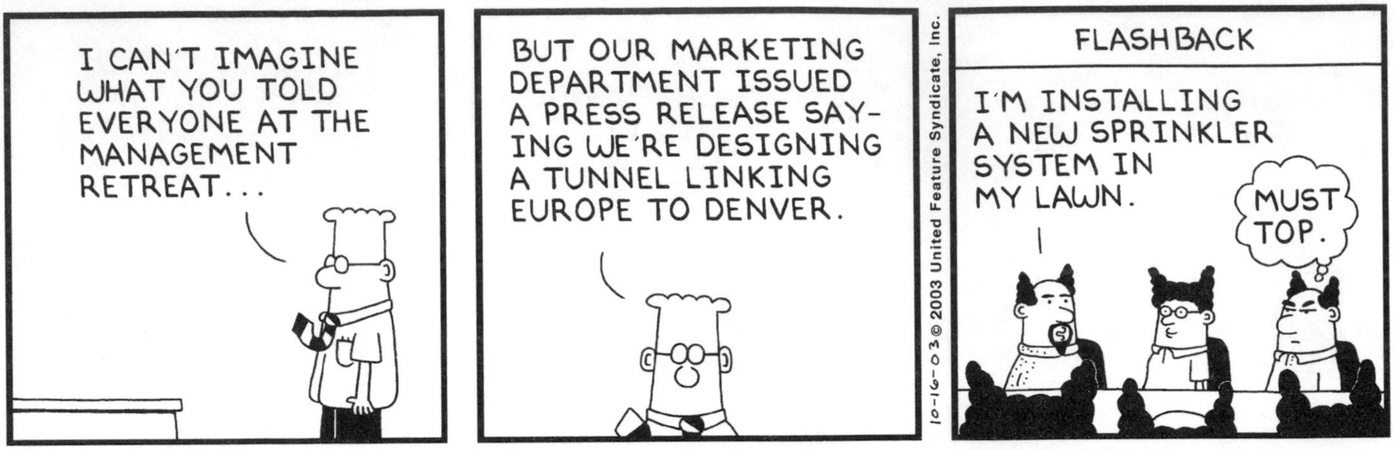
I CAN'T IMAGINE WHAT YOU TOLD EVERYONE AT THE MANAGEMENT RETREAT...
BUT OUR MARKETING DEPARTMENT ISSUED A PRESS RELEASE SAYING WE'RE DESIGNING A TUNNEL LINKING EUROPE TO DENVER.
10-16-03 © 2003 United Feature Syndicate, Inc.
FLASHBACK
I'M INSTALLING A NEW SPRINKLER SYSTEM IN MY LAWN.
MUST TOP.

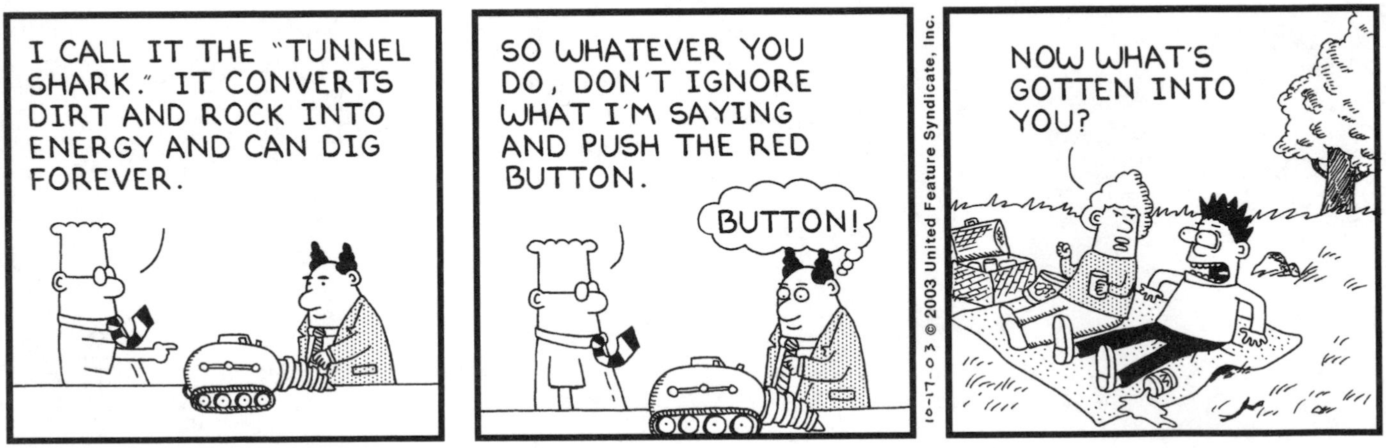
I CALL IT THE "TUNNEL SHARK." IT CONVERTS DIRT AND ROCK INTO ENERGY AND CAN DIG FOREVER.
SO WHATEVER YOU DO, DON'T IGNORE WHAT I'M SAYING AND PUSH THE RED BUTTON.
BUTTON!
10-17-03 © 2003 United Feature Syndicate, Inc.
NOW WHAT'S GOTTEN INTO YOU?

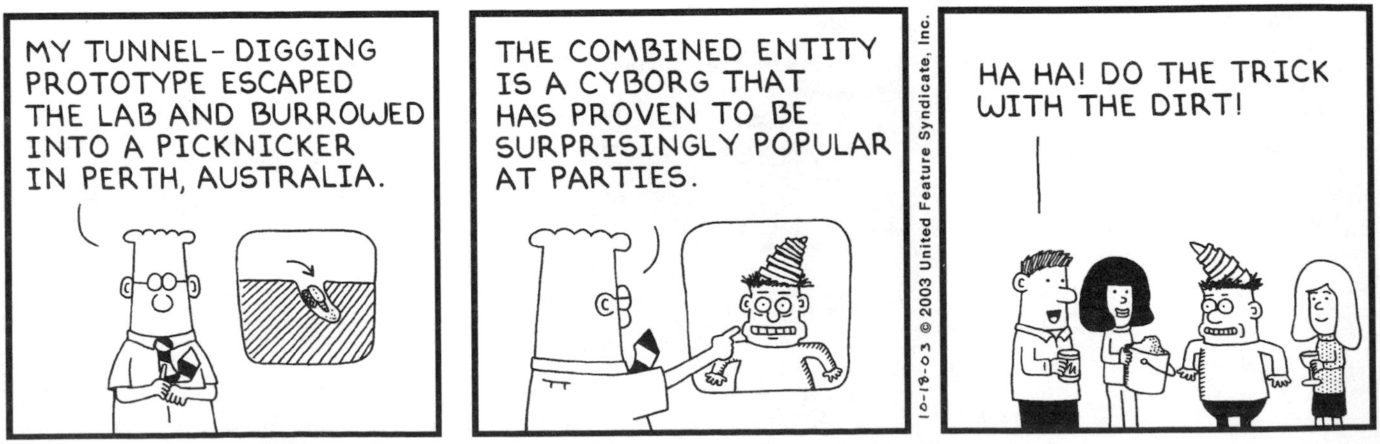
MY TUNNEL-DIGGING PROTOTYPE ESCAPED THE LAB AND BURROWED INTO A PICKNICKER IN PERTH, AUSTRALIA.
THE COMBINED ENTITY IS A CYBORG THAT HAS PROVEN TO BE SURPRISINGLY POPULAR AT PARTIES.
10-18-03 © 2003 United Feature Syndicate, Inc.
HA HA! DO THE TRICK WITH THE DIRT!

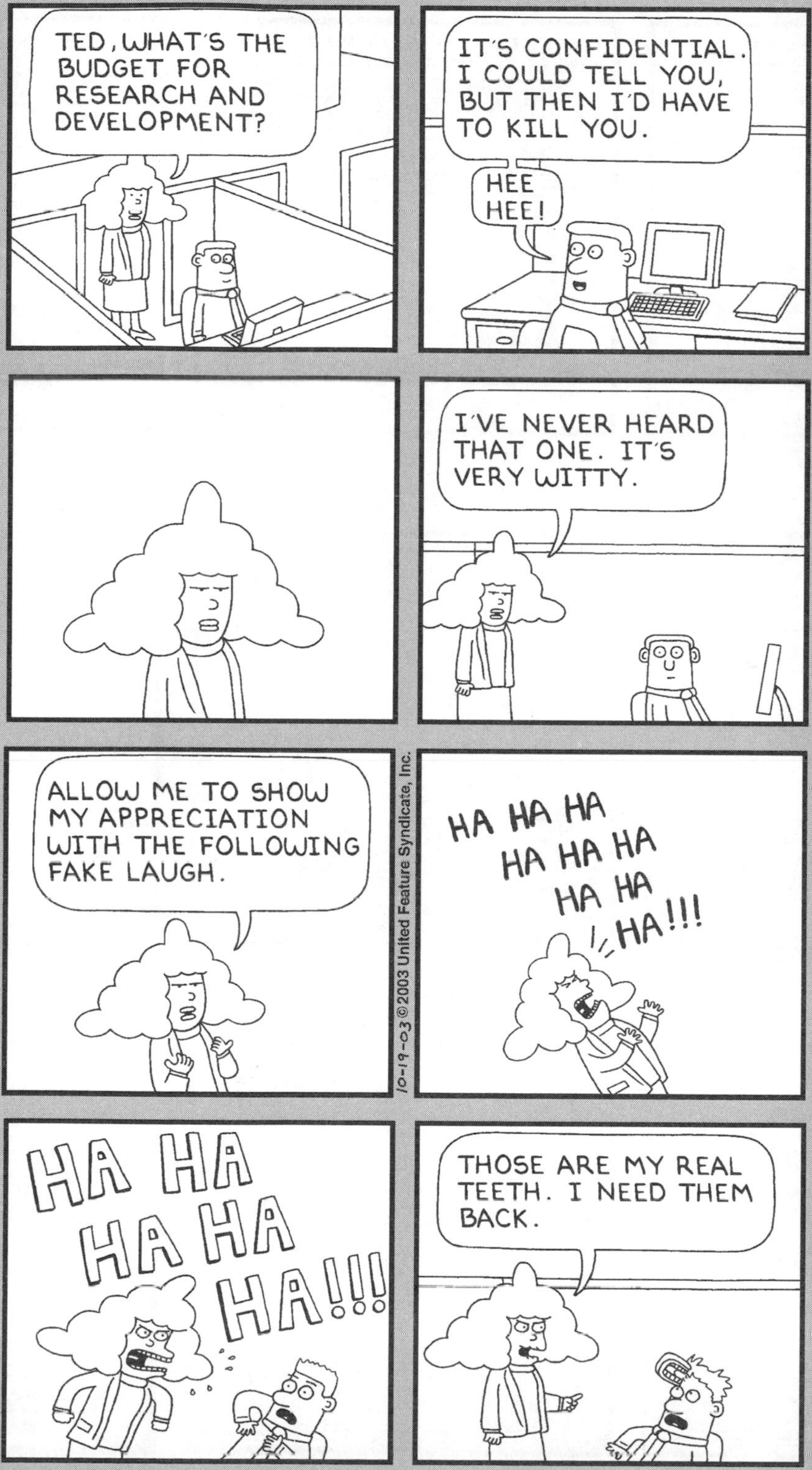
TED, WHAT'S THE BUDGET FOR RESEARCH AND DEVELOPMENT?
IT'S CONFIDENTIAL. I COULD TELL YOU, BUT THEN I'D HAVE TO KILL YOU.
HEE HEE!
I'VE NEVER HEARD THAT ONE. IT'S VERY WITTY.
ALLOW ME TO SHOW MY APPRECIATION WITH THE FOLLOWING FAKE LAUGH.
HA HA HA HA HA HA HA HA HA!!!
HA HA HA HA HA!!!
THOSE ARE MY REAL TEETH. I NEED THEM BACK.
10-19-03 ©2003 United Feature Syndicate, Inc.

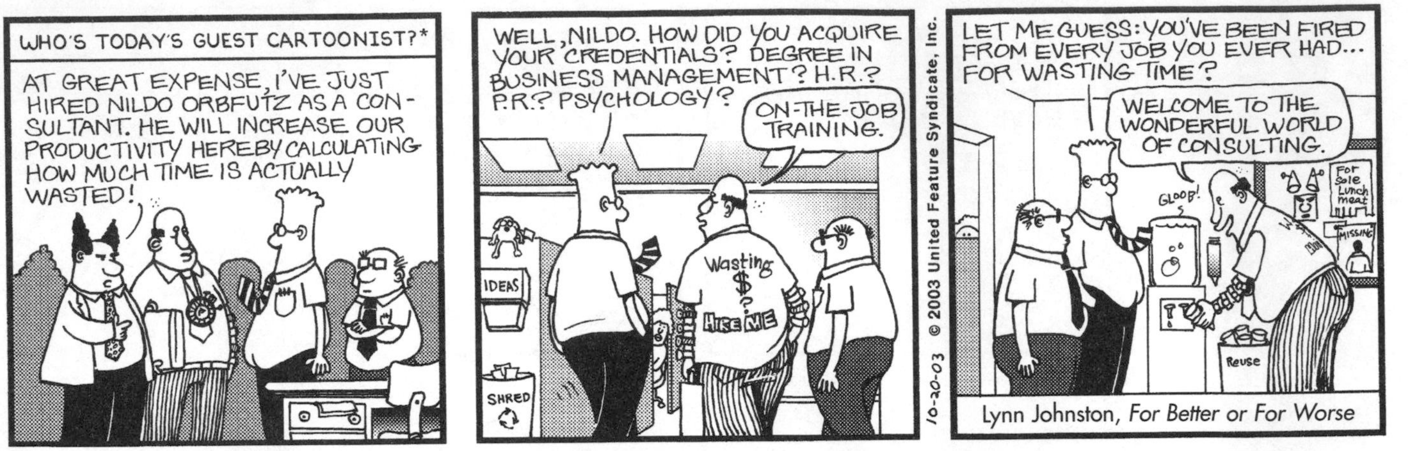
WHO'S TODAY'S GUEST CARTOONIST?*
AT GREAT EXPENSE, I'VE JUST HIRED NILDO ORBFUTZ AS A CONSULTANT. HE WILL INCREASE OUR PRODUCTIVITY HEREBY CALCULATING HOW MUCH TIME IS ACTUALLY WASTED!
WELL, NILDO. HOW DID YOU ACQUIRE YOUR CREDENTIALS? DEGREE IN BUSINESS MANAGEMENT? H.R.? P.R.? PSYCHOLOGY?
ON-THE-JOB TRAINING.
IDEAS
SHRED
Wasting $? HIRE ME
10-20-03 © 2003 United Feature Syndicate, Inc.
LET ME GUESS: YOU'VE BEEN FIRED FROM EVERY JOB YOU EVER HAD... FOR WASTING TIME?
WELCOME TO THE WONDERFUL WORLD OF CONSULTING.
GLOOB!
For Sale Lunch meat
MISSING
Reuse
Lynn Johnston, For Better or For Worse

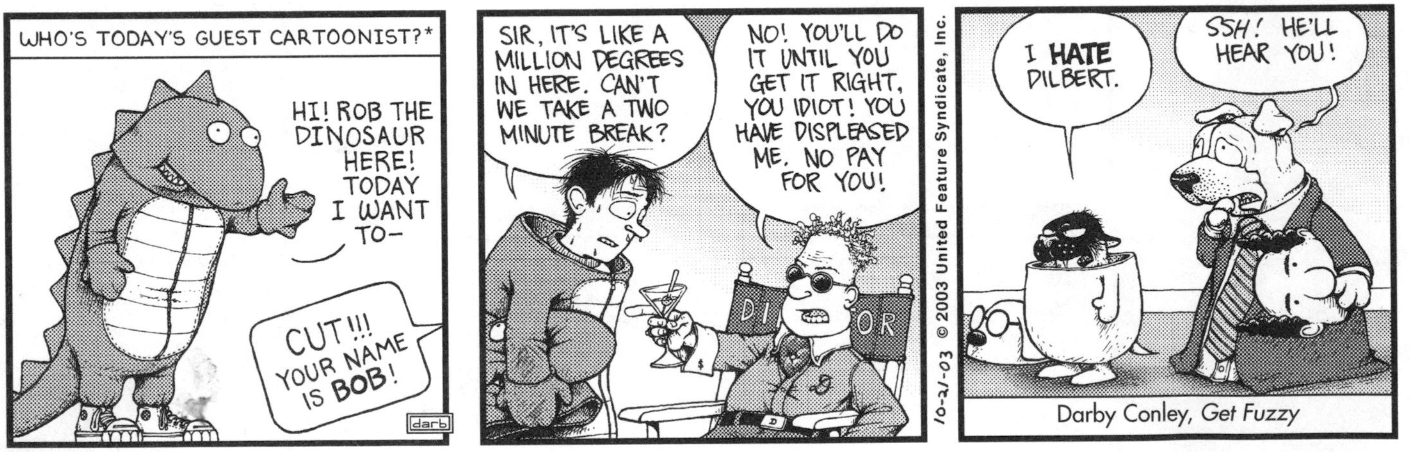
WHO'S TODAY'S GUEST CARTOONIST?*
HI! ROB THE DINOSAUR HERE! TODAY I WANT TO-
CUT!!! YOUR NAME IS BOB!
darb
SIR, IT'S LIKE A MILLION DEGREES IN HERE. CAN'T WE TAKE A TWO MINUTE BREAK?
NO! YOU'LL DO IT UNTIL YOU GET IT RIGHT, YOU IDIOT! YOU HAVE DISPLEASED ME. NO PAY FOR YOU!
10-21-03 © 2003 United Feature Syndicate, Inc.
I HATE DILBERT.
SSH! HE'LL HEAR YOU!
Darby Conley, Get Fuzzy

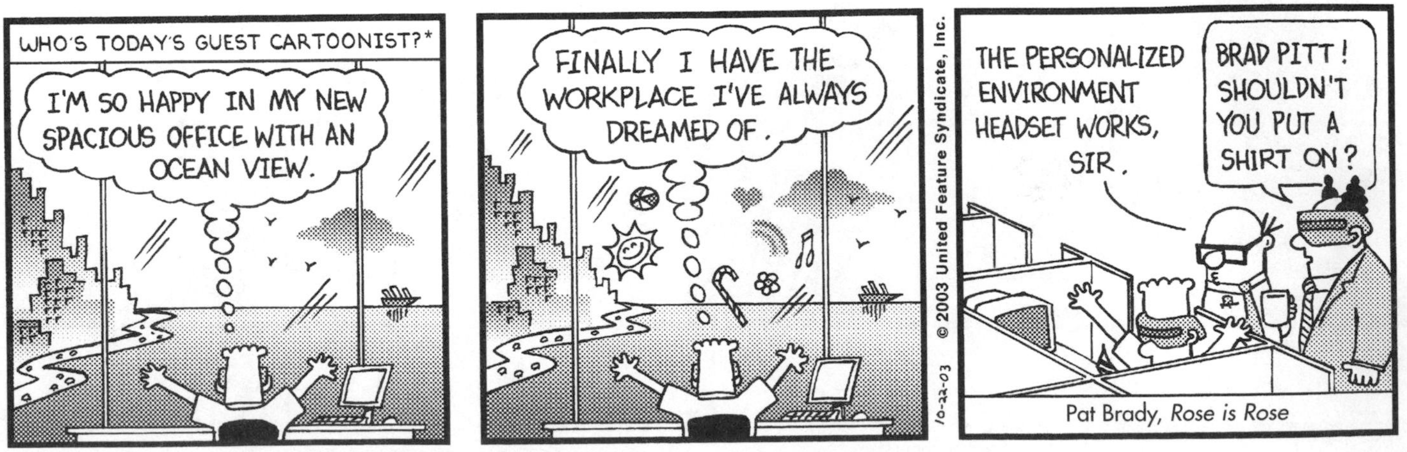
WHO'S TODAY'S GUEST CARTOONIST?*
I'M SO HAPPY IN MY NEW SPACIOUS OFFICE WITH AN OCEAN VIEW.
FINALLY I HAVE THE WORKPLACE I'VE ALWAYS DREAMED OF.
10-22-03 © 2003 United Feature Syndicate, Inc.
THE PERSONALIZED ENVIRONMENT HEADSET WORKS, SIR.
BRAD PITT! SHOULDN'T YOU PUT A SHIRT ON?
Pat Brady, Rose is Rose

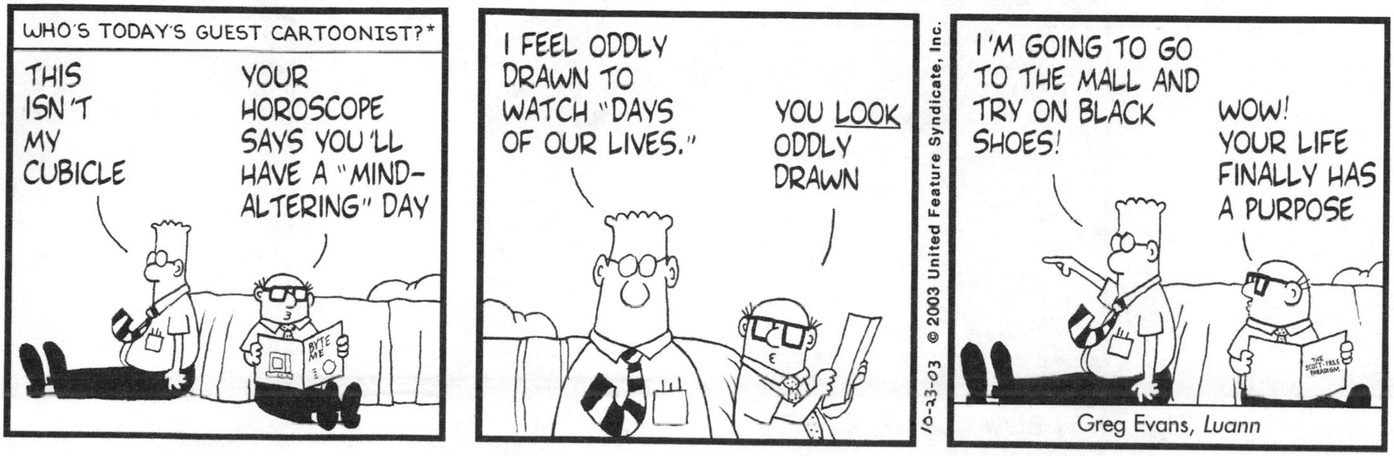
WHO'S TODAY'S GUEST CARTOONIST?*
THIS ISN'T MY CUBICLE
YOUR HOROSCOPE SAYS YOU'LL HAVE A "MIND-ALTERING" DAY
I FEEL ODDLY DRAWN TO WATCH "DAYS OF OUR LIVES."
YOU LOOK ODDLY DRAWN
10-23-03 © 2003 United Feature Syndicate, Inc.
I'M GOING TO GO TO THE MALL AND TRY ON BLACK SHOES!
WOW! YOUR LIFE FINALLY HAS A PURPOSE
Greg Evans, Luann

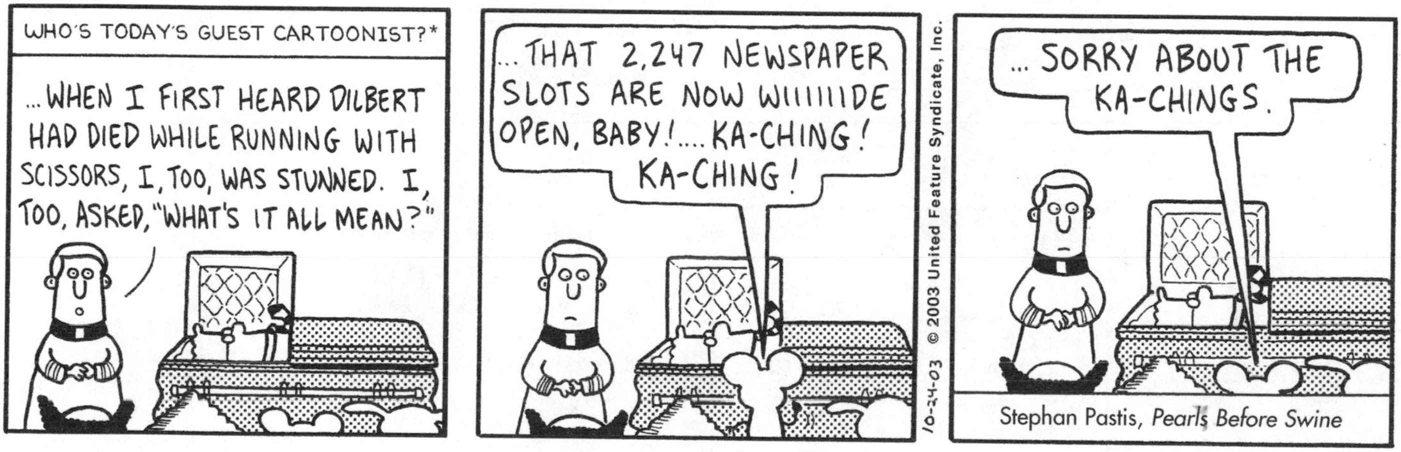
WHO'S TODAY'S GUEST CARTOONIST?*
...WHEN I FIRST HEARD DILBERT HAD DIED WHILE RUNNING WITH SCISSORS, I, TOO, WAS STUNNED. I, TOO, ASKED, "WHAT'S IT ALL MEAN?"
...THAT 2,247 NEWSPAPER SLOTS ARE NOW WIIIIIIDE OPEN, BABY!....KA-CHING! KA-CHING!
10-24-03 © 2003 United Feature Syndicate, Inc.
... SORRY ABOUT THE KA-CHINGS.
Stephan Pastis, Pearls Before Swine

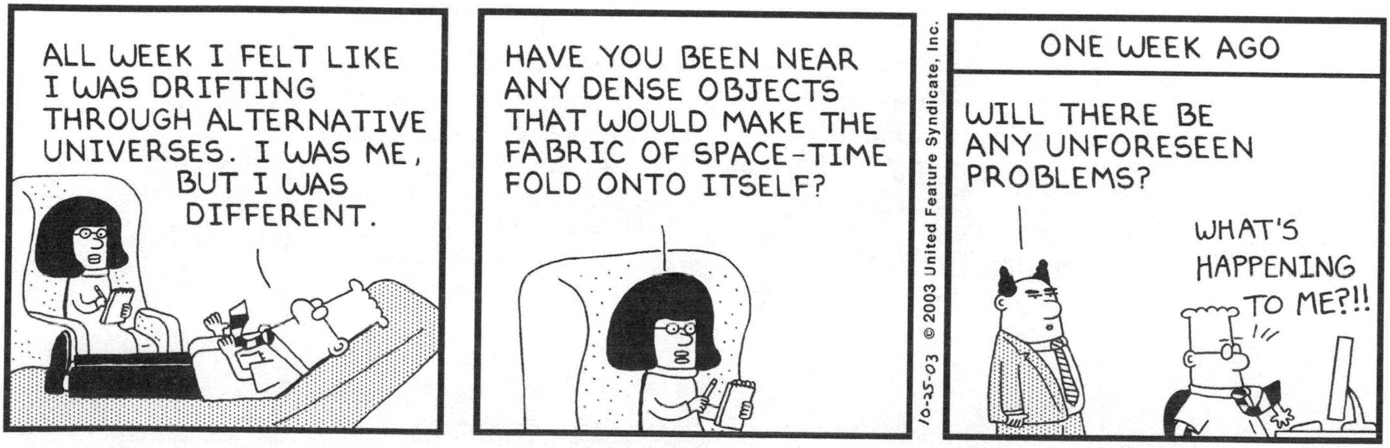
ALL WEEK I FELT LIKE I WAS DRIFTING THROUGH ALTERNATIVE UNIVERSES. I WAS ME, BUT I WAS DIFFERENT.
HAVE YOU BEEN NEAR ANY DENSE OBJECTS THAT WOULD MAKE THE FABRIC OF SPACE-TIME FOLD ONTO ITSELF?
10-25-03 © 2003 United Feature Syndicate, Inc.
ONE WEEK AGO
WILL THERE BE ANY UNFORESEEN PROBLEMS?
WHAT'S HAPPENING TO ME?!!

I HAVE AN IDEA FOR BOOSTING MY PERFORMANCE.
YOU WISELY COACHED US TO USE ALL OF OUR VACATION DAYS EVERY YEAR.
BECAUSE WE COME BACK RECHARGED!
OUR RENEWED MOTI-VATION IS MORE THAN ENOUGH TO COMPEN-SATE FOR THE MISSED DAYS.
MY PLAN IS TO LEVERAGE THAT COMPETITIVE ADVANTAGE.
I'LL TAKE A FIFTEEN YEAR VACATION AND RETURN TEN MINUTES BEFORE RETIREMENT.
THEN I'LL BE SO RECHARGED THAT I'LL POUNCE AND DO TWENTY YEARS OF WORK IN MINUTES!!
UNLESS IT'S NEAR A HOLIDAY, IN WHICH CASE, DO YOU MIND IF I LEAVE EARLY?
10-26-03 © 2003 United Feature Syndicate, Inc.

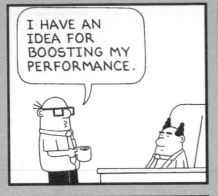

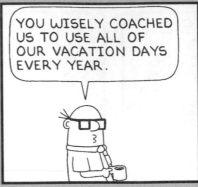

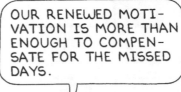

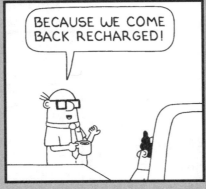

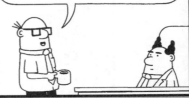

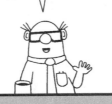

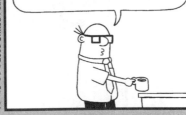

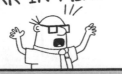

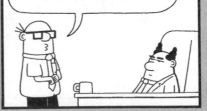

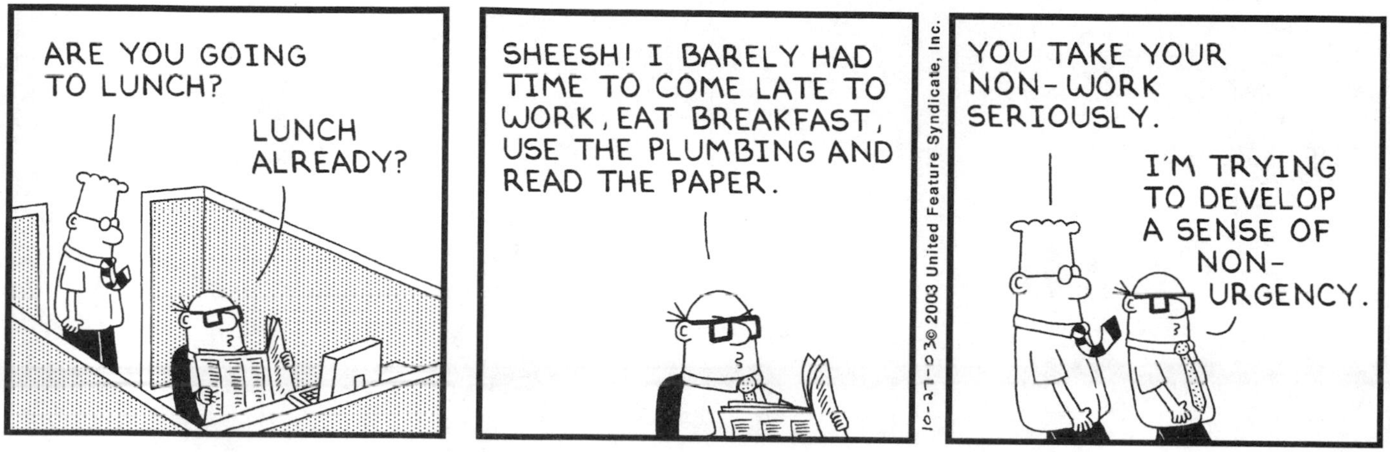
ARE YOU GOING TO LUNCH?
LUNCH ALREADY?
SHEESH! I BARELY HAD TIME TO COME LATE TO WORK, EAT BREAKFAST, USE THE PLUMBING AND READ THE PAPER.
YOU TAKE YOUR NON-WORK SERIOUSLY.
I'M TRYING TO DEVELOP A SENSE OF NON-URGENCY.
10-27-03 © 2003 United Feature Syndicate, Inc.

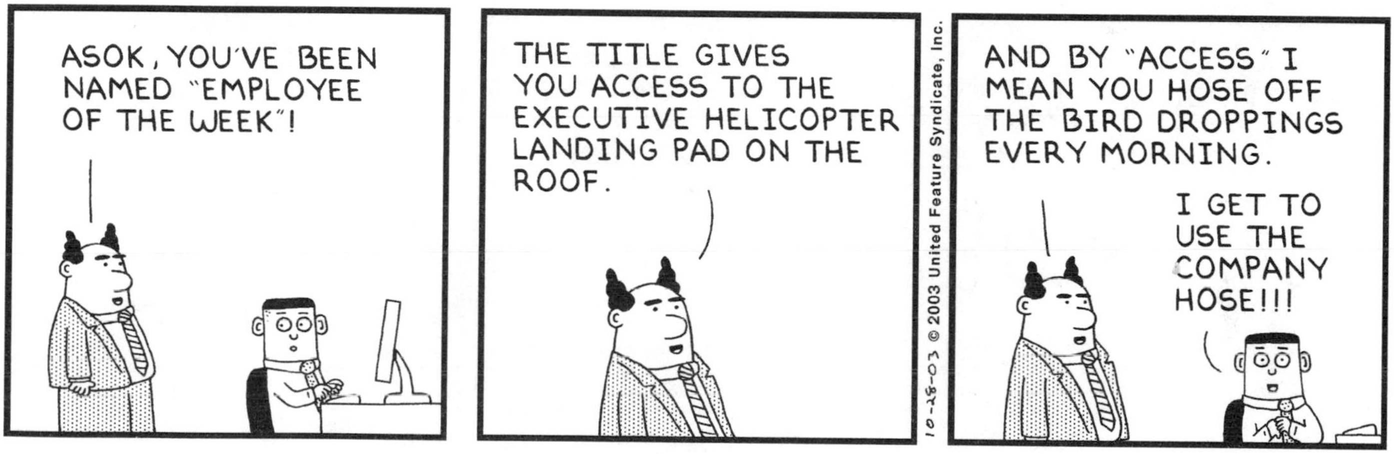
ASOK, YOU'VE BEEN NAMED "EMPLOYEE OF THE WEEK"!
THE TITLE GIVES YOU ACCESS TO THE EXECUTIVE HELICOPTER LANDING PAD ON THE ROOF.
AND BY "ACCESS" I MEAN YOU HOSE OFF THE BIRD DROPPINGS EVERY MORNING.
I GET TO USE THE COMPANY HOSE!!!
10-28-03 © 2003 United Feature Syndicate, Inc.

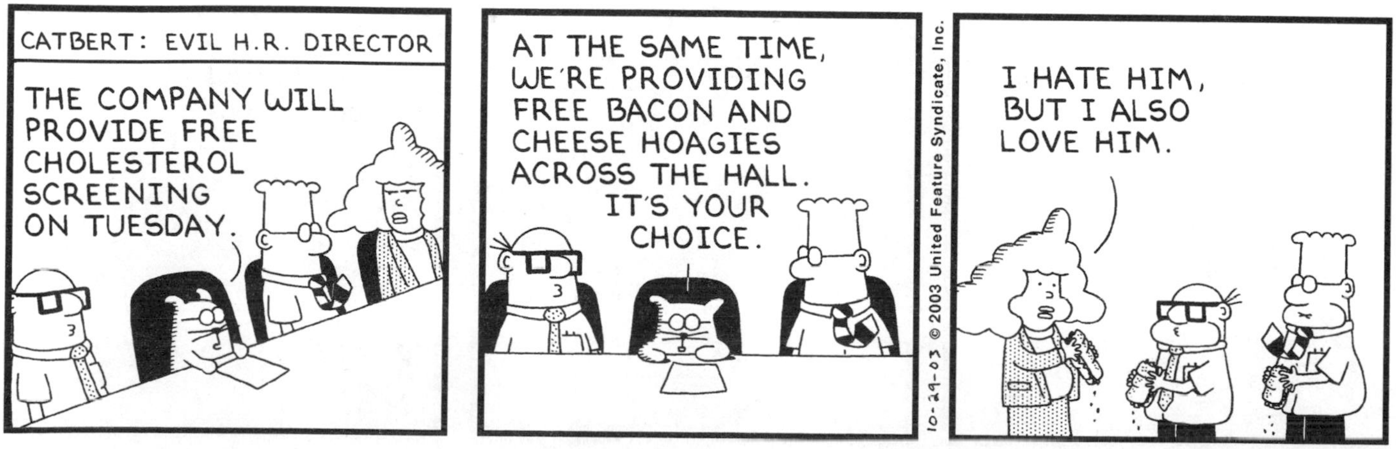
CATBERT: EVIL H.R. DIRECTOR
THE COMPANY WILL PROVIDE FREE CHOLESTEROL SCREENING ON TUESDAY.
AT THE SAME TIME, WE'RE PROVIDING FREE BACON AND CHEESE HOAGIES ACROSS THE HALL.
IT'S YOUR CHOICE.
I HATE HIM, BUT I ALSO LOVE HIM.
10-29-03 © 2003 United Feature Syndicate, Inc.

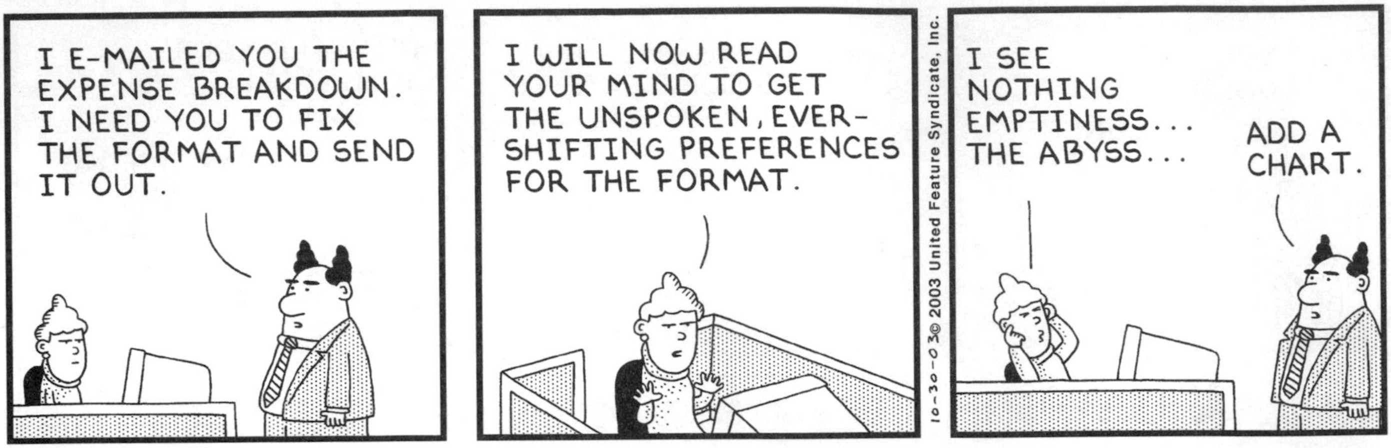
I E-MAILED YOU THE EXPENSE BREAKDOWN. I NEED YOU TO FIX THE FORMAT AND SEND IT OUT.
I WILL NOW READ YOUR MIND TO GET THE UNSPOKEN, EVER-SHIFTING PREFERENCES FOR THE FORMAT.
10-30-03 © 2003 United Feature Syndicate, Inc.
I SEE NOTHING EMPTINESS... THE ABYSS...
ADD A CHART.

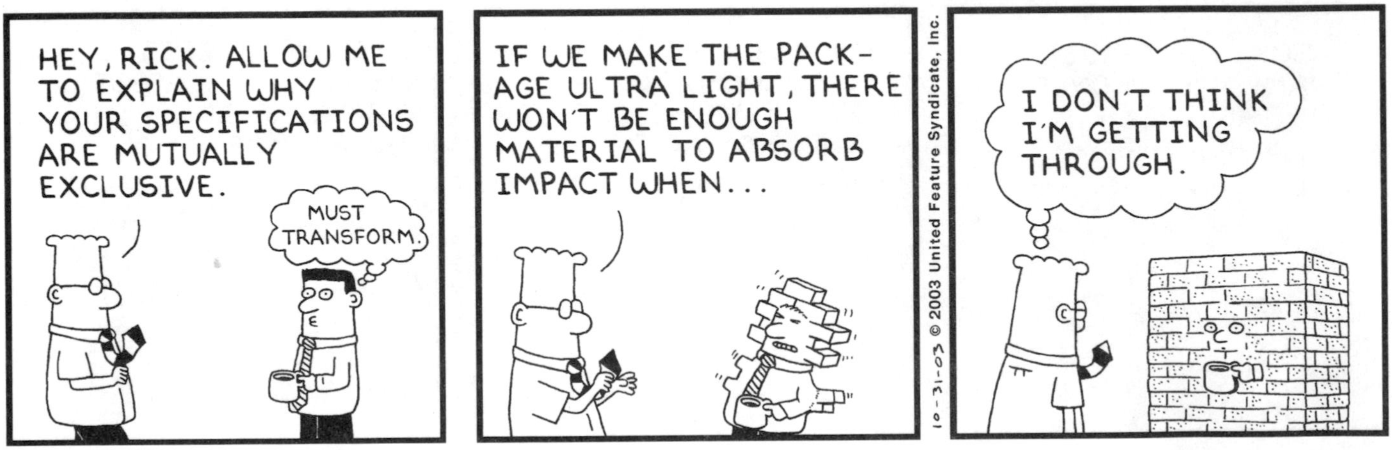
HEY, RICK. ALLOW ME TO EXPLAIN WHY YOUR SPECIFICATIONS ARE MUTUALLY EXCLUSIVE.
MUST TRANSFORM.
IF WE MAKE THE PACKAGE ULTRA LIGHT, THERE WON'T BE ENOUGH MATERIAL TO ABSORB IMPACT WHEN...
10-31-03 © 2003 United Feature Syndicate, Inc.
I DON'T THINK I'M GETTING THROUGH.

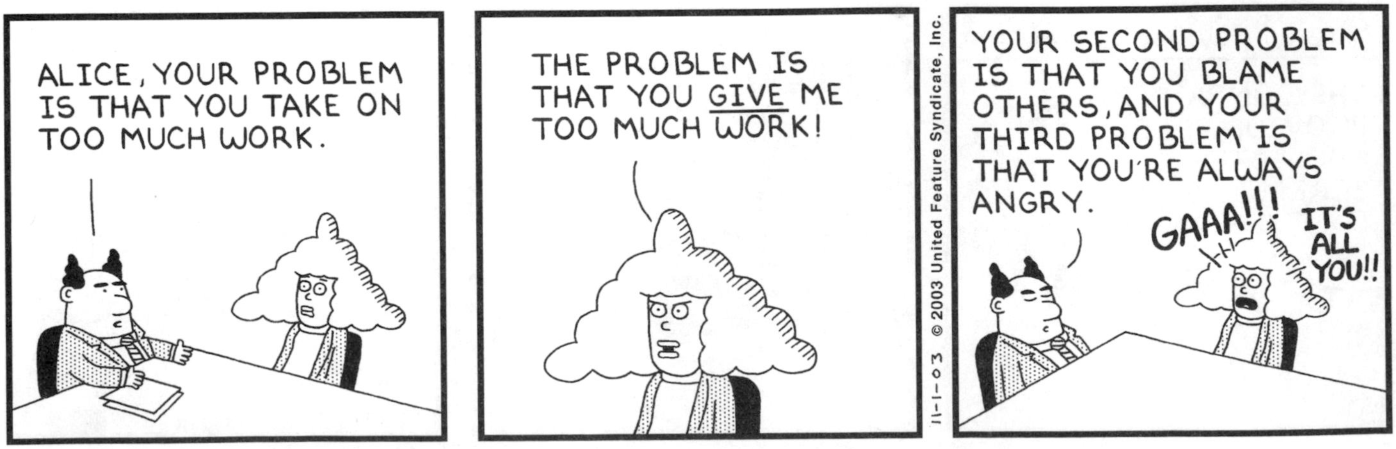
ALICE, YOUR PROBLEM IS THAT YOU TAKE ON TOO MUCH WORK.
THE PROBLEM IS THAT YOU GIVE ME TOO MUCH WORK!
11-1-03 © 2003 United Feature Syndicate, Inc.
YOUR SECOND PROBLEM IS THAT YOU BLAME OTHERS, AND YOUR THIRD PROBLEM IS THAT YOU'RE ALWAYS ANGRY.
GAAA!!!
IT'S ALL YOU!!

WALLY, WHAT'S THE STATUS OF YOUR PROJECT?
DEEP BREATH... CLEAR MY MIND...
I'VE BEEN FOCUSING MY BANDWIDTH ON ORGANIC GROWTH.
I'M GETTING LOTS OF PUSH-BACK, SO I'M TAKING THE DIS-CUSSIONS OFFLINE.
BUT SOMETIMES I TABLE AN ISSUE OR HANDLE IT IN A SIDEBAR.
©2003 United Feature Syndicate, Inc.
NOW I HAVE MY DUCKS IN A ROW, THE DEAL-BREAKERS ARE ON THE BACK BURNER, AND I'M MANAGING EXPEC-TATIONS.
OKAY...KEEP UP THE GOOD WORK.
WALLY, YOU DON'T HAVE A PROJECT.
WHAT? THEN WHY AM I SO TIRED?

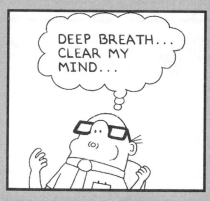

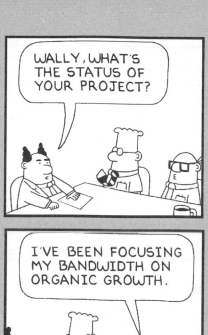

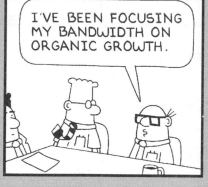

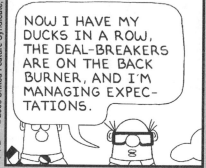

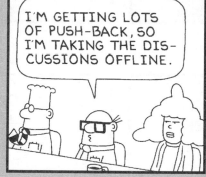

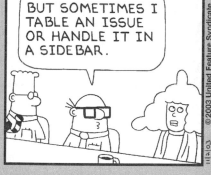

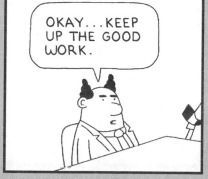

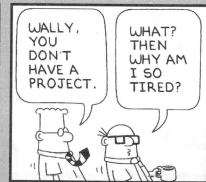

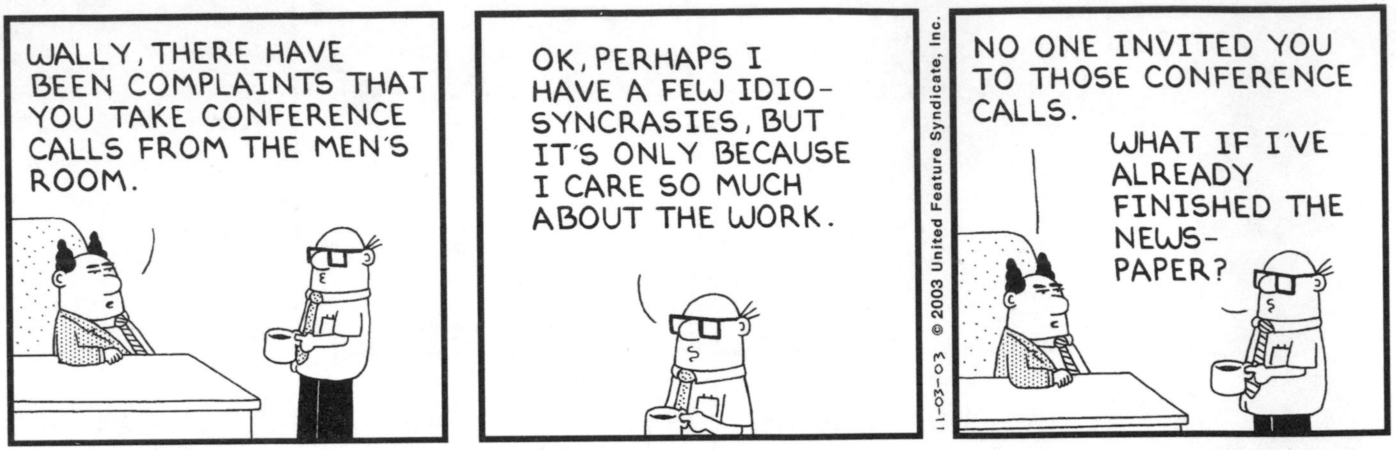
WALLY, THERE HAVE BEEN COMPLAINTS THAT YOU TAKE CONFERENCE CALLS FROM THE MEN'S ROOM.
OK, PERHAPS I HAVE A FEW IDIO-SYNCRASIES, BUT IT'S ONLY BECAUSE I CARE SO MUCH ABOUT THE WORK.
11-03-03 © 2003 United Feature Syndicate, Inc.
NO ONE INVITED YOU TO THOSE CONFERENCE CALLS.
WHAT IF I'VE ALREADY FINISHED THE NEWS-PAPER?

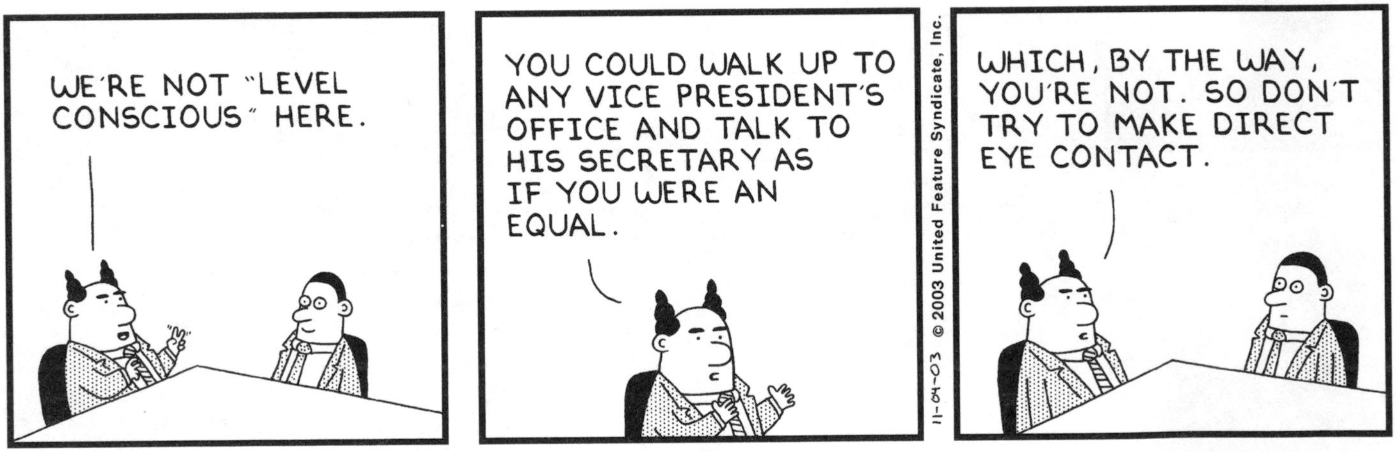
WE'RE NOT "LEVEL CONSCIOUS" HERE.
YOU COULD WALK UP TO ANY VICE PRESIDENT'S OFFICE AND TALK TO HIS SECRETARY AS IF YOU WERE AN EQUAL.
11-04-03 © 2003 United Feature Syndicate, Inc.
WHICH, BY THE WAY, YOU'RE NOT. SO DON'T TRY TO MAKE DIRECT EYE CONTACT.

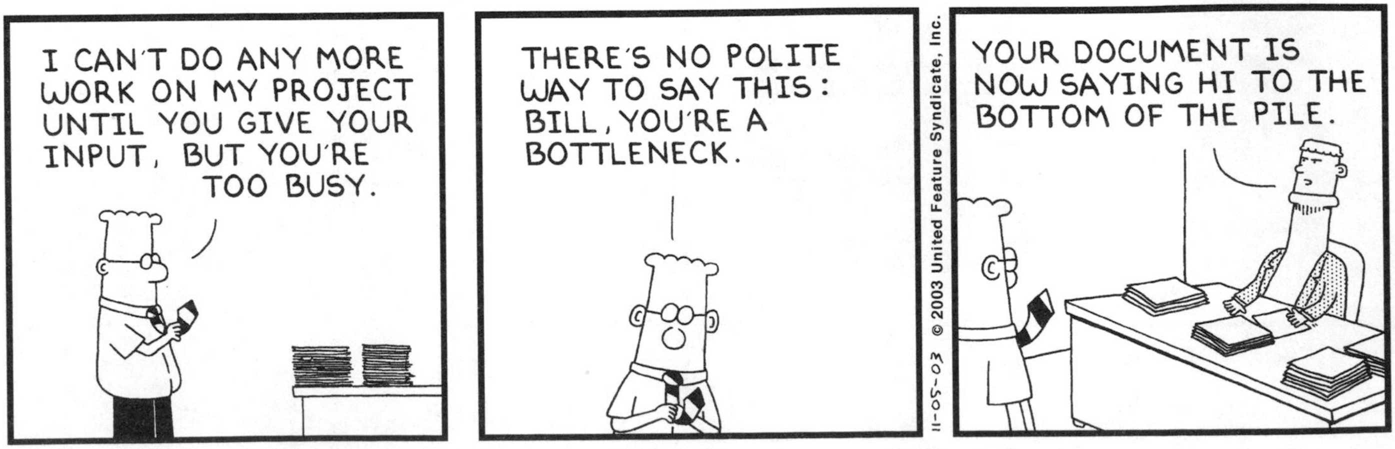
I CAN'T DO ANY MORE WORK ON MY PROJECT UNTIL YOU GIVE YOUR INPUT, BUT YOU'RE TOO BUSY.
THERE'S NO POLITE WAY TO SAY THIS: BILL, YOU'RE A BOTTLENECK.
11-05-03 © 2003 United Feature Syndicate, Inc.
YOUR DOCUMENT IS NOW SAYING HI TO THE BOTTOM OF THE PILE.

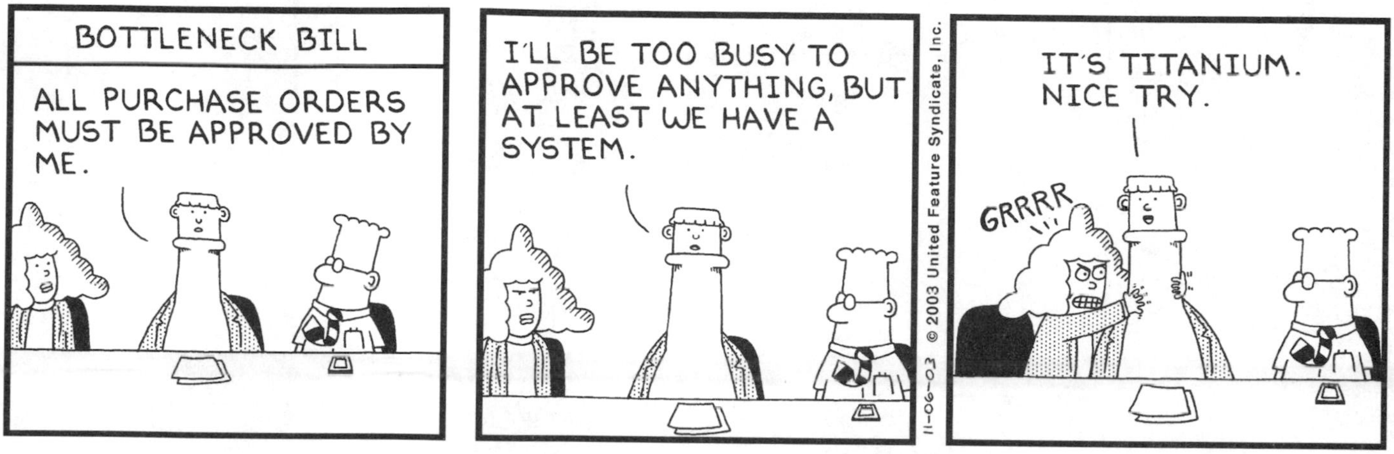
BOTTLENECK BILL
ALL PURCHASE ORDERS MUST BE APPROVED BY ME.
I'LL BE TOO BUSY TO APPROVE ANYTHING, BUT AT LEAST WE HAVE A SYSTEM.
11-06-03 © 2003 United Feature Syndicate, Inc.
GRRRR
IT'S TITANIUM. NICE TRY.

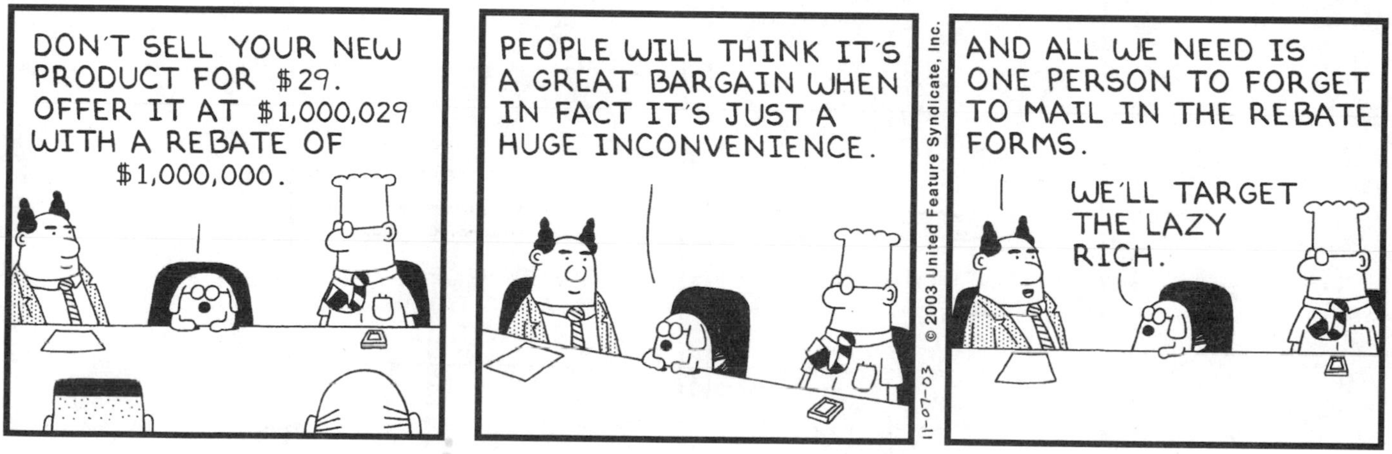
DON'T SELL YOUR NEW PRODUCT FOR $29. OFFER IT AT $1,000,029 WITH A REBATE OF $1,000,000.
PEOPLE WILL THINK IT'S A GREAT BARGAIN WHEN IN FACT IT'S JUST A HUGE INCONVENIENCE.
11-07-03 © 2003 United Feature Syndicate, Inc.
AND ALL WE NEED IS ONE PERSON TO FORGET TO MAIL IN THE REBATE FORMS.
WE'LL TARGET THE LAZY RICH.

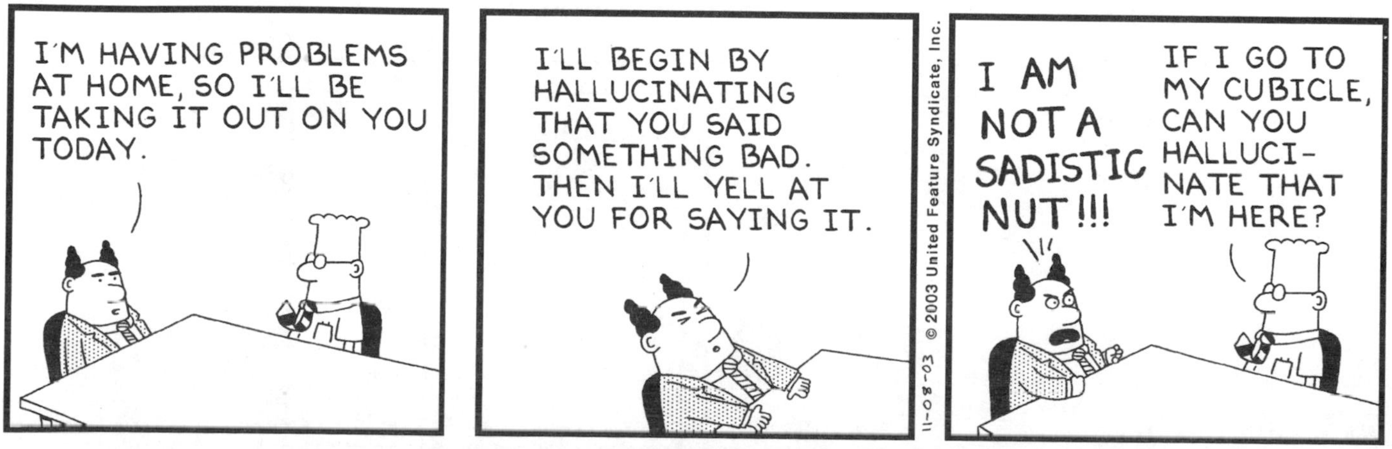
I'M HAVING PROBLEMS AT HOME, SO I'LL BE TAKING IT OUT ON YOU TODAY.
I'LL BEGIN BY HALLUCINATING THAT YOU SAID SOMETHING BAD. THEN I'LL YELL AT YOU FOR SAYING IT.
11-08-03 © 2003 United Feature Syndicate, Inc.
I AM NOT A SADISTIC NUT!!!
IF I GO TO MY CUBICLE, CAN YOU HALLUCI-NATE THAT I'M HERE?

EVERYONE GETS A COMPANY SHIRT!
IT'S GOOD FOR MORALE.
OOPS! NOT FOR TEMPS.
NONE FOR CONTRACTORS.
NOT FOR VENDORS.
NOTHING IN YOUR SIZE.
NOT FOR PEOPLE WHO MIGHT GET DOWN-SIZED ON FRIDAY.
I'LL USE THE LEFTOVERS AS GARAGE RAGS.
DID THE SHIRTS IMPROVE MORALE?
SURE DID! I FEEL GREAT!
11-9-03 ©2003 United Feature Syndicate, Inc.

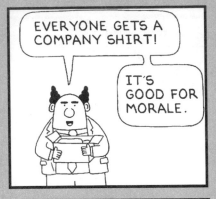

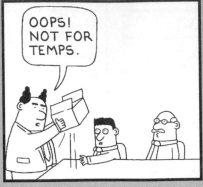

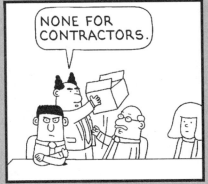

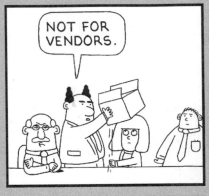

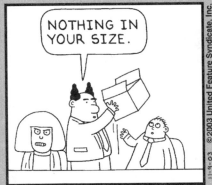

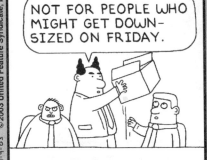

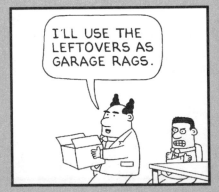

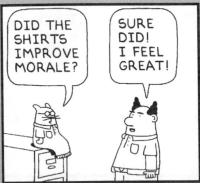

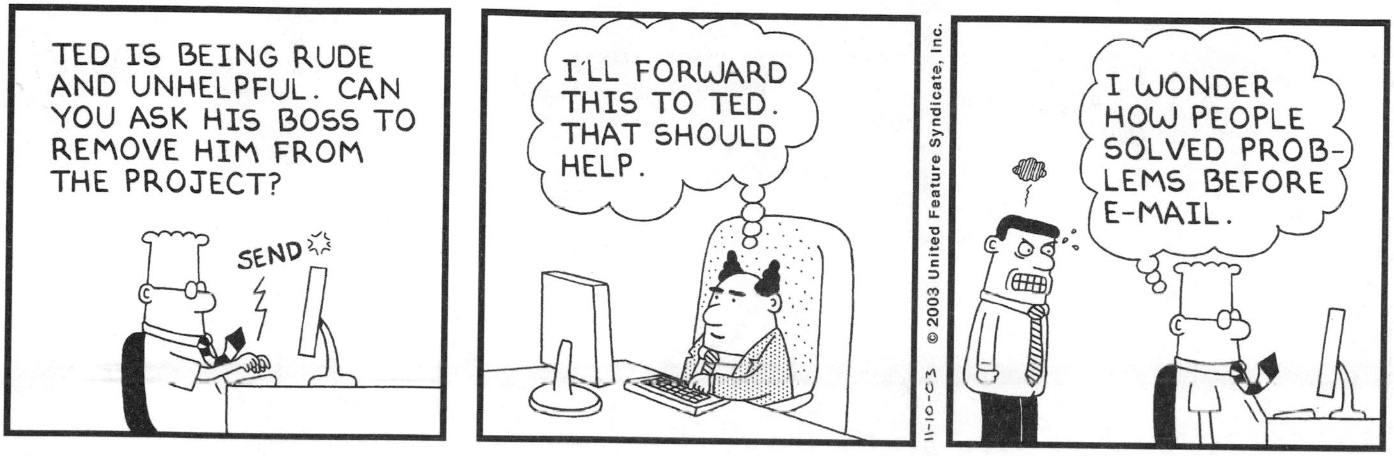
TED IS BEING RUDE AND UNHELPFUL. CAN YOU ASK HIS BOSS TO REMOVE HIM FROM THE PROJECT?
SEND
I'LL FORWARD THIS TO TED. THAT SHOULD HELP.
11-10-03 © 2003 United Feature Syndicate, Inc.
I WONDER HOW PEOPLE SOLVED PROB-LEMS BEFORE E-MAIL.

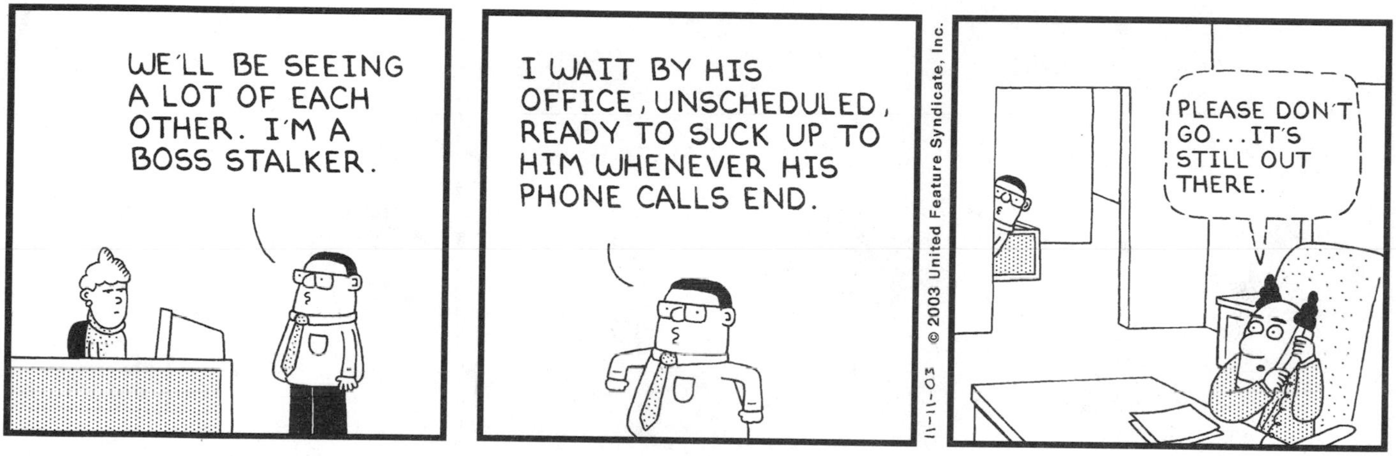
WE'LL BE SEEING A LOT OF EACH OTHER. I'M A BOSS STALKER.
I WAIT BY HIS OFFICE, UNSCHEDULED, READY TO SUCK UP TO HIM WHENEVER HIS PHONE CALLS END.
11-11-03 © 2003 United Feature Syndicate, Inc.
PLEASE DON'T GO... IT'S STILL OUT THERE.

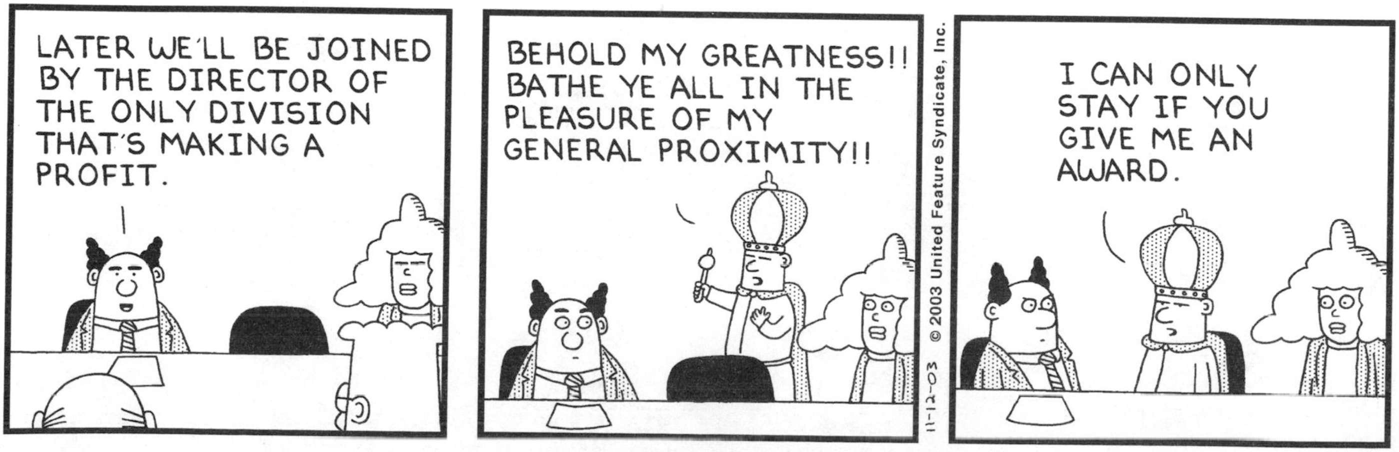
LATER WE'LL BE JOINED BY THE DIRECTOR OF THE ONLY DIVISION THAT'S MAKING A PROFIT.
BEHOLD MY GREATNESS!! BATHE YE ALL IN THE PLEASURE OF MY GENERAL PROXIMITY!!
11-12-03 © 2003 United Feature Syndicate, Inc.
I CAN ONLY STAY IF YOU GIVE ME AN AWARD.

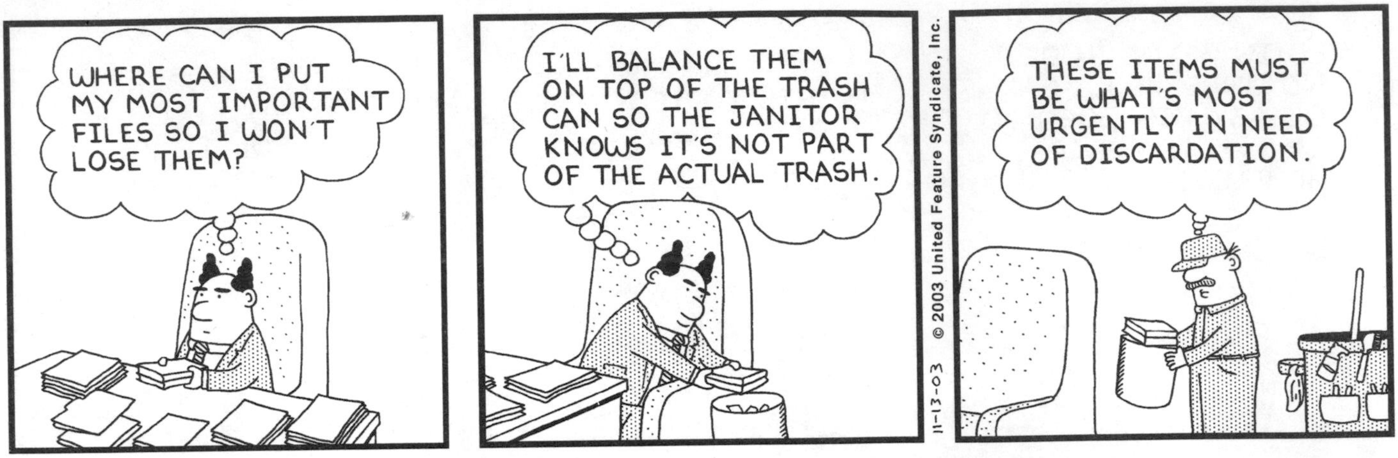
WHERE CAN I PUT MY MOST IMPORTANT FILES SO I WON'T LOSE THEM?
I'LL BALANCE THEM ON TOP OF THE TRASH CAN SO THE JANITOR KNOWS IT'S NOT PART OF THE ACTUAL TRASH.
11-13-03 © 2003 United Feature Syndicate, Inc.
THESE ITEMS MUST BE WHAT'S MOST URGENTLY IN NEED OF DISCARDATION.

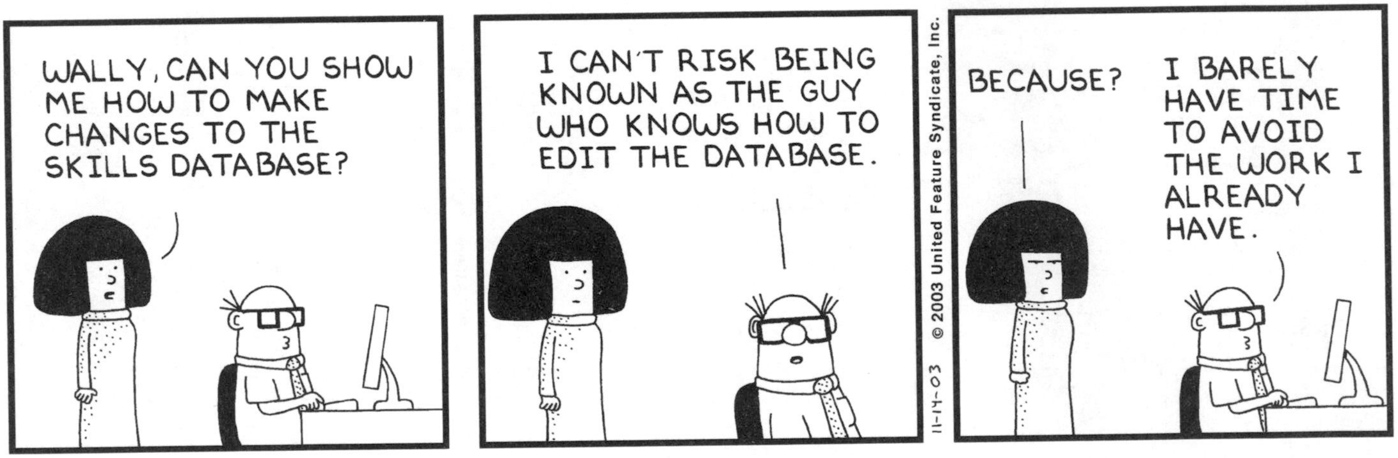
WALLY, CAN YOU SHOW ME HOW TO MAKE CHANGES TO THE SKILLS DATABASE?
I CAN'T RISK BEING KNOWN AS THE GUY WHO KNOWS HOW TO EDIT THE DATABASE.
11-14-03 © 2003 United Feature Syndicate, Inc.
BECAUSE?
I BARELY HAVE TIME TO AVOID THE WORK I ALREADY HAVE.

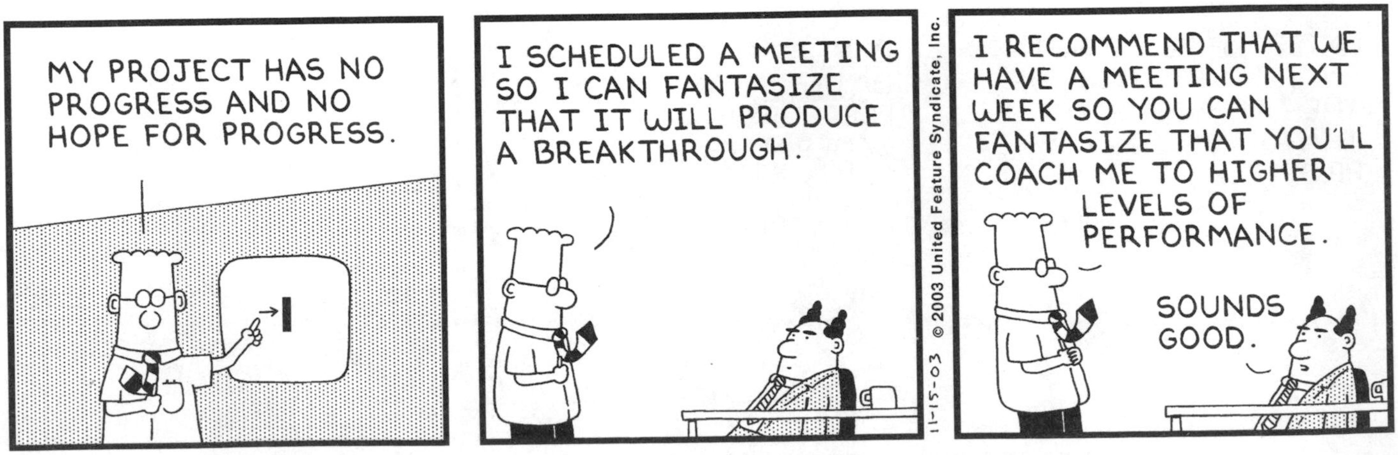
MY PROJECT HAS NO PROGRESS AND NO HOPE FOR PROGRESS.
I SCHEDULED A MEETING SO I CAN FANTASIZE THAT IT WILL PRODUCE A BREAKTHROUGH.
11-15-03 © 2003 United Feature Syndicate, Inc.
I RECOMMEND THAT WE HAVE A MEETING NEXT WEEK SO YOU CAN FANTASIZE THAT YOU'LL COACH ME TO HIGHER LEVELS OF PERFORMANCE.
SOUNDS GOOD.

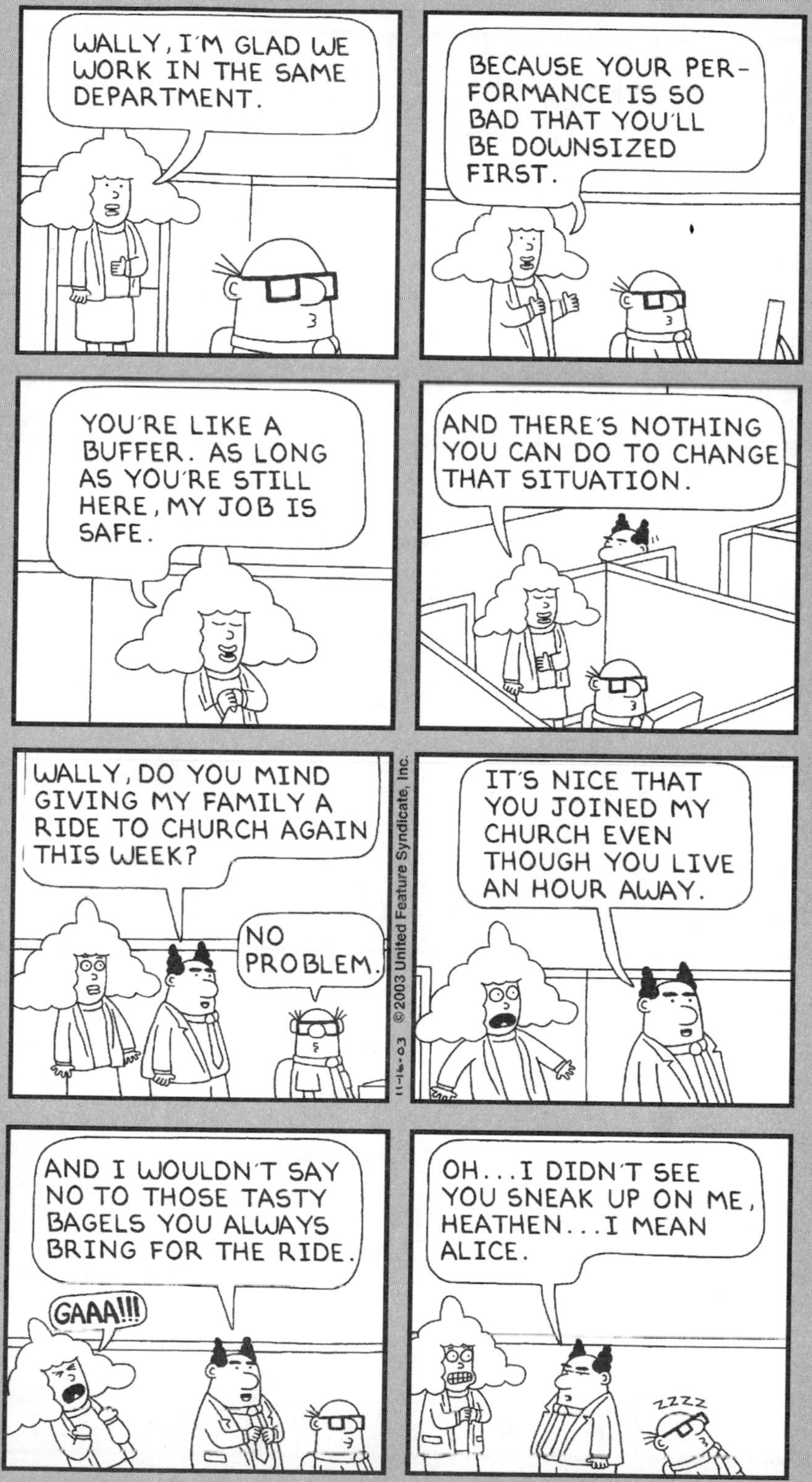
WALLY, I'M GLAD WE WORK IN THE SAME DEPARTMENT.
BECAUSE YOUR PERFORMANCE IS SO BAD THAT YOU'LL BE DOWNSIZED FIRST.
YOU'RE LIKE A BUFFER. AS LONG AS YOU'RE STILL HERE, MY JOB IS SAFE.
AND THERE'S NOTHING YOU CAN DO TO CHANGE THAT SITUATION.
WALLY, DO YOU MIND GIVING MY FAMILY A RIDE TO CHURCH AGAIN THIS WEEK?
NO PROBLEM.
© 2003 United Feature Syndicate, Inc.
11-16-03
IT'S NICE THAT YOU JOINED MY CHURCH EVEN THOUGH YOU LIVE AN HOUR AWAY.
AND I WOULDN'T SAY NO TO THOSE TASTY BAGELS YOU ALWAYS BRING FOR THE RIDE.
GAAA!!!
OH...I DIDN'T SEE YOU SNEAK UP ON ME, HEATHEN...I MEAN ALICE.
ZZZZ

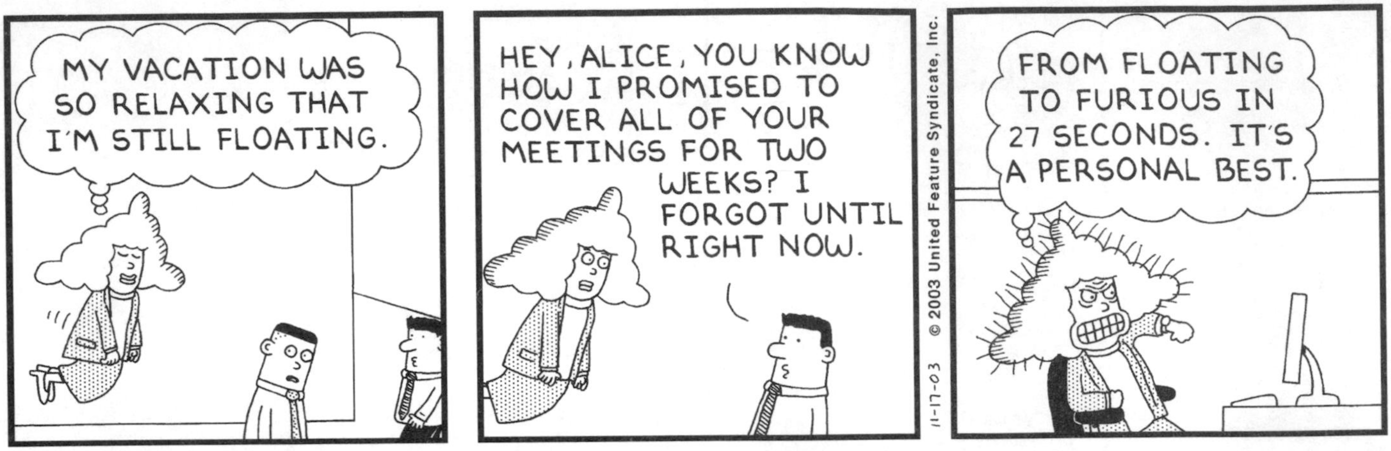
MY VACATION WAS SO RELAXING THAT I'M STILL FLOATING.
HEY, ALICE, YOU KNOW HOW I PROMISED TO COVER ALL OF YOUR MEETINGS FOR TWO WEEKS? I FORGOT UNTIL RIGHT NOW.
© 2003 United Feature Syndicate, Inc.
11-17-03
FROM FLOATING TO FURIOUS IN 27 SECONDS. IT'S A PERSONAL BEST.

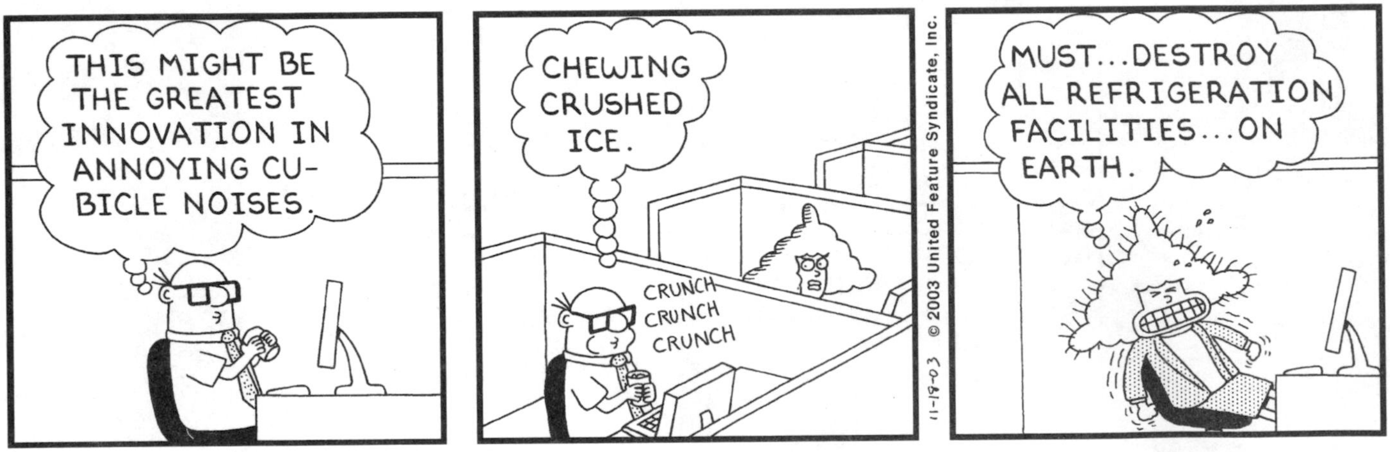
THIS MIGHT BE THE GREATEST INNOVATION IN ANNOYING CUBICLE NOISES.
CHEWING CRUSHED ICE.
CRUNCH CRUNCH CRUNCH
© 2003 United Feature Syndicate, Inc.
11-18-03
MUST...DESTROY ALL REFRIGERATION FACILITIES...ON EARTH.

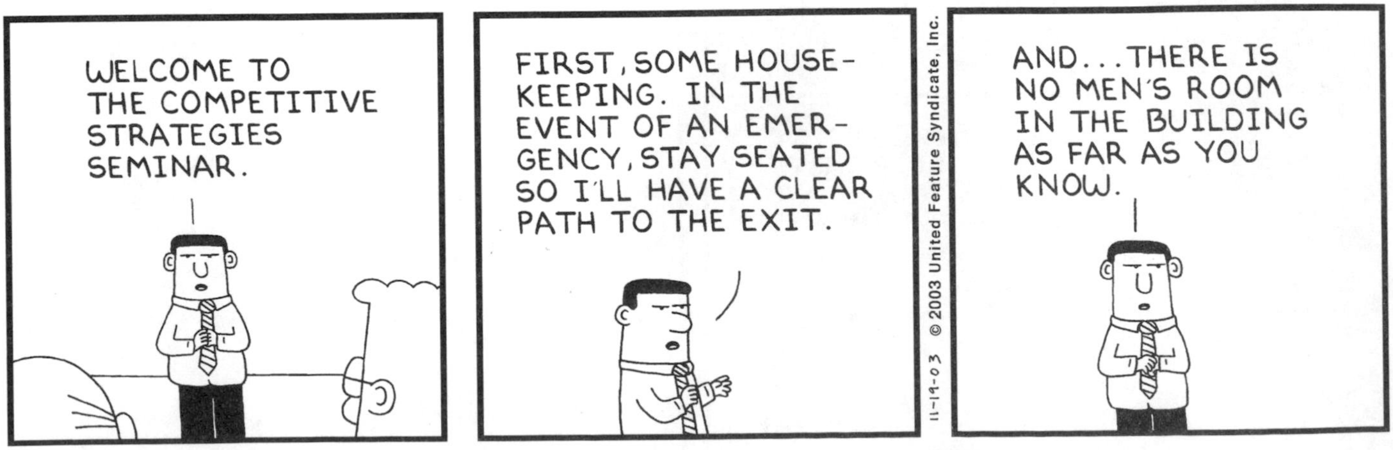
WELCOME TO THE COMPETITIVE STRATEGIES SEMINAR.
FIRST, SOME HOUSEKEEPING. IN THE EVENT OF AN EMERGENCY, STAY SEATED SO I'LL HAVE A CLEAR PATH TO THE EXIT.
© 2003 United Feature Syndicate, Inc.
11-19-03
AND...THERE IS NO MEN'S ROOM IN THE BUILDING AS FAR AS YOU KNOW.

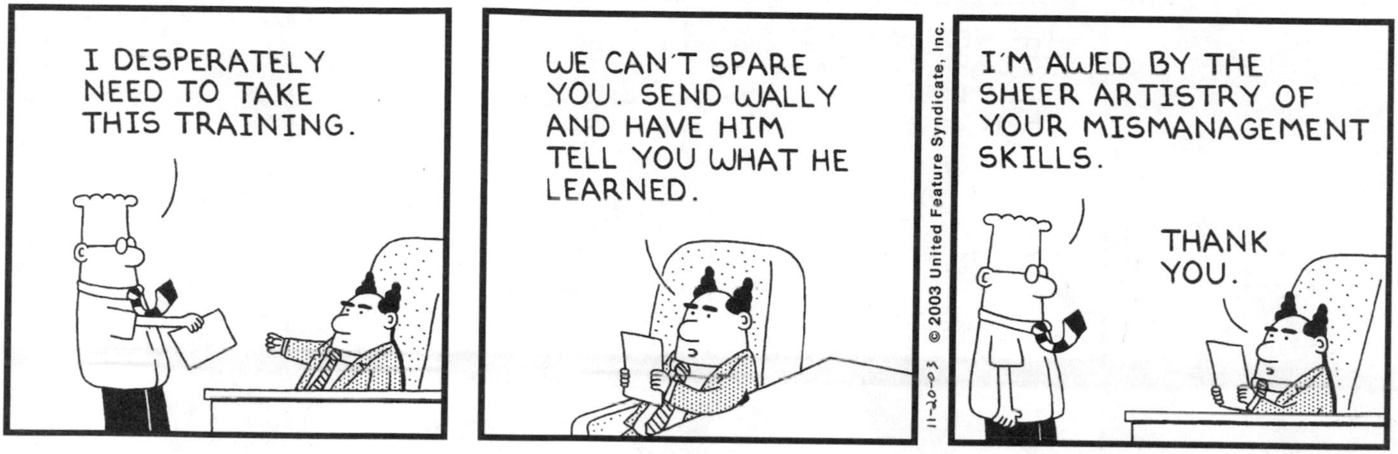
I DESPERATELY NEED TO TAKE THIS TRAINING.
WE CAN'T SPARE YOU. SEND WALLY AND HAVE HIM TELL YOU WHAT HE LEARNED.
11-20-03 © 2003 United Feature Syndicate, Inc.
I'M AWED BY THE SHEER ARTISTRY OF YOUR MISMANAGEMENT SKILLS.
THANK YOU.

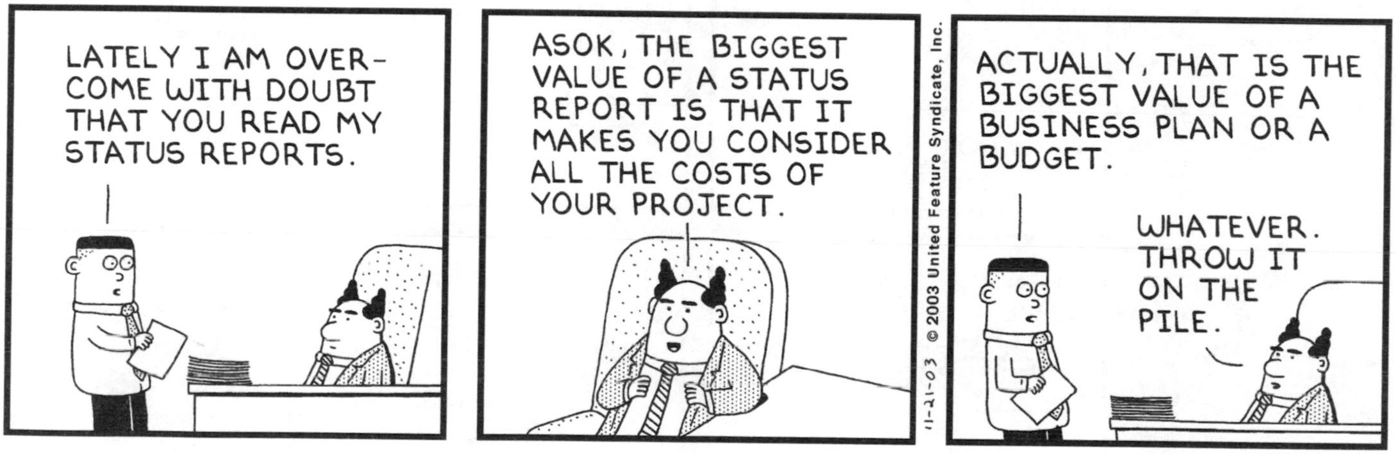
LATELY I AM OVERCOME WITH DOUBT THAT YOU READ MY STATUS REPORTS.
ASOK, THE BIGGEST VALUE OF A STATUS REPORT IS THAT IT MAKES YOU CONSIDER ALL THE COSTS OF YOUR PROJECT.
11-21-03 © 2003 United Feature Syndicate, Inc.
ACTUALLY, THAT IS THE BIGGEST VALUE OF A BUSINESS PLAN OR A BUDGET.
WHATEVER. THROW IT ON THE PILE.

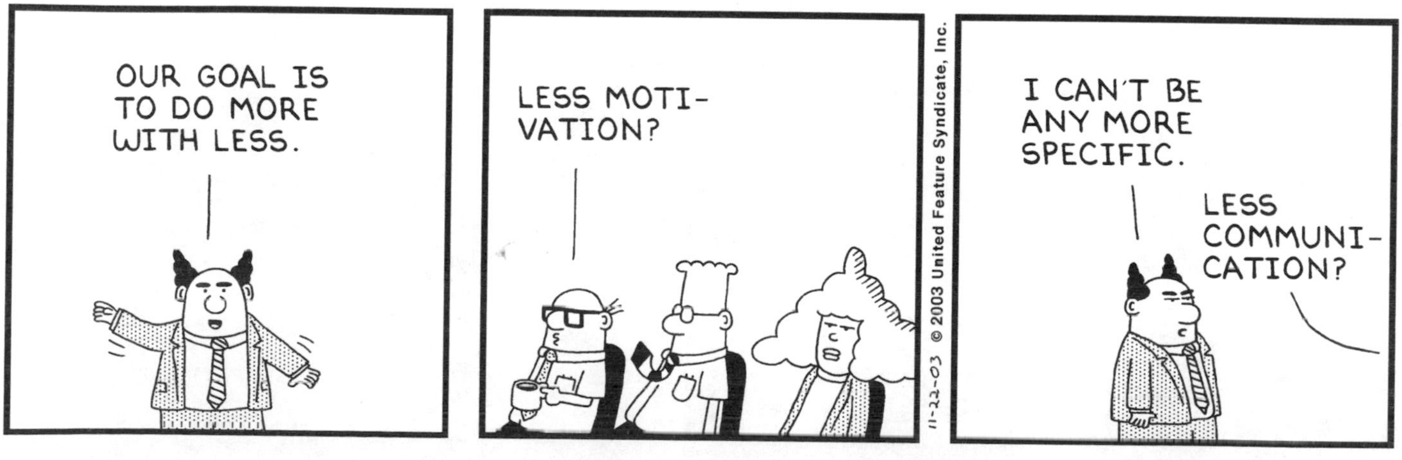
OUR GOAL IS TO DO MORE WITH LESS.
LESS MOTIVATION?
11-22-03 © 2003 United Feature Syndicate, Inc.
I CAN'T BE ANY MORE SPECIFIC.
LESS COMMUNICATION?

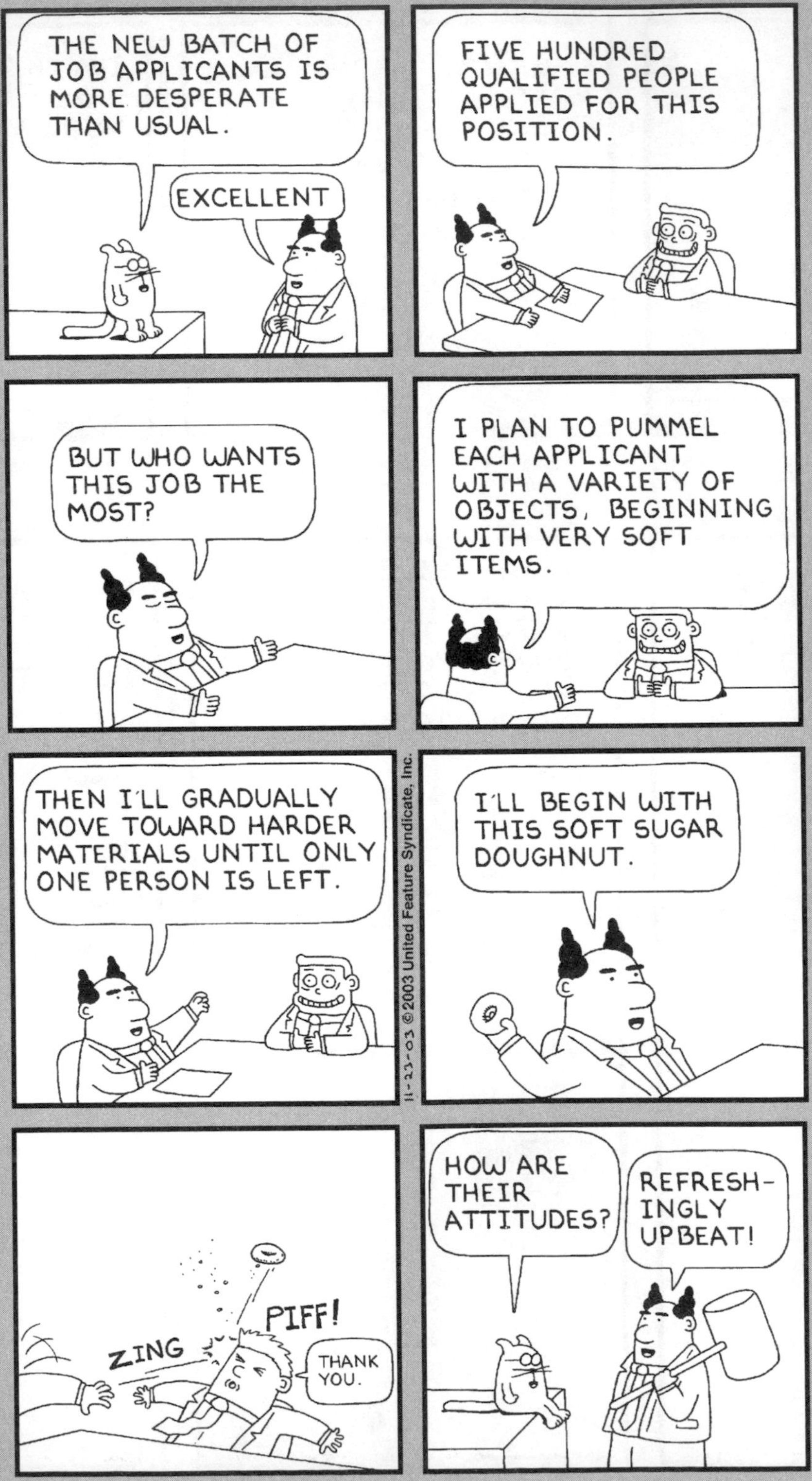
THE NEW BATCH OF JOB APPLICANTS IS MORE DESPERATE THAN USUAL.
EXCELLENT
FIVE HUNDRED QUALIFIED PEOPLE APPLIED FOR THIS POSITION.
BUT WHO WANTS THIS JOB THE MOST?
I PLAN TO PUMMEL EACH APPLICANT WITH A VARIETY OF OBJECTS, BEGINNING WITH VERY SOFT ITEMS.
THEN I'LL GRADUALLY MOVE TOWARD HARDER MATERIALS UNTIL ONLY ONE PERSON IS LEFT.
11-23-03 ©2003 United Feature Syndicate, Inc.
I'LL BEGIN WITH THIS SOFT SUGAR DOUGHNUT.
ZING
PIFF!
THANK YOU.
HOW ARE THEIR ATTITUDES?
REFRESH-INGLY UPBEAT!

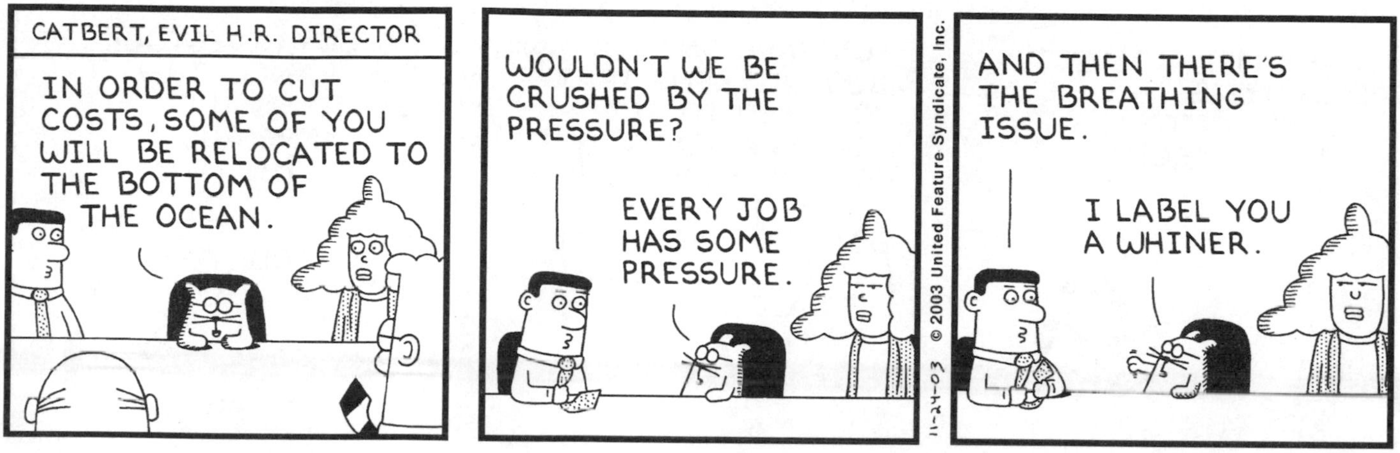
CATBERT, EVIL H.R. DIRECTOR
IN ORDER TO CUT COSTS, SOME OF YOU WILL BE RELOCATED TO THE BOTTOM OF THE OCEAN.
WOULDN'T WE BE CRUSHED BY THE PRESSURE?
EVERY JOB HAS SOME PRESSURE.
11-24-03 © 2003 United Feature Syndicate, Inc.
AND THEN THERE'S THE BREATHING ISSUE.
I LABEL YOU A WHINER.

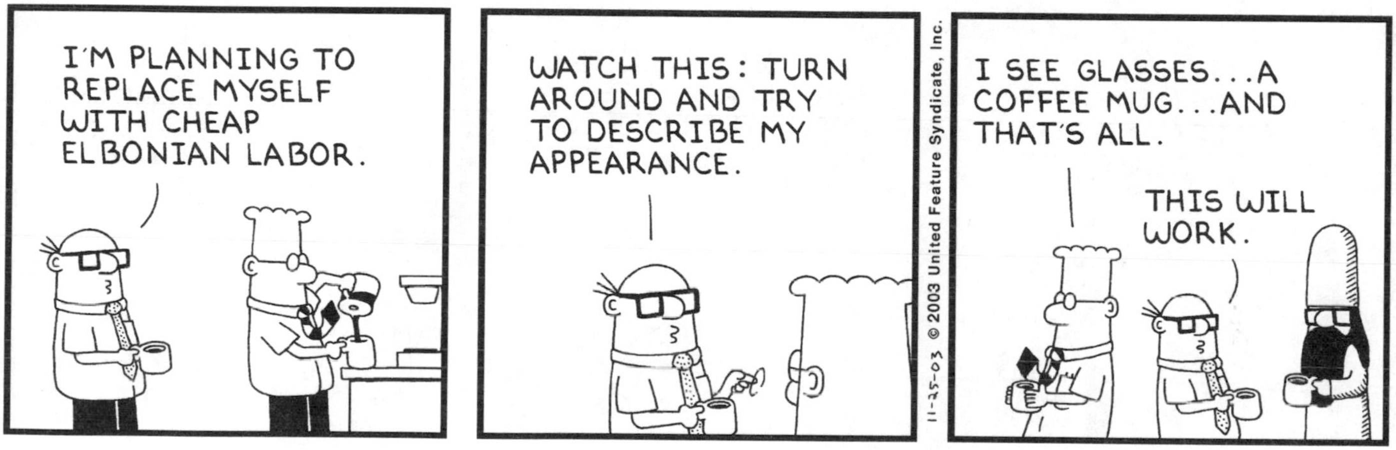
I'M PLANNING TO REPLACE MYSELF WITH CHEAP ELBONIAN LABOR.
WATCH THIS: TURN AROUND AND TRY TO DESCRIBE MY APPEARANCE.
11-25-03 © 2003 United Feature Syndicate, Inc.
I SEE GLASSES...A COFFEE MUG...AND THAT'S ALL.
THIS WILL WORK.

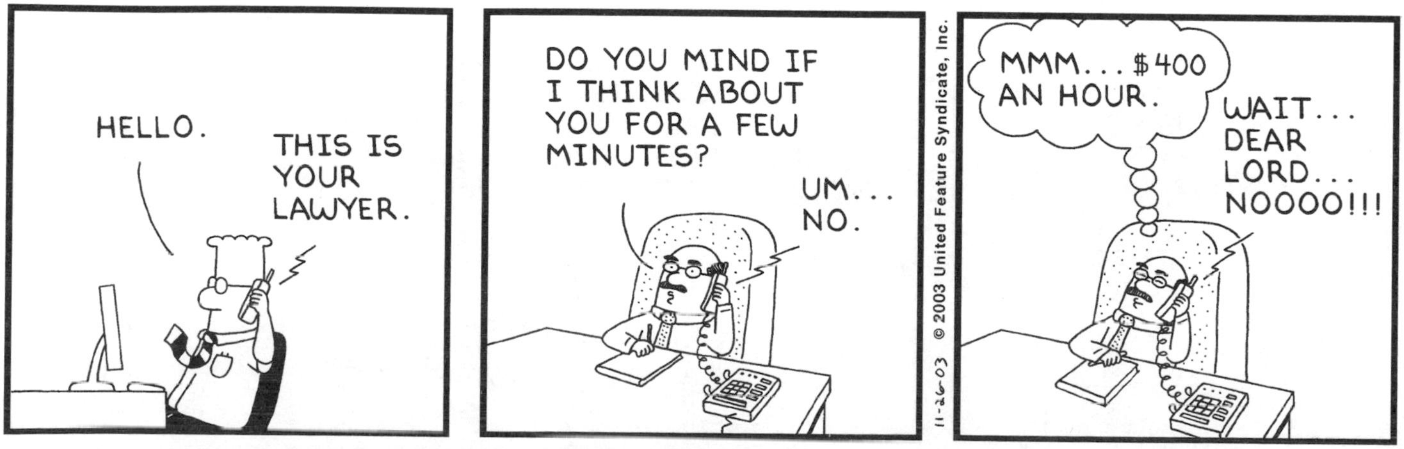
HELLO.
THIS IS YOUR LAWYER.
DO YOU MIND IF I THINK ABOUT YOU FOR A FEW MINUTES?
UM... NO.
11-26-03 © 2003 United Feature Syndicate, Inc.
MMM... $400 AN HOUR.
WAIT... DEAR LORD... NOOOO!!!

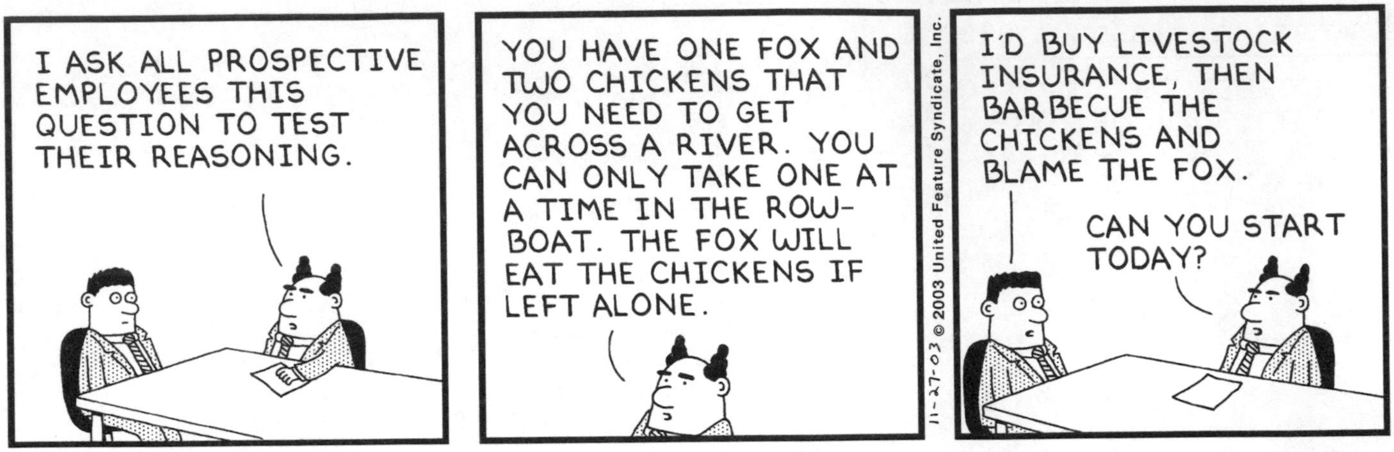
I ASK ALL PROSPECTIVE EMPLOYEES THIS QUESTION TO TEST THEIR REASONING.
YOU HAVE ONE FOX AND TWO CHICKENS THAT YOU NEED TO GET ACROSS A RIVER. YOU CAN ONLY TAKE ONE AT A TIME IN THE ROW-BOAT. THE FOX WILL EAT THE CHICKENS IF LEFT ALONE.
11-27-03 © 2003 United Feature Syndicate, Inc.
I'D BUY LIVESTOCK INSURANCE, THEN BARBECUE THE CHICKENS AND BLAME THE FOX.
CAN YOU START TODAY?

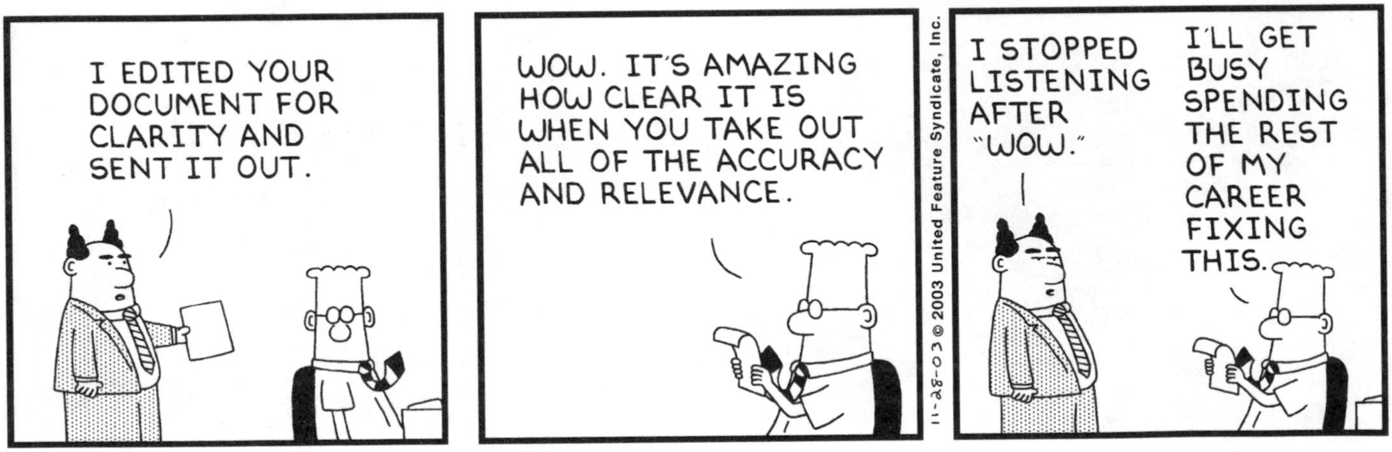
I EDITED YOUR DOCUMENT FOR CLARITY AND SENT IT OUT.
WOW. IT'S AMAZING HOW CLEAR IT IS WHEN YOU TAKE OUT ALL OF THE ACCURACY AND RELEVANCE.
11-28-03 © 2003 United Feature Syndicate, Inc.
I STOPPED LISTENING AFTER "WOW."
I'LL GET BUSY SPENDING THE REST OF MY CAREER FIXING THIS.

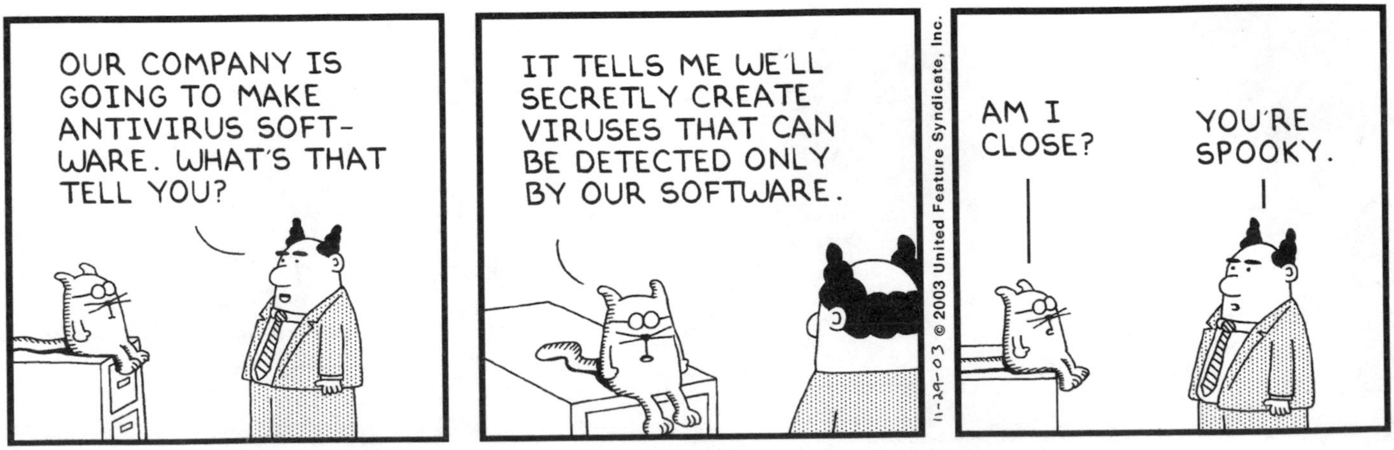
OUR COMPANY IS GOING TO MAKE ANTIVIRUS SOFT-WARE. WHAT'S THAT TELL YOU?
IT TELLS ME WE'LL SECRETLY CREATE VIRUSES THAT CAN BE DETECTED ONLY BY OUR SOFTWARE.
11-29-03 © 2003 United Feature Syndicate, Inc.
AM I CLOSE?
YOU'RE SPOOKY.

I'D LIKE YOU TO MEET BRADLEY, OUR NEW MANAGER OF EXECUTIVE COMPENSATION.
BRADLEY'S JOB IS TO RECOMMEND TO OUR BOARD HOW MUCH TO PAY COMPANY EXECUTIVES SUCH AS ME.
BRADLEY IS TOTALLY OBJECTIVE.
TOTALLY.
THAT WAS A WORLD-CLASS OBSERVATION, SO I'LL RECOMMEND THAT THE COMPANY BUY YOU A PONY.
...A STRONG PONY TO CARRY THE HUGE BAGS OF CASH I RECOMMEND FOR YOU.
11-30-03 ©2003 United Feature Syndicate, Inc.
GOOD WORK, BRADLEY. I'LL RECOMMEND TO THE BOARD THAT YOU GET A HUGE RAISE!
GAAA!!! STOP PRETENDING TO HAVE REASONS!! JUST STEAL THE STUPID MONEY!!!
SEE WHAT I HAVE TO DEAL WITH EVERY DAY?
WOULD AN EXTRA MONTH OF VACATION REDUCE THE STING?

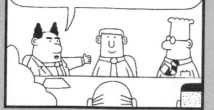

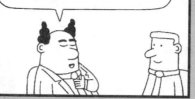

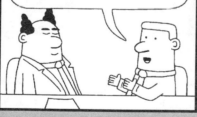

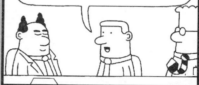

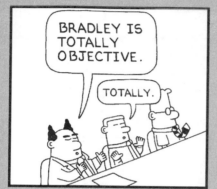

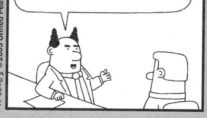

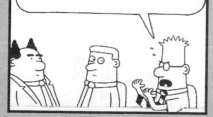

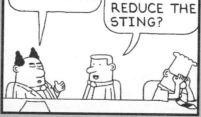

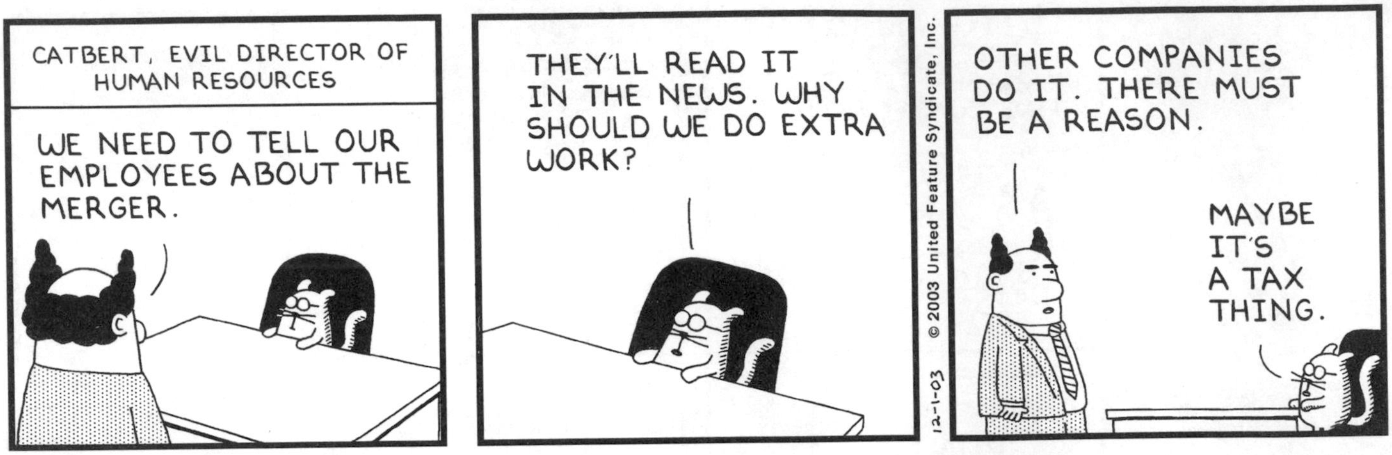
CATBERT, EVIL DIRECTOR OF HUMAN RESOURCES
WE NEED TO TELL OUR EMPLOYEES ABOUT THE MERGER.
THEY'LL READ IT IN THE NEWS. WHY SHOULD WE DO EXTRA WORK?
OTHER COMPANIES DO IT. THERE MUST BE A REASON.
MAYBE IT'S A TAX THING.
12-1-03 © 2003 United Feature Syndicate, Inc.

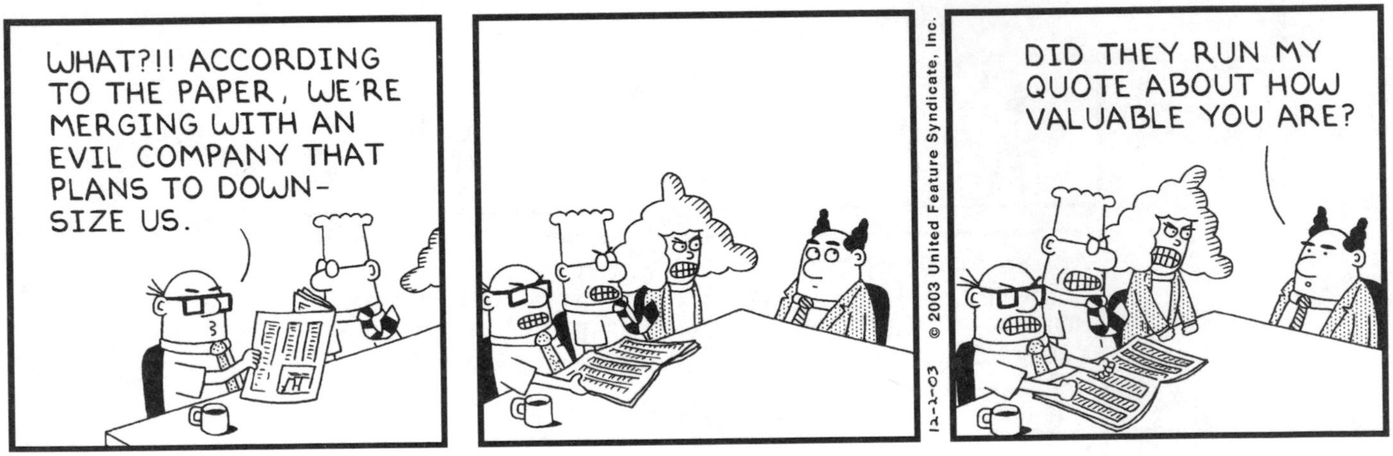
WHAT?!! ACCORDING TO THE PAPER, WE'RE MERGING WITH AN EVIL COMPANY THAT PLANS TO DOWN-SIZE US.
DID THEY RUN MY QUOTE ABOUT HOW VALUABLE YOU ARE?
12-2-03 © 2003 United Feature Syndicate, Inc.

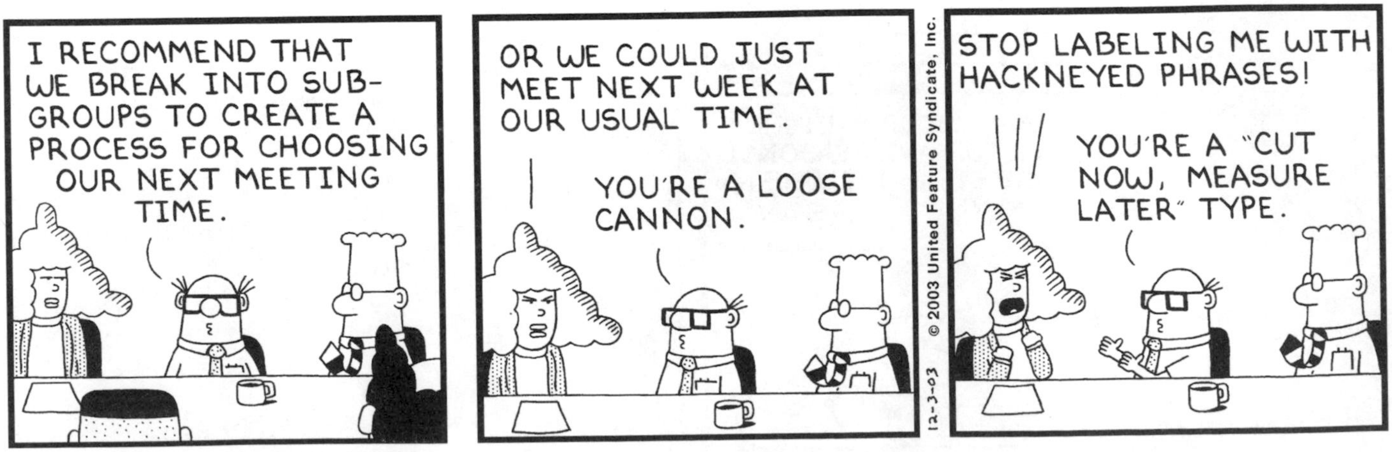
I RECOMMEND THAT WE BREAK INTO SUB-GROUPS TO CREATE A PROCESS FOR CHOOSING OUR NEXT MEETING TIME.
OR WE COULD JUST MEET NEXT WEEK AT OUR USUAL TIME.
YOU'RE A LOOSE CANNON.
STOP LABELING ME WITH HACKNEYED PHRASES!
YOU'RE A "CUT NOW, MEASURE LATER" TYPE.
12-3-03 © 2003 United Feature Syndicate, Inc.

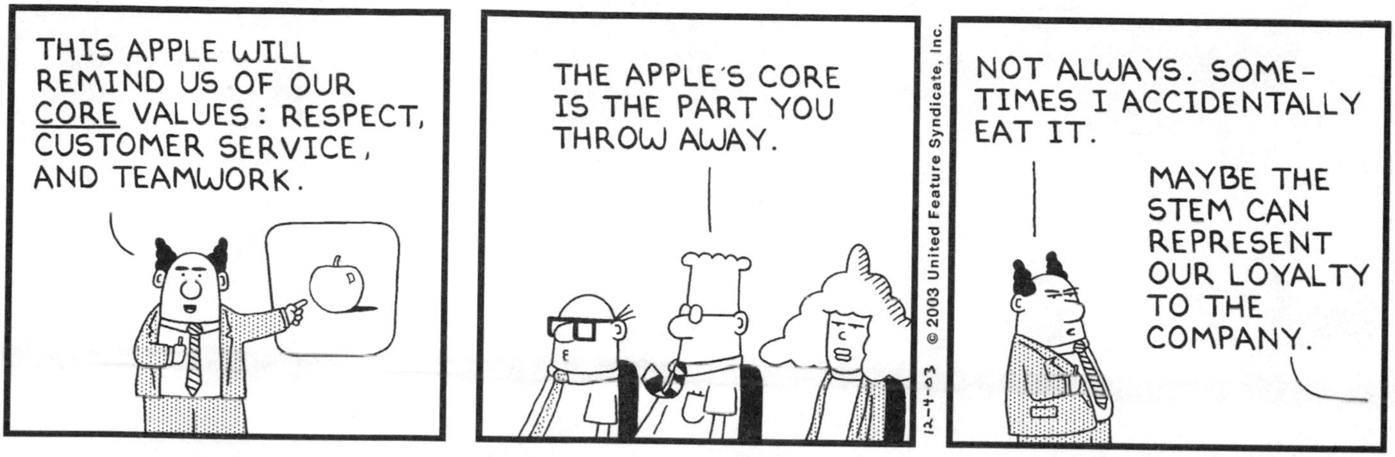
THIS APPLE WILL REMIND US OF OUR CORE VALUES: RESPECT, CUSTOMER SERVICE, AND TEAMWORK.
THE APPLE'S CORE IS THE PART YOU THROW AWAY.
NOT ALWAYS. SOMETIMES I ACCIDENTALLY EAT IT.
MAYBE THE STEM CAN REPRESENT OUR LOYALTY TO THE COMPANY.
12-4-03 © 2003 United Feature Syndicate, Inc.

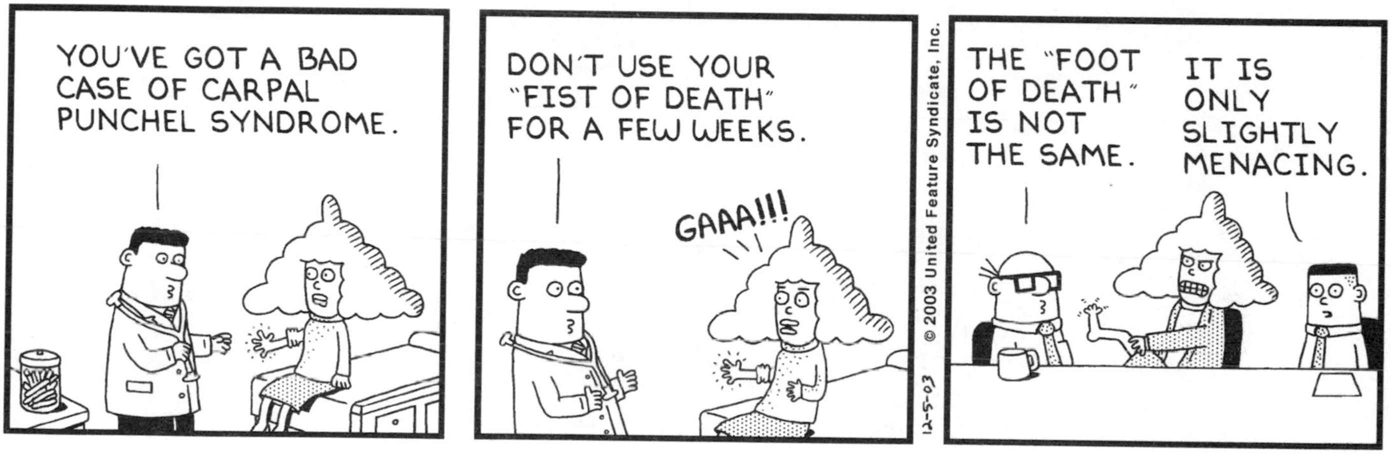
YOU'VE GOT A BAD CASE OF CARPAL PUNCHEL SYNDROME.
DON'T USE YOUR "FIST OF DEATH" FOR A FEW WEEKS.
GAAA!!!
THE "FOOT OF DEATH" IS NOT THE SAME.
IT IS ONLY SLIGHTLY MENACING.
12-5-03 © 2003 United Feature Syndicate, Inc.

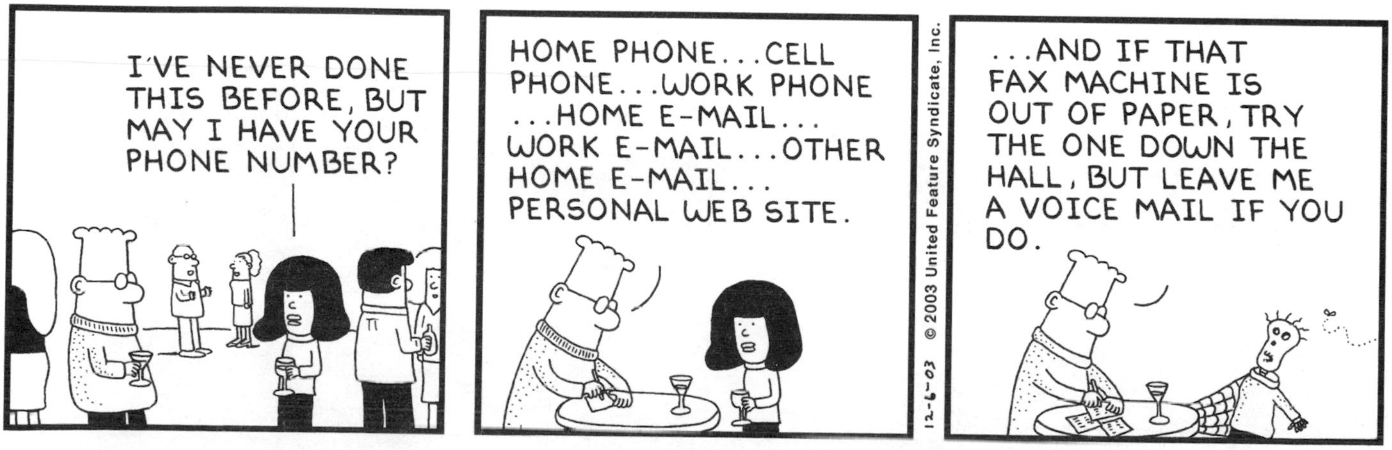
I'VE NEVER DONE THIS BEFORE, BUT MAY I HAVE YOUR PHONE NUMBER?
HOME PHONE...CELL PHONE...WORK PHONE ...HOME E-MAIL... WORK E-MAIL...OTHER HOME E-MAIL... PERSONAL WEB SITE.
...AND IF THAT FAX MACHINE IS OUT OF PAPER, TRY THE ONE DOWN THE HALL, BUT LEAVE ME A VOICE MAIL IF YOU DO.
12-6-03 © 2003 United Feature Syndicate, Inc.

MAY I MOVE TO ONE OF THE EMPTY CUBICLES?
THOSE ARE FULL-SIZE CUBICLES; INTERNS GET HALF-SIZE CUBICLES.
YES...ORDINARILY, BUT THERE ARE HUNDREDS OF VACANT CUBICLES BECAUSE OF DOWNSIZING.
I'M NOT FOLLOWING YOU.
THEY'RE EMPTY! THEY WILL NEVER BE OCCUPIED. I WANT TO USE ONE.
WE DON'T HAVE THE BUDGET TO TURN A FULL-SIZE CUBICLE INTO A HALF-SIZE CUBICLE JUST FOR YOU.
GAAA!!! THAT'S NOT WHAT I... NEVER MIND! FORGET IT!
FURTHERMORE, I DO NOT BELIEVE THIS IS A HALF-SIZE CUBICLE.
12-7-03 ©2003 United Feature Syndicate, Inc.

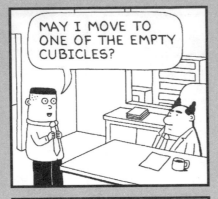

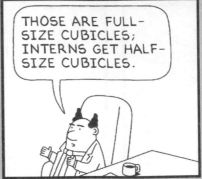

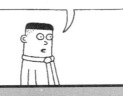

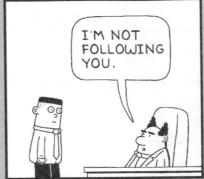

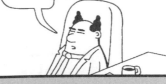

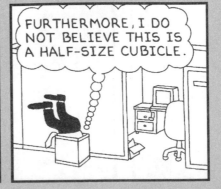

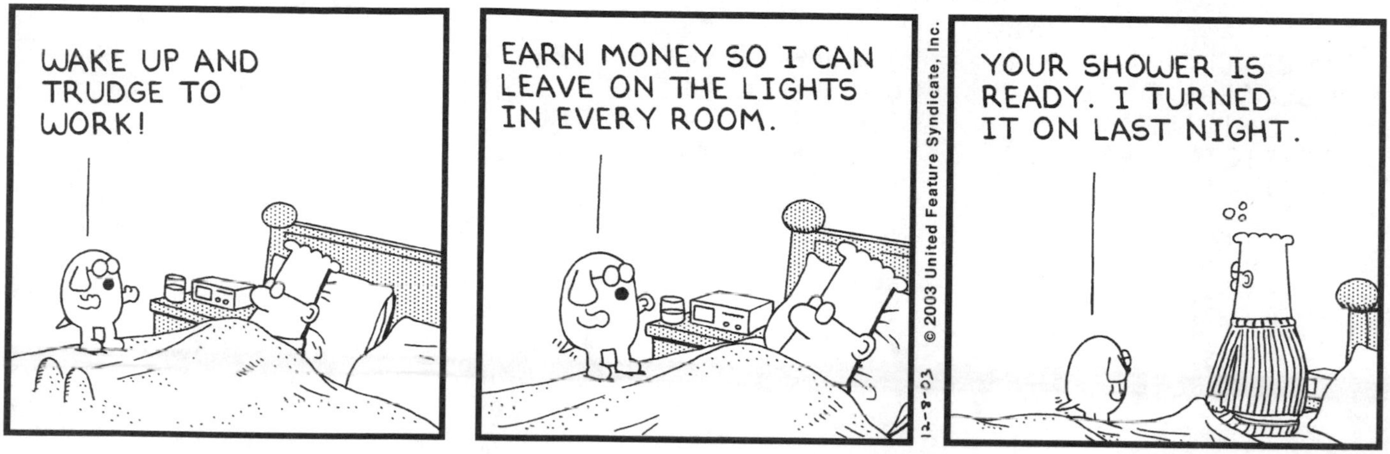
WAKE UP AND TRUDGE TO WORK!
EARN MONEY SO I CAN LEAVE ON THE LIGHTS IN EVERY ROOM.
12-8-03 © 2003 United Feature Syndicate, Inc.
YOUR SHOWER IS READY. I TURNED IT ON LAST NIGHT.

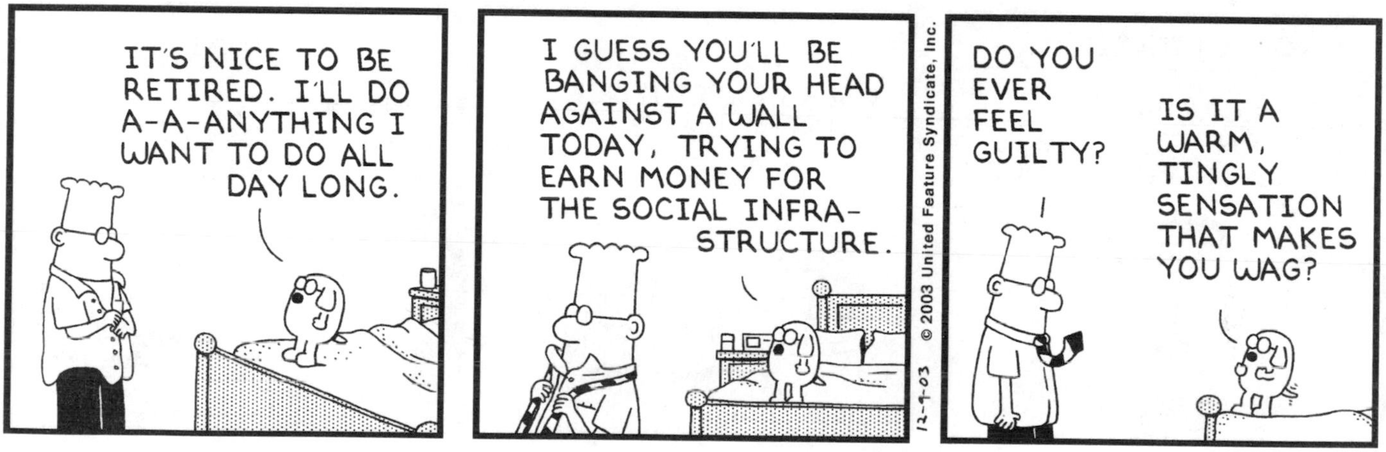
IT'S NICE TO BE RETIRED. I'LL DO A-A-ANYTHING I WANT TO DO ALL DAY LONG.
I GUESS YOU'LL BE BANGING YOUR HEAD AGAINST A WALL TODAY, TRYING TO EARN MONEY FOR THE SOCIAL INFRA-STRUCTURE.
12-9-03 © 2003 United Feature Syndicate, Inc.
DO YOU EVER FEEL GUILTY?
IS IT A WARM, TINGLY SENSATION THAT MAKES YOU WAG?

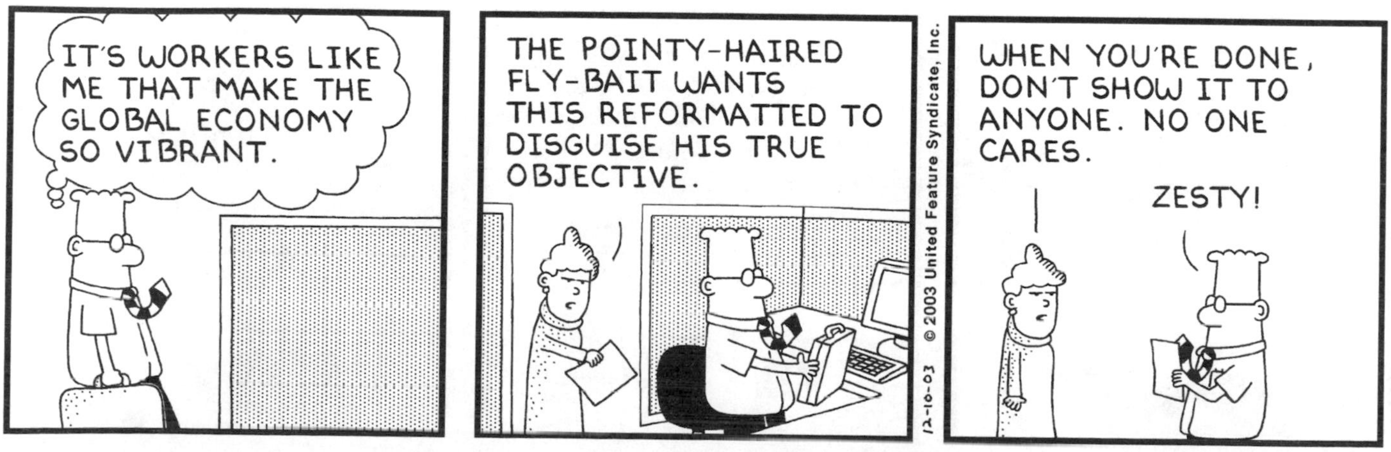
IT'S WORKERS LIKE ME THAT MAKE THE GLOBAL ECONOMY SO VIBRANT.
THE POINTY-HAIRED FLY-BAIT WANTS THIS REFORMATTED TO DISGUISE HIS TRUE OBJECTIVE.
12-10-03 © 2003 United Feature Syndicate, Inc.
WHEN YOU'RE DONE, DON'T SHOW IT TO ANYONE. NO ONE CARES.
ZESTY!

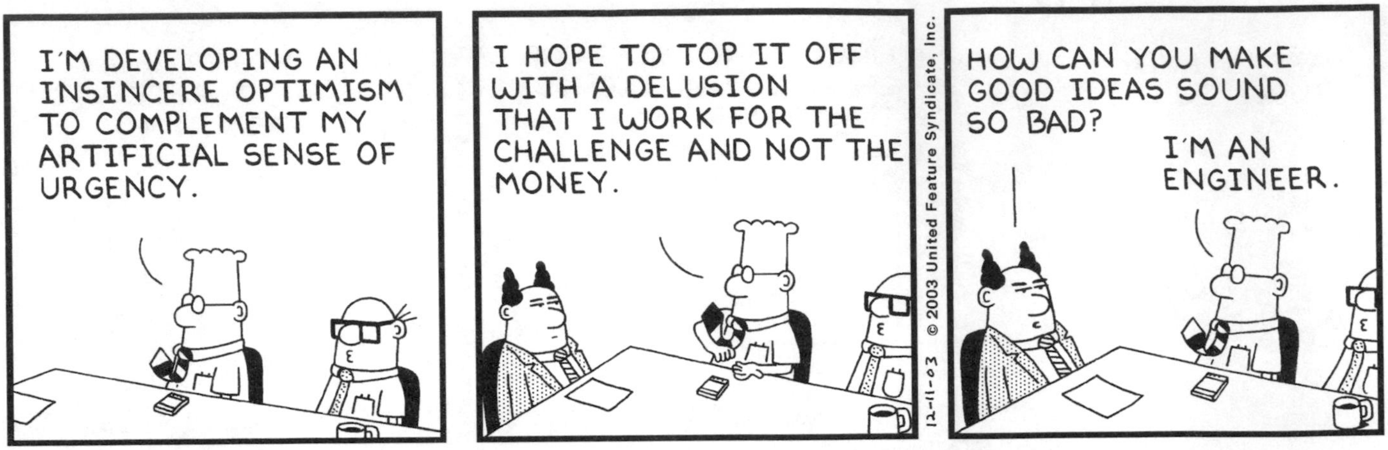
I'M DEVELOPING AN INSINCERE OPTIMISM TO COMPLEMENT MY ARTIFICIAL SENSE OF URGENCY.
I HOPE TO TOP IT OFF WITH A DELUSION THAT I WORK FOR THE CHALLENGE AND NOT THE MONEY.
12-11-03 © 2003 United Feature Syndicate, Inc.
HOW CAN YOU MAKE GOOD IDEAS SOUND SO BAD?
I'M AN ENGINEER.

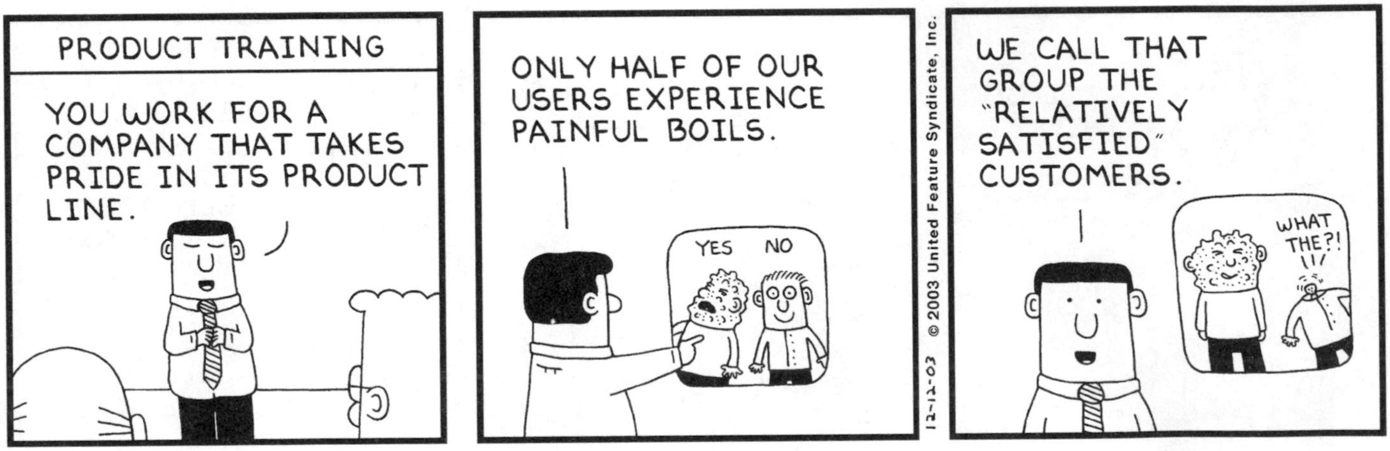
PRODUCT TRAINING
YOU WORK FOR A COMPANY THAT TAKES PRIDE IN ITS PRODUCT LINE.
ONLY HALF OF OUR USERS EXPERIENCE PAINFUL BOILS.
YES
NO
12-12-03 © 2003 United Feature Syndicate, Inc.
WE CALL THAT GROUP THE "RELATIVELY SATISFIED" CUSTOMERS.
WHAT THE?!

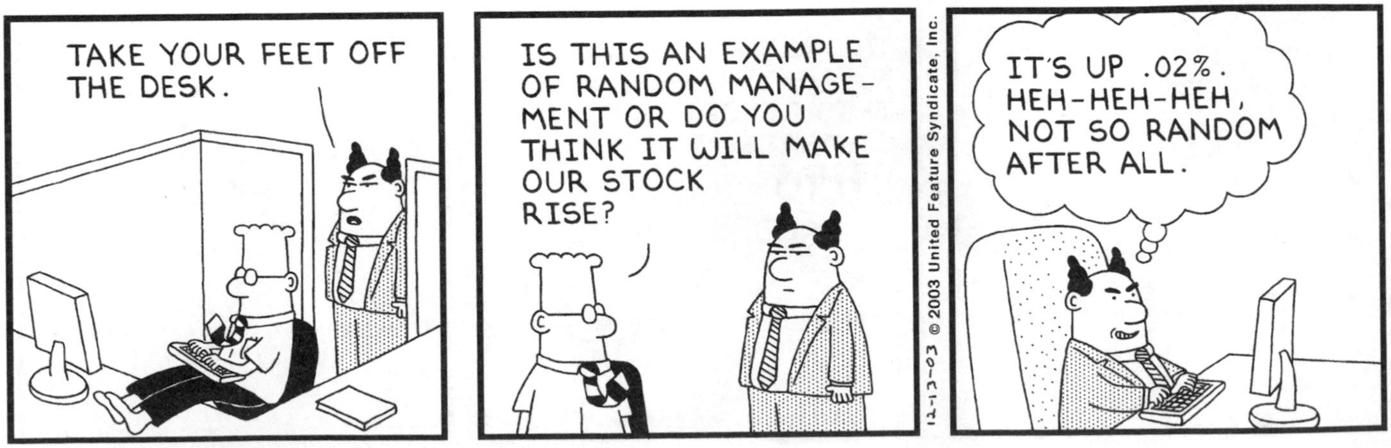
TAKE YOUR FEET OFF THE DESK.
IS THIS AN EXAMPLE OF RANDOM MANAGE-MENT OR DO YOU THINK IT WILL MAKE OUR STOCK RISE?
12-13-03 © 2003 United Feature Syndicate, Inc.
IT'S UP .02%. HEH-HEH-HEH, NOT SO RANDOM AFTER ALL.

IT'S TOTALLY BRILLIANT.
I MUST SHOW THIS TO OUR CREATIVE DEPARTMENT.
I DESIGNED A NEW LOGO FOR THE COMPANY. SEE WHAT YOU CAN DO WITH IT.
WELL, WELL, WELL, AN ENGINEERING MANAGER BECOMES AN ARTIST.
APPARENTLY I WASTED MY TIME GETTING A MASTER'S DEGREE IN GRAPHIC ARTS AND DESIGN.
ALL I NEEDED WAS A DULL PENCIL AND A SCRAP OF PAPER.
ART IS NOT THAT EASY, YOU ARROGANT PILE OF PERFECTLY SYMMETRICAL CRUD!!!
WHAT IF THE LOGO IS INSIDE A RECTANGLE?
SOB
12-14-03 © 2003 United Feature Syndicate, Inc.

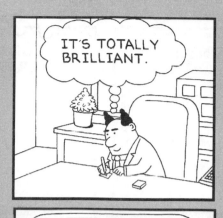

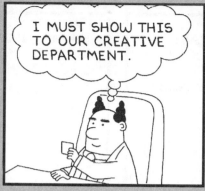

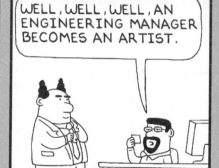

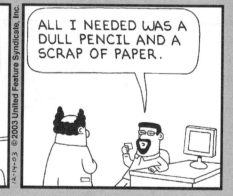

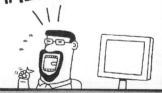

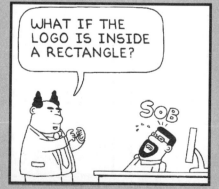

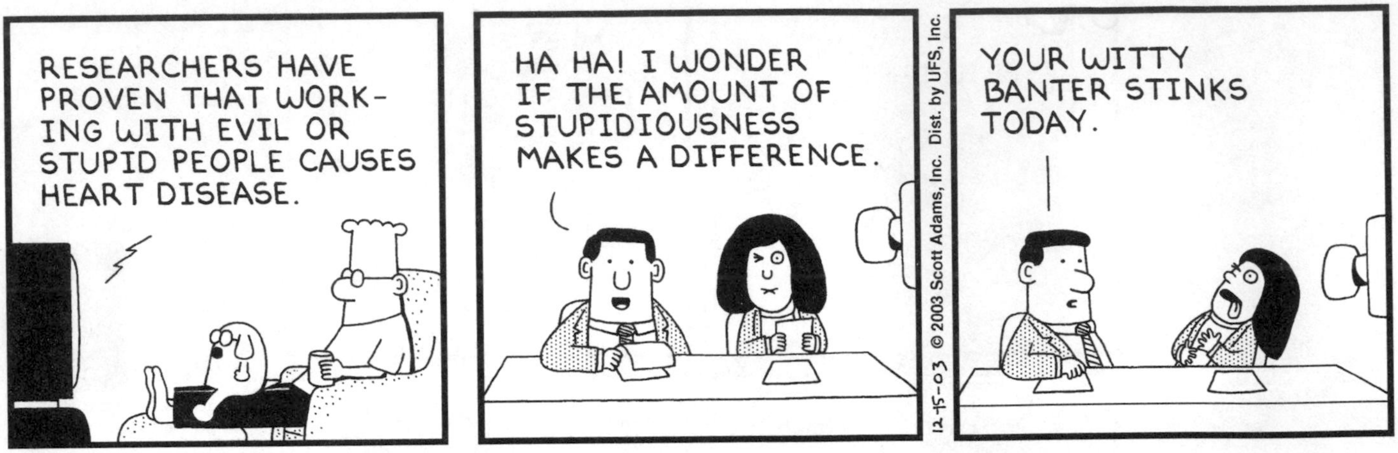
RESEARCHERS HAVE PROVEN THAT WORKING WITH EVIL OR STUPID PEOPLE CAUSES HEART DISEASE.
HA HA! I WONDER IF THE AMOUNT OF STUPIDIOUSNESS MAKES A DIFFERENCE.
12-15-03 © 2003 Scott Adams, Inc. Dist. by UFS, Inc.
YOUR WITTY BANTER STINKS TODAY.

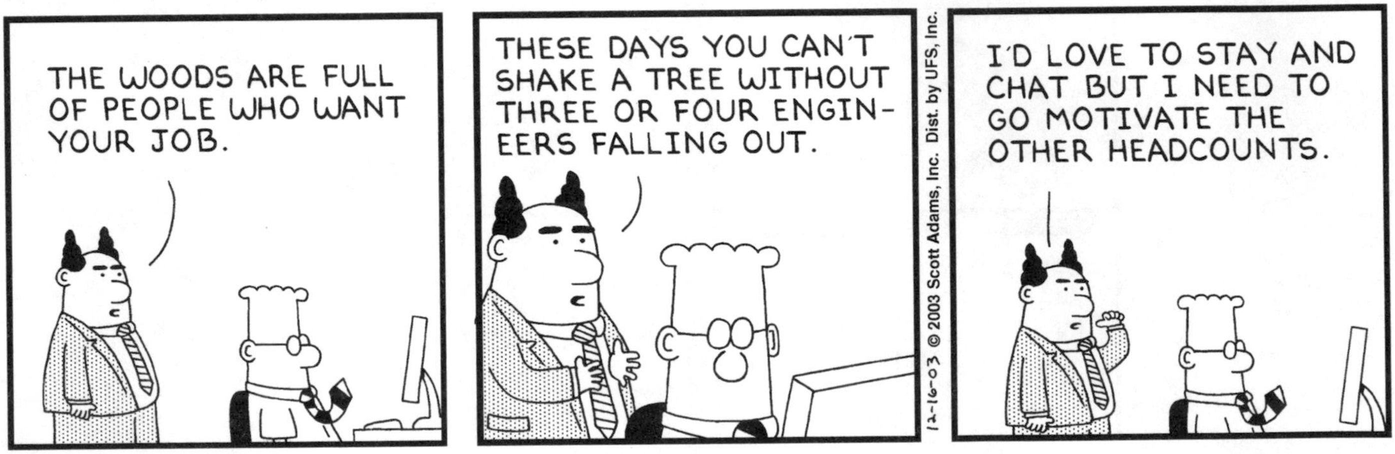
THE WOODS ARE FULL OF PEOPLE WHO WANT YOUR JOB.
THESE DAYS YOU CAN'T SHAKE A TREE WITHOUT THREE OR FOUR ENGINEERS FALLING OUT.
12-16-03 © 2003 Scott Adams, Inc. Dist. by UFS, Inc.
I'D LOVE TO STAY AND CHAT BUT I NEED TO GO MOTIVATE THE OTHER HEADCOUNTS.

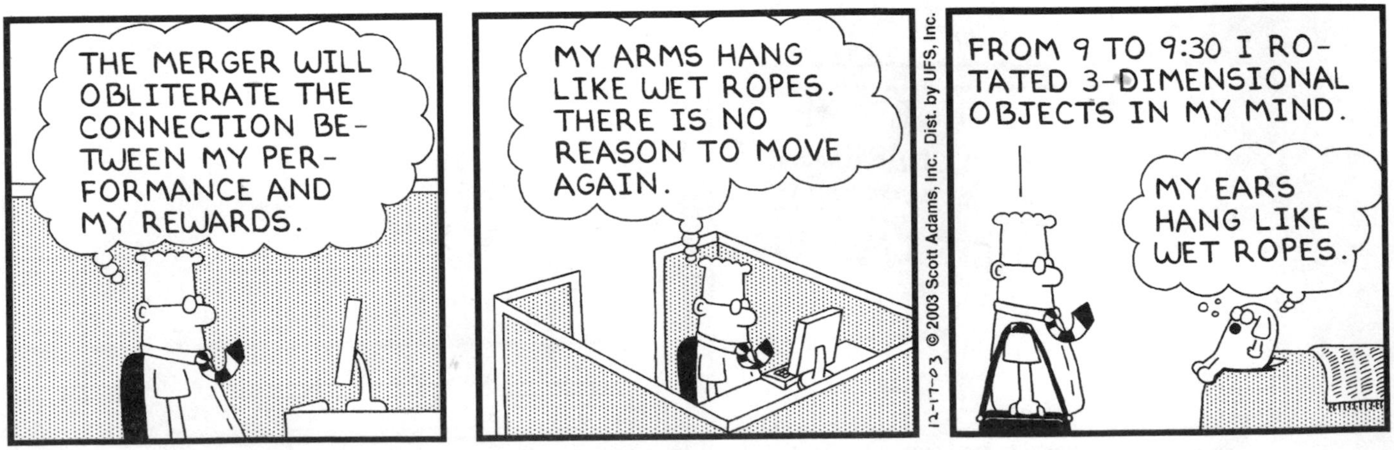
THE MERGER WILL OBLITERATE THE CONNECTION BETWEEN MY PERFORMANCE AND MY REWARDS.
MY ARMS HANG LIKE WET ROPES. THERE IS NO REASON TO MOVE AGAIN.
12-17-03 © 2003 Scott Adams, Inc. Dist. by UFS, Inc.
FROM 9 TO 9:30 I ROTATED 3-DIMENSIONAL OBJECTS IN MY MIND.
MY EARS HANG LIKE WET ROPES.

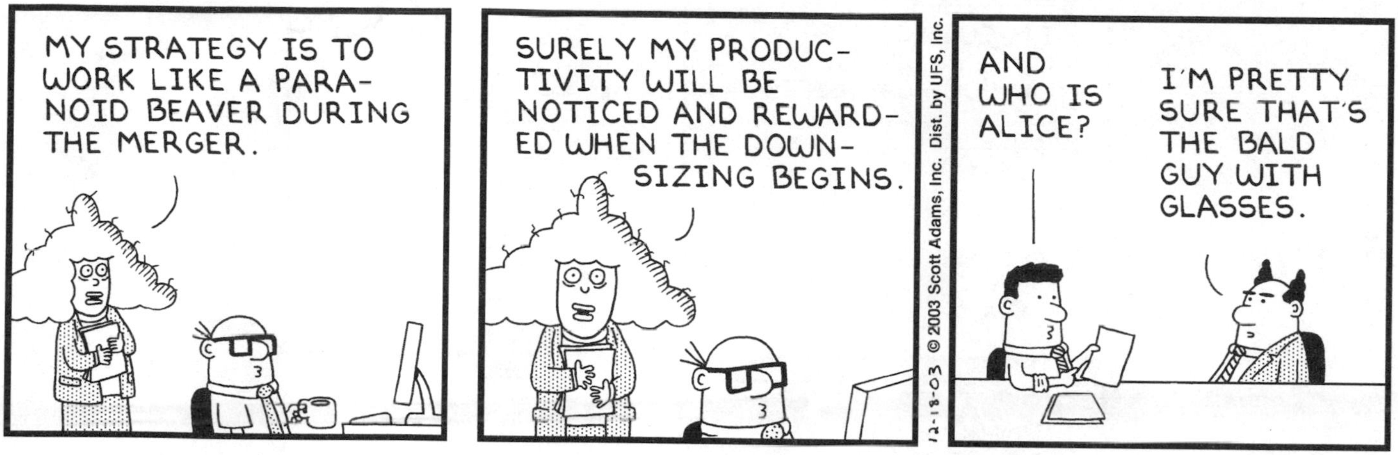
MY STRATEGY IS TO WORK LIKE A PARANOID BEAVER DURING THE MERGER.
SURELY MY PRODUCTIVITY WILL BE NOTICED AND REWARDED WHEN THE DOWNSIZING BEGINS.
12-18-03 © 2003 Scott Adams, Inc. Dist. by UFS, Inc.
AND WHO IS ALICE?
I'M PRETTY SURE THAT'S THE BALD GUY WITH GLASSES.

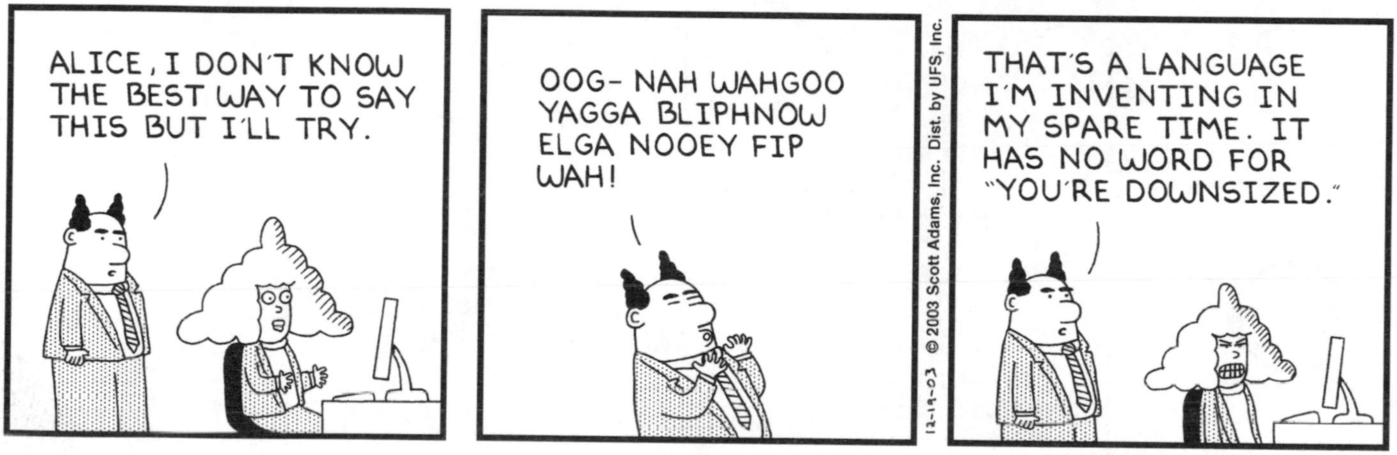
ALICE, I DON'T KNOW THE BEST WAY TO SAY THIS BUT I'LL TRY.
OOG- NAH WAHGOO YAGGA BLIPHNOW ELGA NOOEY FIP WAH!
12-19-03 © 2003 Scott Adams, Inc. Dist. by UFS, Inc.
THAT'S A LANGUAGE I'M INVENTING IN MY SPARE TIME. IT HAS NO WORD FOR "YOU'RE DOWNSIZED."

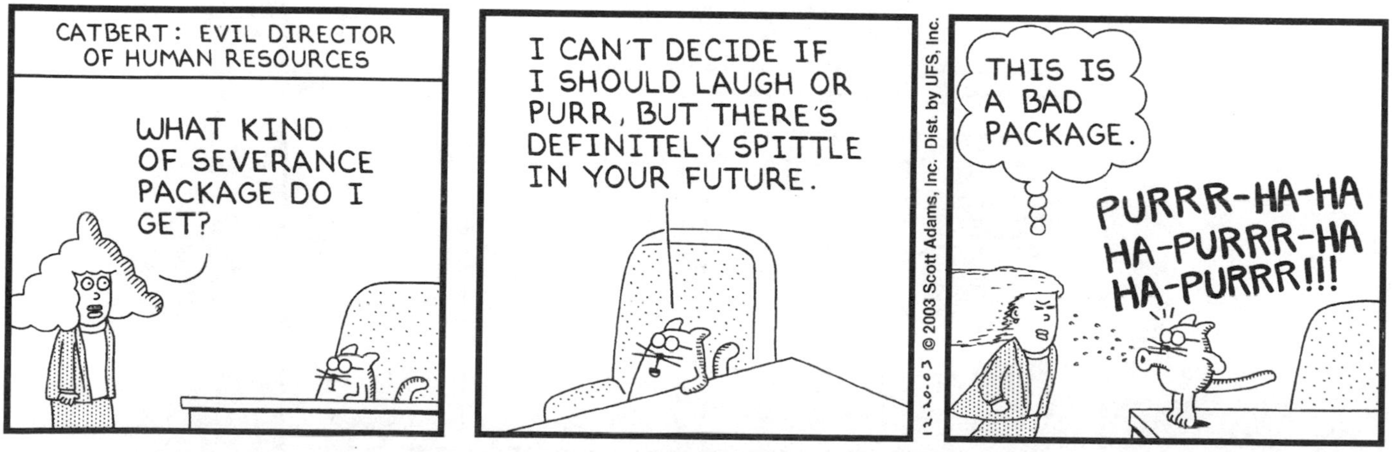
CATBERT: EVIL DIRECTOR OF HUMAN RESOURCES
WHAT KIND OF SEVERANCE PACKAGE DO I GET?
I CAN'T DECIDE IF I SHOULD LAUGH OR PURR, BUT THERE'S DEFINITELY SPITTLE IN YOUR FUTURE.
12-20-03 © 2003 Scott Adams, Inc. Dist. by UFS, Inc.
THIS IS A BAD PACKAGE.
PURRR-HA-HA HA-PURRR-HA HA-PURRR!!!

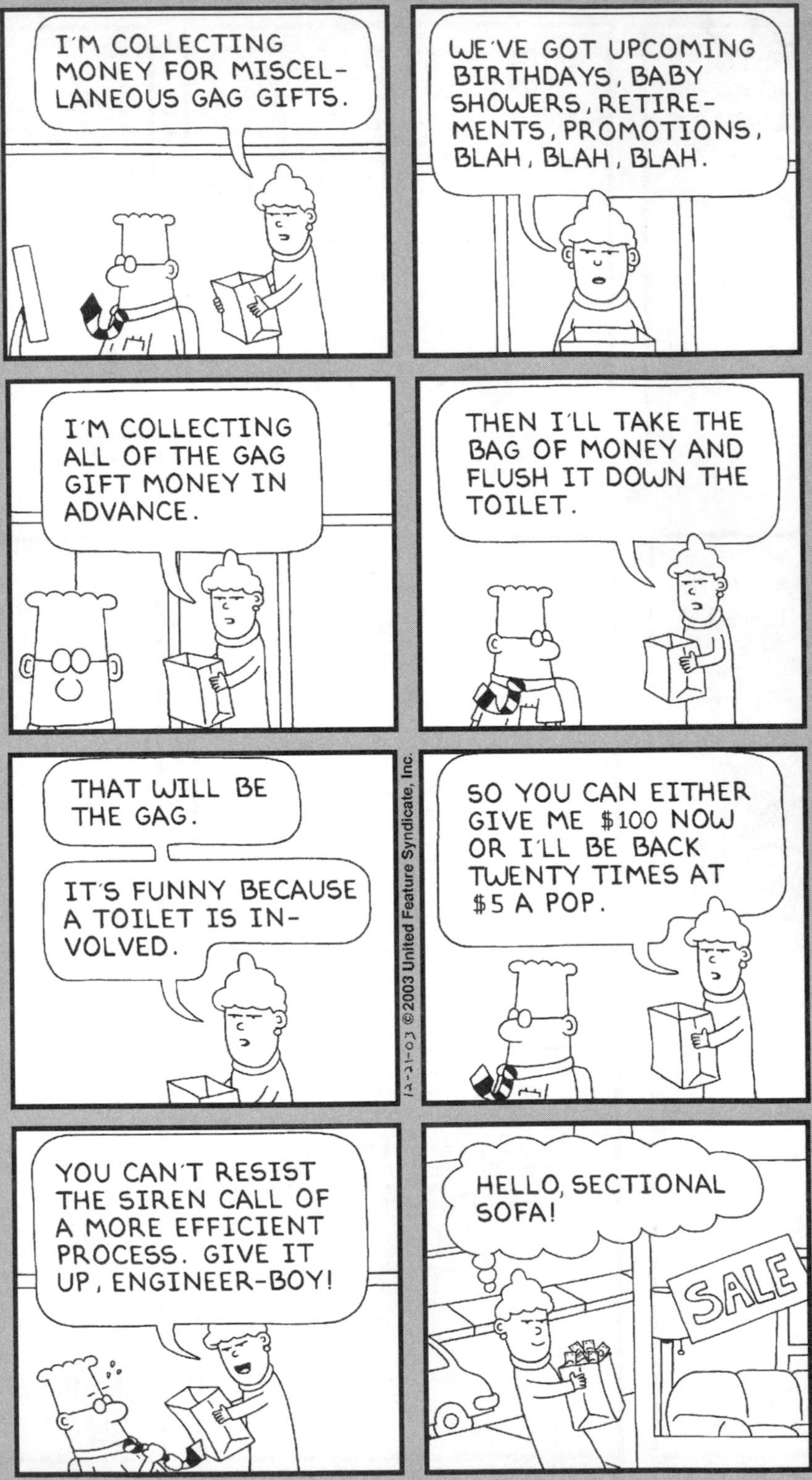
I'M COLLECTING MONEY FOR MISCELLANEOUS GAG GIFTS.
WE'VE GOT UPCOMING BIRTHDAYS, BABY SHOWERS, RETIREMENTS, PROMOTIONS, BLAH, BLAH, BLAH.
I'M COLLECTING ALL OF THE GAG GIFT MONEY IN ADVANCE.
THEN I'LL TAKE THE BAG OF MONEY AND FLUSH IT DOWN THE TOILET.
THAT WILL BE THE GAG.
IT'S FUNNY BECAUSE A TOILET IS INVOLVED.
12-31-03 © 2003 United Feature Syndicate, Inc.
SO YOU CAN EITHER GIVE ME $100 NOW OR I'LL BE BACK TWENTY TIMES AT $5 A POP.
YOU CAN'T RESIST THE SIREN CALL OF A MORE EFFICIENT PROCESS. GIVE IT UP, ENGINEER-BOY!
HELLO, SECTIONAL SOFA!
SALE

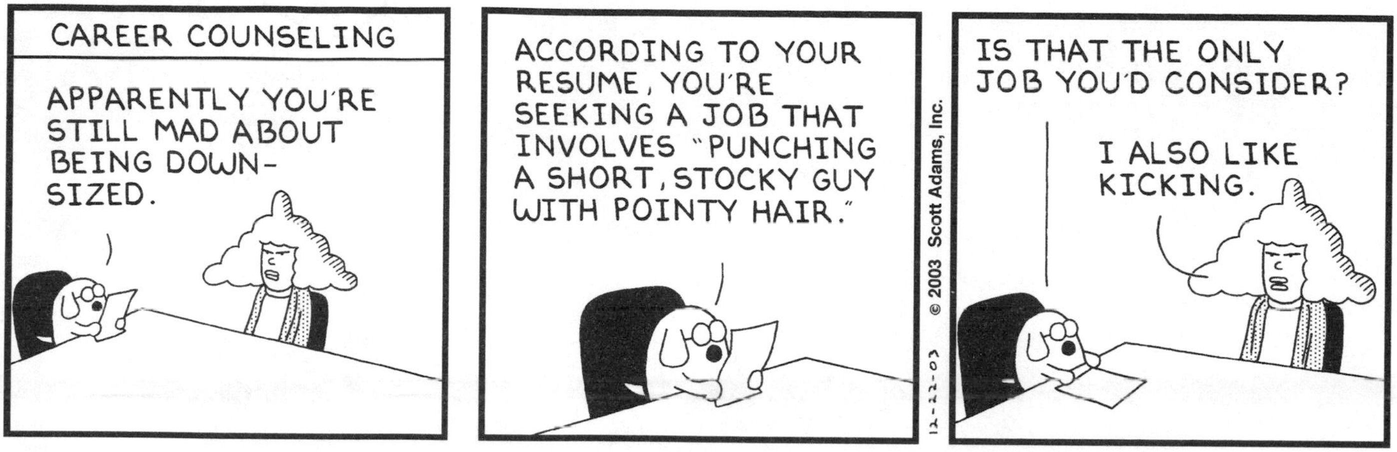
CAREER COUNSELING
APPARENTLY YOU'RE STILL MAD ABOUT BEING DOWN-SIZED.
ACCORDING TO YOUR RESUME, YOU'RE SEEKING A JOB THAT INVOLVES "PUNCHING A SHORT, STOCKY GUY WITH POINTY HAIR."
12-22-03 © 2003 Scott Adams, Inc.
IS THAT THE ONLY JOB YOU'D CONSIDER?
I ALSO LIKE KICKING.

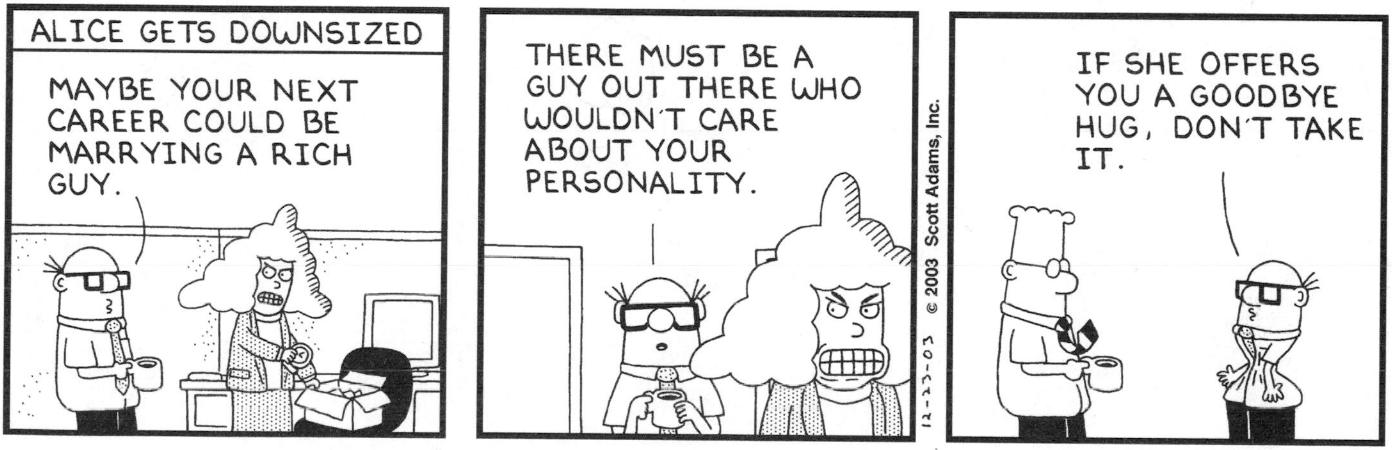
ALICE GETS DOWNSIZED
MAYBE YOUR NEXT CAREER COULD BE MARRYING A RICH GUY.
THERE MUST BE A GUY OUT THERE WHO WOULDN'T CARE ABOUT YOUR PERSONALITY.
12-23-03 © 2003 Scott Adams, Inc.
IF SHE OFFERS YOU A GOODBYE HUG, DON'T TAKE IT.

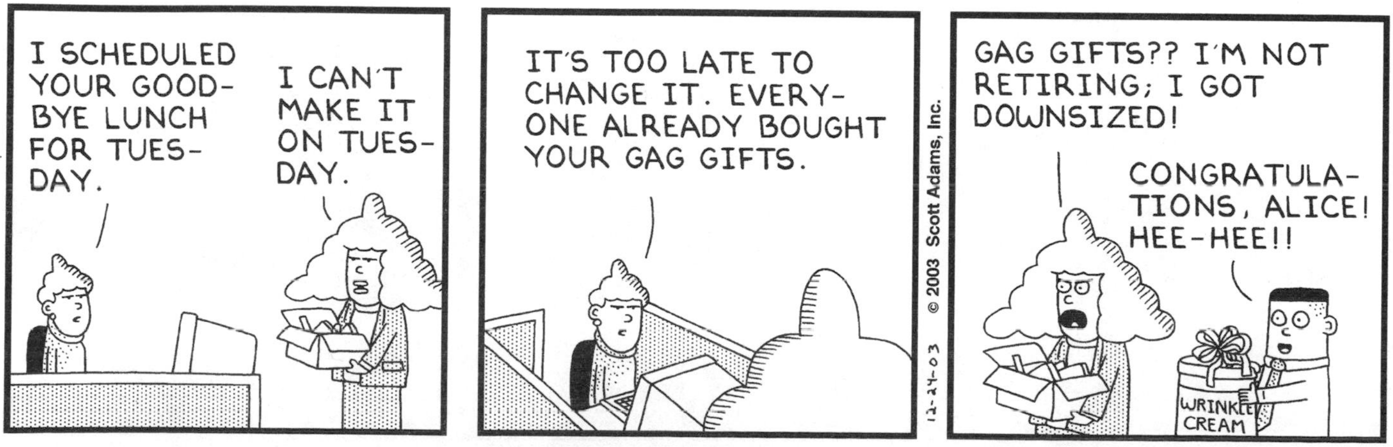
I SCHEDULED YOUR GOOD-BYE LUNCH FOR TUES-DAY.
I CAN'T MAKE IT ON TUES-DAY.
IT'S TOO LATE TO CHANGE IT. EVERY-ONE ALREADY BOUGHT YOUR GAG GIFTS.
12-24-03 © 2003 Scott Adams, Inc.
GAG GIFTS?? I'M NOT RETIRING; I GOT DOWNSIZED!
CONGRATULA-TIONS, ALICE! HEE-HEE!!
WRINKLE CREAM

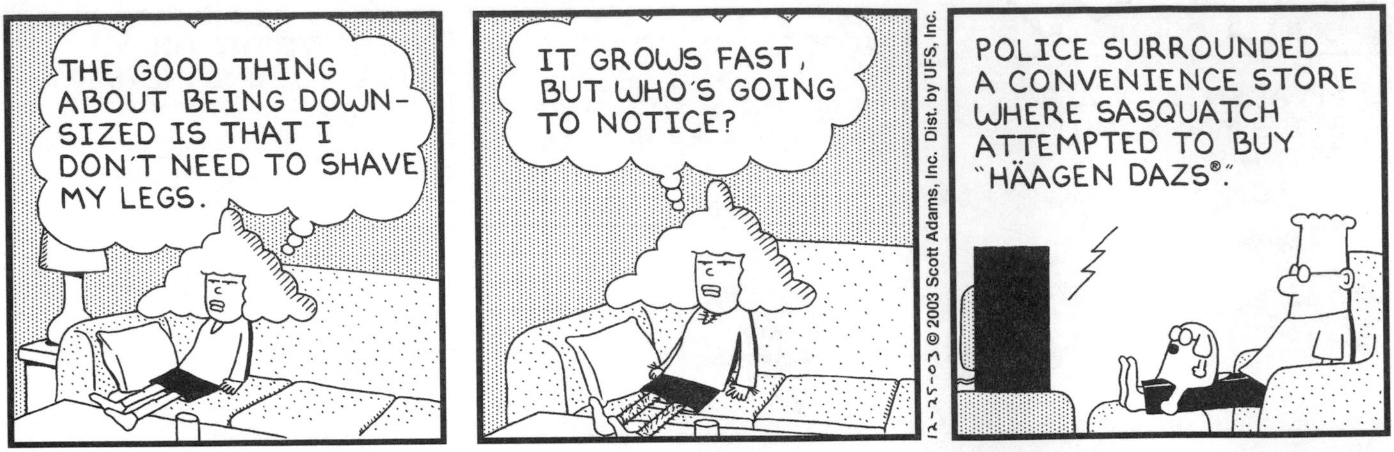
THE GOOD THING ABOUT BEING DOWN-SIZED IS THAT I DON'T NEED TO SHAVE MY LEGS.
IT GROWS FAST, BUT WHO'S GOING TO NOTICE?
POLICE SURROUNDED A CONVENIENCE STORE WHERE SASQUATCH ATTEMPTED TO BUY "HÄAGEN DAZS®."
12-25-03 © 2003 Scott Adams, Inc. Dist. by UFS, Inc.

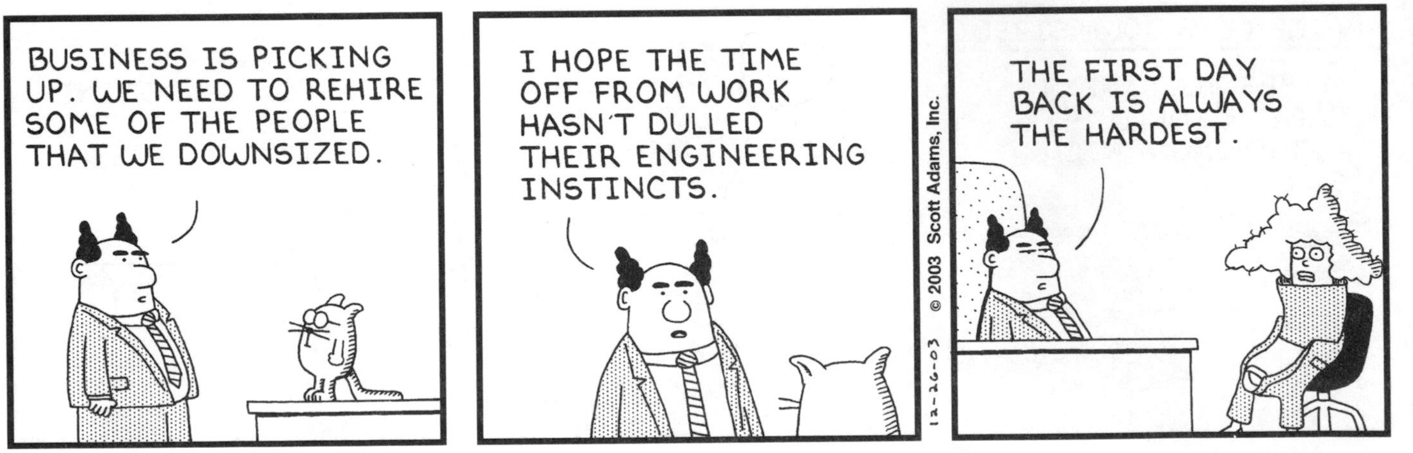
BUSINESS IS PICKING UP. WE NEED TO REHIRE SOME OF THE PEOPLE THAT WE DOWNSIZED.
I HOPE THE TIME OFF FROM WORK HASN'T DULLED THEIR ENGINEERING INSTINCTS.
THE FIRST DAY BACK IS ALWAYS THE HARDEST.
12-26-03 © 2003 Scott Adams, Inc.

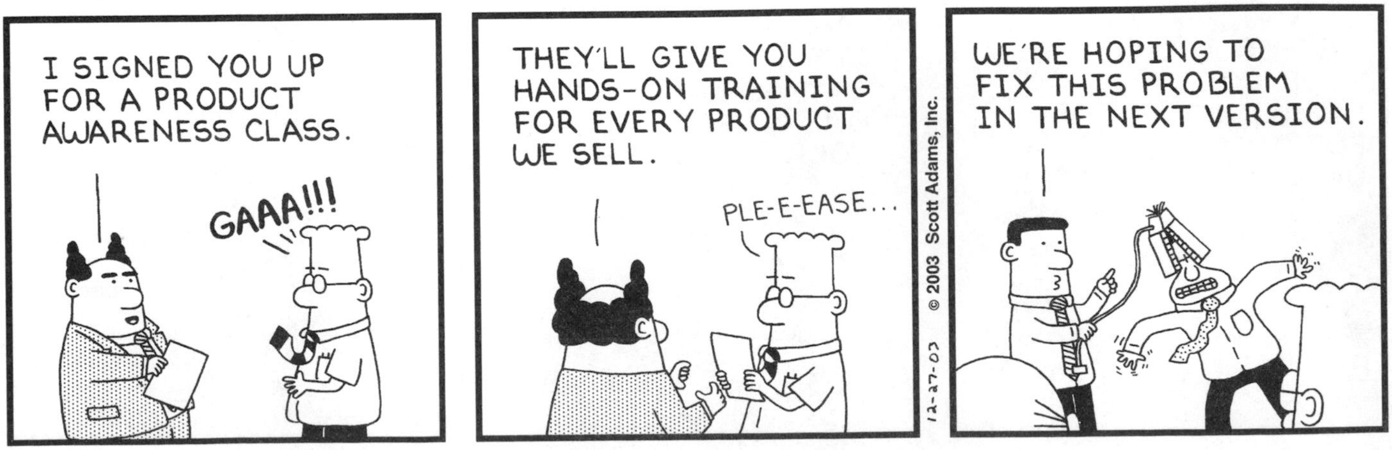
I SIGNED YOU UP FOR A PRODUCT AWARENESS CLASS.
GAAA!!!
THEY'LL GIVE YOU HANDS-ON TRAINING FOR EVERY PRODUCT WE SELL.
PLE-E-EASE...
WE'RE HOPING TO FIX THIS PROBLEM IN THE NEXT VERSION.
12-27-03 © 2003 Scott Adams, Inc.

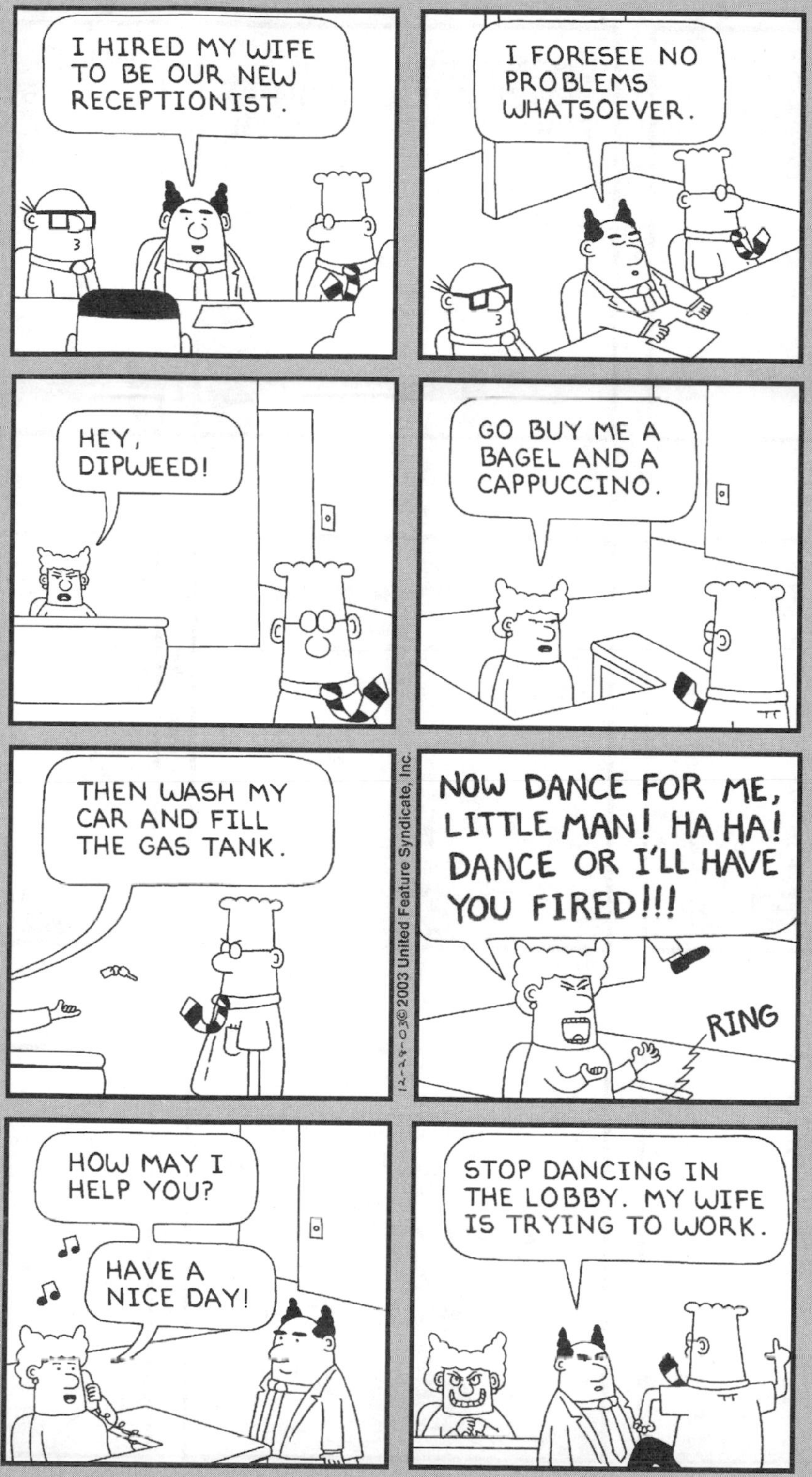
I HIRED MY WIFE TO BE OUR NEW RECEPTIONIST.
I FORESEE NO PROBLEMS WHATSOEVER.
HEY, DIPWEED!
GO BUY ME A BAGEL AND A CAPPUCCINO.
THEN WASH MY CAR AND FILL THE GAS TANK.
NOW DANCE FOR ME, LITTLE MAN! HA HA! DANCE OR I'LL HAVE YOU FIRED!!!
RING
HOW MAY I HELP YOU?
HAVE A NICE DAY!
STOP DANCING IN THE LOBBY. MY WIFE IS TRYING TO WORK.
12-28-03 ©2003 United Feature Syndicate, Inc.

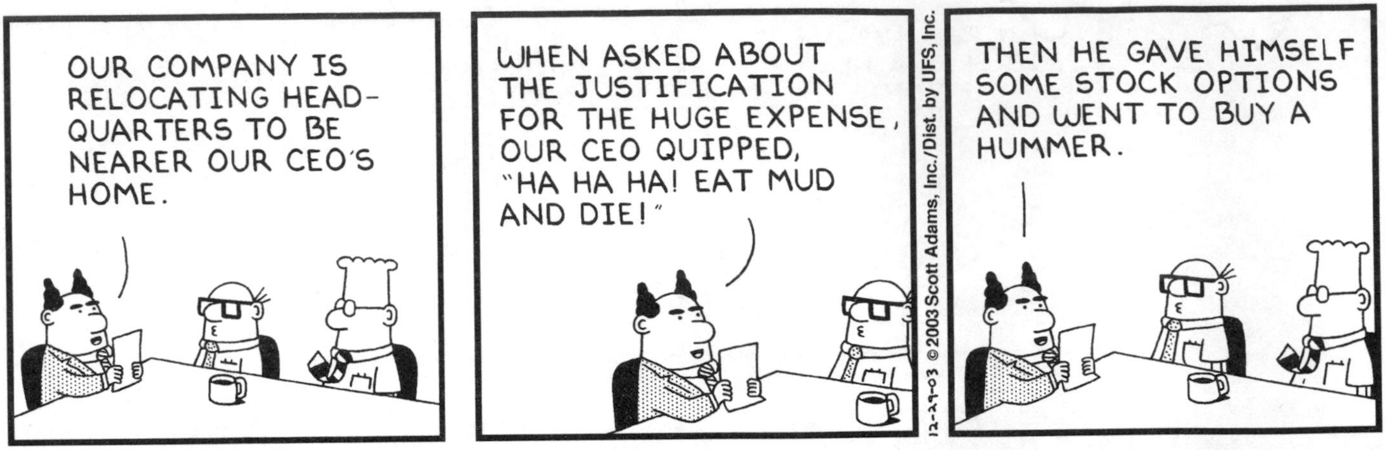
OUR COMPANY IS RELOCATING HEAD-QUARTERS TO BE NEARER OUR CEO'S HOME.
WHEN ASKED ABOUT THE JUSTIFICATION FOR THE HUGE EXPENSE, OUR CEO QUIPPED, "HA HA HA! EAT MUD AND DIE!"
THEN HE GAVE HIMSELF SOME STOCK OPTIONS AND WENT TO BUY A HUMMER.
12-29-03 © 2003 Scott Adams, Inc./Dist. by UFS, Inc.

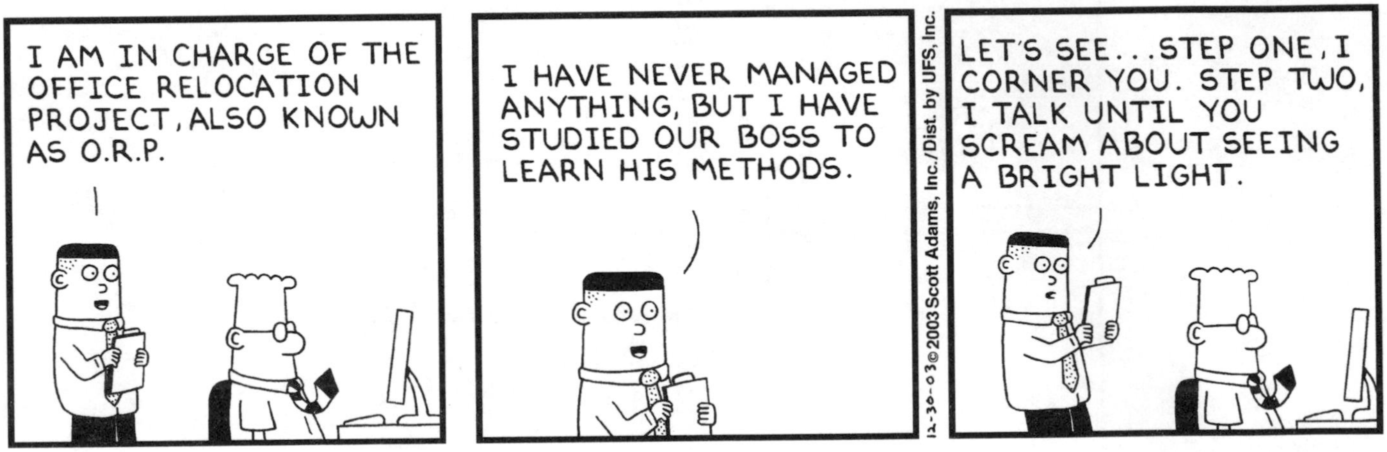
I AM IN CHARGE OF THE OFFICE RELOCATION PROJECT, ALSO KNOWN AS O.R.P.
I HAVE NEVER MANAGED ANYTHING, BUT I HAVE STUDIED OUR BOSS TO LEARN HIS METHODS.
LET'S SEE...STEP ONE, I CORNER YOU. STEP TWO, I TALK UNTIL YOU SCREAM ABOUT SEEING A BRIGHT LIGHT.
12-30-03 © 2003 Scott Adams, Inc./Dist. by UFS, Inc.

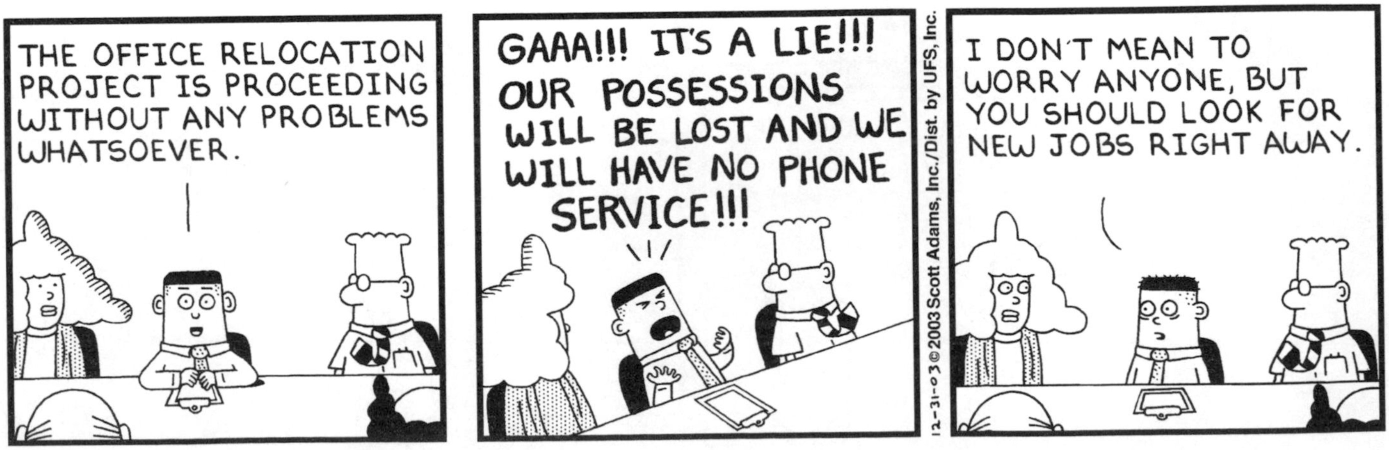
THE OFFICE RELOCATION PROJECT IS PROCEEDING WITHOUT ANY PROBLEMS WHATSOEVER.
GAAA!!! IT'S A LIE!!! OUR POSSESSIONS WILL BE LOST AND WE WILL HAVE NO PHONE SERVICE!!!
I DON'T MEAN TO WORRY ANYONE, BUT YOU SHOULD LOOK FOR NEW JOBS RIGHT AWAY.
12-31-03 © 2003 Scott Adams, Inc./Dist. by UFS, Inc.

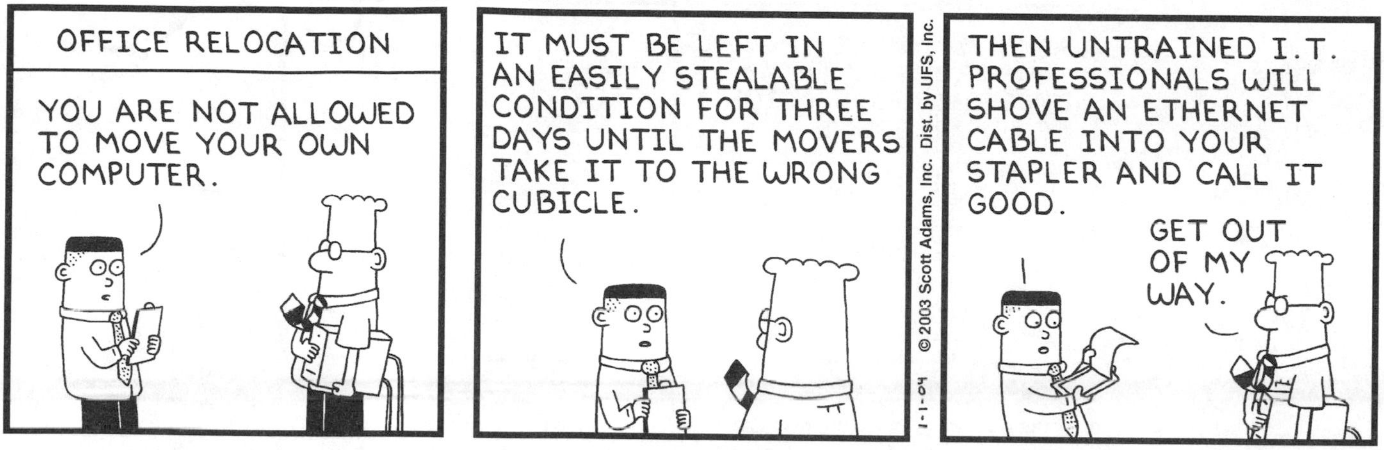
OFFICE RELOCATION
YOU ARE NOT ALLOWED TO MOVE YOUR OWN COMPUTER.
IT MUST BE LEFT IN AN EASILY STEALABLE CONDITION FOR THREE DAYS UNTIL THE MOVERS TAKE IT TO THE WRONG CUBICLE.
1-1-04
© 2003 Scott Adams, Inc. Dist. by UFS, Inc.
THEN UNTRAINED I.T. PROFESSIONALS WILL SHOVE AN ETHERNET CABLE INTO YOUR STAPLER AND CALL IT GOOD.
GET OUT OF MY WAY.

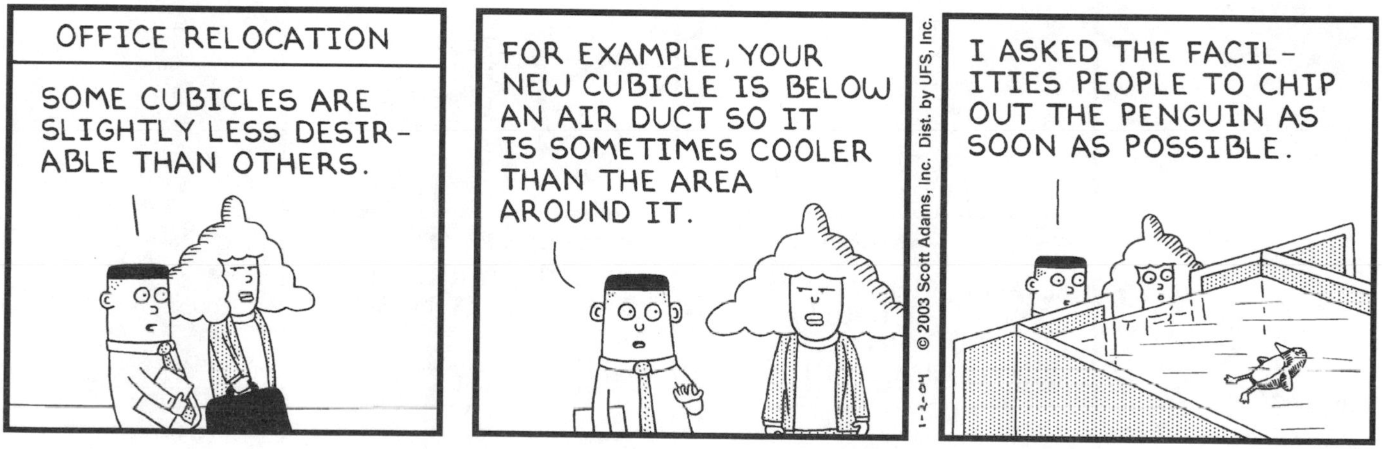
OFFICE RELOCATION
SOME CUBICLES ARE SLIGHTLY LESS DESIRABLE THAN OTHERS.
FOR EXAMPLE, YOUR NEW CUBICLE IS BELOW AN AIR DUCT SO IT IS SOMETIMES COOLER THAN THE AREA AROUND IT.
1-2-04
© 2003 Scott Adams, Inc. Dist. by UFS, Inc.
I ASKED THE FACILITIES PEOPLE TO CHIP OUT THE PENGUIN AS SOON AS POSSIBLE.

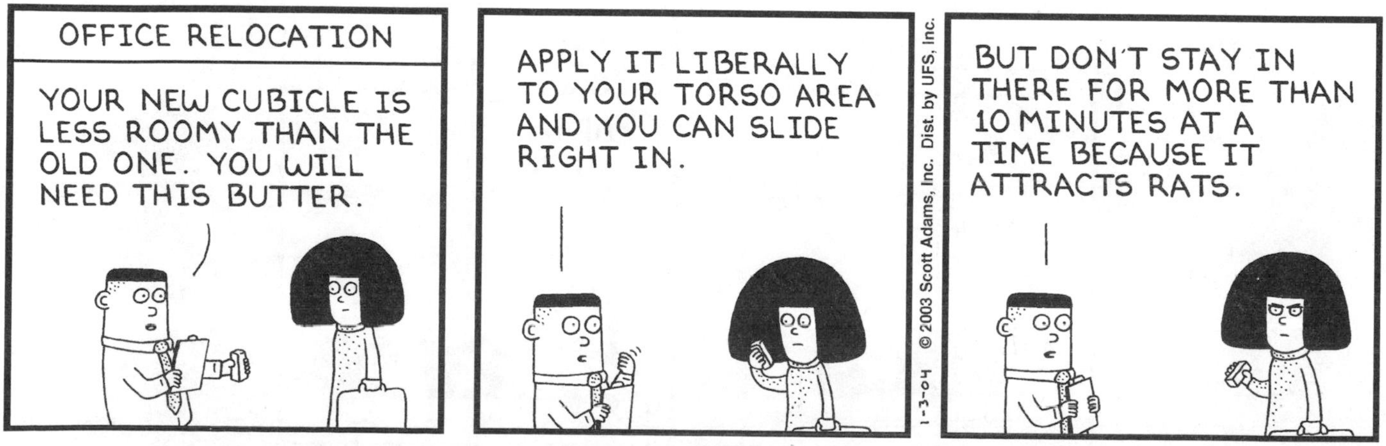
OFFICE RELOCATION
YOUR NEW CUBICLE IS LESS ROOMY THAN THE OLD ONE. YOU WILL NEED THIS BUTTER.
APPLY IT LIBERALLY TO YOUR TORSO AREA AND YOU CAN SLIDE RIGHT IN.
1-3-04
© 2003 Scott Adams, Inc. Dist. by UFS, Inc.
BUT DON'T STAY IN THERE FOR MORE THAN 10 MINUTES AT A TIME BECAUSE IT ATTRACTS RATS.

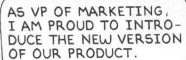

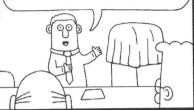

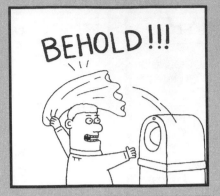

AS VP OF MARKETING, I AM PROUD TO INTRODUCE THE NEW VERSION OF OUR PRODUCT.
BEHOLD!!!
THIS IS A TESTAMENT TO WHAT CAN HAPPEN WHEN YOU LISTEN TO CUSTOMERS.
WE ASKED CUSTOMERS WHAT THEY WANTED THE NEW VERSION TO DO.
SIX MONTHS AGO I GAVE THAT RAW DATA TO YOU ENGINEERS. TODAY WE SEE THE RESULT.
IT'S THE FIRST TIME I'VE SEEN IT MYSELF.
WHAT'S IT DO?
BAM!!
OUR CUSTOMERS SAID THEY HATE US.
SPIT
© 2003 United Feature Syndicate, Inc.
1-4-04

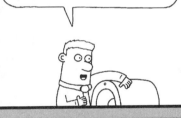

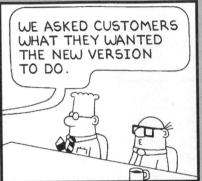

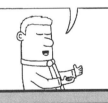

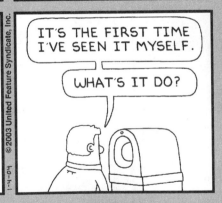

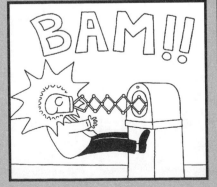

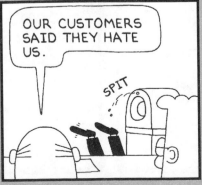

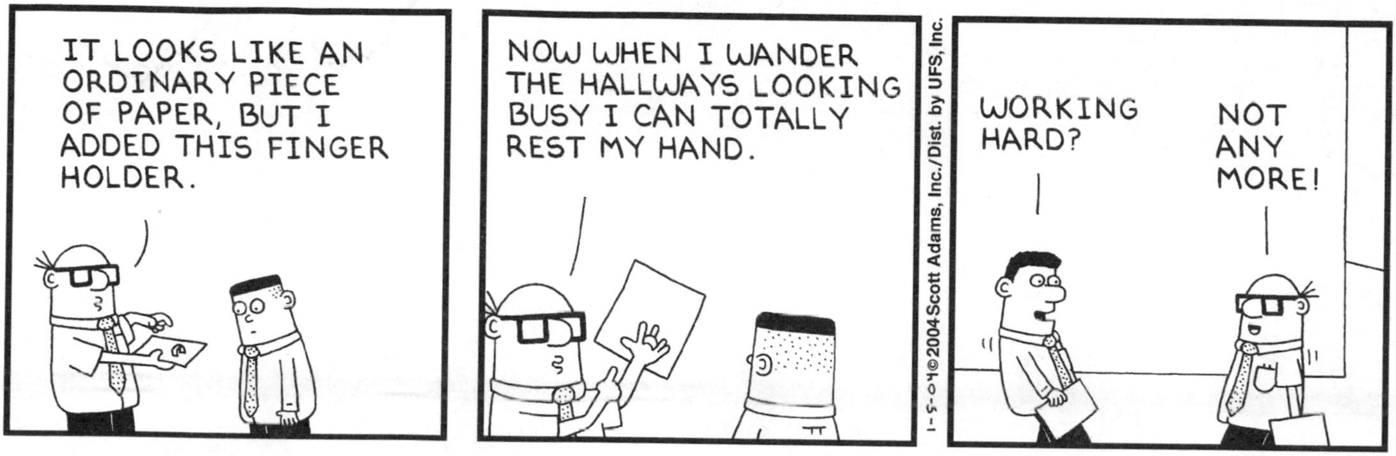
IT LOOKS LIKE AN ORDINARY PIECE OF PAPER, BUT I ADDED THIS FINGER HOLDER.
NOW WHEN I WANDER THE HALLWAYS LOOKING BUSY I CAN TOTALLY REST MY HAND.
1-5-04 ©2004 Scott Adams, Inc./Dist. by UFS, Inc.
WORKING HARD?
NOT ANY MORE!

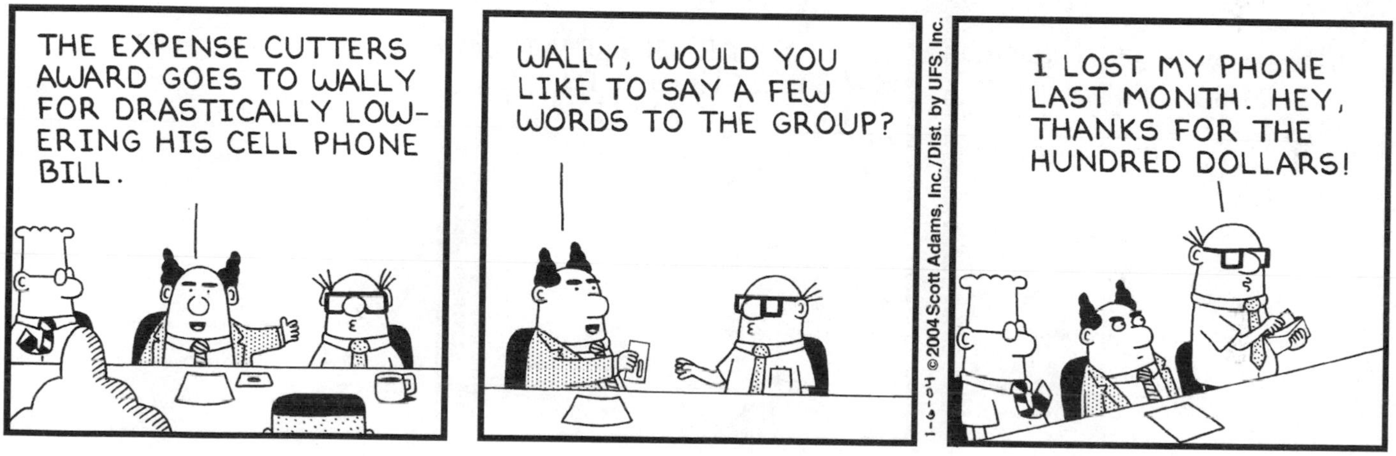
THE EXPENSE CUTTERS AWARD GOES TO WALLY FOR DRASTICALLY LOWERING HIS CELL PHONE BILL.
WALLY, WOULD YOU LIKE TO SAY A FEW WORDS TO THE GROUP?
1-6-04 © 2004 Scott Adams, Inc./Dist. by UFS, Inc.
I LOST MY PHONE LAST MONTH. HEY, THANKS FOR THE HUNDRED DOLLARS!

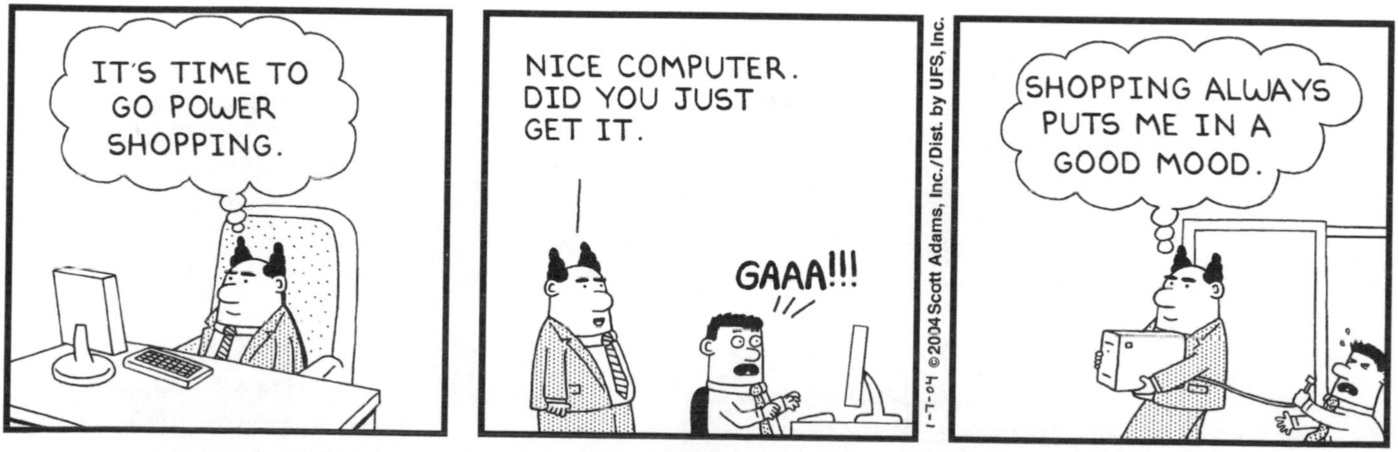
IT'S TIME TO GO POWER SHOPPING.
NICE COMPUTER. DID YOU JUST GET IT.
GAAA!!!
1-7-04 ©2004 Scott Adams, Inc./Dist. by UFS, Inc.
SHOPPING ALWAYS PUTS ME IN A GOOD MOOD.

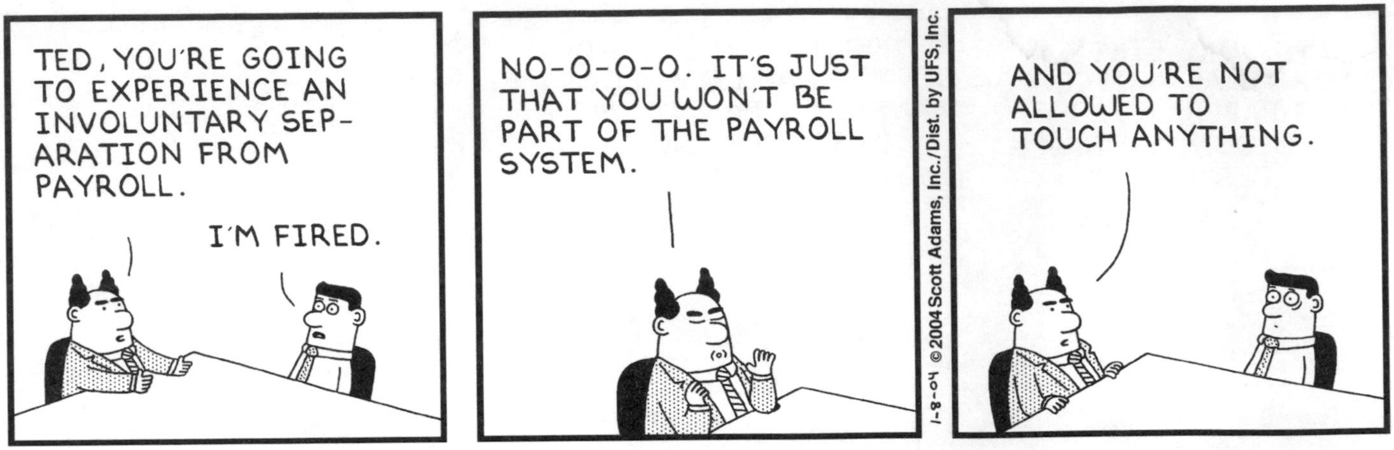
TED, YOU'RE GOING TO EXPERIENCE AN INVOLUNTARY SEPARATION FROM PAYROLL.
I'M FIRED.
NO-O-O-O. IT'S JUST THAT YOU WON'T BE PART OF THE PAYROLL SYSTEM.
AND YOU'RE NOT ALLOWED TO TOUCH ANYTHING.

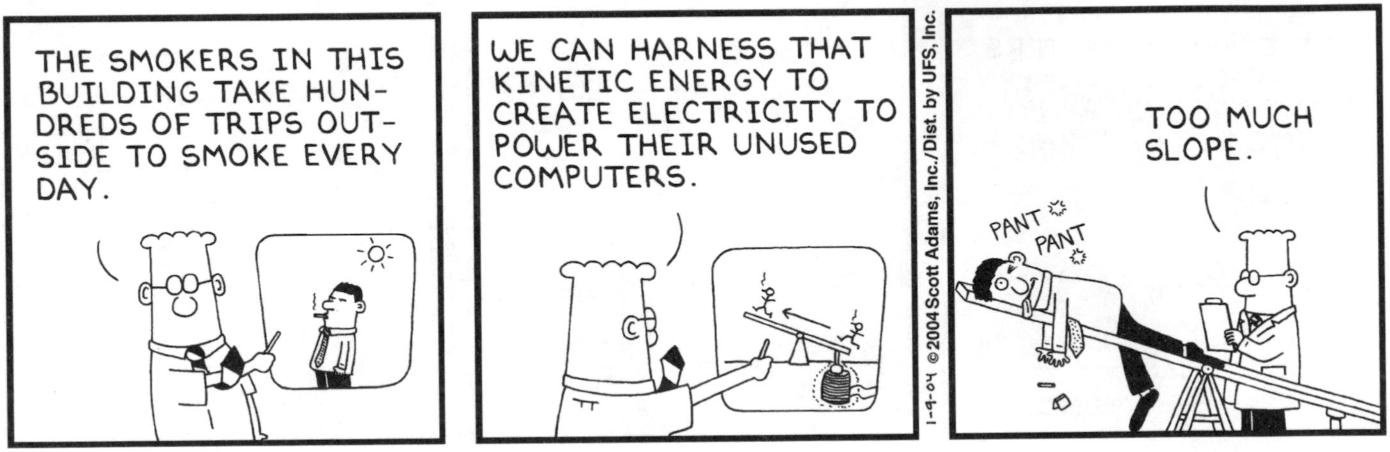
THE SMOKERS IN THIS BUILDING TAKE HUNDREDS OF TRIPS OUTSIDE TO SMOKE EVERY DAY.
WE CAN HARNESS THAT KINETIC ENERGY TO CREATE ELECTRICITY TO POWER THEIR UNUSED COMPUTERS.
PANT
PANT
TOO MUCH SLOPE.

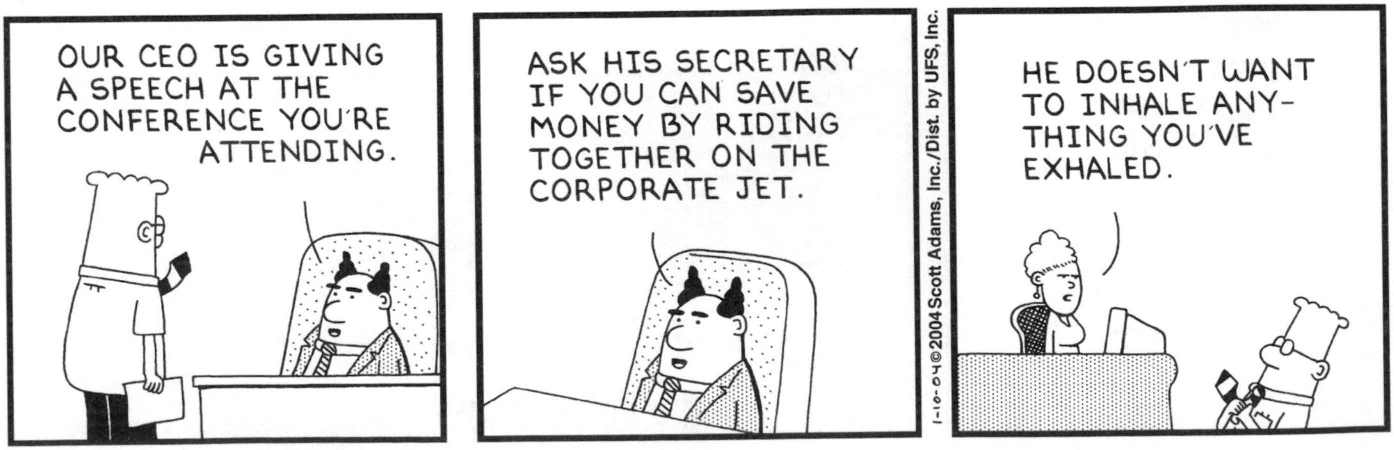
OUR CEO IS GIVING A SPEECH AT THE CONFERENCE YOU'RE ATTENDING.
ASK HIS SECRETARY IF YOU CAN SAVE MONEY BY RIDING TOGETHER ON THE CORPORATE JET.
HE DOESN'T WANT TO INHALE ANYTHING YOU'VE EXHALED.

I DISCOVERED A HOLE IN OUR INTER-NET SECURITY.
WHAT?!!
GOOD GRIEF, MAN! HOW COULD YOU PUT A HOLE IN OUR INTERNET?
I DIDN'T PUT IT THERE. I FOUND IT...AND IT'S NOT...
IT'S YOUR JOB TO FIX THAT HOLE. I WANT YOU TO WORK 24-7!
ACTUALLY, THAT'S NOT MY JOB. BUT I'LL INFORM OUR NETWORK MANAGE-MENT GROUP.
©2004 United Feature Syndicate, Inc.
1-11-04
PASSING THE BUCK!!! YOU'RE A BUCK PASSER!!!
FORGET IT! THERE'S NO HOLE! IT GOT BETTER!
THAT'S MORE LIKE IT.
I FIXED THE INTERNET.

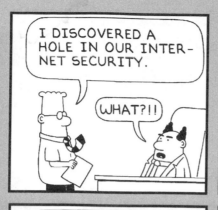

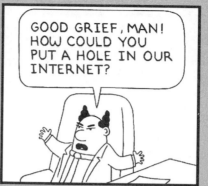

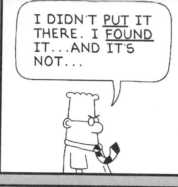

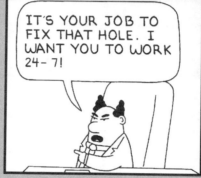

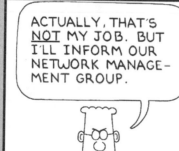

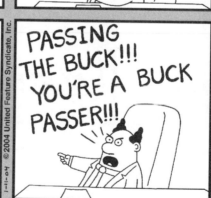

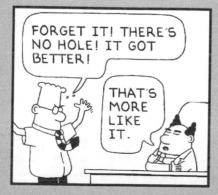

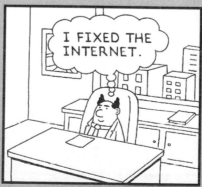

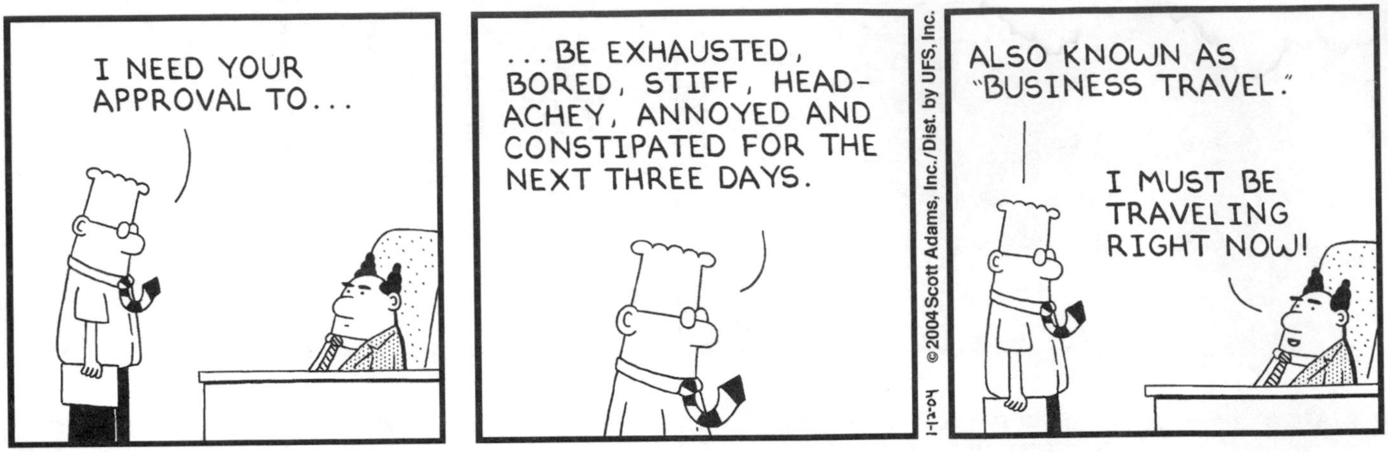
I NEED YOUR APPROVAL TO...
...BE EXHAUSTED, BORED, STIFF, HEADACHEY, ANNOYED AND CONSTIPATED FOR THE NEXT THREE DAYS.
ALSO KNOWN AS "BUSINESS TRAVEL."
I MUST BE TRAVELING RIGHT NOW!
1-12-04 © 2004 Scott Adams, Inc./Dist. by UFS, Inc.

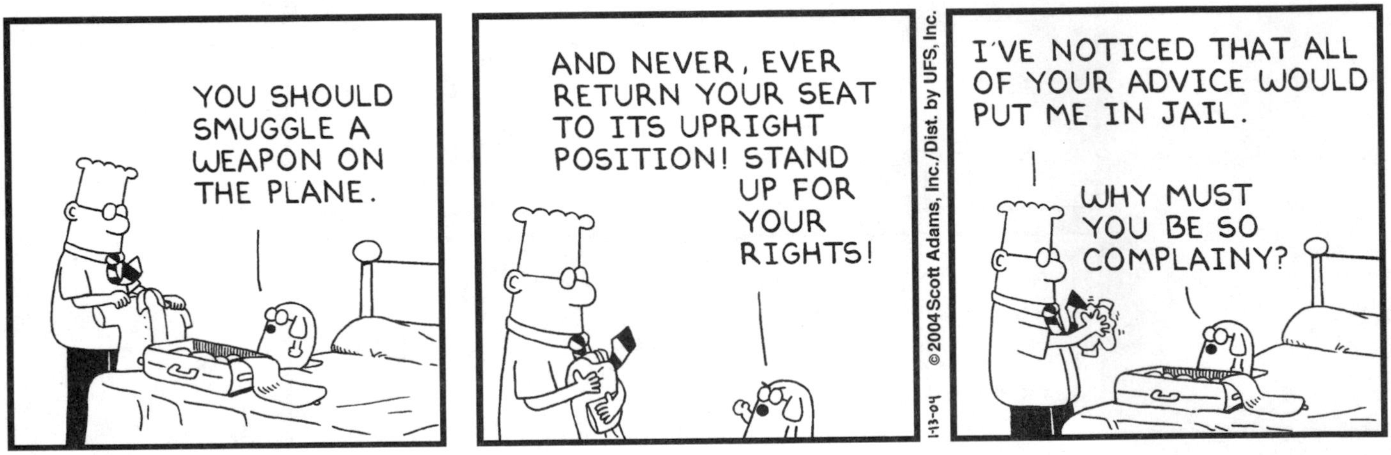
YOU SHOULD SMUGGLE A WEAPON ON THE PLANE.
AND NEVER, EVER RETURN YOUR SEAT TO ITS UPRIGHT POSITION! STAND UP FOR YOUR RIGHTS!
I'VE NOTICED THAT ALL OF YOUR ADVICE WOULD PUT ME IN JAIL.
WHY MUST YOU BE SO COMPLAINY?
1-13-04 © 2004 Scott Adams, Inc./Dist. by UFS, Inc.

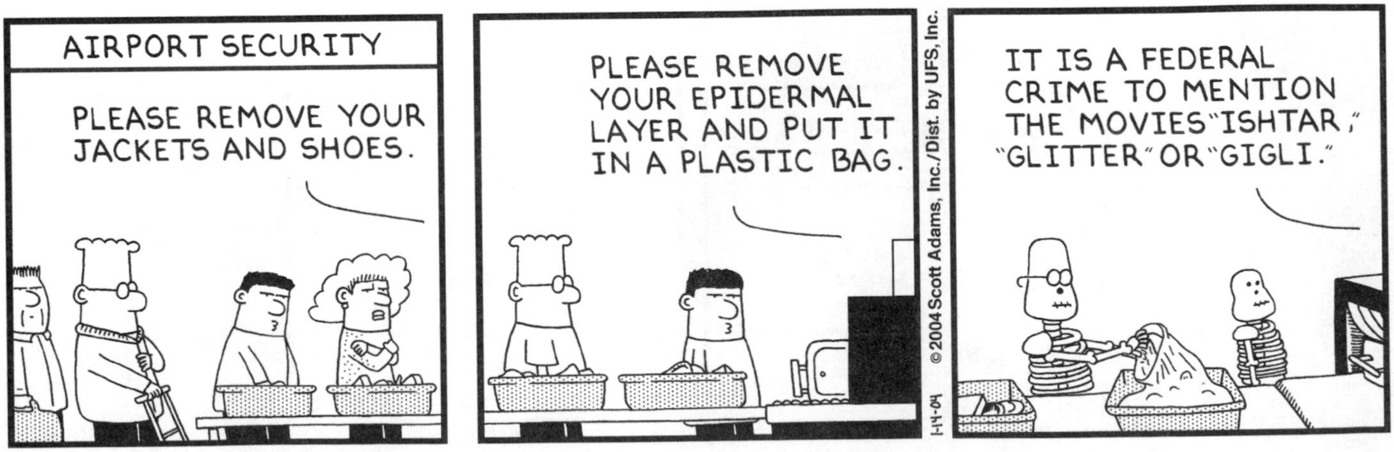
AIRPORT SECURITY
PLEASE REMOVE YOUR JACKETS AND SHOES.
PLEASE REMOVE YOUR EPIDERMAL LAYER AND PUT IT IN A PLASTIC BAG.
IT IS A FEDERAL CRIME TO MENTION THE MOVIES "ISHTAR," "GLITTER" OR "GIGLI."
1-14-04 © 2004 Scott Adams, Inc./Dist. by UFS, Inc.

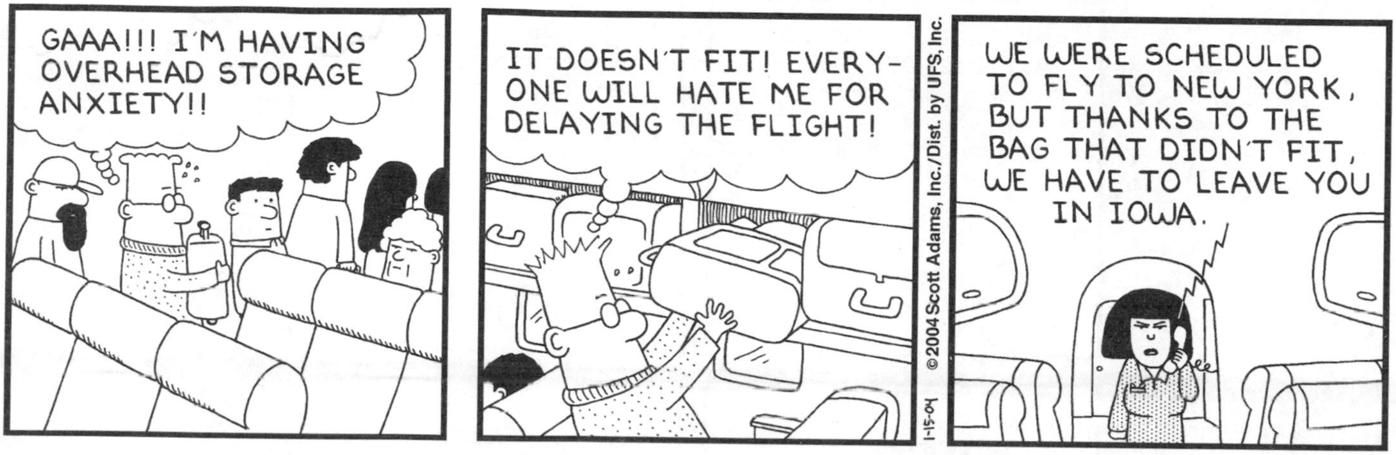
GAAA!!! I'M HAVING OVERHEAD STORAGE ANXIETY!!
IT DOESN'T FIT! EVERYONE WILL HATE ME FOR DELAYING THE FLIGHT!
© 2004 Scott Adams, Inc./Dist. by UFS, Inc.
1-15-04
WE WERE SCHEDULED TO FLY TO NEW YORK, BUT THANKS TO THE BAG THAT DIDN'T FIT, WE HAVE TO LEAVE YOU IN IOWA.

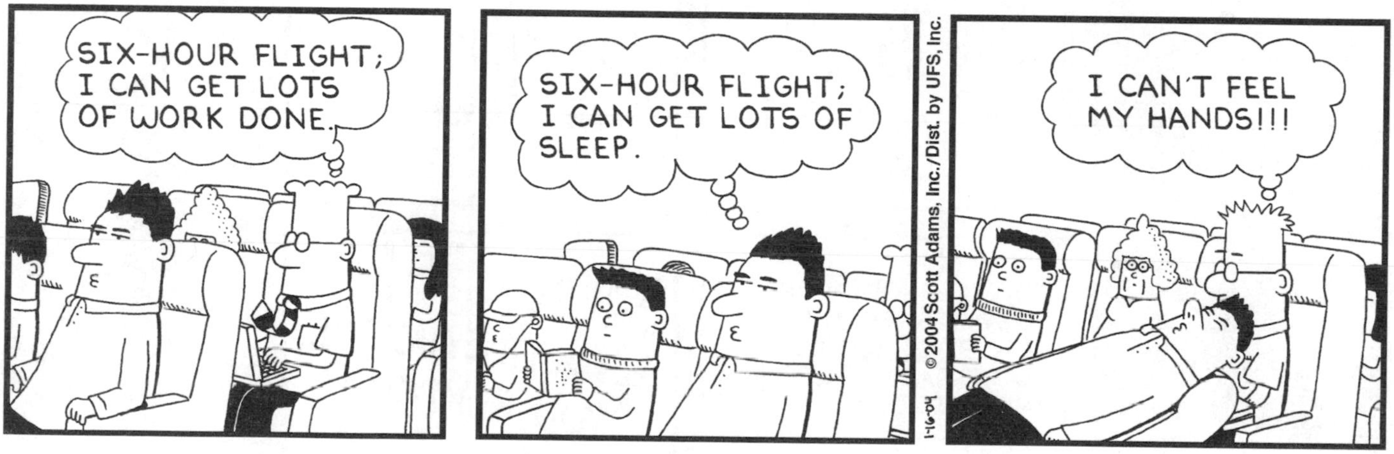
SIX-HOUR FLIGHT; I CAN GET LOTS OF WORK DONE.
SIX-HOUR FLIGHT; I CAN GET LOTS OF SLEEP.
© 2004 Scott Adams, Inc./Dist. by UFS, Inc.
1-16-04
I CAN'T FEEL MY HANDS!!!

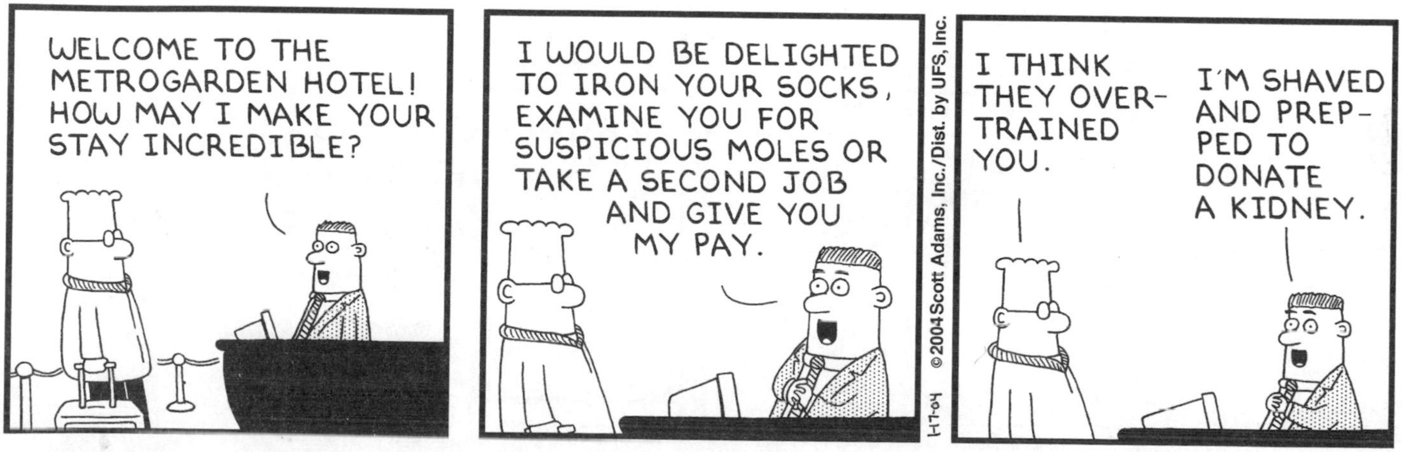
WELCOME TO THE METROGARDEN HOTEL! HOW MAY I MAKE YOUR STAY INCREDIBLE?
I WOULD BE DELIGHTED TO IRON YOUR SOCKS, EXAMINE YOU FOR SUSPICIOUS MOLES OR TAKE A SECOND JOB AND GIVE YOU MY PAY.
© 2004 Scott Adams, Inc./Dist. by UFS, Inc.
1-17-04
I THINK THEY OVER-TRAINED YOU.
I'M SHAVED AND PREP-PED TO DONATE A KIDNEY.

ASK THE VENDOR TO TAKE 20% OFF THE PRICE.
NOW???
YOU ALREADY SIGNED THE CONTRACT. THE PRICE IS SET IN STONE.
IT DOESN'T HURT TO ASK.
IT DOESN'T?
SO...ALTHOUGH WE JUST SIGNED THE CONTRACT, WOULD YOU PLEASE LOWER THE PRICE 20%?
© 2004 United Feature Syndicate, Inc.
1-18-04
HA HA HA!!!
GET A TIME MACHINE, YOU BUMPKIN!!!
GAAA!!! I FEEL STUPID AND FILLED WITH SELF-LOATHING...FUTILITY TUGS AT MY SOUL...MY GUTS ARE CLENCHED!
GOOD.
ASK IF THEY'LL GO FOR 19%.
IT HURTS TO ASK!!!

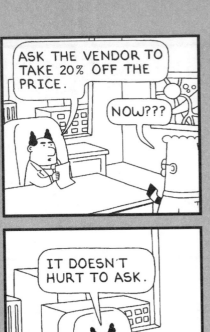

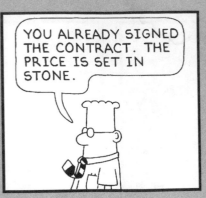

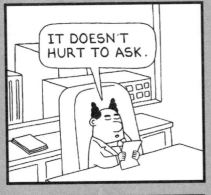

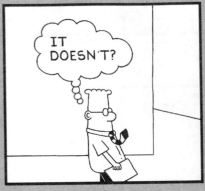

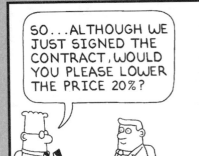

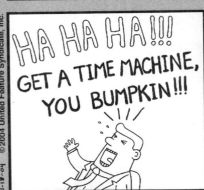

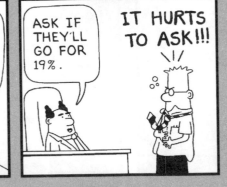

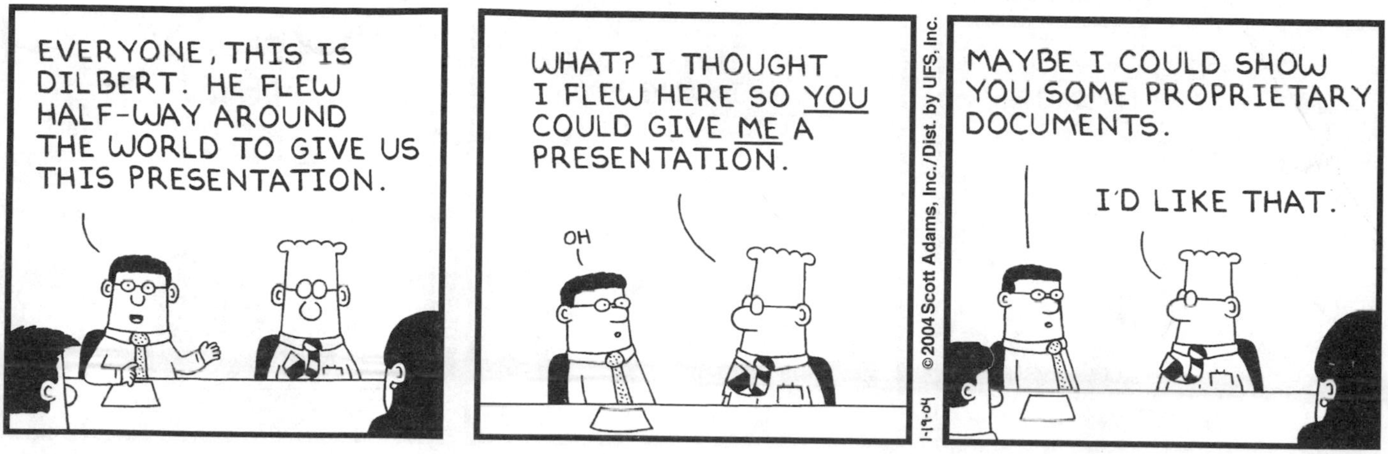
EVERYONE, THIS IS DILBERT. HE FLEW HALF-WAY AROUND THE WORLD TO GIVE US THIS PRESENTATION.
WHAT? I THOUGHT I FLEW HERE SO YOU COULD GIVE ME A PRESENTATION.
OH
MAYBE I COULD SHOW YOU SOME PROPRIETARY DOCUMENTS.
I'D LIKE THAT.

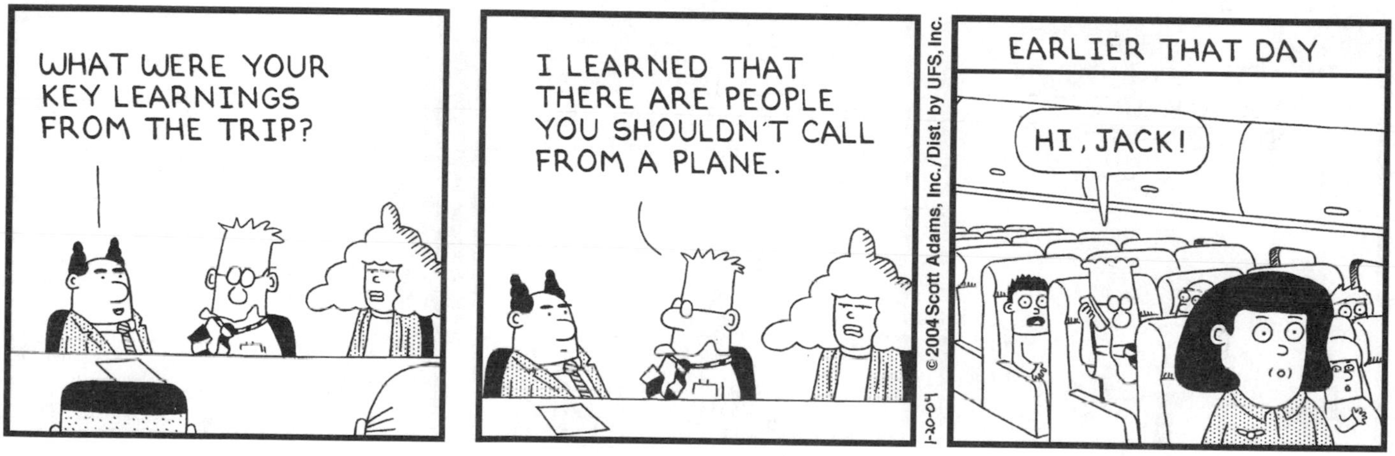
WHAT WERE YOUR KEY LEARNINGS FROM THE TRIP?
I LEARNED THAT THERE ARE PEOPLE YOU SHOULDN'T CALL FROM A PLANE.
EARLIER THAT DAY
HI, JACK!

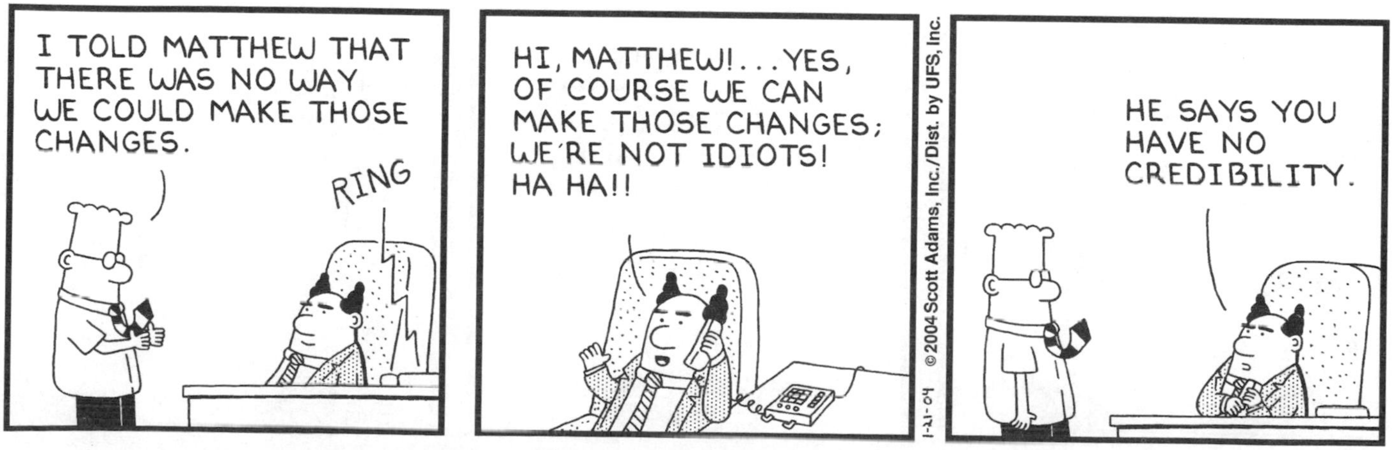
I TOLD MATTHEW THAT THERE WAS NO WAY WE COULD MAKE THOSE CHANGES.
RING
HI, MATTHEW! . . . YES, OF COURSE WE CAN MAKE THOSE CHANGES; WE'RE NOT IDIOTS! HA HA!!
HE SAYS YOU HAVE NO CREDIBILITY.

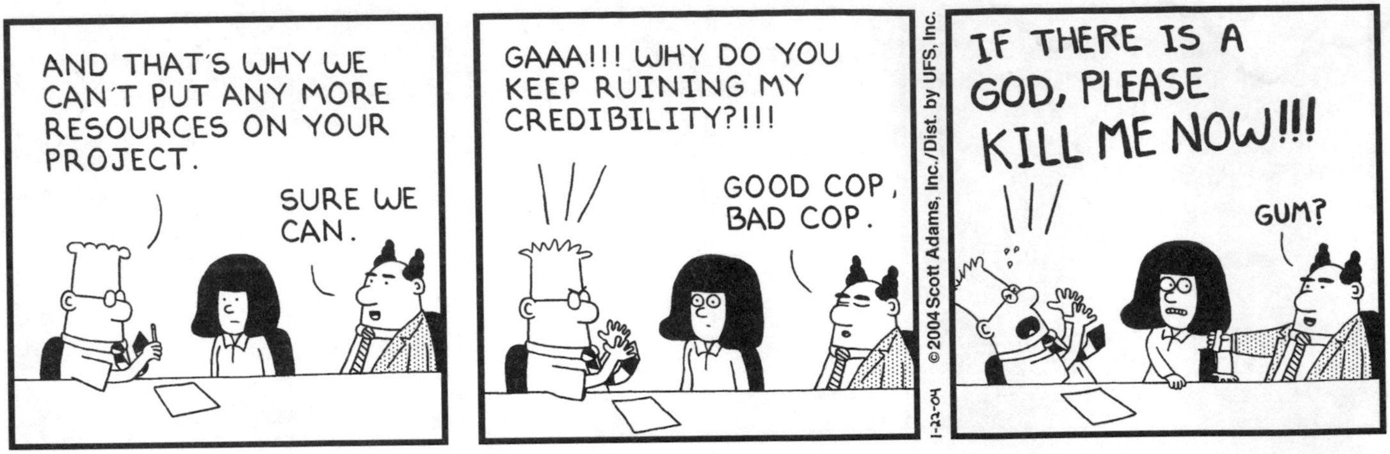
AND THAT'S WHY WE CAN'T PUT ANY MORE RESOURCES ON YOUR PROJECT.
SURE WE CAN.
GAAA!!! WHY DO YOU KEEP RUINING MY CREDIBILITY?!!!
GOOD COP, BAD COP.
© 2004 Scott Adams, Inc./Dist. by UFS, Inc.
1-22-04
IF THERE IS A GOD, PLEASE KILL ME NOW!!!
GUM?

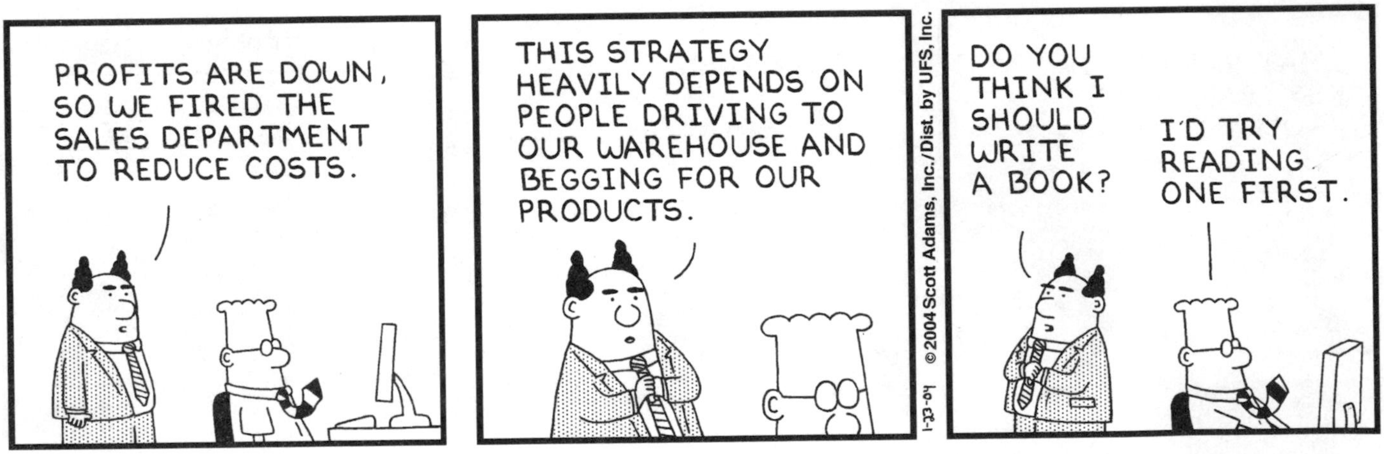
PROFITS ARE DOWN, SO WE FIRED THE SALES DEPARTMENT TO REDUCE COSTS.
THIS STRATEGY HEAVILY DEPENDS ON PEOPLE DRIVING TO OUR WAREHOUSE AND BEGGING FOR OUR PRODUCTS.
© 2004 Scott Adams, Inc./Dist. by UFS, Inc.
1-23-04
DO YOU THINK I SHOULD WRITE A BOOK?
I'D TRY READING ONE FIRST.

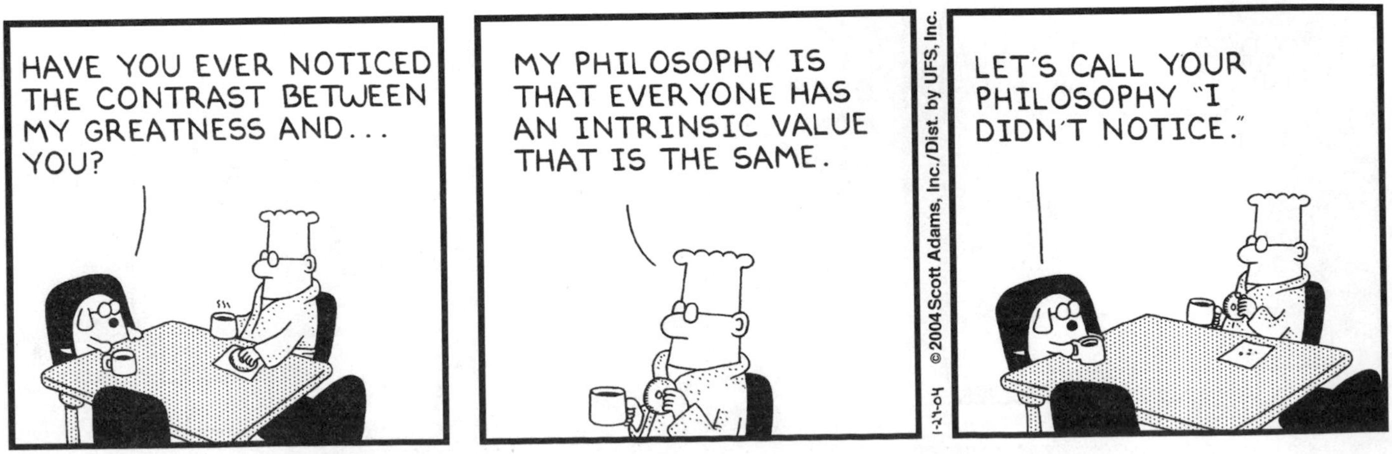
HAVE YOU EVER NOTICED THE CONTRAST BETWEEN MY GREATNESS AND... YOU?
MY PHILOSOPHY IS THAT EVERYONE HAS AN INTRINSIC VALUE THAT IS THE SAME.
© 2004 Scott Adams, Inc./Dist. by UFS, Inc.
1-24-04
LET'S CALL YOUR PHILOSOPHY "I DIDN'T NOTICE."

OUR CEO WILL BE HAPPY TO ANSWER ANY QUESTIONS.
WHY DOES THE COMPANY PAY YOU 40 MILLION DOLLARS A YEAR?
I ASK BECAUSE IT'S 400 TIMES MORE THAN I MAKE. AND I WORK 70 HOURS A WEEK.
DO YOU WORK 28,000 HOURS PER WEEK?
Dist. by United Feature Syndicate, Inc.
OR DO YOU HAVE SOME SORT OF SPECIAL ABILITY THAT ISN'T OBVIOUS?
1-25-04 ©2004 Scott Adams, Inc.
GRRRR RRRRR AAAH-OOGAH!!!
GOLDEN EGG. ONE EVERY TEN MINUTES.
GOOD ANSWER.

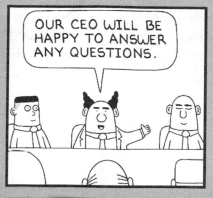

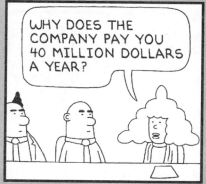

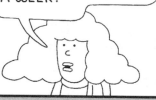

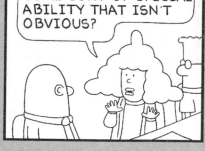

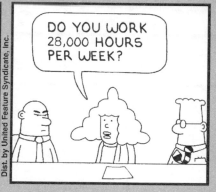

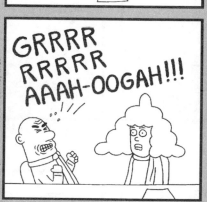

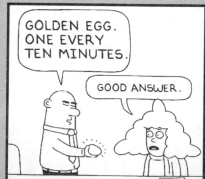

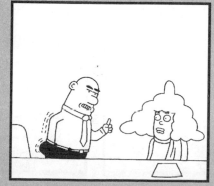

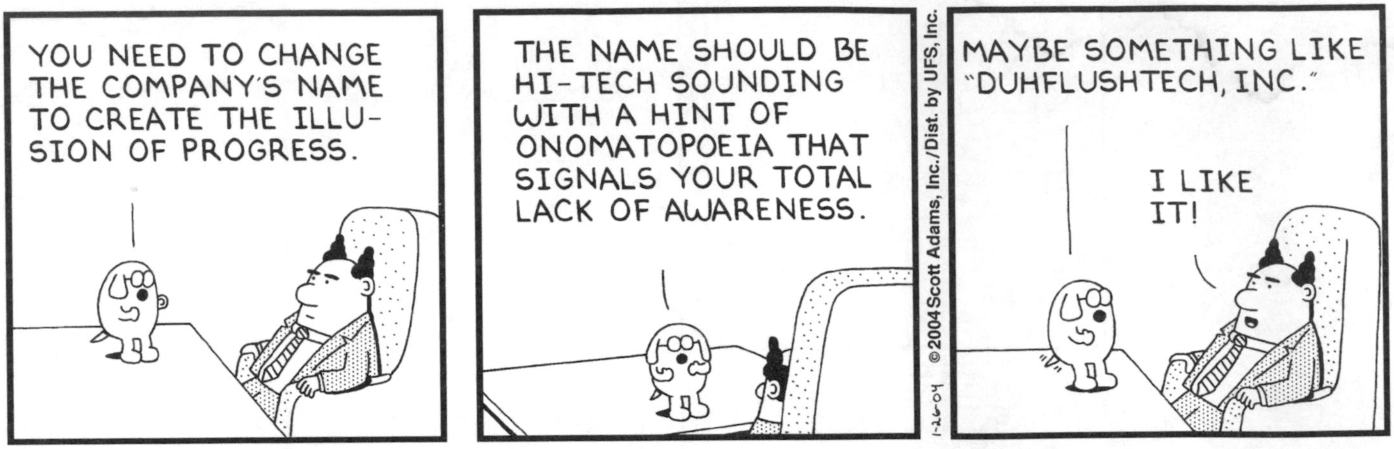
YOU NEED TO CHANGE THE COMPANY'S NAME TO CREATE THE ILLUSION OF PROGRESS.
THE NAME SHOULD BE HI-TECH SOUNDING WITH A HINT OF ONOMATOPOEIA THAT SIGNALS YOUR TOTAL LACK OF AWARENESS.
© 2004 Scott Adams, Inc./Dist. by UFS, Inc.
1-26-04
MAYBE SOMETHING LIKE "DUHFLUSHTECH, INC."
I LIKE IT!

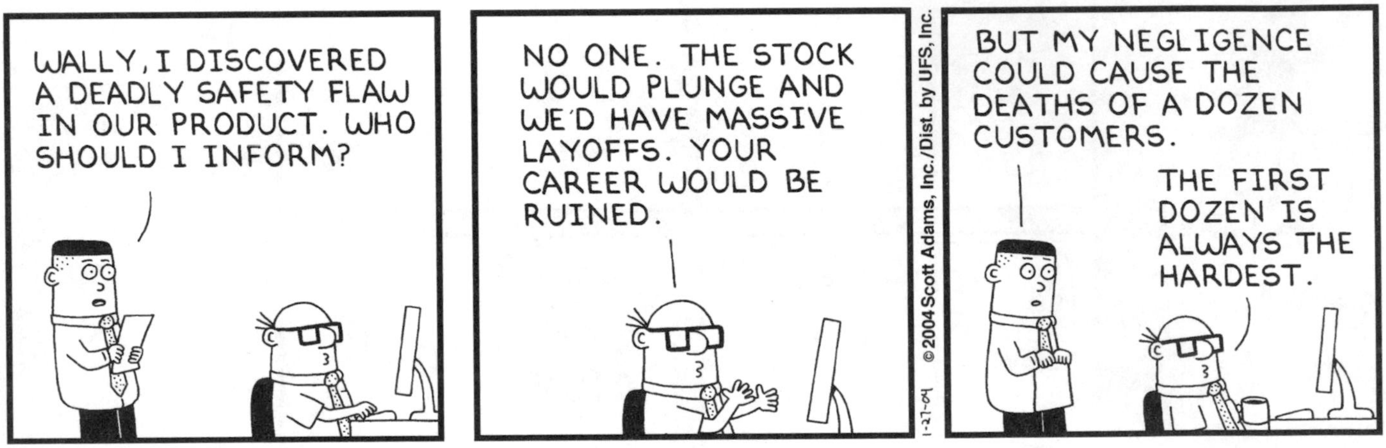
WALLY, I DISCOVERED A DEADLY SAFETY FLAW IN OUR PRODUCT. WHO SHOULD I INFORM?
NO ONE. THE STOCK WOULD PLUNGE AND WE'D HAVE MASSIVE LAYOFFS. YOUR CAREER WOULD BE RUINED.
© 2004 Scott Adams, Inc./Dist. by UFS, Inc.
1-27-04
BUT MY NEGLIGENCE COULD CAUSE THE DEATHS OF A DOZEN CUSTOMERS.
THE FIRST DOZEN IS ALWAYS THE HARDEST.

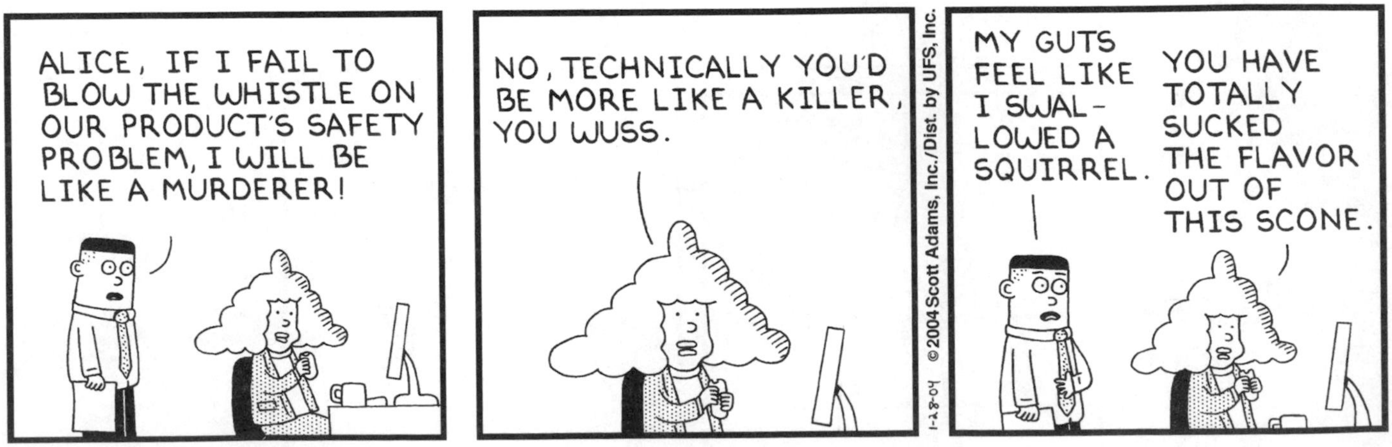
ALICE, IF I FAIL TO BLOW THE WHISTLE ON OUR PRODUCT'S SAFETY PROBLEM, I WILL BE LIKE A MURDERER!
NO, TECHNICALLY YOU'D BE MORE LIKE A KILLER, YOU WUSS.
© 2004 Scott Adams, Inc./Dist. by UFS, Inc.
1-28-04
MY GUTS FEEL LIKE I SWALLOWED A SQUIRREL.
YOU HAVE TOTALLY SUCKED THE FLAVOR OUT OF THIS SCONE.

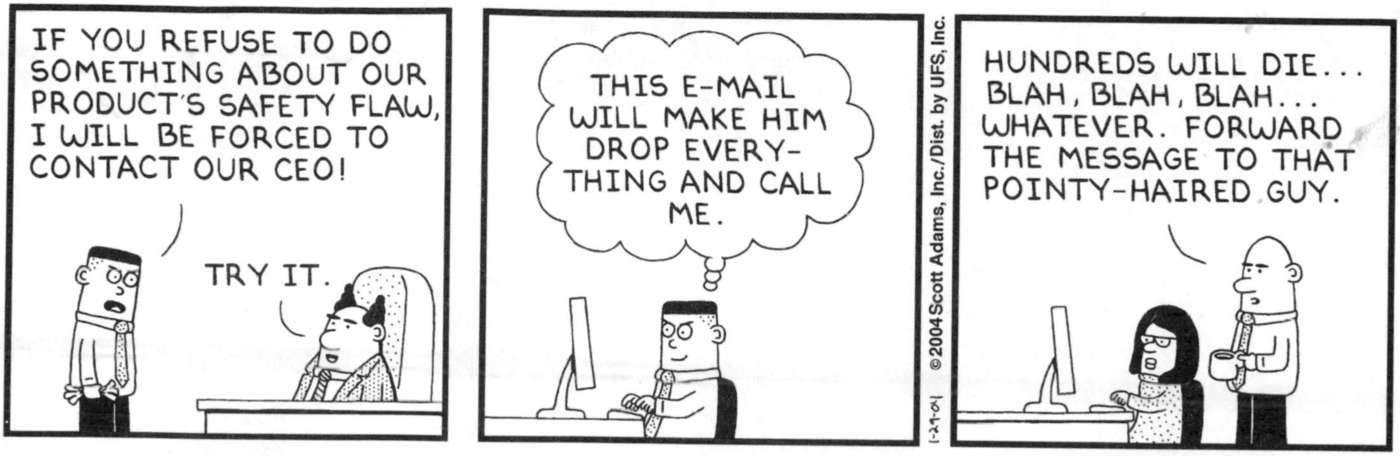
IF YOU REFUSE TO DO SOMETHING ABOUT OUR PRODUCT'S SAFETY FLAW, I WILL BE FORCED TO CONTACT OUR CEO!
TRY IT.
THIS E-MAIL WILL MAKE HIM DROP EVERY-THING AND CALL ME.
© 2004 Scott Adams, Inc./Dist. by UFS, Inc.
1-29-04
HUNDREDS WILL DIE... BLAH, BLAH, BLAH... WHATEVER. FORWARD THE MESSAGE TO THAT POINTY-HAIRED GUY.

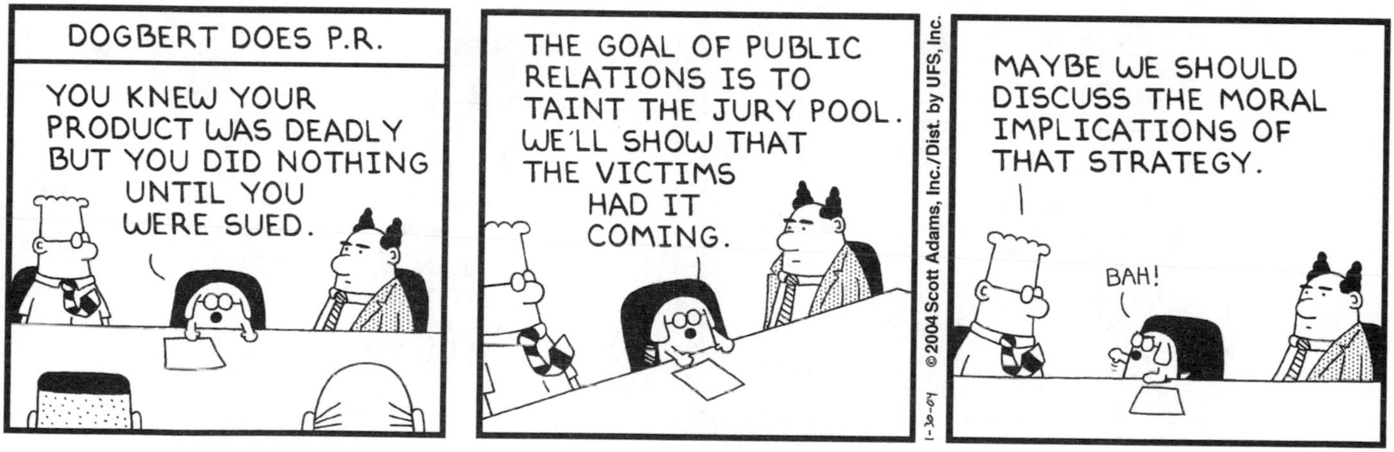
DOGBERT DOES P.R.
YOU KNEW YOUR PRODUCT WAS DEADLY BUT YOU DID NOTHING UNTIL YOU WERE SUED.
THE GOAL OF PUBLIC RELATIONS IS TO TAINT THE JURY POOL. WE'LL SHOW THAT THE VICTIMS HAD IT COMING.
© 2004 Scott Adams, Inc./Dist. by UFS, Inc.
1-30-04
MAYBE WE SHOULD DISCUSS THE MORAL IMPLICATIONS OF THAT STRATEGY.
BAH!

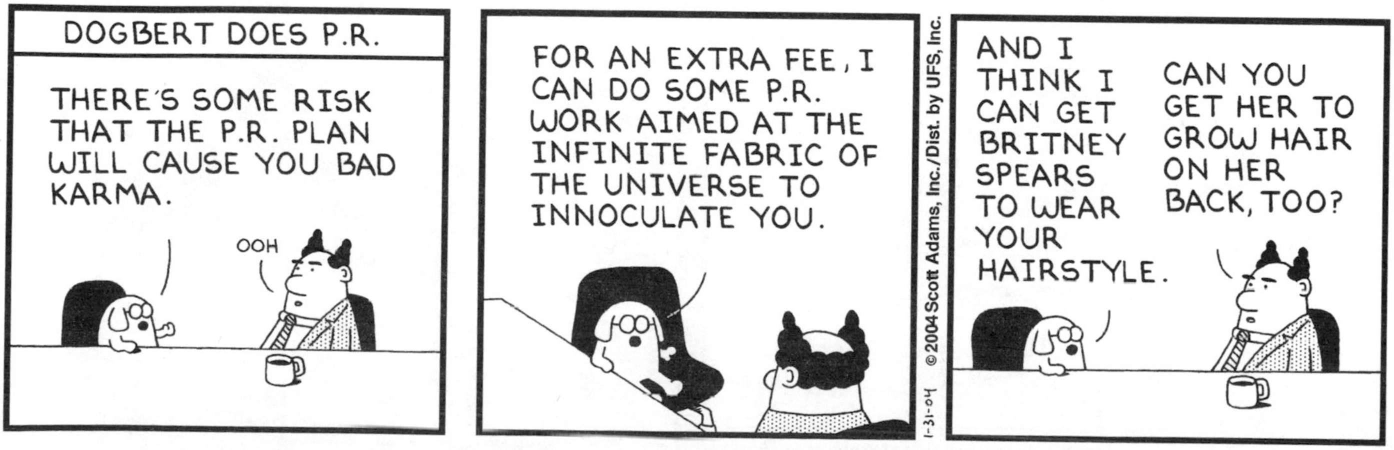
DOGBERT DOES P.R.
THERE'S SOME RISK THAT THE P.R. PLAN WILL CAUSE YOU BAD KARMA.
OOH
FOR AN EXTRA FEE, I CAN DO SOME P.R. WORK AIMED AT THE INFINITE FABRIC OF THE UNIVERSE TO INNOCULATE YOU.
© 2004 Scott Adams, Inc./Dist. by UFS, Inc.
1-31-04
AND I THINK I CAN GET BRITNEY SPEARS TO WEAR YOUR HAIRSTYLE.
CAN YOU GET HER TO GROW HAIR ON HER BACK, TOO?

DILBERT, COME IN HERE.
I KEEP CLICKING ON THIS LINK AND NOTHING HAPPENS.
CLICK CLICK CLICK CLICK CLICK CLICK
SEE?
TRY SOME-THING ELSE.
WHY WOULD I DO THAT?
CLICK CLICK CLICK CLICK
CLICK CLICK CLICK CLICK CLICK CLICK CLICK
THE DEFINITION OF INSANITY IS: DOING THE SAME THING AND EXPECTING A DIFFERENT RESULT.
CLICK CLICK CLICK CLICK CLICK CLICK
HEY, IT WORKED THIS TIME!
WHAT WE HAVE HERE IS A BAD PRECEDENT.
THEY CALLED ME "CRAZY."
Dist. by United Feature Syndicate, Inc.
2-1-04 ©2004 Scott Adams, Inc.

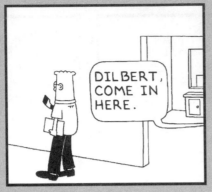

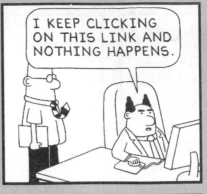

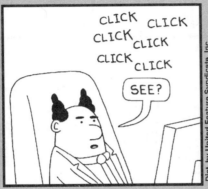

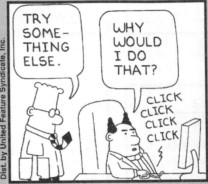

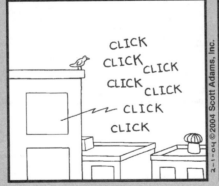

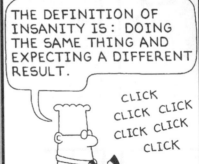

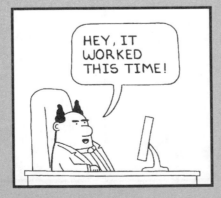

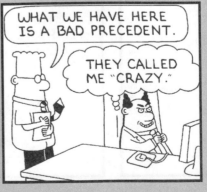

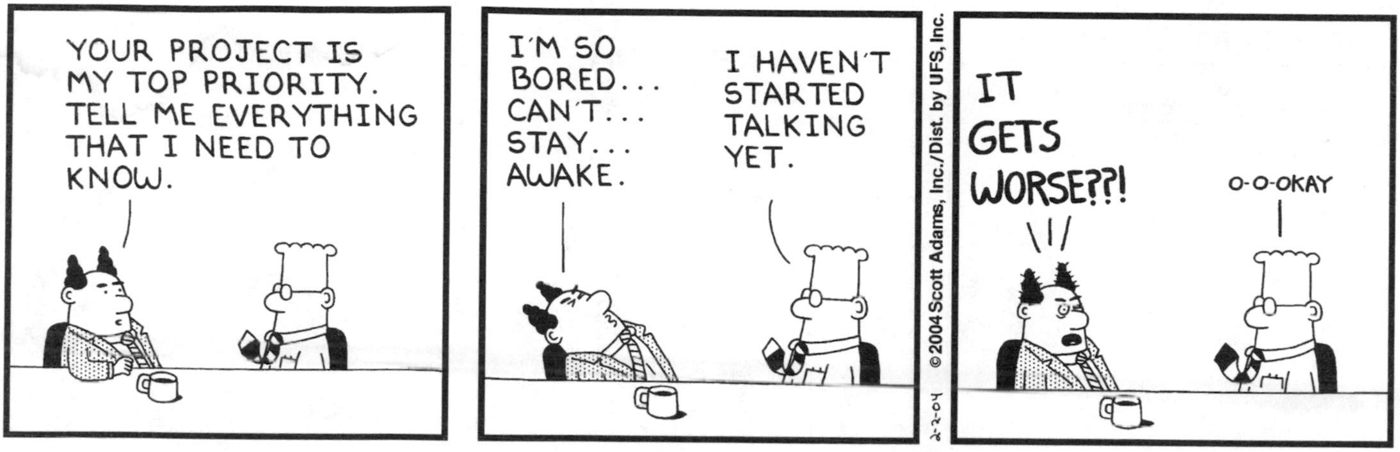
YOUR PROJECT IS MY TOP PRIORITY. TELL ME EVERYTHING THAT I NEED TO KNOW.
I'M SO BORED... CAN'T... STAY... AWAKE.
I HAVEN'T STARTED TALKING YET.
© 2004 Scott Adams, Inc./Dist. by UFS, Inc.
2-2-04
IT GETS WORSE??!
O-O-OKAY

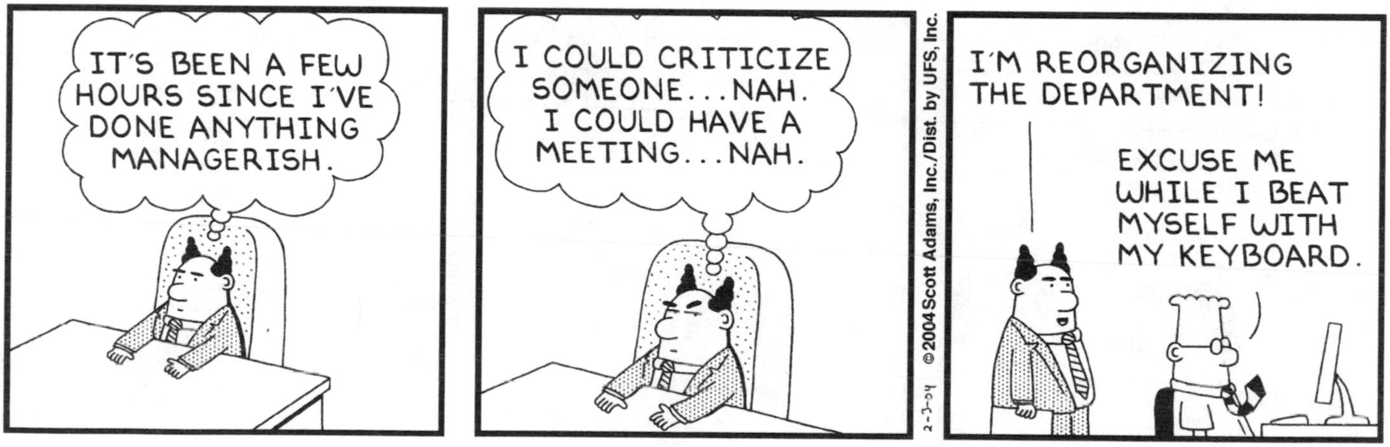
IT'S BEEN A FEW HOURS SINCE I'VE DONE ANYTHING MANAGERISH.
I COULD CRITICIZE SOMEONE...NAH. I COULD HAVE A MEETING...NAH.
© 2004 Scott Adams, Inc./Dist. by UFS, Inc.
2-3-04
I'M REORGANIZING THE DEPARTMENT!
EXCUSE ME WHILE I BEAT MYSELF WITH MY KEYBOARD.

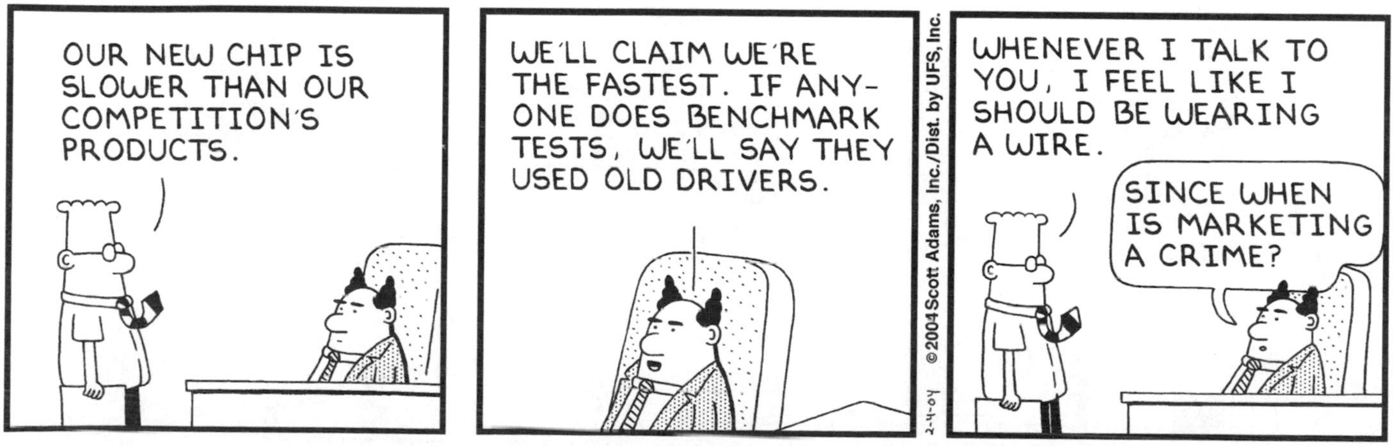
OUR NEW CHIP IS SLOWER THAN OUR COMPETITION'S PRODUCTS.
WE'LL CLAIM WE'RE THE FASTEST. IF ANYONE DOES BENCHMARK TESTS, WE'LL SAY THEY USED OLD DRIVERS.
© 2004 Scott Adams, Inc./Dist. by UFS, Inc.
2-4-04
WHENEVER I TALK TO YOU, I FEEL LIKE I SHOULD BE WEARING A WIRE.
SINCE WHEN IS MARKETING A CRIME?

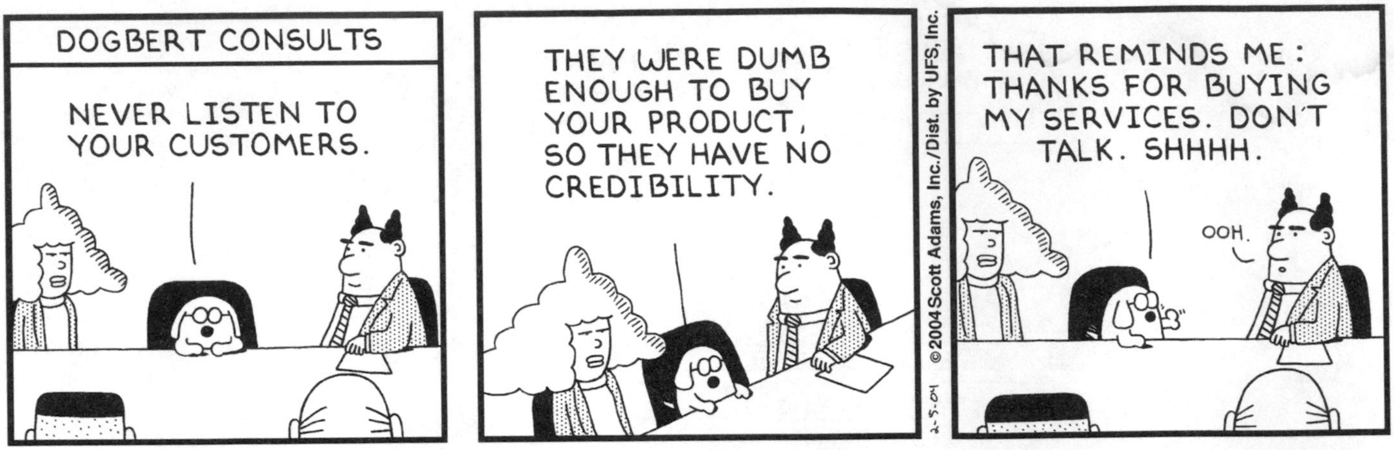
DOGBERT CONSULTS
NEVER LISTEN TO YOUR CUSTOMERS.
THEY WERE DUMB ENOUGH TO BUY YOUR PRODUCT, SO THEY HAVE NO CREDIBILITY.
2-5-04
© 2004 Scott Adams, Inc./Dist. by UFS, Inc.
THAT REMINDS ME: THANKS FOR BUYING MY SERVICES. DON'T TALK. SHHHH.
OOH.

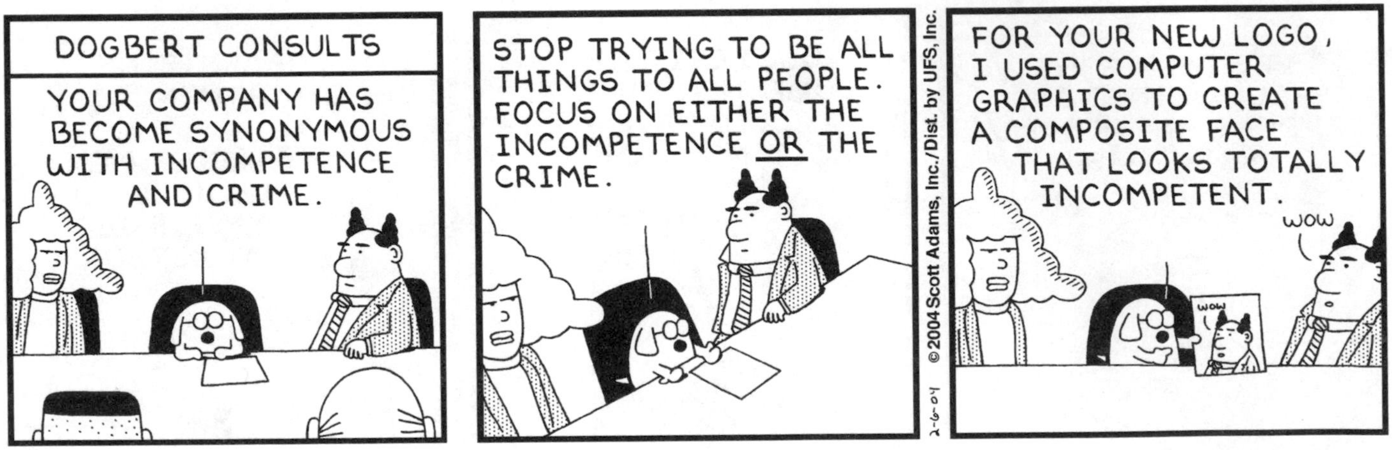
DOGBERT CONSULTS
YOUR COMPANY HAS BECOME SYNONYMOUS WITH INCOMPETENCE AND CRIME.
STOP TRYING TO BE ALL THINGS TO ALL PEOPLE. FOCUS ON EITHER THE INCOMPETENCE OR THE CRIME.
2-6-04
© 2004 Scott Adams, Inc./Dist. by UFS, Inc.
FOR YOUR NEW LOGO, I USED COMPUTER GRAPHICS TO CREATE A COMPOSITE FACE THAT LOOKS TOTALLY INCOMPETENT.
WOW
WOW

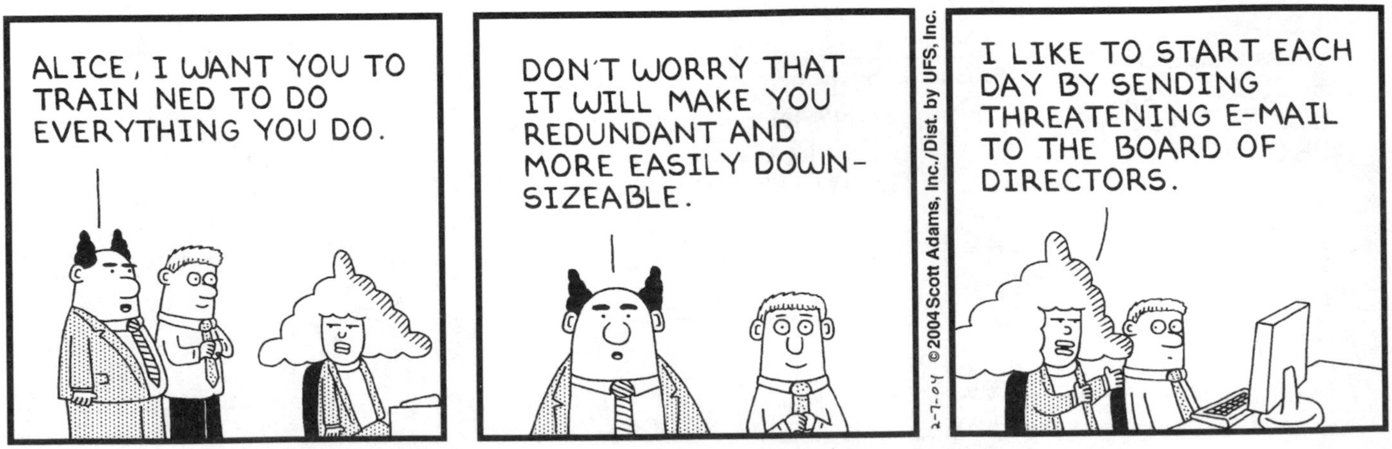
ALICE, I WANT YOU TO TRAIN NED TO DO EVERYTHING YOU DO.
DON'T WORRY THAT IT WILL MAKE YOU REDUNDANT AND MORE EASILY DOWN-SIZEABLE.
2-7-04
© 2004 Scott Adams, Inc./Dist. by UFS, Inc.
I LIKE TO START EACH DAY BY SENDING THREATENING E-MAIL TO THE BOARD OF DIRECTORS.

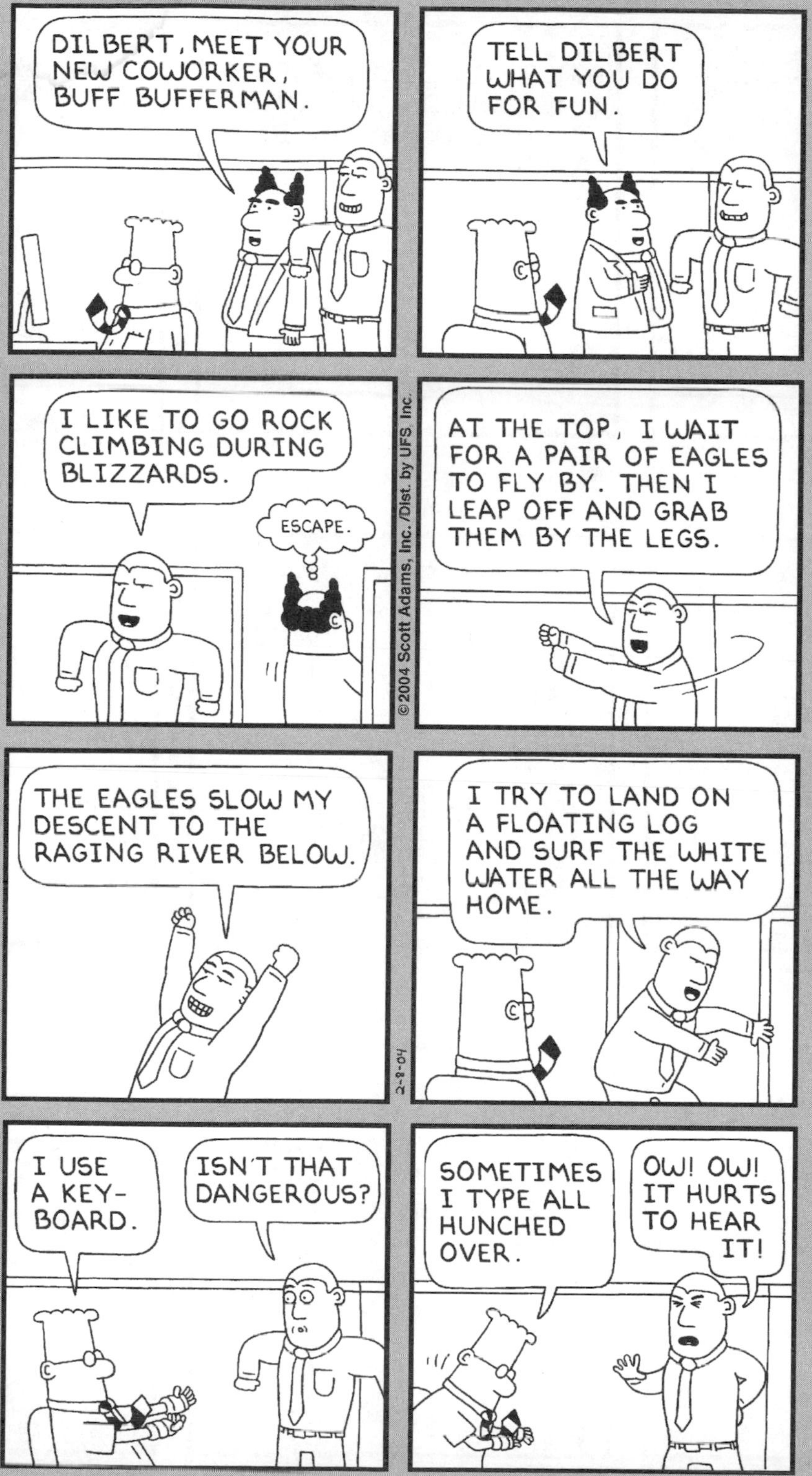
DILBERT, MEET YOUR NEW COWORKER, BUFF BUFFERMAN.
TELL DILBERT WHAT YOU DO FOR FUN.
I LIKE TO GO ROCK CLIMBING DURING BLIZZARDS.
ESCAPE.
AT THE TOP, I WAIT FOR A PAIR OF EAGLES TO FLY BY. THEN I LEAP OFF AND GRAB THEM BY THE LEGS.
THE EAGLES SLOW MY DESCENT TO THE RAGING RIVER BELOW.
I TRY TO LAND ON A FLOATING LOG AND SURF THE WHITE WATER ALL THE WAY HOME.
I USE A KEY-BOARD.
ISN'T THAT DANGEROUS?
SOMETIMES I TYPE ALL HUNCHED OVER.
OW! OW! IT HURTS TO HEAR IT!
©2004 Scott Adams, Inc./Dist. by UFS Inc.
2-8-04

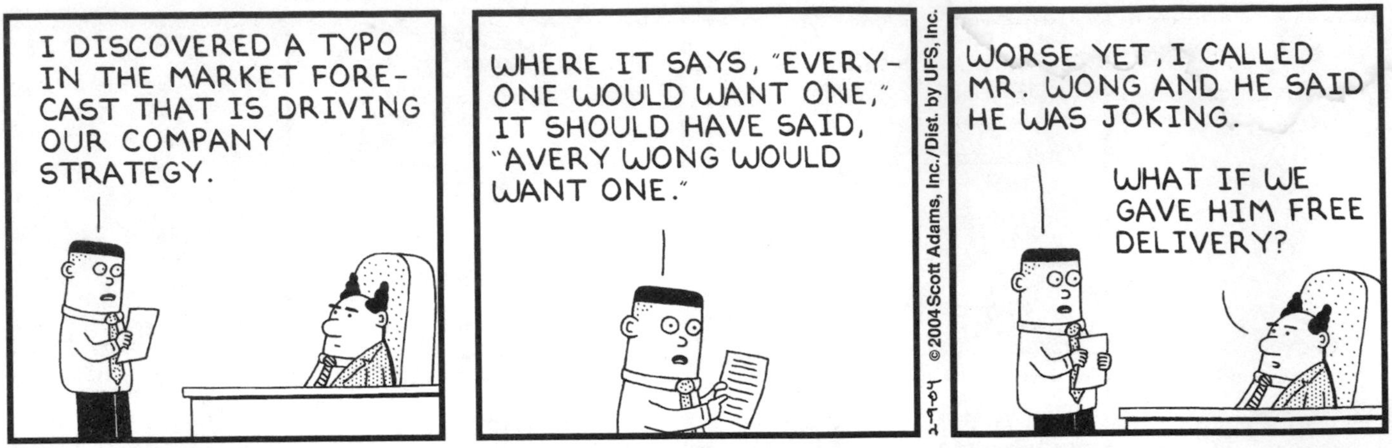
I DISCOVERED A TYPO IN THE MARKET FORECAST THAT IS DRIVING OUR COMPANY STRATEGY.
WHERE IT SAYS, "EVERYONE WOULD WANT ONE," IT SHOULD HAVE SAID, "AVERY WONG WOULD WANT ONE."
2-9-04 © 2004 Scott Adams, Inc./Dist. by UFS, Inc.
WORSE YET, I CALLED MR. WONG AND HE SAID HE WAS JOKING.
WHAT IF WE GAVE HIM FREE DELIVERY?

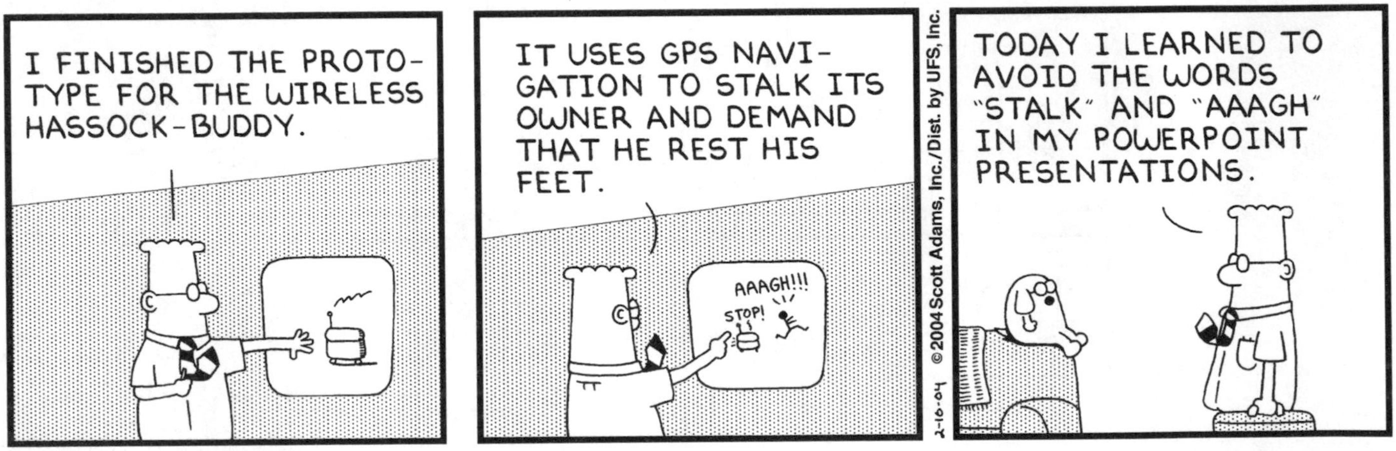
I FINISHED THE PROTOTYPE FOR THE WIRELESS HASSOCK-BUDDY.
IT USES GPS NAVIGATION TO STALK ITS OWNER AND DEMAND THAT HE REST HIS FEET.
AAAGH!!!
STOP!
2-10-04 © 2004 Scott Adams, Inc./Dist. by UFS, Inc.
TODAY I LEARNED TO AVOID THE WORDS "STALK" AND "AAAGH" IN MY POWERPOINT PRESENTATIONS.

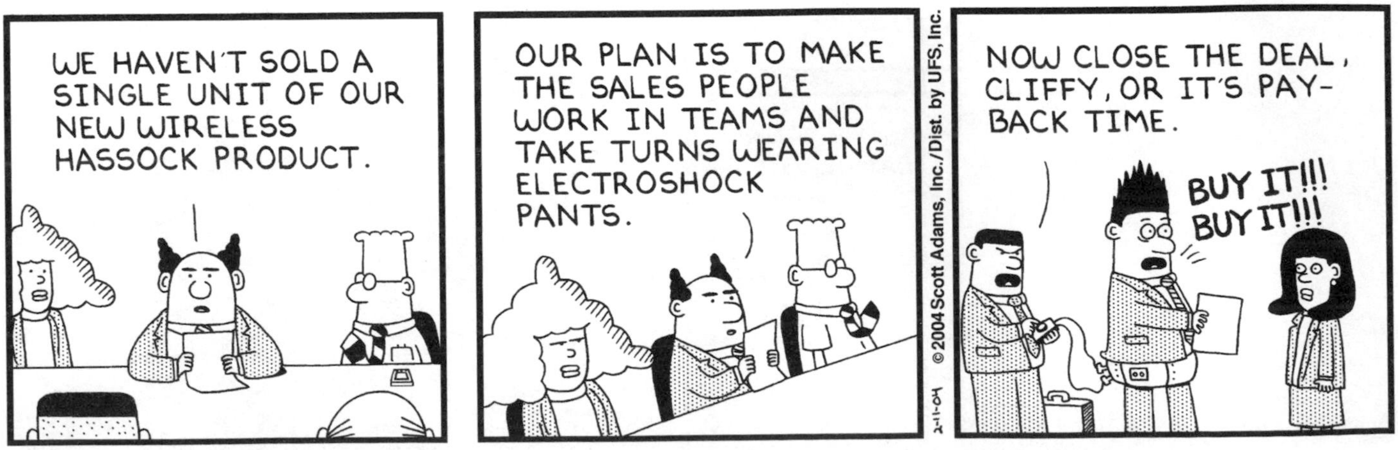
WE HAVEN'T SOLD A SINGLE UNIT OF OUR NEW WIRELESS HASSOCK PRODUCT.
OUR PLAN IS TO MAKE THE SALES PEOPLE WORK IN TEAMS AND TAKE TURNS WEARING ELECTROSHOCK PANTS.
2-11-04 © 2004 Scott Adams, Inc./Dist. by UFS, Inc.
NOW CLOSE THE DEAL, CLIFFY, OR IT'S PAYBACK TIME.
BUY IT!!! BUY IT!!!

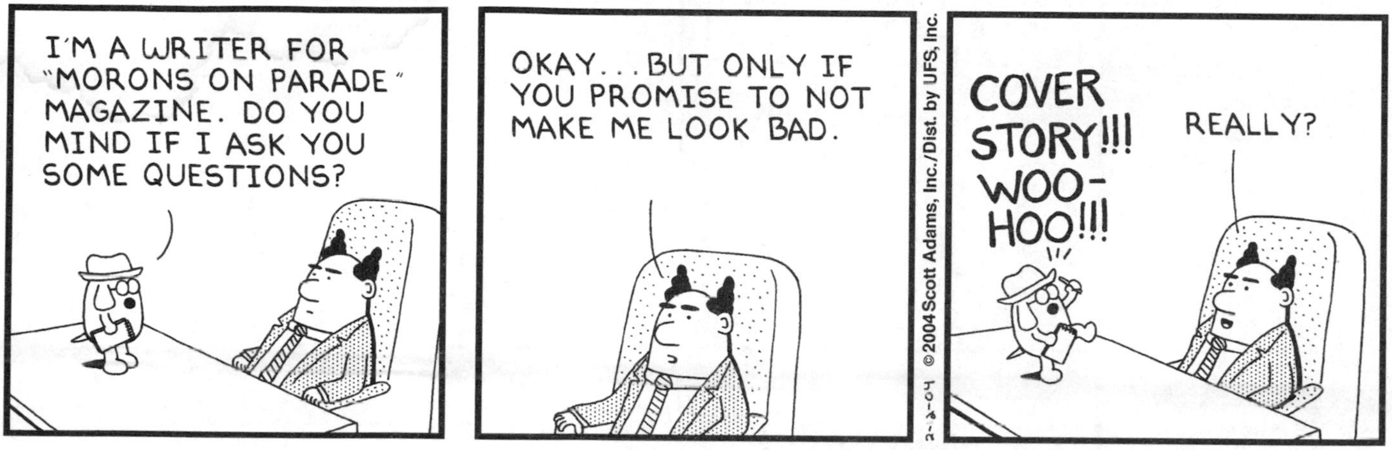
I'M A WRITER FOR "MORONS ON PARADE" MAGAZINE. DO YOU MIND IF I ASK YOU SOME QUESTIONS?
OKAY... BUT ONLY IF YOU PROMISE TO NOT MAKE ME LOOK BAD.
COVER STORY!!! WOO-HOO!!!
REALLY?
© 2004 Scott Adams, Inc./Dist. by UFS, Inc.
2-12-04

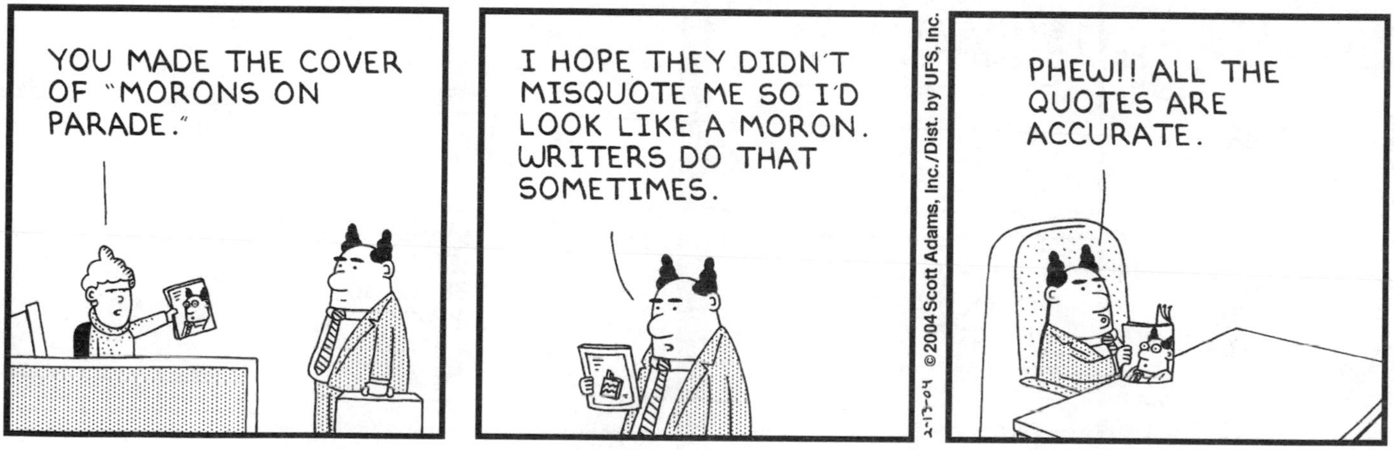
YOU MADE THE COVER OF "MORONS ON PARADE."
I HOPE THEY DIDN'T MISQUOTE ME SO I'D LOOK LIKE A MORON. WRITERS DO THAT SOMETIMES.
PHEW!! ALL THE QUOTES ARE ACCURATE.
© 2004 Scott Adams, Inc./Dist. by UFS, Inc.
2-13-04

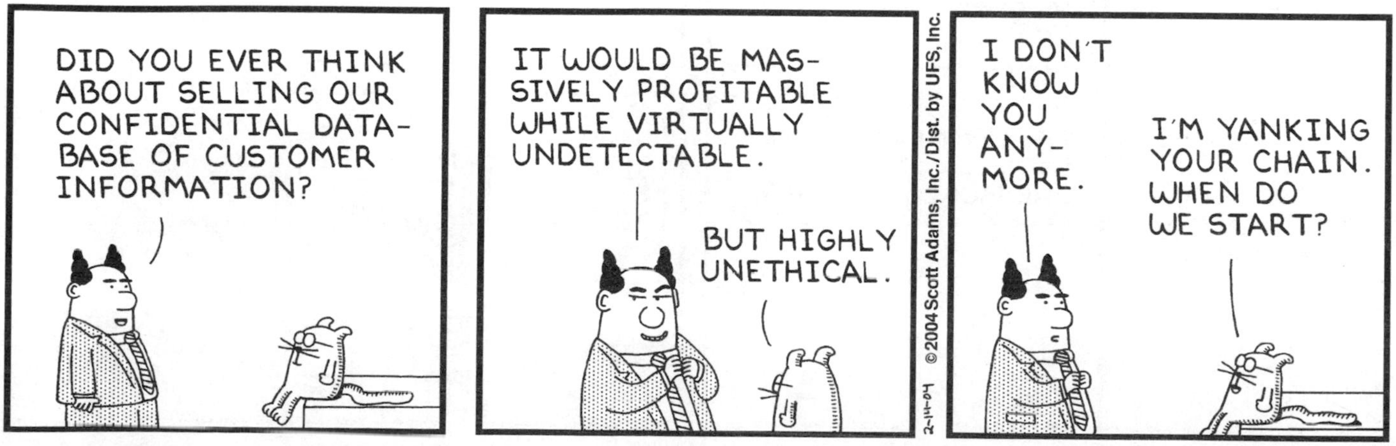
DID YOU EVER THINK ABOUT SELLING OUR CONFIDENTIAL DATA-BASE OF CUSTOMER INFORMATION?
IT WOULD BE MAS-SIVELY PROFITABLE WHILE VIRTUALLY UNDETECTABLE.
BUT HIGHLY UNETHICAL.
I DON'T KNOW YOU ANY-MORE.
I'M YANKING YOUR CHAIN. WHEN DO WE START?
© 2004 Scott Adams, Inc./Dist. by UFS, Inc.
2-14-04

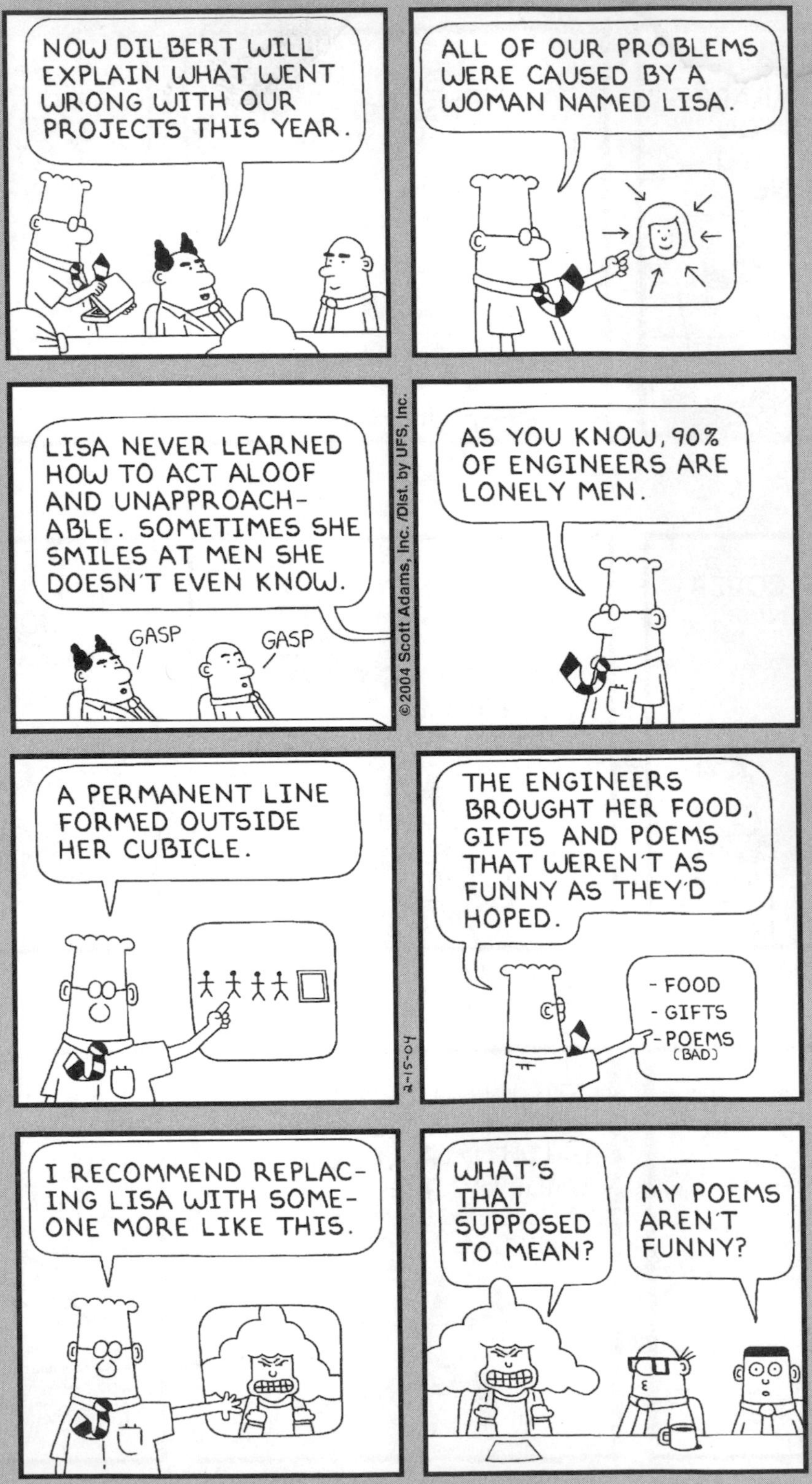
NOW DILBERT WILL EXPLAIN WHAT WENT WRONG WITH OUR PROJECTS THIS YEAR.
ALL OF OUR PROBLEMS WERE CAUSED BY A WOMAN NAMED LISA.
LISA NEVER LEARNED HOW TO ACT ALOOF AND UNAPPROACH-ABLE. SOMETIMES SHE SMILES AT MEN SHE DOESN'T EVEN KNOW.
GASP
GASP
©2004 Scott Adams, Inc./Dist. by UFS, Inc.
AS YOU KNOW, 90% OF ENGINEERS ARE LONELY MEN.
A PERMANENT LINE FORMED OUTSIDE HER CUBICLE.
2-15-04
THE ENGINEERS BROUGHT HER FOOD, GIFTS AND POEMS THAT WEREN'T AS FUNNY AS THEY'D HOPED.
- FOOD
- GIFTS
- POEMS (BAD)
I RECOMMEND REPLAC-ING LISA WITH SOME-ONE MORE LIKE THIS.
WHAT'S THAT SUPPOSED TO MEAN?
MY POEMS AREN'T FUNNY?

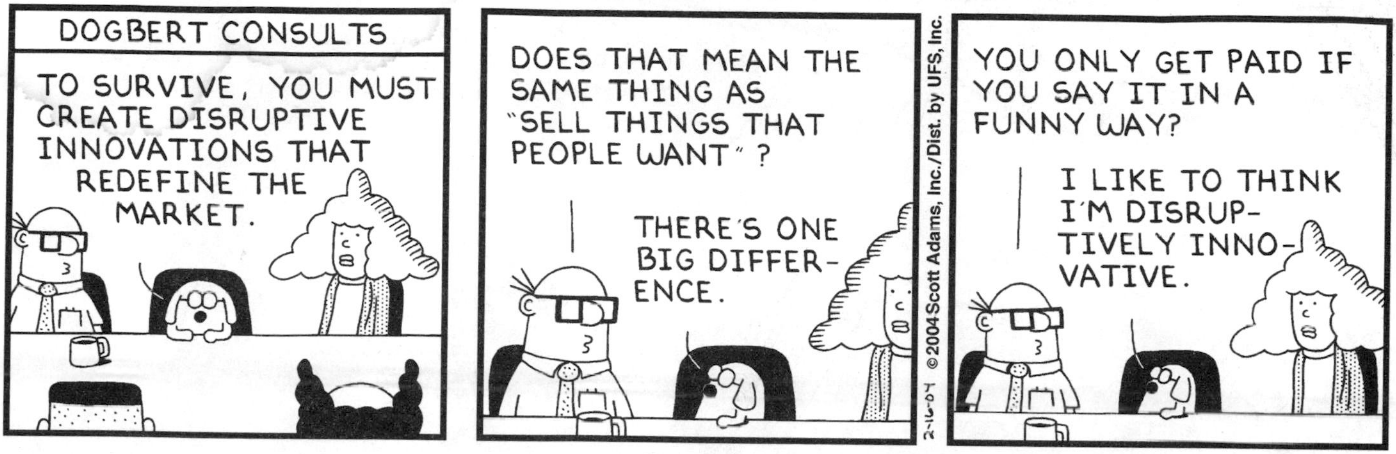
DOGBERT CONSULTS
TO SURVIVE, YOU MUST CREATE DISRUPTIVE INNOVATIONS THAT REDEFINE THE MARKET.
DOES THAT MEAN THE SAME THING AS "SELL THINGS THAT PEOPLE WANT"?
THERE'S ONE BIG DIFFERENCE.
YOU ONLY GET PAID IF YOU SAY IT IN A FUNNY WAY?
I LIKE TO THINK I'M DISRUPTIVELY INNOVATIVE.
2-16-04 © 2004 Scott Adams, Inc./Dist. by UFS, Inc.

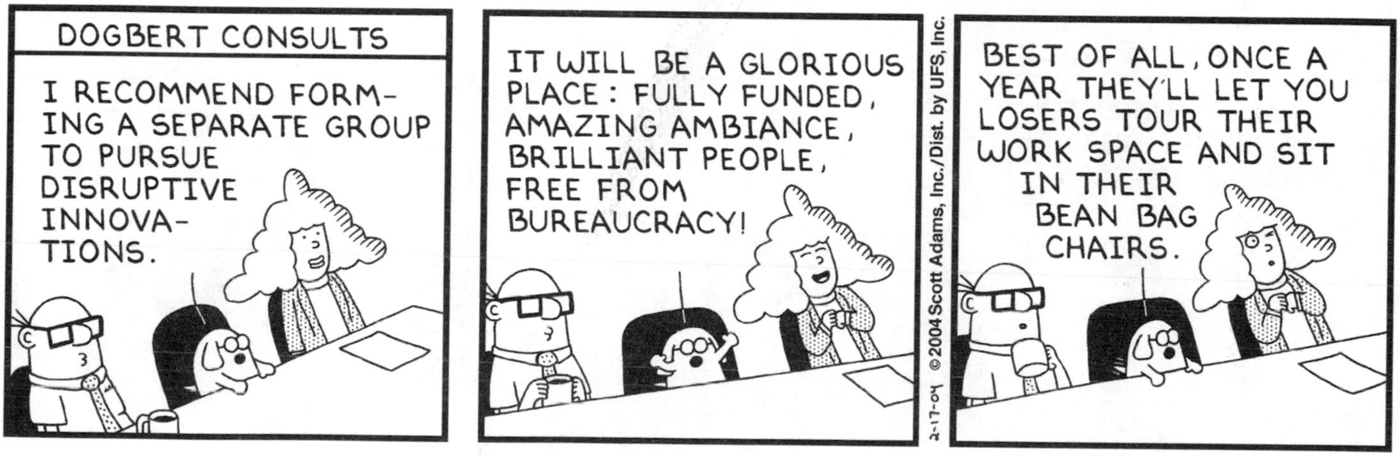
DOGBERT CONSULTS
I RECOMMEND FORMING A SEPARATE GROUP TO PURSUE DISRUPTIVE INNOVATIONS.
IT WILL BE A GLORIOUS PLACE: FULLY FUNDED, AMAZING AMBIANCE, BRILLIANT PEOPLE, FREE FROM BUREAUCRACY!
BEST OF ALL, ONCE A YEAR THEY'LL LET YOU LOSERS TOUR THEIR WORK SPACE AND SIT IN THEIR BEAN BAG CHAIRS.
2-17-04 © 2004 Scott Adams, Inc./Dist. by UFS, Inc.

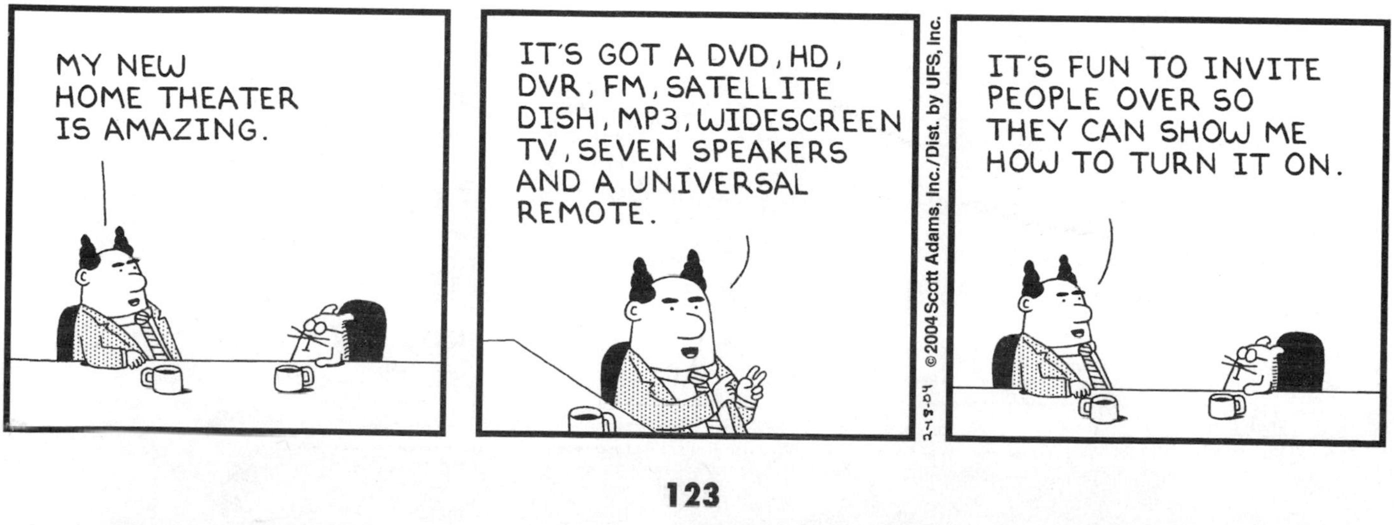
MY NEW HOME THEATER IS AMAZING.
IT'S GOT A DVD, HD, DVR, FM, SATELLITE DISH, MP3, WIDESCREEN TV, SEVEN SPEAKERS AND A UNIVERSAL REMOTE.
IT'S FUN TO INVITE PEOPLE OVER SO THEY CAN SHOW ME HOW TO TURN IT ON.
2-18-04 © 2004 Scott Adams, Inc./Dist. by UFS, Inc.

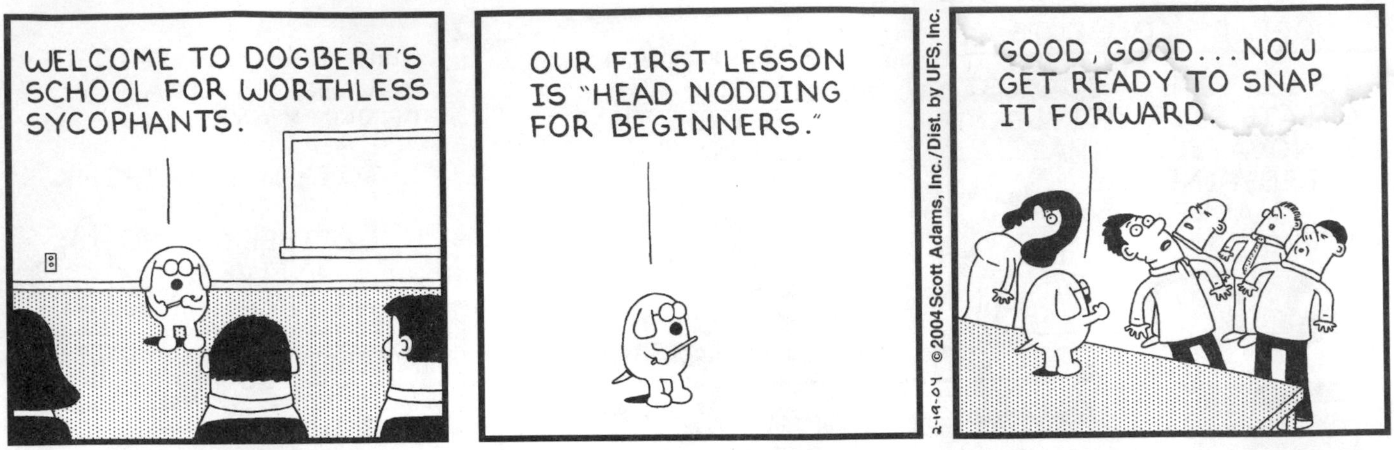
WELCOME TO DOGBERT'S SCHOOL FOR WORTHLESS SYCOPHANTS.
OUR FIRST LESSON IS "HEAD NODDING FOR BEGINNERS."
2-19-04 © 2004 Scott Adams, Inc./Dist. by UFS, Inc.
GOOD, GOOD. . . NOW GET READY TO SNAP IT FORWARD.

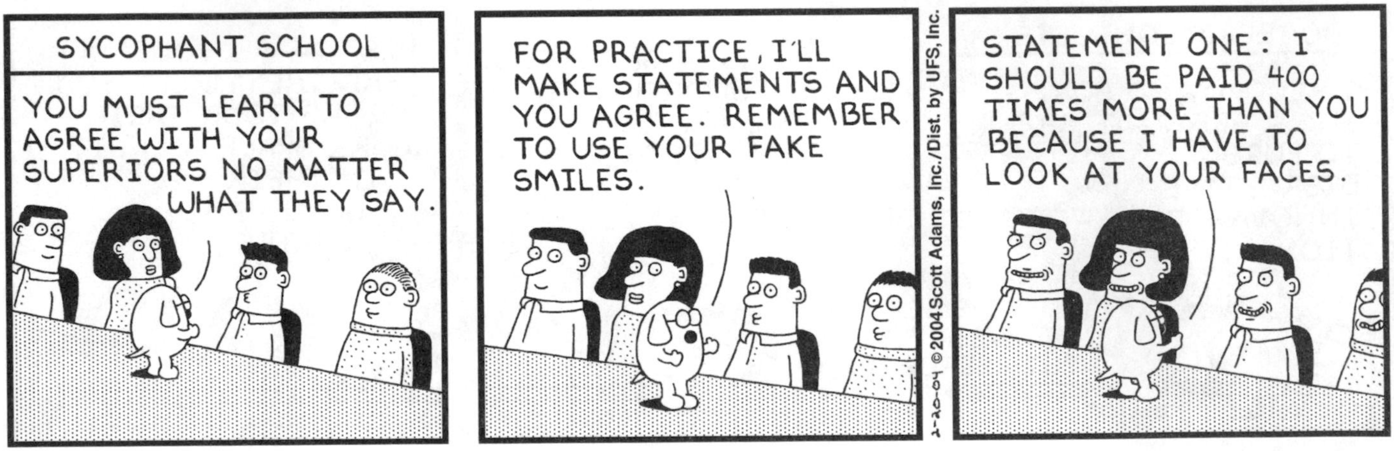
SYCOPHANT SCHOOL
YOU MUST LEARN TO AGREE WITH YOUR SUPERIORS NO MATTER WHAT THEY SAY.
FOR PRACTICE, I'LL MAKE STATEMENTS AND YOU AGREE. REMEMBER TO USE YOUR FAKE SMILES.
2-20-04 © 2004 Scott Adams, Inc./Dist. by UFS, Inc.
STATEMENT ONE: I SHOULD BE PAID 400 TIMES MORE THAN YOU BECAUSE I HAVE TO LOOK AT YOUR FACES.

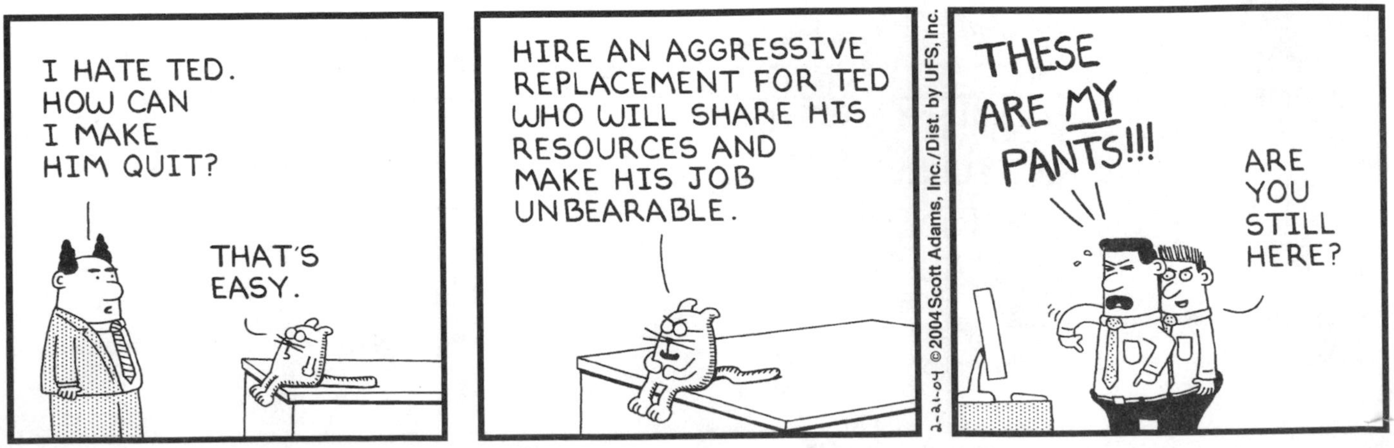
I HATE TED. HOW CAN I MAKE HIM QUIT?
THAT'S EASY.
HIRE AN AGGRESSIVE REPLACEMENT FOR TED WHO WILL SHARE HIS RESOURCES AND MAKE HIS JOB UNBEARABLE.
2-21-04 © 2004 Scott Adams, Inc./Dist. by UFS, Inc.
THESE ARE MY PANTS!!!
ARE YOU STILL HERE?

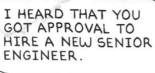
I HEARD THAT YOU GOT APPROVAL TO HIRE A NEW SENIOR ENGINEER.

AS AN INTERN, I HAVE PERFORMED ALL THE FUNCTIONS OF A SENIOR ENGINEER FOR THE PAST FIVE YEARS. I AM NOW READY FOR PROMOTION.

I PLAN TO HIRE SOMEONE FROM OUTSIDE THE COMPANY

MUST...CONTROL... ...TINY...FISTS... OF INTERN FURY.

I HAVE APPROVAL TO FILL THE SENIOR ENGINEER POSITION BUT THERE'S A BAN ON HIRING NEW INTERNS.

SO IF I PROMOTE YOU, MY EMPIRE...OOPS... I MEAN MY DEPARTMENT WON'T GROW.

GAAA!!! MY DESPAIR HAS TURNED INTO A SEARING PSYCHOLOGICAL PAIN!!!

OW! OW! OW!

THAT REMINDS ME; I NEED YOU TO TRAIN THE NEW GUY.

© 2004 Scott Adams, Inc. /Dist. by UFS, Inc.

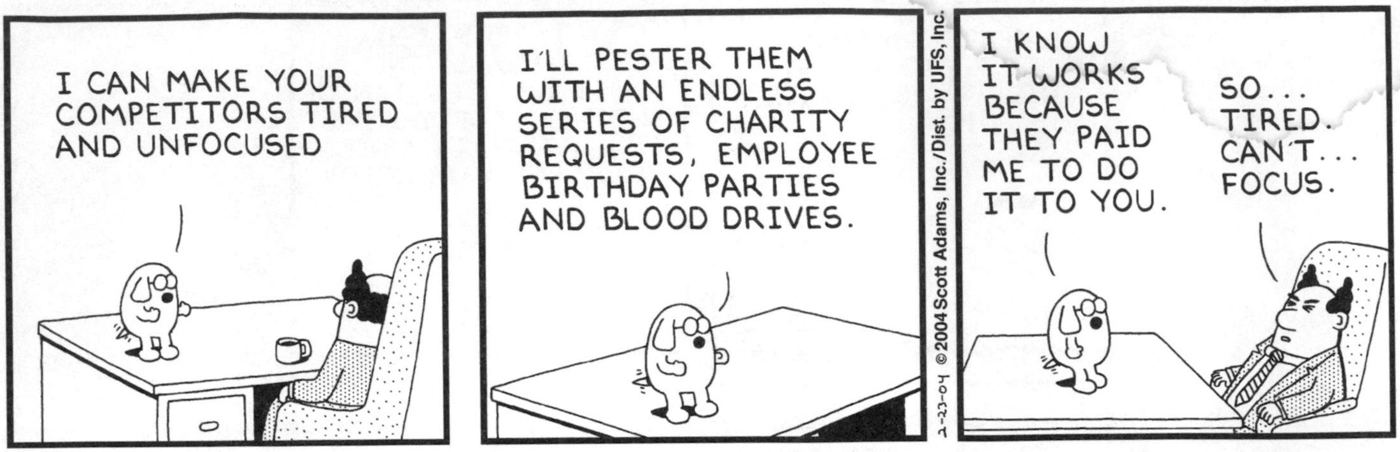
I CAN MAKE YOUR COMPETITORS TIRED AND UNFOCUSED
I'LL PESTER THEM WITH AN ENDLESS SERIES OF CHARITY REQUESTS, EMPLOYEE BIRTHDAY PARTIES AND BLOOD DRIVES.
© 2004 Scott Adams, Inc./Dist. by UFS, Inc. 2-23-04
I KNOW IT WORKS BECAUSE THEY PAID ME TO DO IT TO YOU.
SO... TIRED. CAN'T... FOCUS.

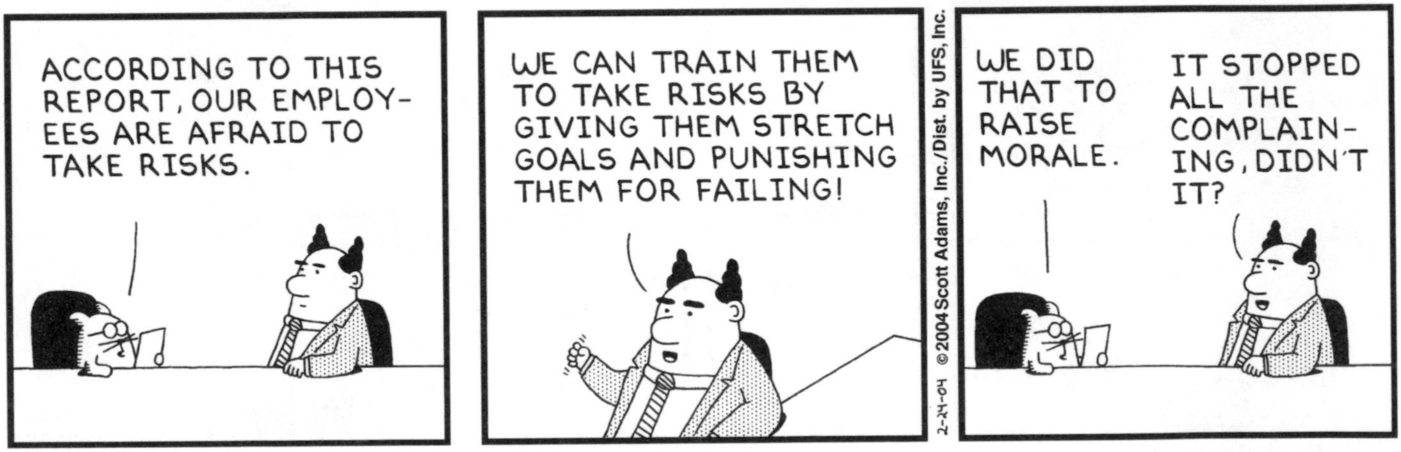
ACCORDING TO THIS REPORT, OUR EMPLOYEES ARE AFRAID TO TAKE RISKS.
WE CAN TRAIN THEM TO TAKE RISKS BY GIVING THEM STRETCH GOALS AND PUNISHING THEM FOR FAILING!
© 2004 Scott Adams, Inc./Dist. by UFS, Inc. 2-24-04
WE DID THAT TO RAISE MORALE.
IT STOPPED ALL THE COMPLAINING, DIDN'T IT?

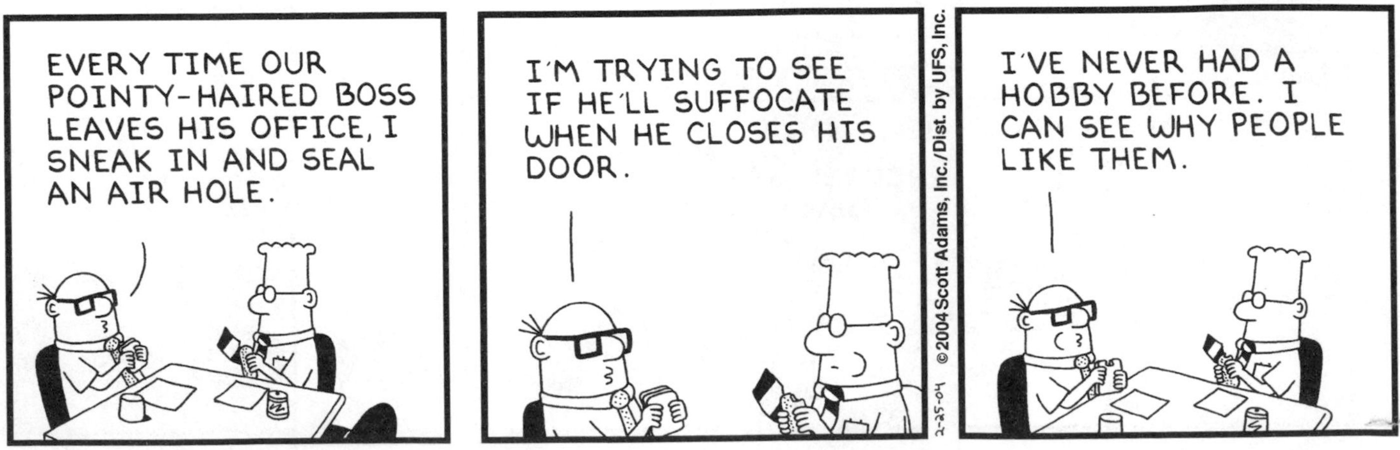
EVERY TIME OUR POINTY-HAIRED BOSS LEAVES HIS OFFICE, I SNEAK IN AND SEAL AN AIR HOLE.
I'M TRYING TO SEE IF HE'LL SUFFOCATE WHEN HE CLOSES HIS DOOR.
© 2004 Scott Adams, Inc./Dist. by UFS, Inc. 2-25-04
I'VE NEVER HAD A HOBBY BEFORE. I CAN SEE WHY PEOPLE LIKE THEM.

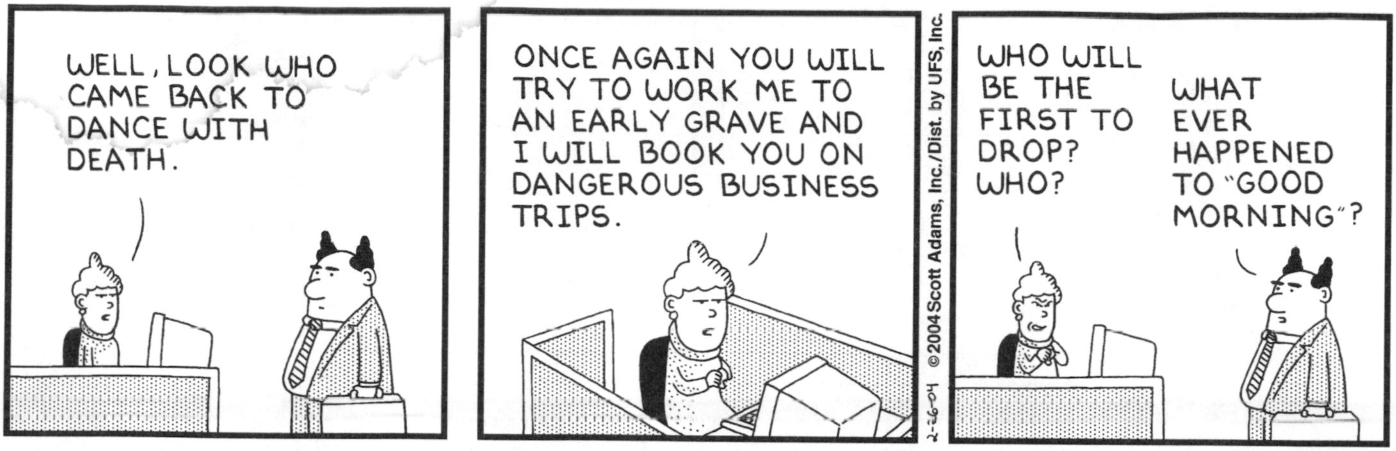
WELL, LOOK WHO CAME BACK TO DANCE WITH DEATH.
ONCE AGAIN YOU WILL TRY TO WORK ME TO AN EARLY GRAVE AND I WILL BOOK YOU ON DANGEROUS BUSINESS TRIPS.
2-26-04 © 2004 Scott Adams, Inc./Dist. by UFS, Inc.
WHO WILL BE THE FIRST TO DROP? WHO?
WHAT EVER HAPPENED TO "GOOD MORNING"?

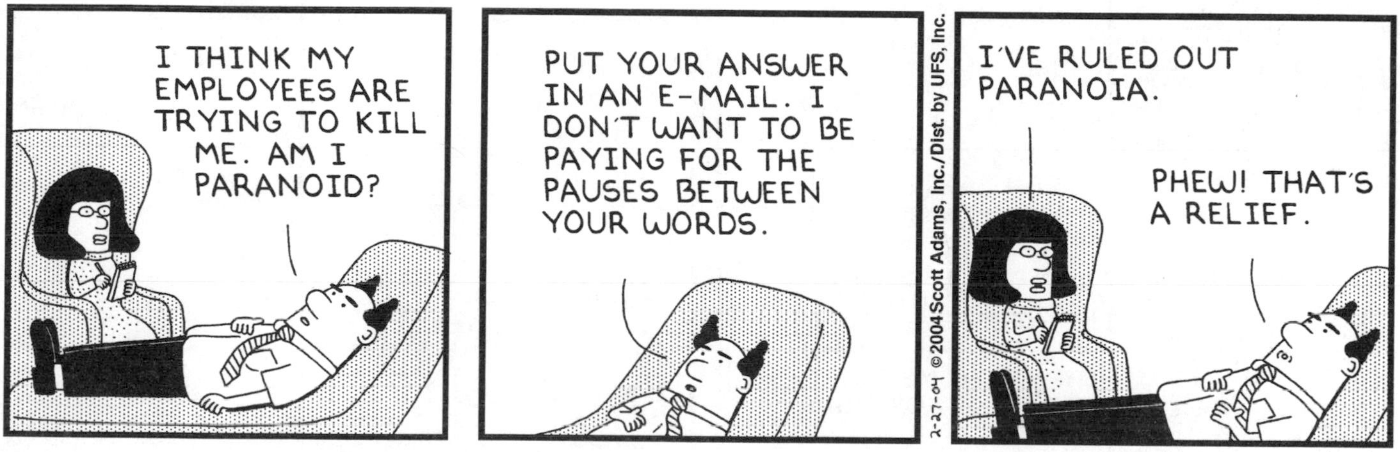
I THINK MY EMPLOYEES ARE TRYING TO KILL ME. AM I PARANOID?
PUT YOUR ANSWER IN AN E-MAIL. I DON'T WANT TO BE PAYING FOR THE PAUSES BETWEEN YOUR WORDS.
2-27-04 © 2004 Scott Adams, Inc./Dist. by UFS, Inc.
I'VE RULED OUT PARANOIA.
PHEW! THAT'S A RELIEF.

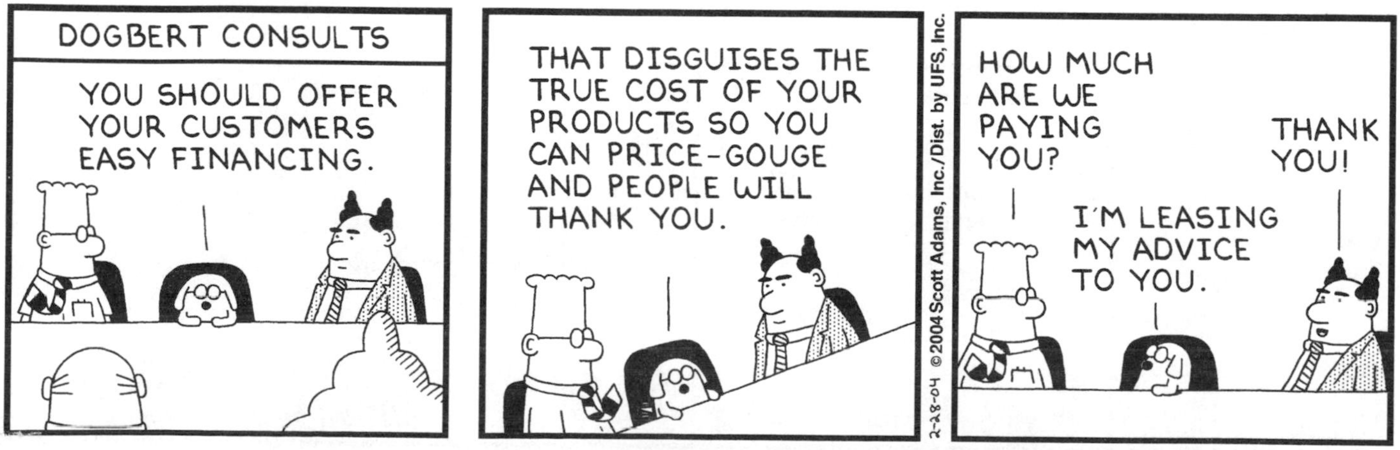
DOGBERT CONSULTS
YOU SHOULD OFFER YOUR CUSTOMERS EASY FINANCING.
THAT DISGUISES THE TRUE COST OF YOUR PRODUCTS SO YOU CAN PRICE-GOUGE AND PEOPLE WILL THANK YOU.
2-28-04 © 2004 Scott Adams, Inc./Dist. by UFS, Inc.
HOW MUCH ARE WE PAYING YOU?
I'M LEASING MY ADVICE TO YOU.
THANK YOU!

GAAA!!! OUR BOSS'S BOSS IS COMING!
WHERE?
ZOOP!
UH- OH.
HELLO, HEAD-COUNT.
I NEED TO RUN. TONS OF WORK.
WHY? ARE YOU POORLY MANAGED?
©2004 Scott Adams, Inc. /Dist. by UFS, Inc.
NO! WE HAVE EVERY-THING WE NEED! EVERYTHING IS PERFECT!
SO...WAS YOUR BOSS CONFUSED, LYING OR MISINFORMED WHEN HE ASKED ME FOR MORE FUNDING FOR YOUR BUDGET?
2-29-04
NOOO!!! IGNORE ME! I DON'T KNOW ANYTHING!!!
HMM.
DILBERT SAYS YOU DON'T COMMUNICATE WITH THE STAFF, AND YOU DON'T NEED MONEY.
PHEW! I'M GLAD THAT'S OVER.